ISRAEL

ISRAEL

AN INTRODUCTION

BARRY RUBIN

Yale UNIVERSITY PRESS

NEW HAVEN AND LONDON

Published with assistance from the foundation established in memory of Amasa Stone
Mather of the Class of 1907, Yale College.

Yale University Press books may be purchased in quantity for educational, business,
or promotional use. For information, please e-mail sales.press@yale.edu (U.S. office)
or sales@yaleup.co.uk (U.K. office).

Designed by Mary Valencia
Set in Minion and Futura type by Newgen North America.
Printed in the United States of America by Sheridan Books.

Library of Congress Cataloging-in-Publication Data
Rubin, Barry M.
Israel : an introduction / Barry Rubin.
p. cm.
Includes bibliographical references and index.
ISBN 978-0-300-16230-1 (pbk. : alk. paper)   1. Israel.   I. Title.
DS126.5.R77 2011
956.9405—dc23
2011028927

A catalogue record for this book is available from the British Library.

This paper meets the requirements of ANSI/NISO Z39.48−1992 (Permanence of Paper).

10 9 8 7 6 5 4 3 2 1

Contents

Preface

The purpose of this book is simple and straightforward: to provide an introductory text about Israel for both students and the general reader. A huge amount of material could be included in such a volume, so selections had to be made. A key goal here has been to present a rounded picture that goes far beyond history and politics. Indeed, materials in English on Israeli culture, for example, have been particularly limited. This book seeks to fill the gap.

A great deal about Israel is controversial. Often, however, the controversies are artificially manufactured myths and rewritings of history that are not borne out by the evidence. We have striven to be as balanced and as accurate as possible on every point.

This book is a place to begin, not an endpoint. The reader is encouraged to follow up with other material for a fuller picture. If something is not mentioned or is given what some might consider too much or too little space, that is a consequence of the need to cover a huge amount of territory, even though Israel itself is a small country.

Nor is this book meant to be a history of the Middle East or of the Palestinians or of the Arab-Israeli conflict or of the peace process. There are enough works on all these subjects. What there is not, however, is a basic survey of Israel itself.

This book is a project of the Global Research in International Affairs (GLORIA) Center, in the Interdisciplinary Center (IDC) in Herzliya, Israel. The GLORIA Center focuses on Middle Eastern issues as well as the relations of other parts of the world with the region. It publishes the *MERIA Journal: The Middle East Review of International Affairs* and has produced numerous books and academic studies. Its website is at http://www.gloria-center.org.

Thanks are due to the staff of the GLORIA Center and the many colleagues who contributed to the chapters in this book and who have read it to offer corrections and suggestions. Special credit here goes to Yeru Aharoni and Anna Melman for editing and, in some cases, writing drafts—a time-consuming and labor-intensive job. I have done my best to edit the collected material into a comprehensive and accurate introductory book on Israel.

A number of individuals produced basic texts used in these chapters, but I am responsible for the editing and the final text. Among the contributors are the following: *Understanding Israel*—Barry Rubin; *History*—Jonathan Spyer; *Land and People*—Tanya Sklar and Leigh Libling; *Society and Politics*—Anna Melman; *Economics*—David Rosenberg; *Dance, Literature, Poetry, and Food*—Keren Ribo; *Theater*—Gil Zarbiv; *Film*—Shmuel Duvdevani; *Art*—Nissim Gal; *Media*—Eytan Gilboa; *Sports*—Israel Rosenblatt. Gary Natan prepared the index.

The contributors and I wish to thank Brandon Weinstock and Lana Osher for their research assistance. Finally, let me note that many people not named here contributed as readers and made suggestions. We are grateful for their assistance and for their additions and corrections. I would especially like to thank Daniel Bachman, Howard Wachtel, Larry Kohn, Boaz Ganor, Judith Colp Rubin, Gabriella Rubin, and Daniel Rubin.

ISRAEL

Chapter One

UNDERSTANDING ISRAEL

Since the establishment of the modern state of Israel in 1948, examinations of its history have usually emphasized its wars, the Arab-Israeli conflict, and diplomatic negotiations. That focus is misleading. Israel has fought wars, and it has been a target of more terrorist attacks than any other country, as well as a constant participant in peacemaking efforts over decades. Yet conflicts and negotiations, though the stuff of daily headlines, are only a small part of the story. This book addresses a broader, ultimately more important question: What is the reality of this country and its people?

The basic answer is that modern Israel has built a fully realized—though not perfect or completed—political system, economy, society, and culture. It is a normal country, although a unique one with many distinctive features.

Although modern Israel grew from one of the world's oldest societies and cultures, its ancient heritage has not necessarily made the task of nation-building easier. On the contrary, religion and secularism, multiple languages, varying levels of economic development within its population, and its citizens' often different historical experiences, among other factors, made its nation-building process exceptionally complex and challenging. Add to this a land with few natural resources surrounded by hostile neighbors, and the relative success story of Israel becomes even more remarkable.

DEFINING MODERN ISRAEL

The idea that Jews are "only" a religious group is a concept that began with the French Revolution but did not become influential in Western Europe until the mid-nineteenth century. It never fully took hold in the Eastern European or Middle Eastern Jewish communities. In Western Europe, sympathetic non-Jews and Jews alike, as well as Jews who wanted to assimilate to the majority culture, sought to portray Jews as ordinary citizens in every way except in the narrow, personal area of religion. Not seeing Jews as a separate people with their own culture, language, and identity was a strategy for trying to gain equality and diminish antisemitism, not a reflection of their actual history and self-image until that time.

This approach contradicted all previous history, as well as the Jewish self-image. In Biblical times and up to the destruction of ancient Israel by the Romans more than 1,900 years ago, Jews functioned as a national people, arguably the first such in history. Thereafter, for more

than seventeen centuries Jews constituted a separate people with their own non-state governing institutions, unique language, special customs, distinct ideas, and different culture, not to
mention such things as clothing and art. Words like "Hebrew" and "Israelite"—used more
commonly than the word "Jews" well into modern times—reflected that national identity and
peoplehood, which extended beyond religion alone.

Religion, then, was only one marker of Jewish identity, and even that was national in nature.
There was thus no contradiction between a religious and a national identity. In the ancient
world, well into modern times, and in many places even today, a distinctive religion has been
one of the main hallmarks of the nation-state. This is especially true in the contemporary
Middle East, where Israel is more typical than different in this respect.

Throughout history, what marked Jews as having a particularly strong national identity was
that they rejected the gods and religious customs of even those, like the Romans and later the
Christians and Muslims, who ruled over them. In many other cases, people accepted the religion, language, and identity of rulers or neighbors and disappeared from history. The lasting
religio-national identity of Jews proved stronger than that of virtually any other group.

This survival was due neither to mere stubbornness nor to restrictions placed on them by
oppression. Rather, the Jews acted more like a modern nation, albeit having lost their control
over or presence in a specific territory. Indeed, the religious prohibition on Jews diluting their
customs or integrating those from other peoples in antiquity was what led to the Jewish revolts against the Greeks—which successfully reestablished a Jewish state—and Romans, which
failed, leading to the destruction of that state and the exile of the Jewish people from the Land
of Israel.

After the shifting of the centers of Jewish life from Israel to the Diaspora—to communities
in exile, away from the historical homeland in the Middle East—Jews continued to function as
much like a nation as possible, even though the cost of distinctiveness was discrimination and
even periodic murder at the hands of their neighbors. Over the centuries, in the framework of
rabbinic leadership, Jews maintained their own community government, laws, calendar, language, and philosophical outlook, as may be seen in the great rabbinic texts and in particular
foods, customs, and clothing.

Yet this was not just a local affair. Individual communities, even when separated by large
distances and living under very different conditions, maintained international connections
throughout the long medieval period and into modern times. Indeed, this was the reason Jews
were able to be so successful in maintaining long-range commerce, relatively (though not
completely) identical customs, and a unified intellectual dialogue.

All Jews, even the least educated and poorest living in the most isolated hamlets, were aware
of their origin in the Biblical Land of Israel; many also maintained ties with the small number
of Jews continuing to live there and believed they were destined to return there with the coming of the Messiah.

Zionism updated all of these existing ideas in the spirit of self-conscious, contemporary
nationalism. It proposed an answer to the "Jewish question," that is, how should Jews, including those whose lives were no longer encompassed by religious observance, meet the modern
world's challenges and opportunities? The response was neither assimilation nor a purely religious existence but a national existence: creating a Jewish state in the historical homeland.

Substituting human action for religious patience, Zionists also argued, would preserve the lives of the Jews themselves and the prospering of their religion.

In Eastern Europe, where the great majority of European Jews were concentrated, a de facto national life still existed throughout the nineteenth century and in many places into the twentieth as well. Most European Jews spoke Yiddish, a language derived from Hebrew and German. They worshipped daily in synagogues, where the Land of Israel was at the center of their religion, and functioned as a community totally separate from their neighbors. Only mass murder by the Nazis and their many allies, along with forcible assimilation under Communism, ended this way of life.

A roughly parallel picture held for the Middle East. Jews lived almost entirely within their own communities, observed the religiously based laws, had distinctive dress and occupations, and spoke a distinctive language that was an Arabic-Hebrew or Spanish-Hebrew (Ladino) equivalent of Yiddish.

Given this history, the common perception today that Jews were always outsiders, kept involuntarily from full integration into the larger communities among whom they lived, is also a relatively recent concept. For Jews in Christian Europe or the Muslim-majority Middle East, there was never—or only very recently—any offer of full integration. Still, the vast majority of Jews did not view their identity in only negative terms but saw themselves as being "inside," that is, part of, their own cohesive community, sharing a worldview with its other members no matter their geographical location or economic status.

Thus, modern Israel is not an arbitrary or accidental creation—it was not merely the result of the Holocaust, for example. Rather, it was the continuation of a long historical process. The creation of the state was not inevitable—far from it—and not all Jews supported such an outcome. But its establishment was just as logical as that of any other state in today's world in being created by a community of people with a shared worldview, history, and desire to share their fate.

The mere existence of proto-Zionist sentiments in Jewish society and religion and worldview, however, would have amounted to nothing without an organized movement. Vanguard thinkers in the mid-nineteenth century—Moses Hess, Leon Pinsker, and others—provided glimpses of the idea of a Jewish state, but Theodor Herzl truly brought the movement into existence in the 1890s.

The movement required complementary action in the Land of Israel itself. Young Russian Jews acting on their own in the 1880s began that work; they were thereafter supported by the Zionist movement.

The physical movement of people to the Land of Israel to join the traditional religious community already present brought about the *Yishuv*. This was the community of Jews in the Land of Israel between the 1880s and 1948, when Israel became an independent state. It laid the foundation for the projected state. While Jewish tradition and history was the first layer in shaping the modern state of Israel, the Yishuv was the second.

Cultural attributes and political-economic structures created during the Yishuv era became basic attributes of Israel's state and society. The best-known pre-state features include: the revival of the Hebrew language, the start of self-defense organizations, the establishment of a socialist-structured industrial economic base, the development of a comprehensive social

Theodor Herzl (1860–1904), founder of the modern Zionist movement, overlooking the Rhine River from the balcony of the hotel he stayed at during the First Zionist Congress, Basel, Switzerland, 1897. (Getty Images / Image Bank.)

service system, the coalescence of a culture principally rising from the intellectual ferment of Eastern Europe, the creation of innovative *kibbutz* (collective) and *moshav* (cooperative) farming communities, and the construction of a predominantly secular national framework with major religious aspects. Many other factors from the pre-state, Yishuv years continue to influence Israel long after its establishment.

Consider, for example, the role of religion. To say that Israel is a Jewish state is by no means merely a declaration of religious identity. It is primarily a declaration of a national identity. The overwhelming majority of the Yishuv leaders, and later the leaders of Israel, were secular. They simultaneously recognized the importance of religion in binding together Jews, respected the beliefs of a minority of the population, and wanted to ensure that religion did not gain too much power over the society and national culture.

Thus, the generation of leadership that dominated the Yishuv and the early state reached a compromise with the rabbinic leadership—which at the time was completely Orthodox—and allowed religion to prevail in certain aspects of society. Today official institutions observe the Jewish dietary laws; stores generally close on the Sabbath (although this practice has eroded over time); the state observes Jewish religious holidays; marriage, divorce, and burial are under rabbinical control; and full-time *yeshiva* (Jewish seminary) students receive military deferments. The compromise is enshrined in the doctrine of the status quo, whereby the existing balance of power between secular and religious is accepted by both sides and is thus maintained.

Nevertheless, Israel is a largely secular society. It is most accurately characterized as a country in which concepts, customs, and history that originated in religion have been put into a secular and national framework. In a sense, a similar process has taken place in Western Christian-based civilization.

In the first three or four decades of statehood, Jewish Israelis continued to think of themselves as sharply divided into separate religious and secular groups. By the 1990s, however, they realized the existence of a broad spectrum of views and levels of religious observance. As society became generally more secular and less ideological, a broad "traditional" population of individuals emerged; they kept elements of observance but were committed to a basically secular lifestyle. This approach is especially strong among *Mizrahi* Jews (Jews from the Middle East and North Africa).

Religious political parties have existed since the birth of modern Zionism. Yet these parties have not sought to transform the country. Instead, they are interest groups that seek to provide their specific communities with jobs and funding while preserving the status quo. Their goal, then, is not change but continuity. As a result, religious-secular conflicts, though sometimes disproportionately passionate, have declined in importance over time.

This discussion of religion is an example of how Israel has worked out original solutions based on its experiences, conditions, and the requirements of successful state-building, all of which are often misunderstood by outside observers. The same formula applies to other aspects of Israel as a society and a polity.

Despite these multiple challenges, Israel today has a pluralist, democratic system designed to accommodate different communities and viewpoints, though not geographical representation. The growing role of the Supreme Court has been controversial, as has Israel's electoral system, which has no individual-member districts, has many small parties, and suffers from the perception—not borne out in practice—that governments are unstable. In fact, during a thirty-two-year period, only seven different people were prime minister, a small number considering that two left office because of illness and one was assassinated.

Israel's economic system was also developed in tune with the specific conditions faced by a people lacking financial capital and modern institutions and trying to establish itself in an underdeveloped country. Public companies and enterprises, initially supported by Jewish capital from abroad, were the tools whereby the Yishuv's economy was created and jobs were

At a lab in the Teva Medical Factory in Har Hotzvim, Jerusalem, 2010. (Nati Shohat/Flash90.)

provided. In the first decades of nationhood Israel's economy was largely dominated by the Histadrut (the trade union federation) and its many associated companies, as well as by cooperative enterprises.

But by the 1990s, as the country outgrew this socialist, statist system, it made a smooth transition to a far larger degree of privatization. Israel also built an economy based on its strong points—computer, agricultural, medical, and scientific technology—despite the lack of such key requirements as viable natural resources, trade with neighbors, and a large internal market. Class and economic issues—often the main theme of other countries' politics—were not core issues in Israeli politics. A 2011 social protest movement over widening economic gaps and rising prices, especially in housing, launched huge demonstrations but so far has hardly affected electoral politics.

Another large challenge was the creation of an armed forces and national security structure to cope with imminent threats of national destruction from all of its neighbors, a virtually unique problem among the 200 countries in the contemporary world. And this task had to be accomplished by a people with virtually no military experience during the previous 2,000 years. In the Yishuv period, four underground forces developed—two of them in opposition to the leadership—but their successful dissolution into the national armed forces after Israel won independence provided a civilian-directed military institution that has prevailed ever since.

Ensuring that the military reflected the country's democratic principles, functioned effectively with minimal disruption of socioeconomic life, and could defend Israel against overwhelming odds was a major undertaking. A unique system was created combining a period of mandatory service with a large reserve that could be quickly mobilized. In addition, Israel had to develop a technological edge to make up for the numerical superiority of its enemies, plus a strategy to deal with potential simultaneous threats on all of its borders.

This military system was extraordinarily successful in defending the country against external threats. It had to be since even a single major defeat would have spelled the end of the state and the probable massacre or expulsion of most of its inhabitants. Despite the importance of military issues and institutions, however, Israel is not a heavily militarized society.

During its first forty years of existence, the conventional armies of all its neighbors—Egypt, Syria, and Jordan directly and Saudi Arabia and Iraq indirectly—posed a daily threat of war, financed by the Arab world and with arms supplied by the Soviet Union. By signing peace treaties first with Egypt in 1979 and then with Jordan in 1994, Israel removed two of the three main Arab armies facing it. Syria's weakness dropped out the third, reducing the likelihood of conventional war on Israel's borders to near zero. The Soviet Union's dissolution, Iraq's turn inward, and the Arab states' preoccupation with the Iranian and revolutionary Islamist threat all further reduced danger on that front.

By 2011, however, that situation appeared to be taking another turn; the proliferation of rockets on its borders in the hands of Hamas and Hizballah, the 2011 revolution in Egypt that might undo the peace treaty, and the lack of an Israel-Palestinian peace settlement, along with the general growth of revolutionary Islamism, show that Israel's security problems are far from over. Undoubtedly, the threats remain high compared to those faced by almost any other country in the world. But Israelis are mostly reconciled to the conflict going on for decades.

Having faced that reality, however, national morale is quite high. In annual polls, the number of people expressing satisfaction with their lives and hope in the future is phenomenally high. Almost 80 percent of Israelis say they would fight for their country, as opposed to 60 percent of Americans and 40 percent of Britons. The proportion of young people ready to volunteer for combat units defies all pessimistic predictions about selfishness and hedonism.

Another element in Israel's development was that Jewish immigrants who had arrived from many different countries and cultures were successfully integrated into a coherent society. Preceding and following Israel's independence in 1948, immigrants came first from Europe, then largely from the Middle East, and much later from the former Soviet Union and also, in much smaller numbers, from Ethiopia. Most of the immigrants arrived as refugees, having lost all of their property as well as suffering personal trauma from dangerous conditions and persecution in the countries they had fled.

On the whole, Israeli society integrated immigrants on an equal basis. This happened despite the tremendous economic pressure of the immediate post-independence period when rationing was in effect. Later on, however, complaints arose that the integrating process had been coercive and discriminatory—too ready to remake Mizrahi immigrants along European lines. This became a heated political and cultural issue in the 1980s, although it has largely faded with the birth of a more integrated and often intermarried generation.

Arabs compose almost 20 percent of Israel's population. They are predominantly Muslim, but there are small Christian and Druze populations too. Whatever shortcomings there are in regard to the Arab minority, there is astonishingly little friction despite problems documented in the Or Commission Report (2003), and there are few limits on their rights despite an ongoing military conflict and the constant threat of terrorism.

Although Israel is defined as a Jewish state, it functions more like a traditionally pluralist Middle Eastern country—with a state religion and partly autonomous minorities—than like a twentieth-century mono-nationalist European state that suppressed all minorities in a process of forced assimilation. Each religious community has control over its own matters of personal status and maintains cultural, religious, and, to a degree, judicial autonomy.

This system, as well as the approach to religion generally, is embodied in the existence of five school systems: state (secular) schools, state-religious (*Datim,* or Modern Orthodox) schools, *Haredi* (traditional Orthodox) schools, Arabic-language schools (for Arabic speakers), and Shas (schools for that political party's supporters, predominantly poor Mizrahi Jews).

Israel emerged from its pre- and post-independence years of challenge with a politics, worldview, economy, and culture fused from many different elements. Among the main early influences were traditional Jewish society along with the Yishuv innovations and borrowings from Eastern European, Western European, and Middle Eastern cultures. Added over time were more Middle Eastern, North American, Mediterranean, and modern Russian cultural elements, as well as an autonomous Arab cultural milieu. Mixed together with all the ethnic, linguistic, religious, and cultural elements were a wide range of political ideologies and degrees of social status.

POLITICS, POLITICAL CULTURE, AND EXTERNAL CONFLICT

Like many nations, Israel went through a heroic phase before arriving at an institutionalized order. Unlike other nations, however, its battle for survival has continued throughout its existence, and any book on Israel inevitably finds itself spending a considerable amount of space on the constant conflict with its neighbors and the impact of that conflict. Still, this issue is only one aspect of Israel's statehood, and it is less influential and important than outside observers might think.

To comprehend Israel, however, it is necessary to understand that the perception of existential threat continues to loom large because of events within living memory—namely, the murder of the overwhelming majority of European Jews in the Holocaust and the displacement of almost all Jews living in Muslim-majority countries, in both cases with the loss of all of their property and savings. Israel's victory in its war against Egypt, Jordan, and Syria in 1967 should not be remembered without equally recalling how grim Israel's situation appeared to be before the war and what would have happened to Israel and Israelis if Israel had been defeated.

From the 1930s until 1977, through the pre-state and independence periods, Israel was governed by the Labor Party. Its vision and institutions—including the Histadrut—had tremendous power because the party had spearheaded the transformation of the Land of Israel to the State of Israel, had masterminded the economic development of the independent state, and had taken a determining role in shaping the nature of its society. Nominally the twenty-nine-year reign of the Labor Party came to an end because of its handling of the run-up to the Yom Kippur War of 1973, although Israel eventually defeated its Egyptian and Syrian attackers. Yet the change in leadership was also due to the Mizrahi majority's support for the conservative Likud Party and its growing frustration with an establishment seen as entrenched and corrupt. The hero they made prime minister was a man very much shaped by his Eastern European background, Menahem Begin.

For the Labor elite, which included the majority of the cultural, political, and military establishment, the electoral defeat was nothing less than seismic. The transition was accepted politically with good democratic grace, but a great deal of anger and contempt remained. Nevertheless, Israel did not develop a clear two-party system, and since 1977, ideological debate has sharply declined in favor of a framework favoring issues and personalities.

In retrospect, the 1977 political shift and subsequent events signaled the end of Israel's founding heroic era and the transition to a more typical, established society. Precisely because of Israel's survival as a state and its normalization and institutionalization, the more socialist, statist concepts and institutions from the pre-state era no longer sufficed. The collectivist, idealistic ethos that had made sovereignty possible gave way to a more individualistic, materialistic ethos typical of Western societies. At the same time, the population became more integrated and homogeneous despite the diversity existing within three frameworks: *Ashkenazic-Mizrahi* (the Jews of European and of Middle Eastern and North African origin, respectively), religious-secular, and Jewish-Arab.

These societal developments were simultaneous with, but relatively unrelated to, the important but abstract debate between 1967 and 1993 about how to deal with the ongoing Arab-Israeli conflict. In the 1967 war, Israel captured the Sinai Peninsula and the Gaza Strip from Egypt, the West Bank and east Jerusalem from Jordan, and the Golan Heights from Syria.

Israel's political left argued that the Arab states and the Palestinians (though not necessarily the Palestine Liberation Organization, PLO) would one day negotiate seriously and, when that happened, Israel should trade much of the territory captured in 1967 in exchange for peace.

The political right said that an offer of genuine peace would never take place and therefore Israel should deal with these territories as part of its patrimony and support Jewish settlements there. The basic national consensus was against annexing the West Bank, the Gaza Strip, or the Sinai, while many, including many on the left, supported incorporating east Jerusalem and the Golan Heights into Israel.

Whatever the view on allowing or encouraging Jewish settlement in the captured territories, neither side in Israeli politics tried hard to stop it. After all, if there were ever a peace agreement, the settlements could be dismantled. And as long as there were no serious peace negotiations with the Palestinians, who were still being led by a PLO that espoused terrorist tactics and rejected Israel's existence, these and other hard decisions could be left to the future.

Such debates notwithstanding, each time a promising opportunity to explore the chances for peace appeared, the Israeli government explored them. The first came when Egyptian President Anwar al-Sadat decided that Egypt's interests required an end to the conflict with Israel. Menahem Begin, then prime minister of Israel, eagerly responded at the Camp David meeting in 1978 by handing back the Sinai Peninsula to Egypt and agreeing to dismantle Jewish settlements there in exchange for a peace treaty. The leadership of Israel's political right, the National Camp, demonstrated pragmatic flexibility on this occasion.

The Israeli internal debate continued but remained largely moot until the Oslo Accords of 1993. That agreement was an experiment, albeit a risky one, to see if peace could be achieved. Israel turned over large parts of the West Bank and the Gaza Strip to PLO rule; it also admitted thousands of Palestinians, including the PLO leaders who had previously waged war on Israel's civilians. The Palestinian Authority (PA), which the PLO created to govern the territory, received billions of dollars in aid from the international community, thousands of weapons, and international legitimacy. Its commitment, in return, was to stop terrorism and incitement to anti-Israel violence while preparing for peace and an end to the conflict.

Would the offer of concessions, including the return of almost all the captured territories and Palestinian statehood, produce peace, or did the roots of the Arab-Israeli conflict lie in the refusal of Palestinian, Syrian, and other Arab leaders to accept Israel's existence?

With Israel engaged in this seven-year-long experiment between 1993 and 2000, the terms of the internal debate shifted. Those Israelis whose views ranged from the center to the left argued that PLO, PA, and Fatah leader Yasir Arafat—if offered an independent Palestinian state comprising the West Bank and the Gaza Strip—would negotiate a peace agreement and keep it. At stake was not only an end to war and a securing of the blessings of peace but nothing less than what the veteran Labor leader Shimon Peres called a "new Middle East" in which everyone would prosper.

The general view from the center to the right was that making concessions to achieve a peace agreement would not work and was likely to raise the level of violence and strengthen the hostile forces. It was believed that when final negotiations took place, the two sides would fail to agree, and the peace process would collapse, with Israel in a far worse security situation than before. And if the two sides did reach an agreement, a Palestinian state would be used as a base for a second round of conflict aimed at wiping Israel off the map.

During the 1990s, passions ran high in this new debate, sharpened by the assassination of Prime Minister Yitzhak Rabin in November 1995. The PA at times—but not always—stopped terrorist attacks, but it also continued to incite anti-Israel attitudes and actions, failed to prepare its people for real peace, and persisted in claiming all the territory of Israel. Still, everyone urged patience: the final round of negotiations would prove the case one way or another.

In 2000, four events occurred. The United States hosted the Camp David summit at which Arafat rejected a framework for future talks, and the Palestinians decided to resume full-scale violence. Next, the PA rejected President Bill Clinton's peace plan, and Syria's government turned down a deal to regain the captured Golan Heights in exchange for full peace.

Despite being offered an independent Palestinian state with its capital in east Jerusalem, almost all the pre-1967 territory, and more than $20 billion in compensation (all dollars here are U.S. dollars), the Palestinian leadership turned down these proposals even as the basis for further negotiations. Similarly, Syria, which had been offered the return of the Golan Heights up to the internationally accepted border of 1923, had insisted on also receiving the territory that it had illegally occupied after 1948. The latter gave Syria access to the Sea of Galilee (called Kinneret in Hebrew) and other strategic territory whose only value to Syria would be to interfere with Israel's water supply or to launch offensive attacks. Israel refused to hand back the additional territory.

By 2001, all of these events had convinced the majority of Israelis that peace was not at hand and could not be won by any conceivable concessions on their part. The problem was Israel's existence, not the details of a peace agreement. Subsequent electoral results, notably in 2001 and 2003, showed how Israeli hopes (or illusions, as many now saw them) had evaporated.

Most no longer believed that taking risks and giving up more would bring peace. This was a change in Israeli perceptions and politics as significant as the "earthquake" of 1977, or even more so.

The other lesson Israelis learned from the experience of the 1990s peace process came from the perception of broken Western promises. The United States and Europe had urged Israel to make concessions and take risks, insisting that such actions were necessary to prove that Israel wanted peace. If its peace overtures failed, Israelis were told, Western support would intensify, since the Western nations would understand that Israel had no alternative but to defend itself and refuse to make further concessions.

In fact, the exact opposite happened. Despite Israeli withdrawals from southern Lebanon and later from the Gaza Strip, despite Israel's cooperation with the PA and its unprecedented peace offers (including the offers to give up the Golan Heights and the Gaza Strip, much of east Jerusalem, and almost all of the West Bank and its readiness to accept an independent Palestinian state), Western criticism of Israel increased after the peace process failed, and Western backing arguably diminished. Indeed, more voices in the West than ever before called for Israel's destruction.

Out of the experiences of the 1990s and the five years of Palestinian violence and terrorism directed at Israel that followed, a new Israeli consensus formed. Much of the left and right moved toward the political center, reshaping the political framework. Doubtful of Arab (or at least Palestinian and Syrian) interest in peace and cynical about foreign attitudes, Israelis adopted a new paradigm. They took one idea from the left—readiness to withdraw from territories captured in 1967 and agree to a Palestinian state—and another idea from the right—doubt that anyone on the Palestinian side was really a partner for peace.

Politicians of both the traditional left and the traditional right accepted the new concept. Peace was not at hand, they agreed; Israel was in a long transition period. It was necessary to cooperate with the Palestinian Authority to limit incitement of terrorism and to ensure that the PA did not collapse—especially after Hamas took control of the Gaza Strip—but these efforts should proceed without illusions or expectations.

Since then, Israelis have voted for successive governments in favor of ceding all of the Gaza Strip, most of the West Bank, and much of east Jerusalem in exchange for a full and lasting peace. At the same time, these governments have demanded that before such a deal could be concluded, the PA must provide convincing proof of a readiness to make concessions of its own.

The 2009 peace plan of a coalition government that included both Likud and Labor called for recognition of Israel as a Jewish state, resettlement of Palestinian refugees in the new state of Palestine, limits on the military forces of that state, security guarantees for Israel, and the insistence that any peace agreement must include the permanent end of the Israel-Palestinian conflict rather than being the prelude to a new stage of conflict.

While Israel prefers peace, its politicians and population have not accepted the notion that a quick deal is more important than the risks or conditions involved. This is true despite—or more accurately because—the conflict itself has entered a new phase. Instead of facing Arab nationalist regimes and movements as its primary foes, Israel is now threatened by radical

Islamists. Revolutionary Islamist forces—including Hizballah and Hamas—and the governments of Iran and Syria are committed to Israel's destruction and reject peace in any form.

Israelis largely interpreted the political upheavals of the Arab world in 2011, often hailed in the West as democratic movements, as marking an advance of revolutionary Islamism. If extremism in the Middle East was on the increase, Israelis concluded, to make concessions would be doubly dangerous, since it would give more strategic assets to Israel's most determined foes.

Outside of the Middle East, Israel faced much antagonism in Western media and intellectual circles. Yet the picture was not only a negative one. The country maintained basically good state-to-state relations with almost every Western democracy. And Israel's relations with such powers as Russia and the other states that emerged from the Soviet Empire, China, India, and many Third World countries were far better than they had been in past decades.

The internal security situation was also better than it had been in the past. Israeli strategy against the *intifada* (Palestinian uprising against Israel) in 2000–2005 and against cross-border operations from Hamas and Hizballah has pushed successful terrorist attacks to a low level compared to previous years. While Israel does face a high level of threat, Israelis have adjusted to this situation as a part of their normal routine. This was evident in 2000–2005, when intense terrorist attacks on Israeli civilians failed to produce any considerable breakdown in societal morale.

The potential for massive rocket attacks from Lebanon and the Gaza Strip remains, and the potential possession of nuclear weapons by Iran poses a new threat, yet Israelis currently enjoy a relatively high level of security given their experiences and expectations. Despite the ongoing Arab-Israeli conflict, Israel has largely succeeded in giving its citizens personal and collective security. If crime statistics in Western countries are factored into the threat assessment, Israelis face fewer dangers overall than do inhabitants of most American and many European cities.

CHALLENGES TO NATION-BUILDING

The challenges that Israel faced after independence included not only ensuring its strategic survival but also establishing itself as a democratic country with an industrial economy; fostering high morale among its citizenry; and maintaining internal peace while wealthier, more populous neighbors voiced their intentions to wipe it off the map. Even aside from problems added by threats to its existence, the hostility of neighboring countries, and the costs of self-preservation, the barriers to development were enormous.

First of all, Israel lacked natural resources useful in manufacturing, with the exception of high-quality phosphates on its eastern border. It had virtually no oil and only a tiny amount of natural gas. It faced periodic water shortages. In addition, the new state lacked infrastructure. There was no good road network; only a minimal railroad system; no transport connections to neighboring states, since their borders were closed to the Jewish state; and not even a national water distribution system.

Second, few of the Jews who came to Israel had the knowledge or experience to build either a state or a modern economy. Most were poor or at least had become so by the loss of their former property. The younger Holocaust survivors had no chance for an education at all. Jews from Middle Eastern countries were in a similar situation, coming as they did from nonindustrialized countries.

Chapter Two

HISTORY

The existence of the modern state of Israel is the culmination of a long process going back almost 4,000 years to the formation of a distinct Jewish people. Jews established a kingdom east of the Mediterranean Sea about 3,000 years ago, regained independence after the Maccabean revolt against Greek-Syrian control 2,100 years ago, and survived the final destruction of ancient Israel's autonomy by the Romans 1,900 years ago.

Although most Jews were forced into exile then, the Jewish presence in the Land of Israel, or Zion, continued after the defeat by the Romans. The production of the Mishnah and the Jerusalem Talmud—two of the main texts for Jewish law and religious practice—took place there during the three centuries after the Roman conquest. As late as 1100, fifty Jewish communities could be found in the Land of Israel, with an especially large one in Jerusalem, whose Jews were massacred by the Crusaders. In the seventeenth century, Safed, in what is now northern Israel, became a leading center for Jewish mysticism and learning. And by the mid-nineteenth century so many Jews lived in Jerusalem that a number of scholars believe they formed the largest community there.

For centuries, Jews took it for granted that they were a people with a common religion—a nation rather than merely a religious sect. They maintained the distinctive language of Hebrew. Those outside the Land of Israel considered themselves to be in exile (*galut*) and prayed daily to return. In the meantime, the exiles maintained a connection to the Land of Israel in both religion and culture. In far-off Poland, Morocco, and elsewhere, the celebration of the cycle of the year accorded with the seasons in the Land of Israel. The laws taught to Jewish students, studied by adults, and providing the basis for the education of rabbis were those to be revived once Israel was reestablished—a future about which many Jews had not the slightest doubt.

The bond between Jews and the Land of Israel in religious terms is a central theme in the Jewish religion. While the Bible can be interpreted in historical terms, for many centuries all Jews and today all of them who are religious believe that the land was promised to Jews by the Supreme Being.

There are many passages in the Torah and the rest of the Bible, canonic books from after the exile—especially the Mishnah and the Talmud—and rabbinic works that assert this view. For instance, Abraham is ordered: "Leave your land, your birthplace and your father's house and go to the land that I will show you. And I will make of thee a great nation. . . . And the Lord appeared unto Abraham, and said: 'Unto thy seed will I give this land.'"

That "promised land" was pledged in turn to Isaac: "Sojourn in this land, and I will be with thee, and will bless thee; for unto thee, and unto thy seed, I will give all these lands, and I will establish the oath which I swore unto Abraham thy father."

The purpose of the exodus from Egypt, the Torah says, is to have Moses lead the Israelites back to the Land of Israel. When they arrive, the Lord says to Joshua: "You and all these people, get ready to cross the Jordan River into the land I am about to give to them—to the Israelites. I will give you every place where you set your foot, as I promised Moses."

It is in this land where the anointed kings, Saul, David, and Solomon, ruled. There, in Jerusalem, the First Temple was built, and then the Second Temple after the first was destroyed. These Temples were each built not merely as another shrine but—as the Bible repeatedly makes clear—as a center of Judaism so overwhelmingly important that no other place of worship should exist. Indeed, the Books of Ezra and Nehemiah describe the return of some of the Jews from Babylon and their rebuilding of the Temple.

All the prophets, too, saw a common identity between the Jewish people, the Jewish religion, and the Land of Israel, to which Jews were fated to return. Psalm 137 says, "If I forget thee, O Jerusalem, let my right hand forget her cunning."

The prophet Ezekiel said the Lord showed him the valley of the bones, and the bones came together and returned to life: "These bones are the whole house of Israel; and they are saying, 'Our bones have dried up, our hope is gone, and we are completely cut off.' Therefore prophesy; say to them that [the Lord] says, 'My people! I will open your graves and make you get up out of your graves, and I will bring you into the land of Israel."

The post-exilic literature continued these themes. Rabbi Shimon bar Yochai said the Land of Israel was one of the great gifts given by the Supreme Being. Rabbi Nachshon Gaon, living in ninth-century Iraq, wrote that every Jew has a personal inheritance of part of the land. Many of the rabbis most respected for religious scholarship repeated the injunction that to live in that land was a duty, and some went to live there themselves.

Whether one accepts this long and deeply held religious view as divinely ordained or as an expression of the history of a community, its power and centrality for the Jewish people should be clear. Only with the rise of assimilationism and other ideologies in the second half of the nineteenth century did any Jew even think to question it. The debate was not over the centrality of the return to Israel but rather over its accomplishment—whether it might be brought about by human action or by the Messiah.

The imagery of Jerusalem and the Land of Israel was thus omnipresent in faith, belief, and texts and was renewed daily by all Jews no matter where they lived. Long before the creation of a Zionist movement, the eyes of Jews everywhere were turned toward Jerusalem. Not until the late nineteenth century, with the development of conscious nationalism in Europe, the entrance of Jews into mainstream society, and the opening of a somewhat secular approach to Jewish identity, did a political nationalist movement develop with the aim of returning Jews to Israel and creating a nation-state there through human organization and action.

Thus, the Zionist idea was simultaneously very modern and based on concepts defining one of the oldest self-identified groups in world history. A half-century of activity by the Zionist movement and by groups and individuals within the Land of Israel helped bring the State of Israel into being in 1948. Diplomacy, education, political organization, economic investment, immigration, settlement, defense, and a vast amount of manual and other labor all contributed to the creation of the state.

Although the Zionist movement had precursors in a variety of places—the idea of a Jewish national homeland was already being raised in the mid-nineteenth century by such thinkers as Moses Hess and Leo Pinsker and activists like those in the Hovevei Zion (Lovers of Zion) movement—its main creator was Theodor Herzl, an Austro-Hungarian Jew. Convinced that Europeans would not fully accept and integrate Jews on an equal basis with other citizens, Herzl proposed a national solution to the "Jewish Question" in his book *The Jewish State.* Building on the enthusiastic response it received, he organized the First Zionist Congress in Basel, Switzerland, in August 1897.

The Jewish population of the Land of Israel had been increasing for decades. A growing number of religious Jews, mainly from Eastern Europe and Yemen, immigrated to Jerusalem and Safed in the nineteenth century. During the 1880s, Jewish settlements with a consciously political goal sprang up in the Ottoman-ruled territory of Palestine—which was approximately coextensive with modern-day Israel and the West Bank plus Jordan. Their founding was sparked mainly by idealistic young Russian-born Jews of the Hovevei Zion group. The development of the Zionist movement accelerated immigration. Then, during World War I, the Ottomans deported many of the Jews who had come from Russia, the Ottomans' wartime enemy. Some of the Jews remaining in Palestine supported the Allied cause by organizing an effective espionage network to help the British. Those who had been deported quickly returned once the fighting ended.

Three key events set the stage for Israel's creation: Great Britain's issuing of the Balfour Declaration on November 2, 1917, which supported the establishment of a Jewish homeland; the area's conquest by British forces in 1917 and the defeat of the Ottoman Empire in the war; and the participation of three Jewish Zionist battalions, organized by Ze'ev Jabotinsky, in the British army. After the war, the League of Nations established Palestine, part of the former Ottoman Empire, as a British mandate, formalizing British rule over the territory. It charged Britain with putting the Balfour Declaration into effect—that is, establishing in Palestine a "national home for the Jewish people." When the League of Nations consented to a division of the British Mandate for Palestine, Transjordan was split off, becoming autonomous. Britain established direct rule over the now-much-smaller Palestine.

Several factors inhibited Jewish immigration and kept the number from growing as fast as it might have. The difficulty of finding jobs was a problem, especially during the 1920s. Mounting Arab opposition, including periodic riots and attacks on Jews, caused many casualties. And after the Nazis took power in Germany, when far more Jews were seeking a safe haven, British policy limited immigration, most notably in the 1939 White Paper with which Britain sought to gain political favor in the Arab world. This last restriction was indirectly responsible for the deaths of hundreds of thousands of Jews trapped in Nazi-ruled Europe.

Nevertheless, the Zionist movement and the Yishuv—the Jewish population of the Land of Israel—persevered. The socialism-oriented factions became the leaders of both the movement and the Yishuv during the 1930s. The centralized organization of resources meant that available funds were utilized relatively efficiently.

Despite many vicissitudes, the Yishuv Jews numbered 600,000 by 1945. They created a web of institutions collectively known as the state-in-the-making. These institutions allowed for an independent, highly organized economy; democratic decision making; a wide variety of political parties; agricultural marketing cooperatives; a self-defense force that included primitive arms-manufacturing workshops; collective (kibbutz) and cooperative (moshav) farming settlements; a strong trade union federation; health funds; employment-providing enterprises; and all the other things necessary for establishing a state structure quickly when the opportunity came. Energetic, charismatic leaders ran the decision-making apparatus, whose flexibility allowed them to navigate a series of highly risky and complex choices. At the same time, the Yishuv succeeded in resurrecting the Hebrew language, which had for centuries been restricted to religious services and study.

During World War II, the Yishuv put the highest priority on defeating Nazi Germany while also trying—despite very limited resources—to save Jews by secretly rescuing them and by battling British restrictions on immigration. As the war was ending, the Irgun, one of the Jewish militias, joined the smaller Lehi group in waging a guerrilla war to force out the British; the Lehi had earlier split from the Irgun over this issue. The British authorities arrested many

A crowd of Jewish immigrants, survivors of the Holocaust, arrive in Haifa harbor on the *Exodus 1947*, March 1947. The British seized the ship and interned the passengers in Cyprus. (Getty Images / Image Bank.)

Jews and continued to block immigration. The punishment for possessing a weapon was death by hanging. A number of Jews were executed, and on one occasion the Irgun killed kidnapped British soldiers in retaliation.

The Jewish Agency for Israel, the Jewish authority established under the Balfour Declaration, and the Haganah, the Jewish paramilitary organization, tried to work with the British toward a political solution, launching the "Saison" operation to help the British capture Irgun and Lehi members in 1943 since it opposed all anti-British operations by the smaller militias as long as World War II continued. But the conflict with Britain restarted the following year when the Haganah joined other organizations in fighting the British, who had continued to repress the Yishuv despite this cooperation.

The most important attack by the Jewish rebellion against British rule in Palestine took place on July 22, 1946, when the United Resistance Movement—made up of the Haganah, Irgun, and Lehi—bombed the King David Hotel in Jerusalem, the British Mandatory government's main office. Ninety-one people were killed—Jewish, British, and Arab employees—and forty-six were injured. The movement claimed that a prior warning had been sent to evacuate the building.

After World War II, the British wanted to divest themselves of this territory. Faced with rebellion there, its own domestic problems, and the need for strategic retrenchment, the British decided to pull out and turned the question of Palestine's future over to the United Nations. A series of investigations and plans culminated in the November 29, 1947, UN General Assembly vote to partition Palestine into two states, one Jewish, one Arab, with implementation to take place on May 15, 1948. Thirty-three members voted for the plan, thirteen voted against it, and ten abstained.

According to the Partition Plan, Jerusalem would be a UN-governed international zone. The Arab state was to take up 43 percent of the land (4,500 square miles, or 11,655 square kilometers), much of it surrounding Jerusalem; 804,000 Arabs and 10,000 Jews lived there. The Jewish state was to take up 56 percent of the land (5,500 square miles, or 14,245 square kilometers); 538,000 Jews and 397,000 Arabs lived there, and hundreds of thousands of additional European Jewish Holocaust survivors were ready to arrive as soon as immigration was open.

Although the Jewish leadership accepted the Partition Plan, Palestinian Arab leaders, whose chief, Muhammad Amin al-Husayni, had recently returned from Berlin where he had collaborated with the Germans during the war, rejected both the Partition Plan and the existence of a Jewish state in any form. They launched the war they had been preparing since 1946. About 1,700 people were killed during the next five months. An estimated 700,000 Arabs fled; some were expelled from the Jerusalem corridor—the territory connecting Jerusalem to the land along the coast allocated to the would-be Jewish state—and from the far north during the last days of the war. The Palestinian elite were the first to leave, setting off a panicked flight throughout Palestinian society.

Although many outside observers thought the Jewish side would inevitably lose a military engagement, the Yishuv's organization, discipline, unity, and preparation paid off. In April 1948, Jewish forces launched a full-scale attack. They had made significant territorial gains by the time the British mandate ended on May 14, 1948.

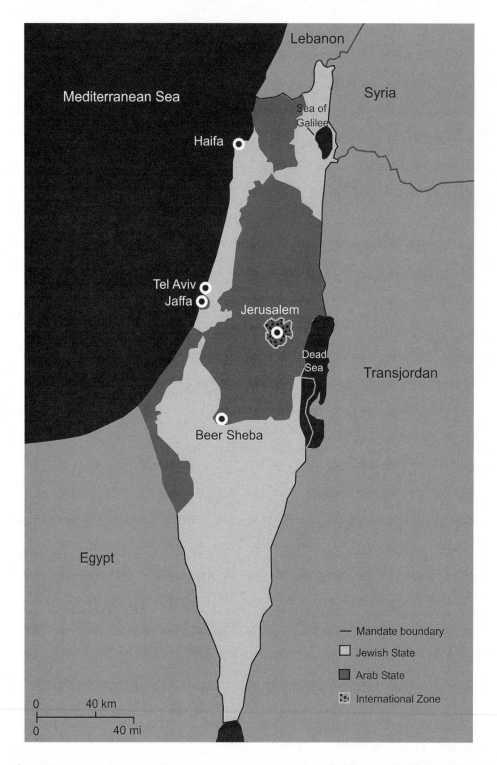

Mediterranean Sea

Lebanon

Syria

Sea of Galilee

Haifa

Tel Aviv

Jaffa

Jerusalem

Dead Sea

Transjordan

Beer Sheba

Egypt

— Mandate boundary

☐ Jewish State

■ Arab State

▒ International Zone

0   40 km

0   40 mi

After an investigation by a special committee, the UN General Assembly voted in 1947 to partition the Palestine Mandate governed by Britain into a Jewish state, an Arab state, and an internationalized district, Jerusalem. This map shows the projected boundaries. (© 2003–2010 Koret Communications Ltd. All rights reserved.)

When fighting began, the Jewish forces were still not entirely unified. Upon declaring independence on May 13 (the day before the mandate ended), the new government of the new Jewish state ordered all militias to be merged into the new national army, the Israel Defense Forces (IDF). The Irgun had agreed to participate. But in June 1948 the Irgun tried to ship in a load of weapons and volunteers on the *Altalena*. The government ordered that the arms be turned over to the new Israeli army. Negotiations failed, and the government ordered its forces, commanded by a young officer named Yitzhak Rabin, to fire at the ship, whose passengers included the Irgun commander Menahem Begin. The *Altalena* caught fire and sank. During the shooting, sixteen Irgun fighters and three soldiers in the IDF were killed.

The battle could have led to civil war, but the matter was quickly resolved, and the Irgun merged into the IDF. This incident established the superiority of the national government and confirmed a willingness to compromise that ensured Israel's unity and survival.

ISRAEL IS BORN, INDEPENDENCE IS WON

The State of Israel was officially declared at a meeting held in City Hall (later, Independence Hall) in Tel Aviv on May 14, 1948. The Declaration of Independence included a call to Arab neighbors for peace and coexistence. The United States and the Soviet Union, as well as other countries, recognized the new state. David Ben-Gurion became the first prime minister, and a broad, multiparty government was formed.

A new stage in the Arab-Israeli conflict began immediately. The moment the British mandate ended, the armies of Iraq, Syria, Jordan, Egypt, and Lebanon crossed into the territory of the former mandate and attacked the Jewish-held sectors. Most observers believed that Israel would be destroyed by the long-established, better-armed professional Arab forces. Israel was surrounded by hostile countries, and an international arms embargo also favored the Arab side. Arab leaders predicted an easy victory, with the Jews being driven into the sea.

But the Arab campaign in the north, conducted mainly by the Syrians, made no gains. In the south, Egyptian forces advanced but were finally halted on May 29, just sixteen miles (10 kilometers) from Tel Aviv. The greatest Arab success came to the British-officered Jordanian army, which captured Jerusalem's Old City on May 28 and expelled the entire Jewish population. The Jewish army, now the Israel Defense Forces, continued to hold Jewish-populated west Jerusalem, but the city was under siege.

On June 11 the United Nations imposed a ceasefire. Just two days earlier, the IDF had finished constructing a steep, circuitous route called the Burma Road, which bypassed Jordanian-held territory, to transport supplies into west Jerusalem. During the ceasefire, Israel received its first weapons from Czechoslovakia. Tens of thousands of Jewish immigrants also arrived, many of whom were immediately sent to the front line with little or no training.

During the ten-day interval between the breakdown of the first ceasefire on July 8 and the imposition of a second one on July 18, the IDF launched an offensive in which it captured the Lower Galilee and two towns—Lod and Ramle—crucial for keeping communications with Jerusalem open. A UN diplomatic effort failed when both sides rejected a proposal to maintain international control that would establish no Arab state and only a tiny Jewish state. Jewish extremists assassinated Count Folke Bernadotte, the UN mediator who had proposed major Jewish concessions, on September 19.

Israel's first prime minister, David Ben-Gurion, reads Israel's Declaration of Independence in Tel Aviv's City Hall, May 14, 1948. Behind him is a portrait of Theodor Herzl, founder of the modern Zionist movement. (Getty Images / Image Bank.)

After the Egyptians shelled an IDF supply convoy, Israel launched an offensive on October 14 that captured Beer Sheba in eight days and drove the Egyptian forces back across the border, except in the Gaza Strip area.

Israeli losses had been heavy. The 6,000 killed amounted to 1 percent of its entire population. Yet Israel had fulfilled its goal of establishing itself as an independent state; furthermore, it now governed 21 percent more territory than had been offered in the UN Partition Plan. The United Nations admitted Israel as a member on March 11, 1949.

Neither the Palestinian Arabs nor the Arab countries created a new state in the former British mandate. In 1950, Jordan's King Abdallah annexed the West Bank, although virtually no countries recognized Jordan's right to the territory. Egypt ruled in the Gaza Strip. Within Israel, military control was maintained over areas of the Galilee, which was populated by 150,000 Arabs; there, Arab citizens ran for office and were elected to the Knesset (Israel's parliament), beginning with the first election, in 1949. But Israel's neighbors had not agreed to the existing borders or to Israel's continued existence. The Arab states accepted only an armistice, not peace. The Arab-Israeli conflict had only begun.

Arab rule prevailed in east Jerusalem and the West Bank (Jordan) and the Gaza Strip (Egypt). During the fighting from November 1947 to May 1948, between the partition resolution and its implementation, about 400,000 Palestinian Arabs had fled to neighboring Arab countries or to territories held by invading Arab armies. The fighting continued, and between May 1948 and January 1949, another 300,000 fled.

Because all the Arab states and Palestinian Arab organizations maintained that Israel's creation was illegitimate and that a state of war continued, national defense remained a high priority for Israel. The new nation had to be prepared to fight a simultaneous attack by Arab states on all of its borders. From the early 1950s on, Palestinian irregular forces made sporadic border crossings, encouraged especially by the Egyptian authorities in the Gaza Strip but also by Syria and Jordan. Israel implemented its basic strategic principles: formation of a relatively small army, which could be enlarged quickly through a reserve call-up system; maintenance of qualitative and technological superiority; and, given Israel's small size, establishment of the ability to take the offensive so that war could be fought on enemy territory.

LARGE-SCALE IMMIGRATION

Besides the hostility that Israel faced on its borders, the small, newly established country faced equally heavy internal challenges. It had to create a stable, democratic governing apparatus; build an economy in a country with few natural resources and no heavy industry; and integrate a huge number of immigrants, who had come empty-handed, into the existing population. During the first eighteen months after independence, 340,000 Jews arrived, a number equaling almost half of the existing citizenry. By 1953, five years after the Partition Plan was proposed, the population had doubled. The newcomers were much needed, but how could they be housed, fed, educated, taught a new language, kept reasonably satisfied, and put to productive work all at the same time?

The first big group to arrive included 270,000 Holocaust survivors from Europe. The trauma they had experienced made their integration potentially difficult. In the country's first two years, about 50,000 Yemeni Jewish immigrants arrived—they, too, had to make a tremendous cultural adjustment—and 113,000 Jews from Iraq followed in the early 1950s. Besides them came large portions of the Jewish communities of Romania, Syria, Libya, Afghanistan, and Egypt.

By 1957, Israel's Jewish population had risen from 712,000 in November 1948 to 1,667,000. After a brief respite, another wave of immigration began in 1958. These newcomers were from North Africa, mainly Morocco: 160,000 immigrated in a very short span of time.

Handling the ensuing housing shortage forced, first, the creation of tent cities, then the construction of transit camps (*ma'abarot*)—127 by the end of 1951—which had better but still very Spartan facilities. Finally, during the second half of the 1950s, immigrants were moved directly upon arrival to places referred to as development towns, often located in the north or south, in order to populate parts of the country close to its borders.

These tent cities, transit camps, and development towns often became places of poverty, alienation, and unemployment. Many of the immigrants faced downward mobility, having lost all of their property in their homelands. Those from Europe had lost everything to the Nazis and the postwar Communist governments; those from the Middle East had seen their property taken by Arab governments or neighbors. Few were able to find jobs in Israel's fledgling economy equivalent to those they had held before emigration.

The new state absorbed hundreds of thousands of immigrants during its first fifteen years as best it could despite limited resources. Still, a sense of resentment and alienation prevailed among the last wave of immigrants to arrive, especially among those from Morocco. Since most of the better-off Jews from North Africa had gone to France, those who migrated to Israel tended to be poorer and less educated. As late arrivals, they had more problems finding jobs and housing, and they were sent to more remote places where living conditions were worse than in other regions. Another grievance was the tendency of government officials—who were sometimes high-handed and arrogant—to press them toward assimilation into a more European culture instead of maintaining their traditional Middle Eastern one.

This gap between European Jews and a part of the Middle Eastern Jews later led to friction. Some considered that the many Mizrahi immigrants became a poorer, less influential "second Israel." The friction peaked in the 1970s and 1980s, becoming a political factor of importance, although it diminished thereafter with political shifts, the broadening culture, and the demographic transition to a third generation, born in Israel, that often intermarried and had no personal memories of the traumatic immigrant experiences.

Both immigrants and the native-born sought to build a new Israeli identity based on reconnection with the land, a goal exemplified by the popular craze for archaeology. Throughout Israel, groups of young people conducted amateur weekend archaeological expeditions. Their chief ambition was to turn up artifacts related to the ancient Jewish presence in the Land of Israel.

A rapidly growing population, together with the economic fallout occasioned by the War of Independence, made austerity unavoidable in the 1950s. Support from Diaspora Jews helped, especially from Jews living in the United States, but the state remained in difficulties.

The issue of German reparations to Israel for the property lost and the suffering endured under the Nazis, first raised in 1950, aroused strong emotions. Some saw the very idea of accepting reparations so soon after the Holocaust as tantamount to taking blood money—that is, as accepting the idea that money could compensate for the mass murder of European Jews. The government took a different view, arguing that Germany had acquired a huge quantity of Jewish assets after the war that should rightfully be in the hands of the people from whom it had been stolen.

After initial talks between Jerusalem and Bonn, the Knesset approved further negotiations in January 1951. These resulted in a March 1953 treaty in which Germany promised $820 million to Israel. A structure was set up to deal with claims for individual restitution. The reparations issue was an agonizing one for the young State of Israel—at one point resulting in a near riot by opponents, led by the Herut Party—but the resulting payments provided a crucial injection of funds into the Israeli economy at a time when this was vital.

THE 1956 SUEZ CRISIS

As Israel was consolidating state and society, its Arab neighbors were undergoing a period of tremendous instability. The most important development was a 1952 military coup overthrowing the Egyptian monarchy and the takeover of Egypt's leadership two years later by Gamal Abdel Nasser. The Egyptian president saw himself, and was widely seen, as leader of the Arab world. A key element in that leadership was a readiness to battle Israel.

Egyptian officers in the Gaza Strip helped recruit and organize Palestinian guerrillas to stage cross-border raids. Israel responded with reprisals. In the largest such attack, carried out on February 28, 1955, the IDF unintentionally inflicted casualties on the Egyptian army as well, producing increased tensions between the two countries.

Another component of Egyptian policy was to develop an alliance with the Soviet Union as a superpower ally that could promote Cairo's regional ambitions. In August 1955, Egypt secured a large arms deal with the Soviet bloc. Israel worried that if those weapons were delivered to the Egyptian army, Cairo might attack Israel along with other Arab states. But Nasser made other enemies. He alienated Britain and France through his radical policies, his turn toward the Soviet Union, and the July 1956 nationalization of the Suez Canal Company. London and Paris were consequently ready to make a secret alliance with Israel. They agreed that Israel would invade the Sinai Peninsula before the Egyptian army could make use of the Soviet arms. Then France and Britain would intervene to end the war and, in doing so, would remove Nasser from power.

Israel kept its part of the bargain, attacking on October 29, 1956. Israeli forces took the Gaza Strip and then raced across the Sinai. But the British and French lost their nerve, the plan was exposed, and British domestic public opinion was very critical. U.S. intervention to save Nasser also put pressure on the allies, as did, to a lesser extent, Soviet threats to intervene militarily. Israel's forces withdrew from the captured territories in early 1957.

One Israeli gain from the war, however, was Egypt's decision to stop organizing cross-border attacks lest Israel retaliate again. Another apparent improvement was a U.S. pledge to guarantee Israel's access to the Gulf of Eilat, reachable by ships passing by Egyptian artillery at Sharm al-Shaykh, at the southern tip of the Sinai Peninsula. International forces were also put into the Sinai to ensure peace. The breakdown of these arrangements in 1967 brought about that year's war: Israel's preemptive strike and victory over its Arab neighbors.

THE DEVELOPMENT OF INFRASTRUCTURE
AND A NUCLEAR PROGRAM

Large-scale immigration from Eastern Europe and North Africa continued through the first half of the 1960s. Israel's population reached 2,384,000 in 1967. The increase made both possible and necessary utilizing the country's natural resources to the fullest extent. Water was especially important. In 1960 a blueprint was in place for a national irrigation scheme. Central to this effort was building a pipeline to tap the waters of the Jordan River.

Despite tensions with Arab states over using water close to the border, the National Water Carrier was completed in 1964. It crossed two-thirds of the country and supplied 84,535 gallons

(320 million cubic meters) of water annually. By 1967, thanks to the efficient channeling of water resources, 140,000 acres (nearly 57 hectares) of wasteland in the Negev desert of southern Israel had been reclaimed and were under cultivation.

The water supply also made possible the growth of the port of Eilat at the southern tip of the Negev. Since the Straits of Tiran, at the mouth of the Gulf of Eilat, were now open as a result of the 1956 war with Egypt, the once-sleepy fishing town began to play a crucial role in promoting Israel's growing trade with newly independent states of Africa and Asia. The Negev's copper ore and potash resources were developed, several new towns were established in the south—Netivot, Dimona, Arad, Yeruham, and Ashdod—and 250,000 new immigrants made their homes in the region.

Despite Israel's internal progress, security needs and historical experience could never be ignored. Generally, Israelis had tried to forget the Holocaust, but there were periodic reminders. Paramount among these was Israeli intelligence's capture of the Nazi war criminal Adolf Eichmann in his hiding place in Argentina on May 23, 1960. His trial and the chilling testimony of survivors focused Israeli attention back on the murder of European Jews. Eichmann was convicted and hanged on May 31, 1962, the only person ever executed by Israel.

The echoes of this affair reverberated in the Israeli determination that "never again" should Jews be helpless in the face of their enemies' genocidal ambitions. In this spirit, Israel's Atomic Energy Agency had been founded in 1952. In 1953 a process for extracting uranium from materials in the Negev desert was perfected, as was a new method for producing heavy water, used in early nuclear reactors. In the late 1950s, Israel received help from France in designing and constructing a nuclear reactor in Dimona, in southern Israel. The complex was initially described as a textile plant, agricultural station, or metallurgical research facility. In 1960, Prime Minister David Ben-Gurion announced that it was a nuclear research center built for "peaceful purposes."

In 1968 the CIA confirmed long-standing U.S. suspicions that Israel had begun to produce nuclear weapons. Israel has hewed to a policy of never openly admitting this, arguing, in the words of Shimon Peres, that the "fog surrounding this question . . . strengthen[s] our deterrent." Reportedly, they are not fully assembled, so Israel can argue that it has no actual nuclear weapons. They could be quickly installed in missile warheads or artillery shells as a last-resort threat to prevent Israel from military destruction, although this has never proven necessary. In 1986, Mordehai Vanunu, a left-wing Israeli who worked in the nuclear installation and later defected, claimed that Israel had between 100 and 200 small nuclear warheads, a figure higher than CIA estimates.

FOREIGN POLICY IN THE 1950S AND 1960S

One of the main problems facing Israeli diplomacy, especially in the early years, has been how to build close or even normal relations with any country when a significant bloc of states, some of them rich in oil and natural gas, promise to reward those countries that boycott or oppose Israel and to punish those friendly toward it. Two statistics from 2010 show this potential disparity in influence, a basic difference that has held throughout Israel's history:

1. The Arab Gulf States—the Arab countries of the Persian Gulf (Saudi Arabia, Qatar, Kuwait, Oman, and the United Arab Emirates)—import six times more Western goods than Israel does.

2. Israel has one vote in the United Nations; Arabic-speaking states have twenty-five; and Muslim-majority states, most of which are not friendly toward Israel, have fifty.

In the 1950s and 1960s especially, there were countervailing forces, including the enthusiasm for Israel in liberal and socialist circles abroad; the post-Holocaust reaction against antisemitism; and respect for Israel's democratic system, economic advances, and military victories. At that time, pro-Israel lobbies among Western Jewish communities were, however, of little importance.

Given the participation by many Arab regimes in Third World movements and, during the Cold War, the nonaligned movement, as well as the alliance of some Arab regimes with the Soviet bloc, Israel's diplomatic task became even trickier. The tide turned, at least for a while, because of two strategic factors. First, by acting as enemies of the West, radical Arab regimes gave Western countries an extra incentive to support Israel. Second, Israel showed through its stability, victory in the 1967 war, and disproportionate regional power that it was an asset in the Cold War struggle between the United States and the Soviet Union.

During the 1950s and up to 1967, Israel's principal ally was France, whose leaders were bound to Israel by a common socialist leadership, wartime links in the anti-Fascist struggle, and French opposition to the Arab nationalism that was subverting its control over its North African colonies. When Charles de Gaulle became president of France in 1958 with a policy of giving up Algeria, however, France's strategy slowly began to shift. The relationship collapsed in 1967, when de Gaulle responded to Israel's preemptive attack by abandoning the alliance in favor of trying to align with the Arab world. As a result, Israel lost its main source of weapons.

A second important Israeli relationship in Europe was with West Germany, based partly on that country's repentance over the Nazis' actions against Jews. But West Germany did not have the same degree of international influence as France or the ability to supply advanced weapons. And since West Germany and its Communist counterpart, East Germany, were competing for international support, the West Germans feared that too close a link to Israel would lead Arab states to align with their Soviet-backed foe. Thus, the strategic value of West Germany's friendship was limited for Israel. Although Israel also had good relations generally with Western European, South American, and smaller Asian states, none of these could provide strategic backup, significant aid, or advanced weapons.

The single most important diplomatic question for Israel was the stance it took on the main issue of the era, the Cold War. Given Israel's democratic orientation and the fact that both China and the Soviet Union backed its most militant Arab foes, neutrality was impossible, and the United States was the obvious choice as a strategic partner. But believing that Israel would not be a valuable ally and that a relationship would alienate all the Arab regimes, the United States was reluctant to build an alliance during the 1950s and well into the 1960s. As key Arab states grew increasingly supportive of the Soviet Union, however, the United States came to believe that an alliance with Israel would serve its interests.

As early as the Kennedy administration, in 1962, the United States began supplying arms to Israel. With Israel's victory in the 1967 war, when it decisively defeated Soviet-armed radical Arab regimes, U.S. policymakers concluded that the alliance should move into the open. And when Israel saved Jordan from invasion by Syria in 1970—by threatening to attack the Syrians if they crossed the border—the U.S.-Israel relationship moved to the status it has held to the present day.

At the same time, though, Israel did not give up on trying to build important relations with Third World countries. Israel perceived itself, like them, as a developing country. It hoped to leap over the surrounding hostile zone and form trade and diplomatic relationships with other countries in Africa, Asia, and Latin America.

A special asset that Israel had to offer was its technological expertise in innovative development techniques and equipment, particularly for agriculture. Israel established relations with many sub-Saharan African, non-Communist Asian, and Latin American countries. Between 1958 and 1970, almost 4,000 Israeli experts served in the Third World, mainly in Africa. Even when Third World countries supported the Arab side diplomatically against Israel, mutually beneficial relations continued. After the 1967 war, however, Arab states pressured African countries to cut relations with Israel and offered them economic benefits in exchange. This campaign was successful in many cases.

THE SIX-DAY WAR OF 1967 AND ITS AFTERMATH

Israel's brief respite from the direct effects of its neighbors' hostility ended in the mid-1960s, when the Arabic-speaking world was swept by a wave of radicalism, propelled by inter-Arab rivalries; Egypt's leadership; and Nasser's popularity, along with revolutionary activity by a number of Palestinian, Arab nationalist, and neo-Marxist groups. Cross-border guerrilla attacks against Israel from Egypt, Jordan, and Syria took place, along with many small shooting incidents on the Israel-Syria border.

In 1959, a group of Palestinian nationalists, Yasir Arafat among them, founded the Fatah movement. The goal of Fatah—and other Palestinian organizations formed during that era—was to wipe out Israel, which members believed would not survive for long if under assault by Arab armies and Palestinian guerrillas or under the Arab economic boycott's pressure. Five years later, the Palestine Liberation Organization (PLO) was founded, largely as an instrument of Egyptian policy. In the Arab political arena, reversing the results of the 1948 war in which Israel had won its independence and eliminating that state was again at the top of the agenda. Arab regimes, politicians, and intellectuals asserted that no price was too high to pay for a total victory ending in Israel's destruction.

The high level of tension and competition among Arab regimes to prove their militant opposition to Israel led to a major crisis in 1967. The Soviets, to make the Arabs feel that they needed Moscow's help, falsely charged that Israel was about to attack Syria. Meanwhile, Nasser, insisting on his eagerness to confront Israel, allied Egypt with Syria and Jordan and then demanded that the UN force patrolling the Sinai since the 1956 war be removed. The United Nations immediately complied, making possible an Egyptian advance to Israel's border. Nasser also imposed a total blockade on Israeli shipping at the Straits of Tiran, regardless of the U.S. promise in 1956 that it would ensure Israeli passage through the straits and also of Israel's assertion that such a step would be a cause for war.

It is generally not realized how reluctant Israeli leaders were to attack in response to these threats. Nasser and other Arab leaders were openly speaking about a final showdown in which Israel would be eliminated. Many outside observers thought that this was precisely what would happen. For Israel, war meant risking a possible defeat leading to the country's destruction and a massacre of its inhabitants. The decision to attack was so fraught with danger that even General Yitzhak Rabin, who favored an Israeli offensive, reportedly had a brief nervous breakdown because of the weight of responsibility on him.

When Prime Minister Levi Eshkol spoke on the national radio about the crisis in May 1967, his apparent indecision stirred up a great amount of concern among the Israeli public, other political leaders, and the army. In response, the Labor Party and the main opposition parties formed a national unity government. Moshe Dayan, a retired general, became defense minister, with Rabin as chief of staff of the armed forces.

In line with the doctrine developed since independence, Israel committed itself to attack rather than face an assault on its own limited territory. The result was a preemptive surprise attack against Egypt beginning early in the morning of June 5, 1967. Israel's enemies, despite their prewar bluster, were caught poorly prepared. The Israeli air force wiped out Egypt's air force on the ground, and the Israeli army advanced quickly into the Sinai and seized that peninsula up to the Suez Canal's eastern bank.

The Israeli forces fighting against Syria benefited from having maps of the defense of the Golan Heights, provided by a spy, Eli Cohen, who had paid with his life for obtaining them. The army moved up the slopes and took all the high ground that long had been used to shell Israeli towns below.

On the Jordanian front, however, Israel hesitated. Prime Minister Eshkol had promised King Hussein not to attack if he kept his country out of the fighting. But the king faced too much public pressure to stay neutral, and Nasser had falsely assured him that the Arabs were gaining a huge victory. As a result, Jordan entered the war; but without help from its allies, it suffered total defeat. Israel captured the entire West Bank and east Jerusalem. Of special significance for Israelis was taking the holiest site for all for Jews, the Old City and the Western Wall, the remaining retaining wall of the Temple. These are located in east Jerusalem, which Jordan had governed since 1948 and where it had deliberately destroyed synagogues and Jewish cemeteries.

Within six days, then, Israel had gone from what had seemed to be imminent annihilation to victory—a victory so total and with such low casualties that Israelis saw the results as close to miraculous.

Would the Six-Day War have any effect on the broader political situation? The answer came from the November 1967 Arab summit conference in Khartoum, Sudan. The countries in

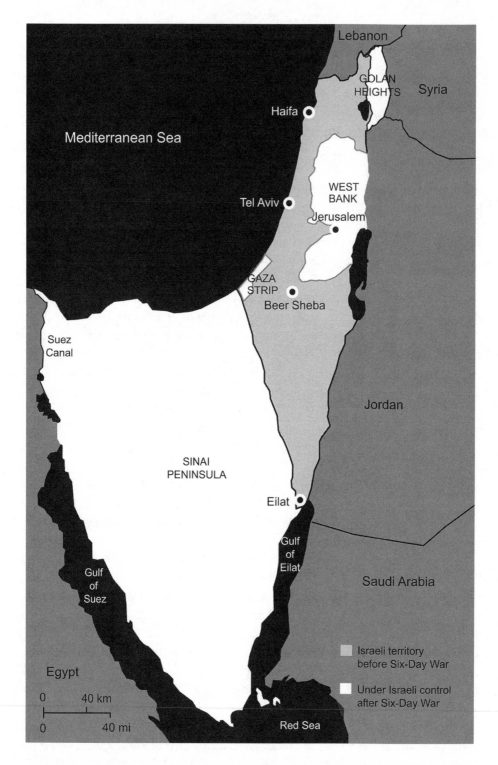

Israel's post-1948 borders were established on the basis of the ceasefire lines ending the War of Independence. During the Six-Day War in 1967, Israel captured five areas: the Sinai Peninsula and the Gaza Strip from Egypt, the West Bank and east Jerusalem from Jordan, and the Golan Heights from Syria. (© 2003–2010 Koret Communications Ltd. All rights reserved.)

Israeli paratroopers at the Western Wall in Jerusalem shortly after capturing it from the Jordanians, June 1967. (Getty Images / Image Bank.)

attendance decided on what came to be known as the "Three No's": they would refuse to make peace with Israel, to recognize it, or to negotiate with it.

Another response came from the UN Security Council, which, on November 22, 1967, agreed to Resolution 242, which set down the basis for a future agreement to achieve a just and lasting peace. The resolution called for Israel to withdraw from territories captured in the war—it did not specify all of those territories—in exchange for a complete end to the conflict.

So 1967 marked the beginning of the decades-long "peace process." The central issue to be resolved was embodied in the two divergent resolutions: the reconciliation of Western attempts to negotiate peace and the Arab refusal to make it. The decision by the authors of the resolution to speak of Israeli withdrawal from "territories" rather than "*the* territories" meant, in Israel's interpretation, that a full withdrawal was not required. The U.S. and British ambassadors to the United Nations, Arthur Goldberg and Lord Caradon, who composed the text, supported that view. Israel also held out for direct negotiations, which would force Arab interlocutors to extend some form of de facto recognition.

This outcome of the war set the framework for Israeli policy and debate during the following decades—a period of high self-confidence but no illusions about the ease of making peace and ending the conflict. The Israeli consensus was that until full peace was achieved—something that would take a very long time—Israel would retain the captured territories as a guarantee of its security and as leverage to obtain a full diplomatic settlement that satisfied its requirements. Those on the political right argued that waiting meant, in practice, permanent retention of the territories, since the Arab side would never make peace and since Israel had its own historical and religious claim to some of the land.

For many years after the war, the issue remained the subject of a passionate but abstract debate; only Arab—especially Palestinian and Syrian—offers to make full peace in exchange for captured territory could resolve the matter. In the meantime, the Labor Party and a national consensus favored establishing settlements in specific areas that Israel might seek to retain—east Jerusalem, the Golan Heights, the Jordan Valley, and areas close to the pre-1967 national borders. The political right favored additional settlement in the Gaza Strip and the West Bank generally.

Another effect of the 1967 defeat was severe damage to the prestige of the USSR in the Arab world. To repair its position, the Soviet Union rebuilt the Syrian and Egyptian armed forces. In 1968, using powerful Soviet-supplied artillery on the Suez Canal's western bank, Nasser began a war of attrition to reduce Israel's presence in the Sinai. Heavy casualties were inflicted on Israeli troops, especially in July and October 1968, and at times Soviet pilots flew missions for the Egyptian air force. Israel retaliated with air and artillery attacks, forcing Egypt to evacuate nearby towns, the canal, and oil refineries, at great cost to Egypt.

The instability inspired Western—and especially U.S.—peacemaking efforts. In June 1970, Secretary of State William Rogers announced an initiative, after consultation with the Arab side but not with Israel, that sought "to encourage the parties to stop shooting and start talking." National Security Advisor Henry Kissinger ridiculed the proposal as too one-sided to achieve anything. Israel agreed only reluctantly to unilateral withdrawal from the east side of the Suez Canal and soon complained that Egypt was violating the ceasefire agreement by moving antiaircraft missile launch sites right next to the canal. The Rogers plan was soon abandoned, and U.S.-Israel relations emerged stronger than ever because of other events.

The key factor in improving relations was the rise of large-scale Palestinian terrorist activity, backed by several Arab regimes and secretly by the Soviet Union, targeting Israel and, in some cases, moderate Arab governments aligned with the United States. The offensive was led by Fatah, which during this period took over the PLO. One of its aims was to force Arab states into a new round of warfare against Israel. The battle had four fronts—the West Bank, Jordan, international terrorism, and Lebanon.

On the first front, Fatah and the PLO, operating from bases inside Jordan, attempted to ignite a guerrilla war in the West Bank and the Gaza Strip and lead terrorist attacks into Israel. Israel quickly defeated this effort by rooting out the armed enemy cells in the territories.

On the second front, which followed, the PLO attacked Israel from bases in Jordan. The Jordanian government was unwilling or unable to stop these operations. Israel responded by hitting PLO safe havens in Jordan, which gave Jordan's government an incentive to act against the Palestinian raids. Facing increased resistance from the Jordanian army and government, which were reluctant to be dragged into an armed conflict with Israel, the PLO sought to take over Jordan itself. In September 1970 the escalating tension led King Hussein and his armed forces to attack and soundly defeat the PLO, expelling them from the country. At a critical moment, when the radical Syrian regime, the PLO's ally, ordered its army to invade Jordan and overthrow the king, Israel warned that it would meet any such invasion by force. The Syrians backed down.

The third front was international. PLO member groups like the Popular Front for the Liberation of Palestine (PFLP) hijacked planes and tried to attack Israeli facilities abroad. After the PLO's expulsion from Jordan, Fatah used similar tactics, creating a front group called Black September as a cover. Among these attacks, planned at the highest levels of Fatah and the PLO, was the 1972 assault on the Olympic village in Munich, Germany, and the kidnapping and killing of Israeli athletes there. In response, Israel initiated a campaign of reprisals, killing Fatah and PFLP representatives in Paris, Rome, Nicosia (Cyprus), and Beirut.

In June 1976 a four-member terrorist team consisting of two Palestinians and two German sympathizers hijacked an Air France plane with 248 passengers and a twelve-member crew, diverting it to Entebbe Airport in Uganda. The hijackers demanded the release of forty Palestinians held in Israel and thirteen others imprisoned in other countries for previous terrorist attacks. The hijackers separated Israeli and Jewish passengers from non-Jewish passengers and released the latter. On July 4, a 100-man IDF task force landed at Entebbe for a successful rescue operation. All the hijackers were killed, as were 3 of the remaining 105 hostages. The assault team's commander, Lieutenant Colonel Yonatan Netanyahu, was also killed.

In the 1970s, on the fourth front, small squads of PLO gunmen left the new PLO bases in Lebanon to infiltrate across the border and attempt to murder as many Israelis as possible before being killed or captured themselves. Two of the most notorious of these terrorist attacks were the massacre of twenty-seven Israelis, twenty-one of whom were children, by members of the Democratic Front for the Liberation of Palestine (DFLP), on May 15, 1974, and the murder of eighteen Israelis, eight of them children, by terrorists of the Popular Front for the Liberation of Palestine, in Kiryat Shmona on April 11, 1974. The end of PLO control of southern Lebanon by Israel's Operation Peace for Galilee in 1982 largely stopped Palestinian groups from carrying out attacks of this kind.

Both the nature of the Palestinian assaults and the success of the Israeli responses—especially in saving Jordan's government from being overthrown by pro-Soviet Syria and the PLO—impressed U.S. and Western policymakers, laying the basis for an emerging alliance.

THE YOM KIPPUR WAR OF 1973

When Prime Minister Eshkol died in February 1969, Golda Meir, the foreign minister, an important member of the founding generation, and a unifying figure in the Labor Party, became prime minister. President Anwar al-Sadat, who ruled Egypt after Nasser's death in September 1970, had been threatening for several years to launch a new war in order to reverse the consequences of Egypt's 1967 defeat. In the fall of 1973, however, Israeli intelligence wrongly assessed Egypt's intentions because of an approach that became known as the "conception": Israeli intelligence assumed that Egypt would not renew its war with Israel after losing so badly the last time it tried. Accepting the "conception" as true and eager to avoid disrupting normal life, Meir and Defense Minister Moshe Dayan did not recognize the danger and did not mobilize the army until mere hours before the attack began.

On October 6, 1973, the Day of Atonement (Yom Kippur), the holiest day in the Jewish calendar, when Israel virtually shuts down, Egypt and Syria attacked simultaneously. At first, the offensive across the Suez Canal in the south and on the Golan Heights in the north pushed back Israeli forces. Israel suffered heavy losses along the canal and in the first counterattack owing to Egypt's possession of new Soviet antitank weapons. For some hours on the Golan Heights, only a half-dozen Israeli tanks stood between Syria's army and the lowlands extending to the Mediterranean.

Israel quickly regained the strategic advantage. The IDF crossed the Suez Canal and surrounded the Egyptian Third Army, and it pushed Syrian forces back toward their own capital of Damascus. On October 25, 1973, a ceasefire agreement was reached. Months of U.S. "shuttle diplomacy" followed, conducted by Kissinger, resulting in disengagement agreements with Egypt and Syria in January 1974. All troops were withdrawn to the prewar lines.

Israeli Prime Minister David Ben-Gurion conferring with senior Mapai politician and future prime minister Golda Meir. (Getty Images / Image Bank.)

Defense Minister Moshe Dayan (with eyepatch) on the Golan Heights during the Yom Kippur War, October 1973. (Getty Images / Image Bank.)

During this period, Israel's lack of international support caused concern in the country. The United States was slow to respond with shipments of military equipment when the war began, and Israelis widely believed that the delay was purposeful, that the United States had assumed that an outcome closer to a tie would make peace negotiations more fruitful. When the U.S. government asked European countries to let their runways be used for the military airlift to Israel, they all refused except for Portugal, which responded to U.S. pressure. During the war, an Arab oil embargo aimed at the United States and the Netherlands for their support of Israel also ushered in an era of high oil prices, giving Arab states a new weapon for intimidation and economic influence.

Although the war lasted barely three weeks, Israel paid heavily: nearly 3,000 were dead or missing. The national mood was far more sober and self-critical than after the 1967 war. The government was widely disparaged for lack of preparation, which set the stage for dramatic internal political changes.

POLITICAL AND SOCIAL TRANSFORMATION

The 1977 election was a turning point in Israel's history, the biggest political change in three decades of independence. A radio announcer called it an "earthquake" when the results were broadcast, and that label stuck. For the first time, not only did the Labor Party lose power, but the loss was by a wide margin. There were several reasons for this outcome, including dissatisfaction with the conduct of the 1973 war, a sense that it was time for a change, and a political upheaval in the thinking of many Mizrahim.

A generation after the mass immigration from predominantly Arabic-speaking countries—especially North African ones—many socially conservative, traditionally religious Mizrahim felt resentment at the predominantly Ashkenazic ruling establishment. Even before independence, the Mizrahim had been strongly represented on the conservative side of the political spectrum. For example, more than 50 percent of the members of the Lehi organization and a considerable proportion of Irgun fighters had a Mizrahi background.

Looking back from the 1970s on the early period of immigration, many Mizrahim felt that the Labor government had scorned them and had pressed them to conform. Their numbers, especially those from North Africa, in top military, economic, political, and cultural positions were still disproportionately low compared with their number in the general population. Consequently, a majority of Mizrahim supported Menahem Begin's conservative nationalist Likud Party, which won the 1977 election. Some corruption scandals in the Labor Party and the rise of a short-lived centrist list also drew votes away from the incumbents.

For many in the dominant, secular, left-of-center Ashkenazic establishment, the Likud's victory was traumatic. Underlying Israeli debates in the following decades was the cultural bitterness caused by the establishment's belief that reactionary forces were transforming and ruining the country. By the 1990s, however, the Ashkenazic–Mizrahi/Sephardic divide was narrowing; arguably, the consensus achieved after the peace process experiment in the 1990s mostly closed it.

The 1970s also saw the radicalization of some of Israel's Arab citizens. The military administration of Arab areas ended in 1966. But the key factor in the shift was the rise of the PLO and Fatah, which promoted both Arab and Palestinian nationalism among the younger generation. The most heated moment came on March 30, 1976, the day of a general strike by Israeli Arabs protesting land expropriations. The demonstrations turned violent, and six Israeli Arabs were killed in clashes with the police.

Voting behavior shifted in the 1970s accordingly. There had always been a strong Arab vote for Labor, but in the 1970s the proportion of Arabs voting for the Communist Party and other left-wing parties grew. Yet very few Israeli Arabs joined in revolutionary activities—the most significant group was the tiny Abna al-Balad (Sons of the Homeland) nationalist movement—and despite the turmoil often going on next door in the captured territories, few violent incidents involved Israeli Arabs.

THE EGYPT-ISRAEL PEACE TREATY

Likud, the nationalist party that gained power in 1977, was generally skeptical about Arab willingness to make peace and reluctant, for both nationalist-religious and strategic reasons, to yield territory captured in 1967. Yet Prime Minister Begin concluded that his Egyptian counterpart, Sadat, wanted a peace agreement. Egypt had broken with the Soviet Union and was seeking U.S. patronage. Moreover, the loss of the Sinai oil fields and the closing of the Suez Canal, filled with wreckage and mines from the 1973 war, was driving Egypt to economic ruin. Finally, Sadat was a risk-taker ready to try a totally different foreign policy in Egypt.

Israeli Prime Minister Menahem Begin (left) greets Egyptian President Anwar al-Sadat on his arrival in Jerusalem in November 1977, a visit that later led to the Egypt-Israel peace treaty. (Getty Images/Image Bank.)

When Begin invited Sadat to Jerusalem, the Egyptian president agreed. In an especially dramatic development, Sadat addressed the Knesset in November 1977. The following year, Sadat and Begin met at Camp David, Maryland, hosted by President Jimmy Carter. The two countries agreed to a transition period during which self-government would be granted to Palestinian residents of the West Bank and the Gaza Strip, a step they hoped would lead to full negotiations and an Israel-Palestinian peace settlement. The Palestinians rejected this opportunity, instead joining almost all the Arab states in declaring Egypt to be a traitor to the Arab cause. PLO leader Yasir Arafat threatened to kill any local Palestinian leaders who accepted the offer.

Nonetheless, Egypt and Israel signed a bilateral peace treaty on March 26, 1979, which provided for an Israeli withdrawal from the Sinai, to be completed by April 25, 1982, followed by an end to the war between the two countries and normal relations. Although Egypt kept the peace a cold one—with commercial, tourist, and other links remaining minimal—this step transformed the regional strategic situation, greatly reducing the chances for a war by Arab states against Israel.

THE LEBANON WAR OF 1982

Besides signing a treaty with Egypt, Israel also destroyed Iraq's nuclear reactor at Osirak in 1981 in an aerial bombing raid without any Israeli casualties. In the June 1981 elections, these successes helped Begin's government win again despite concerns over inflation and a sluggish

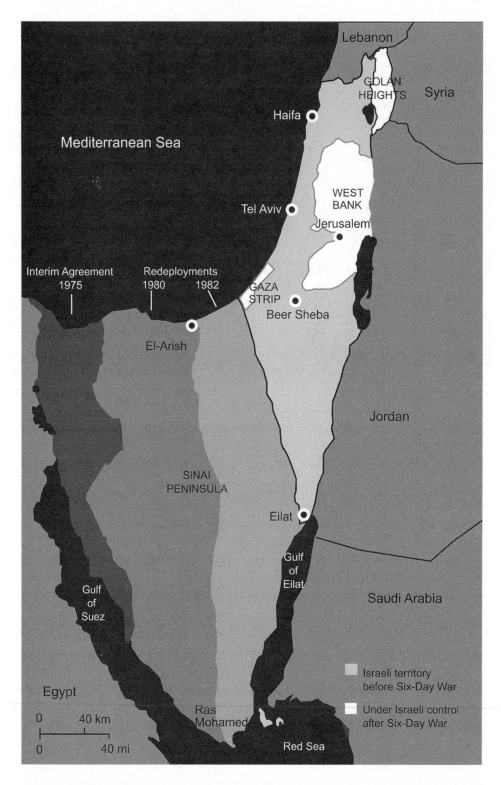

When indirect negotiations with Egypt led to interim agreements and then a peace treaty, Israeli forces withdrew from the Sinai Peninsula, redeploying in stages in 1974, 1975, 1980, and 1982. (© 2003–2010 Koret Communications Ltd. All rights reserved.)

economy. Israel annexed the Golan Heights in December 1981, although this move was not recognized internationally. Other developments in the north would set off the government's greatest crisis.

After being expelled from Jordan in 1970, the PLO had moved its base of operations to Lebanon, where it had created a virtual state within a state. It used south Lebanon for launching cross-border attacks against Israel that often resulted in civilian deaths. By 1981, the PLO was building up forces in the south and creating a regular army—or what nearly amounted to one. After major clashes in the region, the PLO and Israel negotiated a ceasefire indirectly. Fatah generally observed it but allowed or encouraged smaller PLO groups to continue attacks. Israel remained concerned about the buildup there as preparation for a future war.

The situation worsened in June 1982, when an attack by Palestinian terrorists on Israel's ambassador to the United Kingdom, Shlomo Argov, paralyzed him for life. Israel forged a secret alliance with Maronite Christian militias, which had been fighting the PLO and its allies in a Lebanese civil war, and formulated a plan; its chief author was the Israeli defense minister, Ariel Sharon. The plan was for Israel to defeat the PLO and its Syrian partners, thus allowing the Christians to win the civil war, install a government, and make peace with Israel.

The Israeli offensive that began in June 1982 was called Operation Peace for Galilee. Israeli forces advanced quickly, defeating PLO and Syrian troops, and tens of thousands of Lebanese civilians fled northward. Israeli forces soon reached Beirut but stopped there, since an attempt to capture the whole city would have caused high casualties for all concerned. U.S. envoy Philip Habib coordinated diplomatic efforts, and the sides reached an agreement under which Syrian and Palestinian forces would leave Beirut by September 1, to be replaced by an international peacekeeping force composed mostly of American, French, and Italian soldiers. In due course, the Christian leader, Bashir Gemayel, became Lebanon's president. At this point, however, a hitherto successful operation unraveled.

Determined to block Israeli hegemony over Lebanon and ensure its own continued influence, Syria had Gemayel assassinated. To root out the remaining PLO and Fatah infrastructure in refugee camps near Beirut, Israeli forces surrounded the Sabra and Shatila camps and allowed Christian militiamen to enter them. The militiamen, seeking revenge for the assassination of their leader and for massacres of Christians perpetrated in the bloody civil war, killed over a thousand civilians, mostly Palestinians, living in the camps.

This event set off an international outcry and much protest in Israel as well. The war had already been criticized because, unlike its predecessors, it was a war of "choice" rather than necessity, as some saw it. Begin set up a full judicial inquiry under Chief Justice Yitzhak Kahan to investigate the massacre and Israel's role in it. The Kahan Report, published on February 8, 1983, put direct responsibility on the Lebanese militia but blamed several Israeli leaders for failing to control or keep the militiamen out of the camps altogether. It censured Begin and recommended that Sharon be removed from his post.

The plan also faltered in achieving its strategic goals. An Israel-Lebanon agreement ending the war between the two countries was declared on May 17, 1983. But President Amin Gemayel, who had succeeded his murdered brother, was too weak to enforce it over Syrian opposition. In addition, although PLO leader Arafat and his army sailed away to a new headquarters in

Tunisia, Syria refused to withdraw from Lebanon's Beqa'a Valley. A guerrilla war against Israeli forces began and casualties mounted, resulting in increased unpopularity for the Begin government.

Soaring inflation and the institution of austerity measures in the second half of 1983 intensified domestic discontent, and on August 30, 1983, Begin resigned, depressed by the course of events in Lebanon and by the death of his wife nine months earlier. Foreign Minister Yitzhak Shamir replaced him; he was elected on the strength of his promises to maintain Israel's military presence in Lebanon, establish new settlements in the West Bank, and manage the country's economic problems.

As so often happens in times of crisis, a great achievement sends national morale soaring. Two successes changed the national mood: Operation Moses in 1984, in which Jews were smuggled out of Ethiopia through Sudan, and Operation Solomon in 1991, a dramatic thirty-six-hour airlift that brought almost the entire Ethiopian Jewish community still remaining to Israel—8,000 people in the first phase, 14,300 in the second. In the July 23, 1984, elections, Labor won forty-six seats compared to Likud's forty-one, but since neither was able to assemble a parliamentary majority of sixty-one on its own, they agreed to a national unity government: Labor's Shimon Peres would serve as prime minister for two years; then Likud's Shamir would serve for the same amount of time.

Israel's army had remained in Lebanon, withdrawing southward from Beirut. Iran and Syria were backing the new Hizballah and other militant Shi'a Muslim groups to fight the Israeli forces. In 1983, Shamir had maintained the policy of refusing to withdraw fully unless Syria pulled out of eastern Lebanon. The new national unity government established in 1984 altered this stance: it promised to withdraw Israeli forces from Lebanon, unilaterally if necessary. After Israel's peace talks with Lebanon collapsed in January 1985, the government approved a three-phase plan to return IDF forces to the international border. As the IDF withdrew, Hizballah initiated attacks. In March the withdrawal rate accelerated, with phase two completed by the end of April. At this time, Israel also exchanged 1,150 Lebanese and Palestinian prisoners of war for three Israeli prisoners of war.

The final phase of IDF withdrawal was completed ahead of schedule, in June 1985. Total Israeli casualties in Lebanon included more than 650 dead. Israel left behind about 500 soldiers and advisors to aid the newly created, Israel-armed South Lebanon Army (SLA), which patrolled a buffer zone on the Lebanese side of the border about seven–twelve miles (eleven–twenty kilometers) wide. Even though the PLO forces were gone and Hizballah could not attack in Israel itself, the war in south Lebanon continued.

PEACE AND SECURITY ISSUES IN THE 1980S

Although the war in Lebanon had not succeeded in its wider goals and brought heavy costs for Israel, it also reduced the PLO's ability to attack into Israel for some time. The weakening of the PLO also encouraged several peace efforts during the 1980s. Many avenues were tried, but in the end, little progress was made.

The first half of the decade saw the final effort to develop alternatives to engaging the PLO, which was not interested in a compromise peace and continued to express its determination to destroy Israel. Israel's position was that it would negotiate with the PLO only if and when that organization changed its stance, to be signaled by its acceptance of UN Resolution 242—representing recognition of Israel's right to exist as a state—and abandonment of terrorism.

Since negotiation with the PLO was ruled out, Israel tried to proceed in two ways. It sought to give local Palestinians autonomy, as promised in the Egypt-Israel agreement, but this approach ultimately failed because the PLO intimidated West Bank mayors who thought of accepting it—two of them were assassinated. The alternative was the "Jordanian option," an attempt to negotiate with Jordan's government. Returning Jordan's pre-1967 control over the West Bank would, Israel hoped, set the stage for a "Palestinian solution."

In retrospect, it is clear that six Arab-Israeli wars on the state level—in 1948, 1956, 1967, 1968–1970, 1973, and 1982—had sated the appetite of Arab countries for fighting losing wars against Israel. For the next couple of decades, the battles would be fought by non-state actors that were clients of some Arab states and increasingly of Iran. Such groups as the PLO, Hamas, and Hizballah could attack and kill Israeli civilians and disrupt life in the captured territories, but they could not significantly harm, much less defeat, Israel itself. So the country continued to develop internally and, despite appearances at times, enjoyed a far higher degree of security than before.

The Jordanian government was stable and had shown its ability to control the Palestinian forces within Jordan's borders. Moreover, Jordan benefited from Israel's existence, which countered the aggressiveness of its more powerful Arab neighbors and ensured Jordan's sovereignty. Both Jordan and Israel had fought the PLO, and from Amman's standpoint, a West Bank under PLO control would be a threat rather than a cause for celebration.

Shimon Peres, prime minister from 1984 to 1986 and foreign minister for the next two years, was the main advocate of a Jordanian solution. The key initiative during this period was the attempt of King Hussein of Jordan to forge Jordanian-Palestinian cooperation with himself as the senior partner. King Hussein's main effort came in a February 1985 proposal to establish a Jordan-Palestinian delegation to negotiate with Israel, an initiative that PLO leader Arafat told him the PLO accepted. But Arafat reneged on that commitment, and after a year of fruitless attempts, the king announced that he was cutting off political contacts with the PLO. Hussein nevertheless made a second attempt in secret exchanges with Foreign Minister Peres in 1987. Again, no agreement was reached. Unlike Sadat's Egypt, Jordan could not hope to defy virtually all of the Arab states plus the PLO. In early 1988 the king finally and forever dropped Jordan's claim to the West Bank.

The PLO, now ensconced in far-off Tunis, continued its terrorist campaign against Israel during the 1980s although, given the lack of a secure and safe haven on Israel's borders, it staged many of its attacks in other countries. In September 1985, for example, terrorists from Force 17, Arafat's elite bodyguard group, murdered three Israeli civilians who had sailed to Cyprus. In response to this and other attacks, Israel bombed the PLO headquarters in Tunis. Shortly thereafter, in October, a PLO member group carried out a long-planned operation to hijack the *Achille Lauro,* an Italian cruise ship, in the eastern Mediterranean, in the course of which they killed an American Jewish passenger. Arafat negotiated the surrender of the terrorists, ostensibly as a neutral mediator, although radio intercepts showed that he was in command of the group. Italy allowed the group's chief to escape.

THE INTIFADA OF 1987–1991

A Palestinian intifada, or uprising, in 1987 was the biggest revolt in the West Bank and the Gaza Strip during twenty years of Israeli rule. Initially, local forces, unhappy with the PLO's management of the movement, organized and ran the intifada, although soon the PLO stepped in to assert its authority. The new tactic marked the failure of the international terrorist and cross-border operations to have much effect. It also showed the rise of Islamist forces, especially Hamas, which provided an alternative to Fatah and PLO leadership.

The uprising began spontaneously on December 8, 1987, after two Palestinian vehicles collided with an Israeli army truck at a military checkpoint in the Gaza Strip. Four Palestinians died, and a rumor was spread that the accident was a deliberate act of murder planned by Israel, the first in a wave of misinformation whose dissemination became increasingly organized in later years.

Before long, the Unified National Leadership of the Uprising (UNLU), a coalition of Palestinian groups including Hamas but under general PLO and Fatah control, took over direction of the uprising. Hamas originated in the Palestinian branch of the Muslim Brotherhood movement. At the beginning, it engaged only in educational and social activities, so Israel did not bar its activities, but this changed once the group moved to violence. The Hamas Charter, published in August 1988, systematically rejected Israel's existence and presented the Hamas goal of creating an Islamist state. Hamas saw itself as replacing Fatah and the PLO as the Palestinian leadership.

At the same time, Fatah and the PLO saw themselves as replacing Jordan as the rightful proprietor of the West Bank. The PLO called an emergency meeting of its Palestinian National Council (PNC) legislature in November 1988 for three reasons. First, concerned—wrongly—that Israel might respond to King Hussein's decision to drop his claim on the West Bank by annexing the territory, the PLO wanted to put forward its claim to be the rightful government there. Second, the PLO needed to formulate an organizational response to the intifada on a political level, including making it clear to local activists that the Tunis-based PLO was running the show. Third, a U.S. diplomatic initiative suggested that a U.S.-PLO dialogue would ensue if the organization recognized Israel and abandoned the use of terrorism. Both the United States and Israel had set these preconditions for the PLO's entrance into the diplomatic peace process.

The PNC meeting in November 1988 did not end with an agreement to meet the preconditions for negotiation. Although the final resolution of the meeting included some phrases implying acceptance of those terms, the PNC did not accept them, as the U.S. State Department concluded. But soon thereafter, at a Geneva press conference, Arafat offered the minimal language deemed acceptable to the U.S. government, though not by Israel, for at least opening a public dialogue with the PLO. During the period of the dialogue, Fatah did not attack Israel directly, but other PLO member groups did, which showed that the PLO had not altered its strategy.

The outcome of the Israeli elections in 1988 was similar to the outcome in 1984: Likud had forty seats; Labor had thirty-nine. The result was another national unity government, with Shamir as prime minister and Peres as deputy prime minister and finance minister. Having given up on the Jordan option, Peres wanted to explore negotiations with Palestinians who were close to the PLO without being members. Shamir opposed that idea. This government collapsed in March 1990, when Peres walked out in the belief that he could form a majority government on his own.

His walkout became widely known as the "stinking maneuver." Some saw it as devious; others, as a failure. Since Peres could not find the necessary support, on June 8, 1990, Shamir formed a new, more conservative government that rejected a U.S. proposal for direct talks between Israeli and Palestinian delegations. These developments, however, were soon overshadowed by two major events—the Soviet bloc's collapse and the Iraqi invasion of Kuwait—that changed the strategic picture.

The U.S.-PLO dialogue finally ended in May 1990, when Arafat was caught supporting and praising a terrorist attack intended to kill civilians in Tel Aviv but intercepted by Israel's navy off the coast. The operation's deputy commander, Muhammad Ahmad al-Hamadi Yusuf, told interrogators that his order had been "Don't leave anyone alive. Kill them all . . . children, women, elderly people." By this time, too, the intifada had petered out without forcing any change in Israeli policy or causing significant damage to the State of Israel.

THE COLD WAR'S END AND THE WAR OVER KUWAIT

The collapse of the Soviet Union in 1991 and the concomitant end of the Cold War had largely positive implications for Israel. First, the Arab states at war with Israel and the PLO lost their strongest ally and arms supplier, the now-disintegrated Soviet Union. Second, the emergence of democratic countries—formerly part of the Soviet Union or within the Soviet sphere of influence—that wanted to reverse Communist-era policies meant that Israel had new friends in central Europe and the Caucasus. Starting with Hungary in September 1989, the emerging states and Russia itself opened diplomatic and commercial relations with Israel. Third World states—especially in Africa—that had broken relations with Israel after the 1967 war restored them.

Third, the Soviet Union's collapse brought a dramatic increase in Jewish immigration from its former territory. More than one million people, many of them highly skilled, immigrated to Israel from the former Soviet Union in the biggest influx since the early 1950s. The upsurge in population built Israel's confidence and internal markets while presenting its enemies with a stronger Israel that would be more dangerous to confront in war. Perhaps they would be persuaded that time was on Israel's side, not theirs—a possible new incentive to move toward peace.

In August 1990, Iraq seized and annexed Kuwait in a bid to grab that country's oil wealth and to become the Arab world's leader. Most Arab governments, horrified at the perceived threat to their own states, turned to the United States for protection. Building an international coalition, the U.S. government demanded that Iraq pull out of Kuwait by January 15, 1991, or face an attack.

IDF personnel assess damage to apartment buildings following an Iraqi Scud missile strike, January 1991. (Getty Images / Image Bank.)

Arafat and the PLO, with enthusiastic popular support from Palestinians, backed the Iraqi dictator, Saddam Hussein. They believed that the Iraqis would triumph and then turn their guns against Israel, with the Arab world as a whole following suit. This was a tremendous miscalculation since Saudi Arabia, the Kuwaiti government-in-exile, and other Arab governments saw the support for Iraq as a betrayal and turned against the PLO. The Arabs of the Gulf States stopped funding the PLO, sending it into a major financial crisis.

After the multinational force attacked Kuwait, Iraq—mistakenly expecting that an attack on Israel would rally Arab support on its behalf—fired Scud missiles into Israel beginning on January 18, 1991. It fired a total of thirty-nine during the six-week-long war. Israel, worried that the missiles might have chemical or bacteriological warheads, signaled that the attack could bring nuclear retaliation, but Iraq lacked this capability, as it turned out.

Israel would have retaliated immediately against the missile launches in accordance with its own security doctrine, but the United States urged Israel to exercise restraint lest such a strike widen the war. It promised to destroy the launchers itself—a pledge that was not kept—and also to send U.S. air-defense systems to Israel, although these proved ineffective.

Since the warheads were small and the missiles inaccurate, only two people were killed directly in the attacks. But more than 200 were wounded, scores of people died of stress-related heart attacks or other maladies, and the Israeli economy was largely paralyzed. To ensure that Israel remained passive under this attack, the United States promised increased support in compensation after the war, but no specific response of this kind materialized following the Iraqi defeat.

THE OSLO ACCORDS

The defeat of Iraq in Kuwait together with reduced Arab support for the PLO, the divisions opened up in the Arab world, and the growing questioning of traditional Arab policies seemed to benefit Israel. Given the failure of PLO efforts to destroy, defeat, or severely damage Israel over several decades, as well as the PLO's more immediate losses, the assumption was that the Palestinian movement might alter its course. Moreover, the United States, the world's sole superpower, had just saved most of the Arabic-speaking world from potential Iraqi domination. The time seemed ripe for a major peace effort.

After the war ended, U.S. Secretary of State James Baker visited Israel, Egypt, and Syria to promote the idea of a regional peace conference based on UN Security Council Resolution 242. Syria, fearing U.S. global hegemony and bereft of its Soviet patron, agreed for the first time to participate in direct negotiations with Israel. It was further agreed that PLO members would be excluded from the Jordanian-Palestinian delegation, but Israel accepted nominally independent Palestinians whom it knew were secretly Fatah members. On August 4, 1991, the Israeli cabinet agreed to participate in a peace conference on the worked-out terms.

The international conference began with a session in Madrid in October 1991. An attempted Syrian walkout failed when none of the other Arab states joined in. Afterward, negotiations bifurcated. Three sets of bilateral talks were held between Israeli and Syrian, Lebanese, and Jordanian-Palestinian delegations. Another group of talks, held by various combinations of delegations, were organized around specific regional topics, including arms control, economic cooperation, Palestinian refugees, water resources, and the environment. Little actual progress was made in any of these talks, which continued into 1992, even though Israel made the additional concession of meeting the Palestinians without a Jordanian presence. It later emerged that the PLO had given the Palestinian delegates no authority to agree to anything.

In the June 23, 1992, elections in Israel, the Labor Party, led by Yitzhak Rabin, won forty-four Knesset seats compared to Likud's thirty-two. Rabin was able to form a narrow left-center coalition with sixty-two seats. During the campaign, Rabin had called for "separation" between Israel and the Palestinian-inhabited territories. Along with his foreign minister, Peres, Rabin intended to find out whether conditions and experiences had forced the PLO to change its worldview and goals.

The Israeli leaders began secret exchanges with the PLO in Norway and reached a basis for agreement. Then they informed the United States of this development. The actual signing of the Declaration of Principles (informally known as the Oslo Accords) took place in Washington, DC, on September 13, 1993. In a historic moment, Rabin and Arafat shook hands, with U.S. President Bill Clinton, host and sponsor of the agreement, looking on.

For Israel, the agreement was a test of the two-state proposition: Was the PLO ready to make peace with Israel by accepting the existence of two states, one Israeli, one Palestinian, in the Middle East? If all went according to plan, the PLO would be in a hurry to reach a comprehensive compromise, with the existence of a Palestinian state in territory currently occupied by Israel as the eventual goal. The five-year interim period specified in the Oslo Accords, to

PLO leader Yasir Arafat (right) shakes hands with Israeli Prime Minister Yitzhak Rabin as President Bill Clinton watches, after the signing of the Oslo Accords, Washington, DC, September 1995. (Getty Images/Image Bank.)

end by December 1998, would allow for confidence-building measures. Israel believed that having to govern territory and provide for the needs of the population would bring Arafat and the PLO to moderate their stance.

The most important question was whether the PLO would use its new governing authority, large international financial donations, and security forces to stop terrorism and to build a stable political and economic infrastructure. If the PLO and the Palestinians really yearned for a state and wanted to end the long Israeli occupation, they would have a major incentive to make the process work, or so the Israelis hoped.

Israel's assumptions about the PLO were built into the structure of the Oslo Accords and the supplementary agreements made in 1994 and 1996. Israel and the PLO recognized each other, and the accords established a Palestinian Authority (PA) to rule territory currently occupied by Israel, starting with the entire Gaza Strip (except for Israeli settlements there) and the town of Jericho.

The West Bank was divided into three areas: Area A, all of the towns except for Hebron (whose status would be determined in 1996), would be under full PA control. Area B, the villages, was to be governed by the PA politically, but Israel would have the right to enter them for security purposes. Area C, Jewish settlements and unpopulated areas, continued to be under Israeli control. All Jewish settlements, the PLO agreed, would remain where they were until a full peace treaty was signed. Israel stated, without PLO disagreement, that it would not build any new settlements or expand the existing ones territorially, but it retained the right to construct new buildings in existing settlements.

During the course of reaching terms for a full peace treaty, the two sides were to negotiate all issues, including the future of the territories, Jewish settlements, Jerusalem, and Palestinian refugees. An international consortium of donors would provide massive aid to fund the PA's budget.

Rabin and Arafat met in Cairo on October 6, 1993, to agree to the details of implementing the Oslo Accords, including the ground rules for the PA's operation and the establishment of bilateral committees to resolve issues and prepare for the comprehensive negotiations. At the last moment, after agreement was reached and all the leaders were on stage to sign the agreements, Arafat demanded more concessions. Egyptian president Hosni Mubarak, the host, rebuked Arafat, and the Palestinian leader finally agreed, but added a note making his acceptance of the deal conditional on getting more from Israel.

Another crisis occurred when an extremist Jewish settler massacred twenty-nine Muslim worshippers at a Hebron mosque that also marked a Jewish holy site. Nevertheless, on May 4, 1994, Israel and the PLO signed an agreement in Cairo outlining the parameters of Palestinian self-rule in the Gaza Strip and Jericho. According to the agreement, the IDF would withdraw from the Gaza Strip and Jericho, the Palestinians would deploy 9,000 police officers there, and the PA would begin operations. On July 1, 1994, Arafat returned to Gaza City to inaugurate his rule.

From the start, there were worrisome signs. For example, Rabin quickly learned that when Arafat and his entourage entered Gaza, he sneaked in four terrorists who had killed Israelis, the only specific individuals barred by Israel from coming with him. Rabin insisted that they leave, but soon thereafter they returned, heralding the frustrations to come. Rabin and Peres wanted to make the process work if possible and did not want to be blamed for slowing the peace process down. Consequently, they generally remained silent about such complaints.

Although the PLO had signed the Oslo Accords, Arafat had barely gained the majority on its Executive Committee that he needed to support his action. Several leaders resigned; others continued to oppose any negotiations or compromise with Israel. The two Palestinian Islamist groups—Hamas and the smaller Islamic Jihad—took an even harder line, using terrorism to overturn the peace process and build Palestinian support for their own positions.

The PA had to decide how to handle the problem. According to the Oslo Accords, the PA's job was to block attacks on Israel; arrest, prosecute, and imprison the perpetrators of attacks; create the infrastructure for a stable state that could raise living standards; and prepare the Palestinian people to live in peace alongside Israel. Israel monitored progress in these areas.

In dealing with the Islamists, the more radical PLO member groups, and the more radical forces in Fatah, Arafat had several choices. One was to discipline its own ranks, fulfill its commitments to stop terrorism, and either force Hamas to obey its dictates or repress the group. The PA could aim to administer the territory effectively and change its orientation from that of a revolutionary group using violence to attain its goals to that of a government with a state to build.

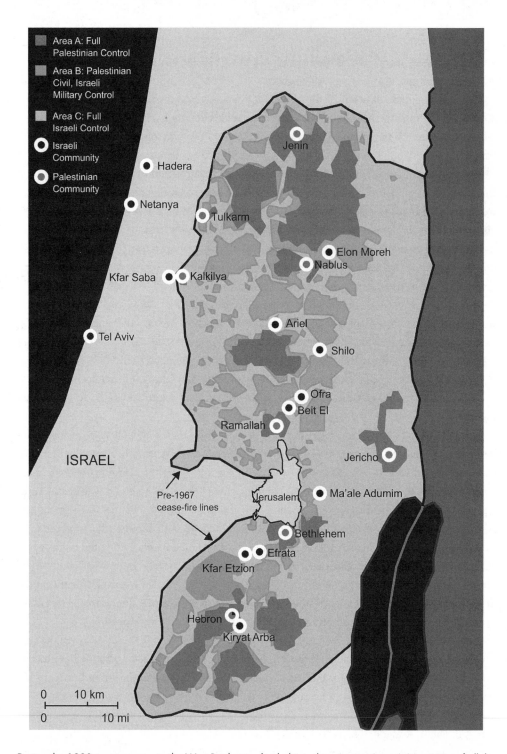

Area A: Full Palestinian Control

Area B: Palestinian Civil, Israeli Military Control

Area C: Full Israeli Control

◎ Israeli Community

◉ Palestinian Community

● Hadera

● Netanya

◉ Tulkarm

Jenin ◎

● Elon Moreh

◉ Nablus

Kfar Saba ◉◉ Kalkilya

● Ariel

◎ Shilo

Tel Aviv ◎

● Ofra

● Beit El

Ramallah ◉

Jericho ◉

ISRAEL

Pre-1967 cease-fire lines

Jerusalem

● Ma'ale Adumim

Bethlehem ◉

● Efrata

Kfar Etzion ●

Hebron ◉

◉ Kiryat Arba

0   10 km

0   10 mi

During the 1990s peace process, the West Bank was divided into three areas: Area A (consisting of all the towns except 20 percent of Hebron) was governed by the Palestinian Authority; Area B (consisting of the villages) was governed by the PA, but Israel had control over security; and Area C (Jewish settlements and unpopulated areas) was governed by Israel. (© 2003–2010 Koret Communications Ltd. All rights reserved.)

At times, the PLO did curb Hamas and stop militants in its own ranks from launching attacks on Israel; at other times, it encouraged or at least was permissive when they engaged in violence against Israel. Those involved in terrorist attacks were jailed but were accused only of bad timing from the standpoint of Palestinian interests and then quietly released. The PA never conducted a serious effort at education toward moderation, but it did deescalate expectations: a two-state compromise, not total victory over Israel, would be the acceptable goal.

Israeli suspicion toward the PA, the PA's and Islamists' continued acceptance of radical action, Palestinian complaints about Israeli policies, and the ongoing violence combined to erode public support for the peace process on both sides. By 1995 public opinion polls reflected this skepticism. The majority of Israelis were displeased with the peace process, and the majority of Palestinians favored suicide attacks against Israel. Nevertheless, Israel's government remained committed to the peace process. Under the interim agreement of September 28, 1995, Israel turned over to the PA all the remaining West Bank towns—Nablus, Ramallah, Jenin, Tulkarm, Kalkilya, and Bethlehem—and part of Hebron (the only West Bank town with Jewish settlers).

NEGOTIATIONS WITH JORDAN AND SYRIA

The Oslo process also brought a dramatic breakthrough with Jordan. Although the Jordanian government had long sought to exit the conflict with Israel, domestic and inter-Arab pressure prevented any such step. But with the weakening of radical states after the Soviet collapse and Iraq's defeat, and with the PLO now negotiating with Israel, Jordan could hold talks as well.

On October 26, 1994, Jordan and Israel signed a full peace agreement near their shared border. They agreed to the boundaries set in 1948—much of the border followed the Jordan River—and began normal trade. Israel also returned a small area of 120 square miles (311 square kilometers) captured from Jordan in 1967; leased a tiny plot of about one square mile (2.6 square kilometers) along the border where Israeli farmers had planted an orchard; and agreed to provide Jordan with water. The two countries signed a commercial treaty in 1996.

Within Jordan, there was much opposition to the agreement, especially from Islamists and Palestinians. Jordan ended up declaring itself disappointed that peace did not bring greater economic rewards, yet that government also minimized contacts with Israel. Still, for Israel the strategic gain of seeing another Arab neighbor removed from the overall conflict was tremendous.

Other such diplomatic gains were also made by Israel during this period. In September 1994, Morocco established low-level diplomatic ties with Israel. Tunisia followed suit, as did Oman and Qatar. Negotiations with Syria were far more difficult. In February 1994, Israel and Syria suspended the bilateral talks that had grown out of the Madrid Conference. Syria had opposed the Israel-PLO agreement and had discouraged Jordan from making peace with Israel, but its influence was too limited to stop these developments, given the loss of its Soviet sponsor and the extent of U.S. power at the time.

In March 1995, U.S.-hosted bilateral talks resumed. The Syrians insisted that they would demand the pre-1967 border as any peacetime frontier, which would have given them small but strategic areas of Israeli territory that they had occupied after the 1948 war. Meanwhile,

Syria was doing everything possible to sabotage the Israel-Palestinian peace process, backing Hamas and supporting radical PLO forces in Lebanon, among other efforts. Despite sporadic negotiations in 1995 and 1996, no real progress was made in Syrian-Israeli talks. The details of a negotiated settlement were not the problem; rather, peace with Israel was not in the Syrian regime's fundamental interest.

RABIN'S ASSASSINATION AND ITS AFTERMATH

On November 4, 1995, Prime Minister Rabin and Foreign Minister Peres attended a peace rally at Tel Aviv's City Hall in the Square of the Kings of Israel. As the two leaders left the stage, a young religious nationalist named Yigal Amir fatally shot Rabin, believing the assassination would sabotage the peace process and prevent Israeli withdrawal from the West Bank. The act traumatized the nation in a way perhaps unequaled in its history. The passionate disputes over policy and the extreme right-wing's demonization of Rabin were both blamed. Thereafter, the national debate over the peace process deescalated amid awareness that things had gone too far. Peres, who immediately became acting prime minister, renewed Rabin's coalition eighteen days later. Believing that the country's mood had swung to support the peace process wholeheartedly, in part because of revulsion over the assassination, Peres called new elections for May 1996.

At this point, a new element entered the picture and turned public opinion in the opposite direction. In late February and early March 1996, following the killing of a bomb maker who had been responsible for many previous attacks, Hamas launched a wave of suicide bombings in Jerusalem, Ashkelon, and Tel Aviv, killing more than fifty Israelis and causing a suspension of the peace process. Israel once again closed its borders with the West Bank and the Gaza Strip, this time for an indefinite period, and demanded that the PA rein in Hamas and the Islamic Jihad.

While Rabin's assassination had reinforced support in Israel for the peace process, now seen as the fallen leader's legacy, the Palestinian attacks made Israelis question the effectiveness and direction of events. After all, if creating the PA and making concessions had led only to an increase in terrorism—when it was supposed to decrease it—how effective was this strategy? In response to doubts, the government tried to rally support with the argument that letting the terrorists succeed in stopping the peace process altogether would be giving them a victory.

The February 1996 elections were a referendum on the peace process as well as the first direct elections for prime minister. Peres was expected to win, but escalating Palestinian terrorism and the candidate's low personal popularity, among other factors, gave the victory to Likud leader Binyamin Netanyahu, albeit in a close vote. Netanyahu formed a broad coalition government with a half-dozen centrist, religious, and right-wing parties.

While Netanyahu had been critical of the Oslo process, as prime minister he accepted the framework, merely asserting that he would negotiate more effectively. A key element in his approach was the concept of "reciprocity," meaning that the PA would have to meet its commitments more fully and clearly to receive more Israeli concessions. Yet Israel's conduct of the process changed in no major way, which ultimately led right-wing parties to bring Netanyahu's government down.

Investigators checking debris following a Hamas terrorist bombing in Jerusalem, 1996. (Getty Images/Image Bank.)

When the Israeli government reopened an ancient tunnel in the Jewish Quarter of Jerusalem in September 1996, the PA, perhaps to test or discredit the government, organized violent demonstrations. For the first time, PA security forces fired at the IDF. The clashes ended after Netanyahu threatened to use more force, with fifty Palestinians and eighteen Israelis killed and hundreds wounded.

Once again, the seemingly endless and virtually stagnant talks continued over confidence-building measures, additional Israeli turnovers of territory to the PA, Israeli complaints of PA incitements to violence against Israel, and all the other short-term issues and efforts to define what a full peace agreement would include. In October 1996 the two sides made a deal over Hebron, the only West Bank town where Israel retained a presence. The PA would control 80 percent of Hebron; Israel, the remaining 20 percent.

At a meeting hosted by the United States two years later, in October 1998, Netanyahu and Arafat agreed to the Wye River Accord, according to which Israel would turn over 13.1 percent of the West Bank to the PA in a three-step military redeployment. In exchange, the PA promised to amend the sections of the Palestinian National Charter denying Israel's right to exist and would intensify security measures to prevent terrorism. The Knesset ratified the Wye River Accord on November 17 by a seventy-five to nineteen vote. Three days later, the first stage of the IDF's deployment from the West Bank was implemented, and 250 Palestinian prisoners were released.

When the PLO called a meeting of its PNC to revise its charter by removing the sections calling for the use of violence and the elimination of Israel, President Clinton attended the session to urge change. A resolution was passed that seemed to fulfill the request, but the PNC merely appointed a committee to decide how to handle the issue. In practice, no action was taken, and another of the purported confidence-building measures served instead to reduce Israel's confidence that the PLO and the PA were changing course. This factor and others, including lax security efforts by the PA, led Netanyahu to announce that Israel would not implement the second phase of troop deployment from the West Bank, scheduled for December 18, 1998. Two days later, the Knesset voted to suspend implementation of the Wye River Accord altogether.

Netanyahu, skeptical of the PA's record of fulfilling commitments, its efforts to create a stable regime, and its moves toward stopping terrorism and attacks against Israel, was walking a political tightrope. His party's own right wing and smaller coalition parties opposed even his policy of limited concessions.

One of the key forces he had to court to stay in power was the Shas Party. In January 1997 he had appointed Roni Bar-On as attorney general. Three months later, allegations surfaced that Netanyahu had brought in Bar-On to facilitate a plea bargain for Aryeh Deri, the Shas leader facing corruption charges, in order to gain Shas's support for Israeli withdrawal from Hebron. Bar-On resigned; Deri was indicted for obstruction of justice; and Elyakim Rubenstein, Bar-On's successor, ruled that because of lack of evidence, no charges would be brought against Netanyahu. The affair showed how strenuously Netanyahu had to work to hold his coalition together.

By December 1998, Netanyahu was facing a great deal of opposition from within his own Likud Party and the governing coalition over the concessions he had made in implementing the Wye River Accord. Right-wing members walked out, and it was clear that Netanyahu could not continue as prime minister. An opposition motion to call new elections passed, and elections were set for May 17, 1999.

THE BARAK PRIME MINISTERSHIP

The elections in 1999 were the second elections in which Israelis were able to vote directly for prime minister, with a straight choice between Netanyahu and Ehud Barak, the former military chief of staff who had been Rabin's protégé. Barak won by 56 percent, compared with only 44 percent for Netanyahu—a wide margin. In the Knesset elections, Barak's One Israel bloc took twenty-six seats and Likud held on to nineteen, a sharp decline from the thirty-two it had held in the previous Knesset. The other major winner was the Sephardic religious party Shas, which won seventeen seats, up from ten despite the corruption charges against some of its leaders. Netanyahu resigned as head of his party and from the Knesset. Ariel Sharon became the new Likud Party chair.

Negotiations with Syria

Just as Rabin's election in 1992 was the basis for starting the Israel-PLO and Israel-Syria peace processes, Barak's 1999 election set the stage for trying to conclude them successfully. In the election campaign, Barak had vowed to do everything possible to reach agreements with the PLO and Syria. After six years of effort, and well beyond the original deadline for reaching a peace treaty, it was time to finish the process, especially since Western governments kept telling Israel that Arafat needed a material outcome to satisfy his constituents and remain in power.

Clinton held Israel-Syria negotiations in Shepherdstown, West Virginia, starting in December 1999, but no progress was made. As a last resort, on March 25, 2000, Clinton met with Syrian president Hafiz al-Asad to make Israel's U.S.-sponsored offer. Barak proposed an Israeli withdrawal from the entire Golan Heights to the international border. As a step toward meeting the inevitable Syrian demand for more, he proposed giving Damascus fishing rights on the Sea of Galilee and creating a joint peace park on the northeastern shore. Asad said no.

The almost decade-long Israel-Syria peace process begun in Madrid in 1991 came to an unsuccessful close. Most Israelis concluded that even if Israel offered big concessions, the Syrian regime simply was not prepared to make peace.

Withdrawal from Lebanon

Barak's Lebanon policy followed the Netanyahu government's April 1, 1998, decision to accept UN Security Council Resolution 425, which called for Israel's full withdrawal from Lebanon. PLO invasions from Lebanon in the 1970s had led Israel to attack in 1978 and 1982, preserving in the end a buffer zone for security along the border. Israel's government conditioned its withdrawal on Lebanon's government guaranteeing security on their common border, which Lebanon refused to do. Consequently, the IDF remained in the security zone; otherwise, Palestinian groups, as well as Hizballah, the new threat, could have continued to stage cross-border attacks.

In 1998 twenty-three IDF soldiers were killed in the security zone in Lebanon, mainly in Hizballah attacks, but the IDF succeeded in blocking attacks from Lebanon into Israel that might have been even more costly. As time went on, the Lebanon operation became increasingly unpopular within Israel as casualty lists continued to grow. The Four Mothers group, begun by mothers of IDF soldiers, sparked a movement favoring withdrawal.

On July 15, 1999, soon after taking office as prime minister, Barak stated that even if no accord was reached with Syria, he would unilaterally withdraw IDF soldiers from Lebanon. This withdrawal took place on May 24, 2000, and the United Nations confirmed that Israel was now compliant with the Security Council resolutions mandating a pullout.

Within Israel, the actual implementation of the move was perceived as damaging Israeli deterrence power. The withdrawal took place quickly, leaving the allied South Lebanese Army in the lurch. That army collapsed, and Hizballah took over southern Lebanon. The radical Islamist group's fortification of the area and claims of victory made Israel's action appear more a defeat than the tactical readjustment it was supposed to be.

Hizballah made new territorial claims: that the tiny Shaba Farms area, universally regarded as part of Syria, was occupied Lebanese territory, which meant that Israel was still occupying part of Lebanon. It began attacking Israel in small operations, firing rockets and trying to send squads across the border. Once again, a hostile force ready to go to war controlled Israel's northern border. To the perception that concessions to Syria had not brought peace, many or most Israelis added the conclusion that giving up territory worsened Israel's strategic situation and actually increased the possibility of war.

Camp David

Barak tried to bring the peace process to a successful conclusion. On September 4, 1999, he met with Arafat in Sharm al-Shaykh, Egypt, to sign a revised Wye River Accord proposing that a Framework Agreement on Permanent Status issues be reached by February 13, 2000, and a comprehensive peace treaty be secured by September 13, 2000. In the interim, Israel would turn over small additional pieces of the West Bank to the PA.

Israel opened a Gaza–West Bank "safe passage" for Palestinians on October 25, 1999. But then Arafat raised objections: the maps that Israel had given him were inadequate, he said, and the areas it was turning over were too sparsely populated and not in a prime location. Although talks broke down, in March 2000, Israel pulled out of another 6.1 percent of the West Bank.

In November 1999, Barak, Arafat, and Clinton met in Oslo to discuss the best way to reach a full peace agreement to end the conflict, which had always been the goal of the peace process. For years, Israel had been told that to move toward peace Arafat needed to achieve dramatic progress and have the prospect of establishing a Palestinian state. Clinton also knew that he himself would be a lame duck after November 2000, when a successor was elected, and his term would end in January 2001. Time was running out for him to broker a deal. Both the United States and Israel were certain that the moment had come to go all out to reach full and final peace. So Clinton invited the two sides to Camp David for what was intended to be the last act of a successful peace process.

Fearing that Barak would offer too much to Arafat at the summit, three right-wing parties left the government, breaking the coalition and necessitating a close vote of confidence on the eve of Barak's departure. But Barak had accepted this risk for peace and acquired a mandate to go ahead to the talks as prime minister. For the first time, an Israeli government would even offer to give up most of east Jerusalem, a hitherto unthinkable concession, to achieve peace. Danny Yatom, Barak's chief of staff, explained the leadership's thinking: "We went to Camp David because it was clear that that was the only way to find out if there was the possibility of striking a deal." Barak himself said he hoped that "Arafat would rise to the occasion and display something of greatness, like Sadat and King Hussein at the moment of truth."

Negotiations at Camp David began on July 11, 2000, and continued intensively for two weeks. All of the issues were discussed, including Jerusalem, Palestinian refugees, borders between the two states, and Israeli settlements. In the end, Clinton presented Israel's proposals for further talks. For its opening bid Israel offered all of the Gaza Strip, 92 percent of the West Bank (the exact places were not specified), and most of east Jerusalem for a Palestinian state. The United States offered $21 billion in compensation for the Palestinians. Arafat rejected this proposal but presented no initiative of his own. It was clear that Arafat had no intention of making a deal, and Clinton blamed him for the collapse of negotiations.

The events of 2000 changed the Israeli worldview more than any development since the victory in the 1967 war. Israel had assumed that if it offered enough, the Palestinian side would make peace. Did Arafat's rejection of the proposals mean that Israel's assumption was wrong? Was some detail or Israeli action causing the peace process to fail? Was the Palestinian side, at least its leadership, not ready for a deal? These were questions around which Israeli politics and policy developed after 2000, especially given the Second Intifada, which was about to start.

The idea that concessions would bring peace was challenged by both Syria's and the PA's rejection of unprecedented Israeli offers of well over 90 percent of their demands. Mainstream politicians and groups could no longer persuasively argue that Syria merely wanted the Golan Heights back and that Palestinians simply sought a state of their own. This view was reinforced when Arafat also rejected Clinton's final Israeli offer, presenting even more unilateral concessions, in December 2000.

In addition, withdrawals from southern Lebanon, the West Bank, and the Gaza Strip had increased the level of terrorist attacks on Israel while reducing Israeli deterrence. The consequences undercut the assumption that giving up territory would reduce neighbors' enmity, a conclusion reinforced by the onset of the Second Intifada in late 2000 and, several years later, by the effect of the total Israeli pullout from the Gaza Strip.

The high level of Western and international criticism of Israel not long after Camp David failed, combined with weakened Western governments' support, also belied what Israel had been told for years: that if it only made concessions and took risks, the world would recognize that Israel genuinely wanted peace and would rally to its side.

THE SECOND INTIFADA

U.S. attempts to salvage negotiations continued after the Camp David talks collapsed, but the Palestinian leadership was already planning a violent second intifada, organized by Fatah's West Bank grassroots leader Marwan Barghouti. The September 28, 2000, one-hour visit of Likud leader Ariel Sharon to the Temple Mount / Haram al-Sharif compound in Jerusalem's Old City provided both pretext and occasion for starting the uprising. Barghouti's Tanzim group in Fatah led the uprising with Arafat's support. Arafat chaired coordinating meetings, which included Hamas. Barghouti later explained, "I knew that the end of September was the last period" before the uprising could occur, "but when Sharon reached the al-Aqsa Mosque, this was the most appropriate moment for the outbreak of the intifada."

Because Barak was still focused on reviving the negotiations, he did not want to respond too harshly to the violence, especially since at first it was not clear whether the Palestinian response to Sharon's visit to the mosque—rioting and clashes between Palestinians and the Israeli police and military—was a brief incident or part of a campaign. So he was slow to adjust his policy to the new development. For many Israelis, his hesitation made the government more unpopular.

With Palestinian violence and IDF actions in the West Bank and the Gaza Strip escalating, Arafat and Barak went to Paris on October 4, 2000, to meet with U.S. Secretary of State Madeleine Albright and CIA director George Tenet, as well as with UN Secretary-General Kofi Annan and French President Jacques Chirac. Eventually Barak and Arafat agreed that Israel's army would withdraw to its pre–September 28, 2000, positions and Arafat would quiet the protests and violence. But differences on other issues precluded any agreement to have a ceasefire. At one point, Arafat tried to leave the talks, and Albright had to run after him and persuade him to return.

On October 12, PA police took into custody two Israeli army reservists who had become lost and accidentally drove into downtown Ramallah, a town under PA control. A Palestinian mob seized, lynched, and mutilated them. The events, filmed by an Italian crew, were shown on Israeli television, and the public perceived this incident—along with other such deliberate murders of unarmed Israeli civilians—as showing the extent of Palestinian hatred and PA disinterest in fulfilling its commitments.

Another round of diplomacy led to an emergency summit at Sharm al-Shaykh, on October 16–17, at which both sides agreed to end the violence and establish a commission of inquiry. Although Israel released a number of Palestinian prisoners, reopened borders, and pulled back military forces, Arafat made little or no apparent attempt to stop the uprising. Barak responded by formally suspending the peace process on October 22.

Barak, who had been expecting to be leading the country to full peace just weeks earlier, was now fighting a war. By mid-November 2000, Israel had tripled the number of troops in the West Bank and the Gaza Strip and taken other measures to pressure the PA to stop the fighting. In November and December, Barak authorized the targeted assassinations of ten Palestinians whom Israeli intelligence identified as ordering and organizing terrorist attacks.

Clinton and Barak made one more effort to save the peace process in a remarkable negotiating strategy. Arafat had rejected the opening Israeli offer at Camp David. Now, even though the Palestinian leader had made no concessions, Israel made its best offer. On December 23, 2000, Clinton set forth these terms to Arafat: The Palestinian state would include between 94 and 96 percent of the West Bank plus 1–3 percent more land swapped between Israel and Palestine. The Palestinians would thus receive roughly the equivalent of the entire pre-1967 land area of the West Bank. Israel's goal was to incorporate into Israel's territory small areas near the border where up to 80 percent of the Jewish settlers in the West Bank were concentrated. Israel would give Israeli territory to the Palestinians in exchange for the lands where the settlements were while also maximizing the territorial contiguity of the Palestinian state.

In addition, Israel proposed to maintain three early-warning stations near the Palestine-Jordan border to ensure that foreign Arab armies did not cross into that area. Palestinian officials would be present to ensure the proper use of these facilities.

In Jerusalem, the Palestinians would have total sovereignty over the Arab neighborhoods, as well as the Haram al-Sharif area atop the Temple Mount. Israel would get only the Jewish Quarter of the Old City, the Jewish neighborhoods, and the Western Wall of the Temple. Israel's only influence over the Temple's site would be that its permission would be required to excavate there; Palestine would have the same veto rights over digging behind the Western Wall.

Finally, an international commission would be established to facilitate the return of Palestinian refugees to "historic Palestine" and "their homeland," meaning that they would be resettled in the new state of Palestine or elsewhere. A multibillion-dollar fund raised internationally would be used to compensate refugees.

The Clinton plan gave the Palestinians about 99 percent of their demands, aside from the demand to resettle refugees in Israel, while reducing Israel's demands and security considerations beyond any previous minimum. Clearly, it was a package tailored to win Arafat's acceptance.

The Israeli cabinet approved Clinton's proposal on December 28, 2000, on the condition that the Palestinians accept it, too. But Arafat rejected the proposal, merely repeating his old demands that all Palestinian refugees and their descendants have a "right of return" to live in Israel; that the PA should have total control of the entire Temple Mount, the whole West Bank, and east Jerusalem; and that there should be no Israeli observers along the border with Jordan.

Even before Arafat's repudiation of the deal, Barak was facing rising domestic criticism at the failure of his diplomatic strategy. Desperate to make some progress, he had authorized his own left-wing supporters to talk informally with a Palestinian delegation in Taba, Egypt. This effort, too, ended without any agreement. The clock had run out for the process, Clinton's term in office, and Barak. Criticized from right and left, with his coalition eroding and the public seeing him as weak or uncertain, Barak was in serious political trouble. After failed attempts to persuade Sharon to join a national unity government—the Likud leader would do so only if he was an equal partner on security decisions, which Barak refused to contemplate—the prime minister resigned on November 28, 2000. The Knesset, however, voted not to dissolve itself, so the election was not for Knesset seats but only for prime minister, with Barak and Sharon as the candidates.

THE SHARON PRIME MINISTERSHIP

Ariel Sharon won the February 6, 2001, election in a landslide, gaining 62 percent of the votes, compared to Barak's 38 percent. Many who traditionally voted for the left supported Sharon in reaction to the outcome of the peace process and the ongoing intifada. An election boycott called by many Arab voters further added to Sharon's victory margin.

Since only the prime minister had been elected, the old Knesset remained, the only time in Israel's history this has happened, and the situation provided an impetus to return to the old system of holding Knesset instead of national elections and choosing the prime minister indirectly. Since the Likud controlled only 19 of the 120 Knesset seats, Sharon had to build a very wide coalition including Labor and three religious, one centrist, and three right-wing parties.

Sharon took office in March 2001. The intifada continued and even escalated in 2001, with heavy Israeli civilian casualties from terrorist attacks. National morale was low after the disappointed expectations of great progress in the 1990s. Having yielded much of the West Bank and most of the Gaza Strip, as well as having provided or permitted the arming and training of PA security forces, Israel also faced a more difficult security situation than before. It was now far easier to infiltrate Israel and stage high-casualty suicide bombing attacks, for example. In addition, since the world had been repeatedly told (even by Israeli sources) that the Palestinians now sought only their own state, rather than Israel's destruction, international criticism of Israel reached unprecedented levels. Not surprisingly, many Israelis, even strong advocates of the peace process, thought that the whole seven-year-long effort had backfired.

Another effect of the 1990s peace process was that Western countries now accepted and even advocated the creation of an independent Palestinian state as the only solution to the conflict. On October 2, 2001, for example, U.S. President George W. Bush announced support for the creation of a Palestinian state through negotiations.

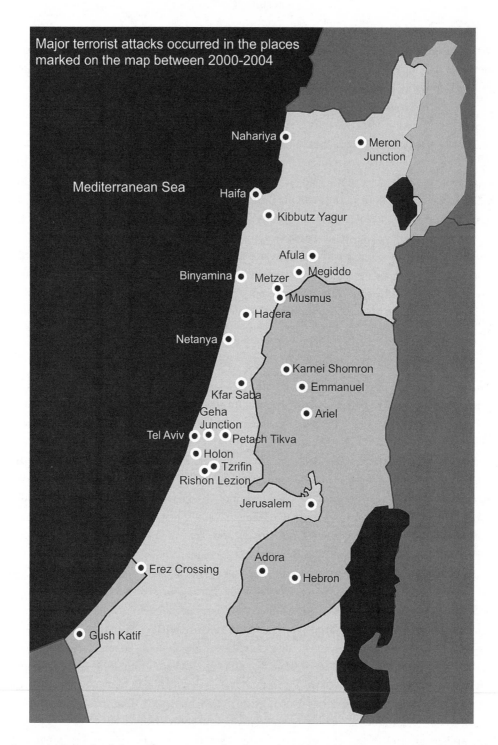

During the Second Intifada, major terrorist attacks were made within Israel and against Jewish settlements in the West Bank and the Gaza Strip. (© 2003–2010 Koret Communications Ltd. All rights reserved.)

Palestinian youths burn tires during an anti-Israel demonstration at El-Bireh, West Bank, March 2000. On the right is Amana Jawad, later convicted and jailed for the murder of an Israeli teenager whom she had lured to the PA-ruled town of Ramallah. (Getty Images / Image Bank.)

Finally, the terrorist attacks and Palestinian refusal to accept terms to end the conflict also signaled the growing challenge to the traditional nationalist leadership from even harder-line Islamist groups, mainly Hamas. Arafat had tried to use these organizations as his tools, but they were increasingly gaining as much support as his Fatah group. This trend paralleled what was happening elsewhere in the Middle East and even the world, as signaled by the September 11, 2001, terrorist attacks on the United States.

Meanwhile, Palestinian terrorist attacks against Israeli civilians continued, causing more casualties within Israel than ever before. For example, twenty-five Israelis were killed and many more were wounded in attacks in Haifa and Jerusalem on December 1–2, 2001. Diplomatic efforts to end the fighting repeatedly failed, for Arafat, despite what he said publicly, continued to order and encourage assaults. Arafat even tried to escalate the fighting by purchasing a large amount of arms from Iran. But on January 3, 2002, Israeli naval commandos captured a freighter, the *Karine A,* in the Red Sea carrying 55 tons (50 metric tons) of heavy weapons. These included rockets that would have allowed the PA to target Israel's airport and major cities. On February 10, 2002, Hamas fired rockets from the Gaza Strip into Israel for the first time.

In the eighteen months of violence between September 2000 and March 2002, a total of 1,065 Palestinians and 344 Israelis were killed. In March 2002 alone, 130 Israelis died in a spate of suicide bombings and armed attacks. The attacks culminated on March 27, when a Hamas suicide bomber entered a hotel in Netanya, just north of Tel Aviv, killing twenty-nine Israelis participating in a Passover seder.

The fighting also affected others. On April 2, 2002, Fatah, Hamas, and the Islamic Jihad seized control of one of Christianity's most revered sites, the Church of the Nativity in Bethlehem. The group took the Christian clerics there hostage and fired on IDF soldiers. The siege lasted until a compromise was reached on May 10. The gunmen accepted deportation to the Gaza Strip or Europe.

With casualties rising, no hope of a diplomatic solution, and the PA clearly unwilling to stop the fighting, Israel's government launched a major offensive on March 29, 2002, named Operation Defensive Shield, to defeat the insurgency. The PA and its institutions seemed to be the conflict's source, so Israeli tanks attacked the installations of the PA security forces, entered Palestinian towns, and took control of most of them for the first time since 1994. Arafat was besieged in his headquarters compound.

The heaviest fighting during Operation Defensive Shield occurred at the Jenin refugee camp in the northern West Bank, where IDF soldiers fought Palestinian gunmen in house-to-house combat. To follow the rules of engagement, meant to prevent civilian casualties, often put Israeli soldiers' lives at risk. On April 9, thirteen Israeli army reservists were killed upon entering a booby-trapped building in the refugee camp. In all, twenty-three Israeli soldiers died in the fighting there. Afterward, elements of the international news media reported that Israeli forces had destroyed large portions of the camp, even though aerial photographs showed this to be untrue. Palestinian spokespeople also spread the story that Israeli troops had massacred up to 500 Palestinian civilians in Jenin, a story picked up uncritically by much of the Western media. Later, a UN investigation showed that these claims were untrue and that very few Palestinian civilians had died in the fighting.

Exaggerations and misrepresentations of its military actions were a growing problem for Israel. Not only were Palestinian forces originating claims of war crimes and other misdeeds, often deliberately fabricating them, but the stories were gaining credibility with the international media, foreign groups, and even Western governments.

To save the PA, the United States urged Israel to limit its offensive. On April 6, the UN Security Council adopted Resolution 1403 urging a ceasefire and IDF withdrawal from Palestinian towns once the PA accepted a ceasefire. But U.S. attempts to broker a ceasefire failed, since Sharon would not agree to a withdrawal timetable and Arafat would not pledge to control the terrorist groups.

When Sharon announced that Israel would keep fighting until the terrorist forces were destroyed, the United States again, on April 9, asked Israel to withdraw. The Israeli army pulled out of Kalkilya and Tulkarm but continued operations elsewhere. In response to U.S. requests and pressures, Israel allowed Arafat to leave his Ramallah compound and travel freely in the PA-ruled territories on May 2, after he agreed to try the murderers of the Israeli tourism minister, Rehavam Ze'evi, assassinated by the Popular Front for the Liberation of Palestine at a Jerusalem hotel in October 2001. Arafat did not keep this pledge.

About 4,000 Palestinians had been arrested during Operation Defensive Shield, including Barghouti, who was later tried and convicted for organizing and leading the intifada. The operation was over, although violence, albeit diminished, continued. In June 2002, twenty-six Israelis were killed in two suicide attacks in Jerusalem. Afterward, the Israeli army began to reoccupy large sections of the West Bank to stop further attacks.

In 2003 and into 2004 terrorist attacks in Israel fell sharply in number, although PA promises of a ceasefire went unimplemented. Between the intifada's start on September 27, 2000, and March 23, 2004, there were 2,728 Palestinian and 917 Israeli fatalities. Some 35 percent of the Palestinian dead were noncombatants, as were 78 percent of the Israeli dead. Women accounted for nearly 5 percent of the Palestinian deaths compared to 31 percent of Israeli deaths. The majority of the Palestinian victims were militants; most of the Israeli victims of Palestinian suicide bombers were civilians.

Israel continued its targeted assassinations of those leading and carrying out terrorist attacks on Israel. The most significant assassinations were of the Hamas spiritual leader Ahmad Yassin, killed in Gaza on March 22, 2004, and the head of Hamas, Abd al-Aziz al-Rantisi, killed on April 17. As late as August 31, 2004, the same day that Sharon announced the timetable of his disengagement plan, Hamas suicide bombers killed 16 and wounded 93 in attacks on two buses in Beer Sheba. Two major attacks took place at Sinai vacation resorts on October 7, in which 33 people—mostly Israeli tourists—were killed and more than 120 were injured. By this point, however, the intifada had been largely suppressed and was petering out.

Domestic Politics

Despite the tremendous pressure from terrorist attacks and Israeli deaths in 2001–2004 and the resulting low morale, the public did not hold the government responsible. No clear military or diplomatic alternative existed. Nevertheless, the Sharon government had big economic issues and complex coalition commitments to deal with.

In May 2002, to boost the economy, the government proposed an austerity package that would cut benefits to poor Israelis. The Haredi community would be particularly hard hit. Coalition members of the Knesset (MKs) from two religious parties, Shas and United Torah Judaism, whose constituents relied on the benefits, refused to support the measure and it failed in a forty-seven to forty-four Knesset vote. Sharon dismissed the two Haredi parties from his cabinet. At the end of October 2002, Labor withdrew from the coalition over the 2003 budget; it especially opposed the allocations to West Bank settlements. Sharon was forced to call early elections, which were held in January 2003 only for Knesset seats. Likud won by a large margin over Labor and put together another complex, five-party coalition.

Defense against Terrorism

Given the ongoing violence and the inadequacy of military measures alone, the cabinet approved a new tactic to prevent terrorist attacks: the construction of a security fence separating the West Bank from Israeli towns and cities. Construction began in June 2002. By October 2003 a large majority—83 percent—of the Israeli public supported this project, with the main criticism coming from left-wing Meretz Party supporters, who argued that the fence took in too much land, and right-wing National Union supporters, who complained that it included too little land. Placed mainly with security considerations in mind, which were determined by

An IDF vehicle patrolling the security fence to stop terrorists crossing from the West Bank into Israel, October 2008. (Jorge Novominsky.)

the nature of the terrain, the fence did not always follow the 1967 frontier—only 19 percent of the public thought it should—but Israel's government made it clear that the fence was in no way intended to mark a future border and could be moved if necessary after any future agreement on borders.

Although the fence attracted international criticism, it did protect Israelis. Successful Palestinian attacks into Israel fell sharply, and the cabinet approved the second stage of construction, costing $1 billion, in September 2003. The fence shielded 80 percent of the Jews living in the West Bank—those in the large Jewish settlements adjacent to the 1967 boundary lines—but placed only 8 percent of the West Bank territory on the Israeli side of the barrier. Most settlements remained outside the fence. Lawsuits by West Bank Palestinians in the Israeli Supreme Court and urgings by the United States brought route changes on several occasions.

On the security fence issue, as with the allegations of a massacre at Jenin and as in many other instances, international criticism promoted solidarity among Israelis. They perceived the criticism as made without evidence and as indicating disinterest in Israeli security. When in July 2004, for example, the majority of judges on the International Court of Justice issued a nonbinding judgment condemning the security barrier and calling for it to be dismantled, their statement mentioned terrorism only twice. Immediately after the decision, 78 percent of Israelis said they favored the fence, and 62 percent added that it improved their personal sense of security.

On April 30, 2003, what became known as the Quartet—the United States, the European Union, the United Nations, and Russia—unveiled a new three-phase peace plan intended to produce a Palestinian state by 2005 or 2006. Under the first phase of this "road map" plan, both sides would acknowledge the other's right to exist. Then Palestinians would cease causing violence, and Israel would withdraw to the September 28, 2000, lines and dismantle settlement outposts built since March 2001. A projected second phase would include peace talks establishing provisional Palestinian borders and recognition of Israel's right to exist by all Arab states. The final phase would be a peace agreement and creation of a Palestinian state. Israel accepted the plan in May, but as so often before, nothing happened despite hundreds of meetings, speeches, and visits. Having seen so many Western plans lead nowhere, Sharon and the rest of Israel's government were looking for an initiative of their own.

Plans for Unilateral Disengagement

The intifada and the failure of the peace process led most, though certainly not all, Jewish Israelis to rethink policy. The new consensus had two main points: On one hand, Israelis were ready to give up almost all the territory captured in the 1967 war and accept an independent Palestinian state. On the other hand, they did not believe that there was a real Palestinian partner for peace. Many or most of those from the center to the left still advocated a peace agreement to end the conflict and produce a stable two-state solution but had abandoned hope that this was going to happen anytime soon. Many or most of those from the center to the right still preferred that Israel retain most of the West Bank but had abandoned the belief that this was likely to happen in the long run and saw it as more of a necessity than as a benefit in its own right.

Barak had introduced a new approach in the 1999 election, that of separation—the idea that Israel would disengage from the West Bank and the Gaza Strip. In Barak's case, separation was largely meant as an interim step toward a full peace agreement. During the 2003 campaign, when Sharon was reelected, the Labor Party had proposed a unilateral withdrawal from the West Bank and the Gaza Strip, including the dismantling of more than fifty settlements.

Ehud Olmert, a Likud MK from a centrist background and a close associate of Sharon's, later floated a similar idea, which gained support from about half of the Israeli populace. Sharon officially presented the proposal to withdraw unilaterally from the Gaza Strip in a December 18, 2003, speech at the Interdisciplinary Center in Herzliya. The prime minister explained that withdrawal would not preclude an eventual two-state solution but that it would be a long time before that solution was likely to be attained. Steps needed to be taken to create the best strategic situation in the interim. The IDF endorsed this idea, since it was easier to defend a long and clearly defined frontier than to send troops into hostile territory on a daily basis.

Sharon thus planned to pull out from the entire Gaza Strip and dismantle all seventeen settlements there, plus four more in the northern West Bank. The Israeli pullout would present an opportunity for the PA to demonstrate its commitment to ruling the Gaza Strip as a peaceful neighbor and focus on economic development there. At best, then, the withdrawal would prove to be an important bilateral confidence-building measure.

In April 2004, President George W. Bush endorsed the plan. But Sharon ran into trouble within his own coalition. In a May 2, 2004, referendum, 60 percent of Likud members rejected the plan. When the cabinet approved it, two right-wing parties walked out of the government coalition. After Sharon proposed a coalition deal with Labor to preserve his parliamentary majority, 58 percent of Likud members rejected this idea at their August 18, 2005, conference. These experiences shaped Sharon's later decision to set up a separate political party.

Sharon's plan was, however, popular among the general public. A June 2004 poll found that 68 percent of the population supported unilateral withdrawal. On the Palestinian side, an opinion poll that same month found that 34 percent of Palestinians welcomed the disengagement plan, whereas 65 percent opposed it. Further, 59 percent of Palestinians said that they would support attacks against civilians in Israel even after disengagement. On October 25, 2004, the Knesset approved the disengagement plan by a large margin. Another law was passed to compensate settlers who were displaced.

Sharon's coalition was further weakened by the departure of the anticlerical Shinui Party in December. Although the party supported disengagement, it objected to the budget allocations to the Haredim and voted against the bill. Sharon fired Shinui ministers from his cabinet and turned to Labor, which entered the coalition in January 2005.

On November 11, 2004, Arafat died. Toward the end of his life, both the international community and Palestinians had increasingly criticized him for corruption. Many saw his death as a chance for a new direction in Israel-Palestinian relations. Although Arafat had never appointed a successor, Mahmoud Abbas won the elections to lead the PA on January 9, 2005, and power was smoothly transferred. After Abbas took office, a new sense of optimism emerged. Israel released 500 Palestinian prisoners on February 21, 2005, as part of a confidence-building measure to strengthen Abbas, and the PA tried to exercise greater control over its security forces. In general, relations between the two sides seemed to be improving.

Part of the improvement included the first productive high-level meeting between Palestinians and Israelis since the Second Intifada had begun in September 2000. Held at Sharm al-Shaykh on February 8, 2005, the meeting between Abbas and Sharon resulted in a joint ceasefire declaration and a call for a complete cessation of violence. After the meeting, Egypt and Jordan sent their ambassadors, recalled after the outbreak of violence in 2000, back to Israel. Hamas and the Islamic Jihad were not party to the ceasefire declaration, but the overall level of attacks declined.

The Intifada Quelled

The last obstacle to Sharon's disengagement plan fell when a bill to force a national referendum prior to unilateral withdrawal was defeated on March 28, 2005. There was a campaign against the plan, with protesters pleading that "Jews do not expel Jews" from their homes. On August 7, before the cabinet vote authorizing the first stage of the plan, Netanyahu, who was critical of it, resigned as minister of finance. He censured the government for failing to obtain anything in return for the withdrawal, claiming that it would damage the country's security. Sharon appointed Olmert to replace Netanyahu. Netanyahu announced that he would challenge Sharon for leadership of the Likud Party.

Implementation of the plan began on August 15, 2005, with the closing of the Gaza Strip to Israelis to prevent more protesters from arriving. For the next two days, Israeli residents

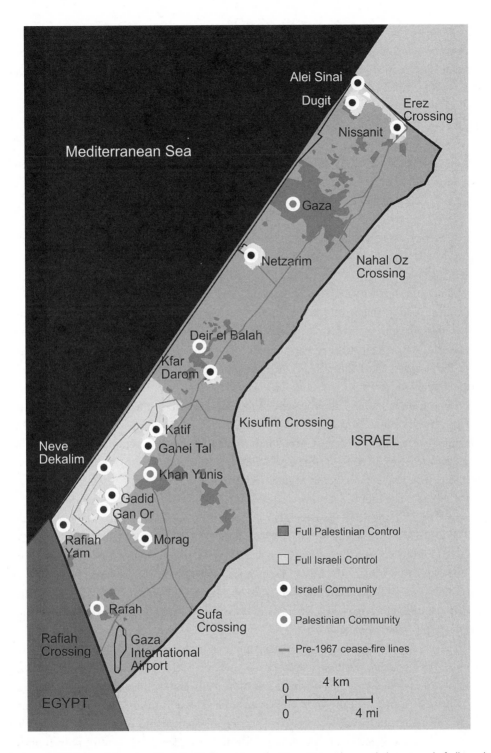

In August 2005, Israel completed its full withdrawal from the Gaza Strip, along with the removal of all Israeli settlements and settlers there. The area was handed over to the Palestinian Authority, but Hamas seized control in June 2007. (© 2003–2010 Koret Communications Ltd. All rights reserved.)

willing to leave the Gaza Strip did so. Removal by force began on August 17. About 14,000 IDF soldiers and Israeli police were deployed to ensure that the transition went smoothly. By August 22 the last residents remaining in the settlement of Netzarim left. Demolition crews began destroying the homes in the settlements. The evacuation of four settlements in the northern West Bank was carried out on August 23. The last IDF forces left the Gaza Strip on September 12, 2005.

With the lesson of the Rabin assassination in sharp focus and with all groups determined to avoid violence, the evacuation of the Gaza settlements passed without serious incident. This became a point of pride for Israeli society because it showed continued strength and unity.

Formation of the Kadima Party

The withdrawal issue had deeply disrupted the Likud's unity and Sharon's leadership of that party. The last straw was when Sharon tried to appoint two of his allies, Ze'ev Boim and Roni Bar-On, as ministers. The Knesset rejected these appointments in a vote of sixty to fifty-four, with Likud ministers who had opposed disengagement voting with the opposition. Then, on November 20, 2005, Sharon announced that he was leaving the Likud because of the infighting and would form a new centrist party, later named Kadima. Thirteen Likud ministers joined him, as did several senior Labor Party members, including Shimon Peres, Dalia Itzik, and Haim Ramon, as well as Shinui's Uriel Reichman, lending credibility to and broadening the appeal of the Kadima Party.

Events within the Labor Party the same month had sparked the defections. The chair of the Histadrut trade union, Amir Peretz, who replaced Shimon Peres as party leader, had pushed aside many of the party's veterans. Peretz had tried to force early elections by resigning from the government on November 21, the day after Sharon's announcement. Within Likud, Netanyahu was elected to replace Sharon as chair in December.

A new national election was scheduled for March 28, 2006. From the outset, Sharon's new party was ahead in the polls. On December 18, 2005, however, Sharon had a stroke. Two days later he was released from the hospital, but on January 4, 2006, he suffered a second stroke, which left him in a coma. Minister of Finance Ehud Olmert took over as acting prime minister. The election campaign proceeded as scheduled, with Olmert as Kadima's leader; and support for Kadima in the opinion polls remained steady. By mid-January, Kadima was the only party in the cabinet. Netanyahu had convinced the four Likud ministers to resign in protest over the government's policies.

The election campaign in Israel for the March 28 elections was notably restrained. The Labor Party's campaign was based almost exclusively on social and economic issues, Peretz's main interest. Likud focused on warning that more unilateral withdrawals would damage Israel's security. During the campaign, Olmert announced that if elected, he would carry out a second unilateral withdrawal and removal of some Jewish settlements on the West Bank, which he called the convergence plan. He proposed retaining under Israeli control only about 10 percent of the West Bank as a security zone, including the three main settlement blocs—Gush Etzion (south of Jerusalem), Ma'ale Adumim (just east of Jerusalem), Ariel (east of Tel Aviv and north of Jerusalem)—and the Jordan Valley.

In the election, Kadima secured the most seats, twenty-nine, with Labor second at nineteen and Likud, with only twelve seats, suffering a very heavy defeat. The new government formed under Prime Minister Ehud Olmert, approved on May 4, 2006, was dominated by the Kadima-Labor coalition. Peretz became deputy prime minister and defense minister, and Tzipi Livni became foreign minister.

HAMAS'S ELECTION VICTORY AND THE LEBANON WAR OF 2006

Events outside Israel were undermining Olmert's convergence plan as well as the success of Sharon's disengagement. In the Palestinian election on January 25, 2006, Hamas won 74 of the 132 seats in the parliament with 45 percent of the popular vote. Hamas opposed Israel's existence; it sought an Islamist state in the area between the Jordan River and the Mediterranean Sea and employed openly antisemitic and genocidal rhetoric.

The Israeli government refused all contact with the new Hamas-led administration until the group committed itself to accepting the existing agreements between Israel and the PA, abandoned the use of terrorism, and accepted Israel's right to exist—steps laid out by the road map plan of the Quartet. Hamas was uninterested in changing its policy.

On the day that Olmert's new cabinet was sworn in, a Palestinian suicide bomber from Hamas blew himself up in Tel Aviv, killing nine Israelis. Hamas and its smaller allies began firing rockets into Israel from the Gaza Strip, which made withdrawal from the Gaza Strip seem a mistake to many Israelis and made them less willing to support more withdrawals. The crisis escalated with the June 25, 2006, kidnapping of an IDF soldier, Corporal Gilad Shalit, by Hamas in a cross-border raid from the Gaza Strip into Israel in which two other soldiers were killed.

Another challenge came in the north from the Lebanese Hizballah, which had taken advantage of Israel's withdrawal from southern Lebanon to seize control of the area. In its third attempt to do so, Hizballah launched a July 12 cross-border attack, kidnapping two soldiers and killing three others. Israel responded with airstrikes and artillery fire, some targeting Hizballah-controlled neighborhoods in Beirut. The Israeli government announced that it was not making war on the moderate Lebanese government but only against Hizballah.

Hizballah responded by firing hundreds of rockets against Israeli civilians, around 4,000 in all, during the ensuing conflict. The small, inaccurate rockets usually landed in open fields, but they still closed down economic activities and normal life in the north. Israeli bombing attacks destroyed Hizballah's longer-range missiles and many of the weapons being sent in by Hizballah's patrons, Iran and Syria, across the Lebanon-Syria border. Large numbers of civilians on both sides were displaced by the fighting.

The management of the war by Olmert, the inexperienced Peretz, and the chief of staff, General Dan Halutz, the first air force officer ever to hold the top military post, drew much criticism. Among other issues, questions were raised about the decision to go to war in the first place, the lack of clear strategic goals, the attempt to use air power almost exclusively in the earlier stages, improper preparation of reserve units, and the late commitment of ground troops without proper support to attack entrenched Hizballah positions. The Olmert government did gain U.S. support for delaying imposition of a ceasefire, but it did not use the time to achieve any great objective.

The UN Security Council unanimously approved Resolution 1701 for a ceasefire on August 11, 2006. The resolution called for the Lebanese army's deployment along the border and the creation of a greatly expanded UN force to block Hizballah's return to the south and its building of fortifications there. In addition, the UN force was assigned to help the Lebanese government block Hizballah's arms imports from Syria and even to disarm the Hizballah militia. None of these steps were taken, augmenting Israelis' disillusionment with the pledges of Western governments and international organizations.

Israeli troops generally succeeded in their intense combat with Hizballah, though with high casualties. Preventing Hizballah from firing the highly mobile rockets proved especially difficult. Overall, 119 Israeli soldiers were killed in the fighting, and 43 Israeli civilians died in rocket attacks. Around 1,000 Lebanese died, of whom Israel estimated 600 were Hizballah fighters. Although Israel defeated the Hizballah forces, showed that it could send troops into Lebanon at will, and killed a high proportion of Hizballah's active-duty soldiers, many in the Arab world celebrated the war as a strategic victory because Hizballah had survived, caused Israeli casualties, and showed its ability to strike within Israel using rockets.

Israelis were dissatisfied with the government's performance. Demobilized reserve IDF soldiers demonstrated, demanding an investigation. A protest tent was set up close to the prime minister's office. Under public pressure, Olmert accepted the necessity of an investigation; Judge Eliyahu Winograd headed the investigating committee.

The committee's interim report of April 30, 2007, was harshly critical of Olmert, Peretz, and Halutz, the last of whom had already resigned in January. Both Olmert and Peretz refused to resign. Olmert was aware that few in his party wanted new elections, since polls indicated that Kadima would not do well. Foreign Minister Tzipi Livni was widely criticized in the media for her perceived indecisiveness. Despite criticizing Olmert, she refused to resign or to battle him for the leadership, which helped deflate the campaign for Olmert's removal. A large demonstration on May 3, 2007, of 100,000 calling for Olmert's resignation came to nothing, and the protest campaign faded.

Peretz was not so fortunate. Primaries to choose the Labor Party's leader had long been scheduled for May 29. Barak, claiming that only he with his centrist and security credentials could beat Netanyahu in an election, gained a majority in the second round. He became defense minister in Olmert's government while making it clear that he believed Olmert should resign.

A NEW NATIONAL CONSENSUS

For many Israelis on both the left and right, the events of the summer of 2006 discredited the strategy of unilateral withdrawals. The flaw in the policy seemed to be its inability to create deterrence. Unilateral withdrawals appeared to persuade the other side that Israel was weak and in retreat; aggressive attacks were the result, not steps toward peace. Iran's and Syria's sponsorship of Palestinian and Lebanese groups that rejected Israel's existence made the situation threatening, since land from which Israel withdrew came under the influence of such groups. Even Kadima's leaders acknowledged that any more disengagement steps had to be taken off the agenda.

These developments strengthened the new public consensus that even though Israel no longer wanted the West Bank and the Gaza Strip and was willing to trade them for full peace and a Palestinian state, the option would not work. Land could not be successfully exchanged for peace. Thus Labor, Kadima, and Likud—the three main parties—all accepted the same basic policy framework, ending the old debate begun in 1967 and carried on through the end of the peace process between those ready to trade territory for peace and those who wanted to keep territory. Danny Seaman, director of the Foreign Press Office, supplied a summary of the Israeli national consensus in a November 2010 interview:

> There were certain "truths" that we were told: That if we adopt UN resolutions, there'll be peace. If we recognize the Palestinian right to self-determination, there'll be peace. If we remove settlements, there'll be peace. And over the past 25 years, there's been a progression in the Israeli position: Israel recognized the PLO as the only legitimate representative of the Palestinian people; relinquished territory; removed settlements. Regarding Lebanon, Israel fulfilled all the UN resolutions. Yet the end result was not the peace that we were promised. . . . Peace is a strategic necessity for the State of Israel. But . . . these "truths" that we were promised never came about. On the contrary, it only increased violence, increased extremism.

Such thinking was reinforced by the emergence of an Iran-led Islamist bloc that was even more intransigent toward Israel, openly denied that the Holocaust had happened, and called for Israel's extermination. Iran's accelerating drive to obtain nuclear weapons and support for Hamas and Hizballah were additional factors making the Iran issue the top priority in the Israeli debate. This, too, encouraged consensus in Israel.

Ensuring U.S. and Western support to counter Iran's drive toward obtaining nuclear weapons was also very important to Israel's strategic interests, especially since Tehran's leaders spoke frequently about wiping Israel off the map and sponsored Hamas, Hizballah, and other terrorist groups that attacked Israel. Israel's primary enemies were no longer neighboring Arab states, Arab nationalist movements, and the PLO, but rather Islamist movements and Iran. Thus, after so many years of peacemaking efforts, the emphasis was now on national defense. The status quo seemed more desirable than before and—despite real concerns over Iran—sustainable.

The sense of a renewed existential threat, deriving from Iranian nuclear ambitions, diminished deterrence after the Lebanon War of 2006, and criticism of the leadership from within Kadima and Labor led to the rapid revival of the fortunes of Likud and its leader, Netanyahu. That Netanyahu was widely judged to have been a very successful finance minister in privatizing large elements of the economy helped rehabilitate him as a potential leader. Events in the Gaza Strip reinforced all of these trends.

HAMAS SEIZES THE GAZA STRIP AND ISRAEL RESPONDS

In June 2007, Hamas defeated Fatah-led forces in the Gaza Strip and seized control of the entire territory. The existence of two Palestinian entities now made the idea of successful negotiations to resolve the Israel-Palestinian conflict seem even less likely. It also, however, made

Israeli leaders see the Fatah-dominated West Bank PA as the lesser of two evils. Even if they doubted that peace could be made with the PA, Israeli leaders knew that its PA counterparts wanted to survive Hamas's challenge and avoid renewed warfare. Israel used its intelligence service, military forces, and economic leverage to help achieve this goal.

Following a November 2007 meeting in Annapolis, Maryland, hosted by the United States, Israel-PA talks restarted, as did indirect exchanges with Syria. Here, too, Israeli leaders doubted that Syria intended to make a deal, but exchanges were nonetheless seen as a way to show Israel's desire for peace, satisfy the United States, and give Syria an incentive to restrain Hizballah.

After taking over the Gaza Strip, Hamas stepped up its campaign of cross-border raids and rocket and mortar attacks on Israel. During 2008, Hamas fired 1,700 rockets at southern Israel. While casualties were low, life in the region was severely disrupted, and by the end of 2008, fifteen Israeli civilians had been killed.

Israel frequently retaliated after the attacks. It also periodically and temporarily blocked the shipping of goods other than food or medicine into the Gaza Strip because Hamas was using imports to consolidate its rule and to strengthen its military capacity. Israel's minimum goal was to keep the Hamas regime weak and unstable; its maximum goal was to topple the regime.

In June 2008, Hamas agreed under pressure to a six-month ceasefire, but it used the time to smuggle in weapons, usually through tunnels passing through the porous Egyptian border blockade. It allowed such smaller allied groups as the Islamic Jihad to violate the ceasefire by continuing to fire rockets and mortars at Israel. Hamas also rejected Israeli offers to release hundreds of Palestinian prisoners in exchange for Shalit, the captured IDF soldier.

In December 2008, Hamas announced that it was ending the ceasefire and began shooting large numbers of rockets into Israel again. Consequently, on December 27, Israel launched Operation Cast Lead, an aerial campaign against Hamas targets, which was followed by a ground attack on January 3. On January 17, Israel declared a unilateral ceasefire, to which Hamas responded by announcing a cessation of rocket attacks for one week. Israel's troops were out of the Gaza Strip four days later.

Operation Cast Lead was quick and focused, and Israeli casualties were minimal. Unlike Hizballah, Hamas did not fight well. It also suffered heavy casualties and had major losses of equipment. In this brief Gaza War, Israeli deterrence was reestablished, and Hamas was forced to be more cautious about attacking Israel thereafter. But Hamas was not forced out of power and was not hit as hard as it could have been, because the Israeli government decided not to go into the most densely populated areas where Hamas troops were hiding. It wished to avoid heavy casualties both in its own army and among Palestinian civilians.

International reaction to the offensive was another consideration. Frequently before, in Israel's conflicts with the PLO and Arab states, the West—including the United States—had moved to prevent a full Israeli victory. Israel did not want to open its relationship with the newly elected U.S. president, Barack Obama, with friction.

Unable to beat Israel on the regular battlefield, Hamas tried different tactics. It used Palestinian civilians as human shields by placing the main Hamas headquarters in a hospital

A rocket fired at Israel from a residential area in the Gaza Strip, December 2008. (Getty Images / Image Bank.)

basement and by firing missiles from schools, houses, and hospitals or closer nearby. It portrayed killed Hamas fighters as if they were civilian victims. And it began a largely successful propaganda campaign against Israel, accusing it of deliberately killing civilians, retaliating with disproportionate destruction, and even committing war crimes.

A UN Human Rights Council delegation, known as the Goldstone Commission, among whose members were people who had previously strongly criticized Israel, came to the Gaza Strip, took Palestinian testimony, and reported the Palestinian testimony as fact. Israel, which had refused to cooperate with the investigation, argued that the report was biased. The report

IDF soldiers operating in the Gaza Strip during Operation Cast Lead, January 2009. (Getty Images / Image Bank.)

had little practical impact even though the UN General Assembly endorsed it. Richard Goldstone, the chief author, himself later denounced the report.

But questions about the report and many other efforts, including coverage by foreign media, remained: Was Israel being demonized and delegitimized? Were Western politicians, intellectuals, media, and public opinion starting to see Israel as an aggressor rather than as the defender of its citizens?

THE PEACE PROCESS DEADLOCKED

Although Israelis generally supported Olmert's foreign and strategic policy, they were skeptical about him personally, given both the mismanagement of the Lebanon War and several personal financial scandals. Throughout his tenure, Olmert was accused of corruption. When evidence and testimony accumulated about bribe-taking and an indictment seemed possible, he announced, in July 2008, that he would not seek reelection as the Kadima Party's leader. In September 2008, Livni narrowly won internal party elections, defeating former chief of staff Shaul Mofaz. After Livni's election, Olmert resigned as prime minister, making him the interim prime minister until Livni could form a government. When she was unable to do so, national elections were scheduled for February 2009.

In the elections, Kadima won one seat more than Likud, twenty-eight compared to twenty-seven. Although it had the largest number of seats, Knesset members from smaller parties preferred Netanyahu, giving him the parliamentary majority needed to form a government.

The new coalition included Likud and Labor plus smaller parties. Barak became defense minister. In January 2011, Barak split off from the Labor Party in order to head off internal pressure to quit the coalition. He instead became head of a new centrist party called Atzmaut (Independence).

Netanyahu, now a centrist himself, explicitly accepted the existence of a Palestinian state if a comprehensive peace agreement could be reached that incorporated Israel's requirements. Netanyahu, Barak, Livni, and Peres all had similar positions. But Israel had no interest in making a two-state agreement that would leave it less safe than before. Despite all the problems that Israel faced regionally and internationally, its current situation was far better than it had so often been in the past.

The following month, Israel's government produced a new peace plan reflecting the country's consensus stance on these issues. There were five things that Israel would insist be incorporated into any peace agreement producing a two-state solution. These were recognition of Israel as a Jewish state by the Palestinians, who would have their own Arab, Muslim state; a clear ending of the conflict and of all Palestinian claims on Israel; strong security arrangements and serious international guarantees for implementing them; a non-militarized Palestinian state; and resettlement of all Palestinian refugees in Palestine unless they wished to remain where they were already living.

The presidency of Barack Obama posed special challenges to the Israeli coalition government, which was concerned that the new U.S. government would be less friendly to Israel than many of its predecessors had been. At the same time, the Obama administration expressed an urgent desire to press forward with an Israel-Palestinian diplomatic process and a strong belief that the issue could be resolved quickly.

This is not what actually happened. When President Obama took office in January 2009, the PA had already suspended talks because of the Israel-Hamas fighting in the Gaza Strip. The new U.S. administration put the emphasis on freezing new Israeli construction in existing West Bank settlements. In exchange, it attempted to convince Arab rulers to give something to Israel. Contrary to U.S. expectations, Arab regimes showed themselves to be far more concerned about an expansionist Iran than the Israel-Palestinian conflict. The PA itself was not eager for talks and vetoed an announcement by Obama in September 2009 that Israel and the Palestinians would start intensive talks within two months.

After months of U.S. efforts, Prime Minister Netanyahu agreed on November 25, 2009, to a ten-month construction freeze, calling the move "a painful step that will advance the peace process." This decision was praised by U.S. Secretary of State Hillary Clinton, who called it an "unprecedented" concession. In the official response to the Israeli government's construction freeze, the U.S. State Department defined its goal as an outcome that "reconciles the Palestinian goal of an independent and viable state based on the 1967 lines, with agreed swaps, and the Israeli goal of a Jewish state with secure and recognized borders that reflect subsequent developments and meet Israeli security requirements." This was an important statement because it indicated U.S. support for alterations of the pre-1967 borders in Israel's favor, the incorporation of some settlements into Israeli territory, security guarantees acceptable to Israel, and recognition of Israel as a Jewish state. But would the U.S. government keep to those commitments?

An indication of the answer to that question came in March 2010, when Washington became angry over a Jerusalem zoning board decision that gave routine approval for future construction of a large housing development, Ramat Shlomo, in northeast Jerusalem, across the pre-1967 border. Jerusalem, as the U.S. government knew, had not been included in the construction freeze. To accommodate U.S. demands, the Israeli government extended the freeze to apply to Jerusalem as well.

Nevertheless, the PA still refused to negotiate with Israel. Not until September 2010, just before the freeze expired, did this change briefly. But the PA walked out again within a few days. Once the ten-month freeze ended on September 27, 2010, the PA again refused to talk. In December, after attempts to secure an additional three-month freeze failed, the U.S. government abandoned this effort. One reason was that the Netanyahu coalition would have collapsed if Netanyahu had accepted an additional freeze that included Jerusalem without having achieved results with the previous freeze.

In any case, several problems with the strategy of freezing construction had become apparent right away. First, the PA had negotiated with Israel for sixteen years without ever seriously challenging Israel's position, stated when the Oslo agreement was signed, that it interpreted the Oslo Accords as permitting construction within existing settlements. That is, the Obama administration had gone further than the PA, which could hardly demand less as a condition for renewing talks. Since the PA had broken off contacts with Israel in response to the Gaza War, requiring a freeze ensured that talks would not restart for a long time. Second, by taking such a tough stand at the outset and offering Israel nothing in return, the United States had not given Israel an incentive to make concessions. Third, when the United States did promise some compensation from Arab states, it could not deliver, since these regimes refused to cooperate.

Israel was quite capable of maintaining peace and prosperity at home without a comprehensive resolution of the Israel-Palestinian conflict. Despite the absence of a diplomatic process, the situation in the West Bank remained generally stable, and Israeli countermeasures—including the security fence—kept terrorism at low levels. In fact, the deployment of Western-trained Palestinian security forces in the West Bank, general calm, foreign aid, and Israel's lifting of some travel restrictions brought increased economic activity there. Fewer IDF troops were deployed in the West Bank than at any time since the First Intifada broke out in 1987.

In the Gaza Strip, however, the situation was different. Hamas continued to rule that area as a virtually independent state. It sent Hamas cadres or allowed allied groups to make cross-border attacks using rockets, mortars, and armed bands. Western nations backed the split in the West Bank, with part ruled by the PA and part ruled by Fatah, and Iran and Syria supported a Hamas-ruled Gaza Strip, making diplomatic progress unlikely and of limited value, since the PA had no control over almost half the territory for which it claimed to speak.

Although the diplomatic process was halted, and violence was generally absent, the conflict with Israel took on new forms. Opponents of Israel focused on delegitimizing the country by using propaganda, boycotts, sanctions, and other methods. The principal goal was to erode support for Israel in the democratic West by portraying the country as oppressive.

One of the most significant such actions came in May 2010. Israel—and also Egypt, which feared that a revolutionary Islamist entity on its border would subvert its own people—had put heavy import and export sanctions on the Gaza Strip. The goal was to keep the Hamas regime weak and, if possible, bring it down through a loss of public support. The Turkish Islamist IHH group organized a six-ship flotilla, ostensibly to bring humanitarian aid to the Gaza Strip. Because its political goal was to help Hamas by breaking the sanctions, the organizers refused an offer to bring the aid to Israel's port of Ashdod, where it would be checked and then transported into Gaza. On May 31, to prevent the ships from landing in Gaza, Israeli forces boarded five of the ships and steered them into Ashdod without injury. But about forty Turks associated with Islamist groups violently resisted attempts by Israeli navy commandos to board the sixth ship, the *Mavi Marmara* flagship, and took some soldiers hostage. In the ensuing gunfight, nine Turkish jihadists were killed.

From the organizers' standpoint, the flotilla was a success. The incident led to much international criticism of Israel; and the Islamist government in Turkey, which had already moved to end the previous close relations between the two countries, became outspokenly hostile. Particularly because of U.S. pressure, Israel narrowed its sanctions to ban just the smuggling of weapons and items of military use. The lifting of these sanctions, along with the inflow of foreign aid, facilitated the survival of the Hamas regime, with its stated goal of destroying Israel and sabotaging any Israel-PA peace process.

The dramatic developments in the region during 2011 only confirmed the post-2000 Israeli worldview that there was no partner for peace, that Western security guarantees were not trustworthy, and that revolutionary Islamist forces determined to attack and desiring to wipe out Israel were increasingly powerful in the Middle East. Where many Western observers perceived an "Arab Spring" of moderate democratic change, Israelis saw—especially in Egypt—a growing extremism, even the undoing of the Egypt-Israel peace treaty.

In an indicative June 2010 poll, 77 percent of Israelis opposed returning to the pre-1967 boundaries even if that led to a peace agreement; 85 percent wanted to maintain a united Jerusalem under Israeli sovereignty in any peace deal. About 60 percent believed that defensible borders were more likely to ensure peace than any peace agreement, while 82 percent considered security concerns more important than any diplomatic deal. All of these figures had climbed upward because of this worldview shift following the failure of the 1993–2000 Oslo peace process, the ensuing intifada, and other developments.

Assessing the overall situation of Israel in the early twenty-first century involves both positive developments and problems. The threat that had prevailed for many decades—conventional warfare against a broad alliance of neighboring and other Arab states—has receded. Israel has developed into a prosperous society with a military that has demonstrated its edge over potential foes. It has strong defenses against terrorism and is developing a multilevel defense system against rockets and missiles. The number of rocket attacks on Israel from the Gaza Strip declined from 2,048 in 2008 to 569 in 2009 and to 150 in 2010. Despite the absence of a diplomatic process, the situation in the West Bank remained generally stable, and Israeli countermeasures—including the security fence—kept terrorism at low levels. The total number of attacks on Israel—including those from the Gaza Strip—declined from 1,354 in 2009 to 798 in 2010.

At the same time, however, the Arab nationalist antagonists—both states and radical groups—have been replaced by revolutionary Islamists determined to sustain the conflict with Israel until Israel is destroyed. The new enemies have developed three new tactics to use against Israel: Hamas and Hizballah fire massive numbers of rockets at Israeli civilians and cities; Iran has undertaken a drive to develop nuclear weapons and long-range missiles that might be used against Israel; and various governments and nongovernmental organizations try to delegitimize Israel. Israelis have ample reason to believe both that the attempts to injure or destroy the nation will continue and that Israel will continue to meet the challenges.

AN ALTERED BUT STABLE SOCIETY

Having firmly established a government and a society—and having weathered war, terrorism, and conflicts of every description in the process—the State of Israel evolved beyond its heroic phase. Austerity and socialist-oriented policies were replaced by more individualistic, materialistic policies with the same characteristics, but now the aspiration was, not to achieve a utopian society, but to be successful in other ways. Preservation of Israel as a Jewish and democratic state remains the core objective. Indeed, despite erosion over time, a remarkable 70 percent of Israeli Arabs—who have seen rising Islamism and instability in the surrounding region—also accept a definition of Israel, in the polling question's words, as a "Jewish and democratic state, in which Jews and Arabs live together."

Certainly, there is deep concern about the volatility of the Middle East, Iran's growing power, and the burgeoning strength of Islamist insurgent movements on Israel's northern and southern borders. Israelis, with their ever-active self-criticism, also find much in society about which to complain, especially political corruption and government inefficiencies. There is a cynicism toward ideology that undercuts past idealism but equally dilutes tendencies toward intolerance and fanatical certainties.

Yet Israelis generally have a positive belief that their lives are good and will get better. Indeed, the country's gross domestic product (GDP) in 2009 stood at $28,400 per capita, about the same as Italy's. Living standards have improved for most Israelis over the years, as has the national infrastructure. The country is far more united both socially and politically than at any time in the past half-century.

Today, almost one-half of the world's Jews are Israelis, compared to only 10 percent when the state was founded. Israel, which was predominantly agricultural at first, has become a world leader in a number of fields, including medicine, science, and agricultural and military technologies and high technologies of various kinds. What was a beleaguered garrison state with an uncertain future is now a stable democracy with a diverse culture, a solid postindustrial economy, and a creative, thriving citizenry.

BIBLIOGRAPHY

Ajami, Fouad. *Dream Palace of the Arabs: A Generation's Odyssey.* New York: Vintage, 1999.

Arens, Moshe. "Consequences of the 2006 War for Israel." *MERIA Journal: The Middle East Review of International Affairs* 11, no. 1 (March 2007). http://www.gloria-center.org/meria/2007/03/arens.html.

Begin, Menachem. *The Revolt.* New York: Nash Publishing Co., 1977.

Ben-Aharon, Yossi. "Negotiating with Syria: A First Hand Account." *MERIA Journal: The Middle East Review of International Affairs* 4, no. 2 (June 2000). http://www.gloria-center.org/meria/2000/06/ben-aharon.html.

Ben-Gurion, David. *Like Stars and Dust: Essays from Israel's Government Year Book*. Sede Boker: Ben-Gurion Research Center, 1997.

Catignani, Sergio. *Israeli Counter-Insurgency and the Intifadahs: Dilemmas of a Conventional Army*. Abingdon, UK: Routledge, 2008.

Chafets, Ze'ev. *Heroes and Hustlers, Hard Hats and Holy Men: Inside the New Israel*. New York: William Morrow, 1986.

Cohen, Stuart. *Israel and Its Army: From Cohesion to Confusion*. London: Routledge, 2008.

Collins, Larry, and Dominique La Pierre. *O Jerusalem*. New York: Touchstone Books, 1988.

Dershowitz, Alan. *The Case for Peace: How the Arab-Israeli Conflict Can Be Resolved*. Hoboken, NJ: John Wiley, 2005.

Elon, Amos. *The Israelis: Founders and Sons*. New York: Penguin, 1983.

Friedman, Thomas. *From Beirut to Jerusalem*. New York: Anchor, 1990.

Gelber, Yoav. *Palestine 1948: War, Escape and the Emergence of the Palestinian Refugee Problem*. Brighton, UK: Sussex Academic Press, 2000.

Gluska, Ami. "Israel's Decision to Go to War, June 2, 1967." *MERIA Journal: The Middle East Review of International Affairs* 11, no. 2 (June 2007). http://www.gloria-center.org/meria/2007/06/gluska.html.

Harel, Amos, and Avi Issacharoff. *34 Days: Israel, Hizballah and the War in Lebanon*. New York: Palgrave Macmillan, 2008.

Hertzberg, Arthur. *The Zionist Idea: A Historical Analysis and Reader*. Philadelphia: Jewish Publication Society of America, 1997.

Herzl, Theodore. *The Jewish State*. New York: Dover, 1989.

Hourani, Albert. *A History of the Arab Peoples*. London: Faber and Faber, 1991.

Israel Security Agency. *2010 Annual Summary: Data and Trends in Terrorism*. December 25, 2010. http://www.shabak.gov.il/SiteCollectionImages/english/TerrorInfo/reports/2010summary-en.pdf.

Jabotinsky, Ze'ev. *The Political and Social Philosophy of Ze'ev Jabotinsky (Selected Writings)*. London: Vallentine Mitchell, 1999.

Johnson, Paul. *A History of the Jews*. New York: Harper Perennial, 1988.

Karsh, Efraim. *Arafat's War: The Man and His Battle for Israeli Conquest*. New York: Grove Press, 2003.

Kimmerling, Baruch, and Joel S. Migdal. *The Palestinian People: A History*. Cambridge, MA: Harvard University Press, 2003.

Kramer, Martin. *Arab Awakening and Islamic Revival: The Politics of Ideas in the Middle East*. New Brunswick, NJ: Transaction, 1996.

Kramer, Martin. "Israel vs. the New Islamist Axis." *MERIA Journal: The Middle East Review of International Affairs* 11, no. 1 (March 2007). http://www.gloria-center.org/meria/2007/03/kramer.html.

Laqueur, Walter. *A History of Zionism: From the French Revolution to the Establishment of the State of Israel*. New York: Schocken, 2003.

Laqueur, Walter, and Barry Rubin. *The Israel-Arab Reader*. 7th ed. New York: Viking/Penguin, 2008.

Lasensky, Scott B. "Friendly Restraint: U.S.-Israel Relations During the Gulf Crisis of 1990–1991." *MERIA Journal: The Middle East Review of International Affairs* 3, no. 2 (June 1999). http://www.gloria-center.org/meria/1999/06/lasensky.html.

Levitt, Matthew. *Hamas: Politics, Charity and Terrorism in the Service of Jihad*. New Haven: Yale University Press, 2006.

Lewis, Bernard. *The Crisis of Islam: Holy War and Unholy Terror*. New York: Random House, 2004.

Lewis, Bernard. *The Middle East: A Brief History of the Last 2,000 Years*. New York: Touchstone Books, 1997.

Lozowick, Yaakov. *Right to Exist: A Moral Defense of Israel's Wars*. New York: Doubleday, 2003.

Makiya, Kanan. *Cruelty and Silence: War, Tyranny and Uprising and the Arab World*. London: Penguin, 1994.

Melman, Yossi, and Meir Javedanfar. *The Nuclear Sphinx of Tehran: Mahmoud Ahmedinejad and the State of Iran*. New York: Carroll and Graf, 2007.

Morris, Benny. *1948: A History of the First Arab-Israeli War*. New Haven: Yale University Press, 2008.

Morris, Benny. *Righteous Victims: A History of the Zionist-Arab Conflict, 1881–1999*. New York: Alfred A. Knopf, 2000.

Netanyahu, Benjamin. *A Durable Peace: Israel and Its Place Among the Nations*. New York: Grand Central Publishing, 2000.

Norton, Augustus Richard. *Hezbollah*. Princeton, NJ: Princeton University Press, 2007.

Oren, Michael. *Six Days of War: June 1967 and the Making of the Modern Middle East*. Oxford: Oxford University Press, 2002.

Oz, Amos. *In the Land of Israel*. Orlando, FL: Mariner Books, 1993.

Qassem, Naim. *Hizbullah: The Story from Within*. London: Saqi, 2005.

Rabinovitch, Abraham. *The Yom Kippur War: The Epic Encounter That Transformed the Middle East*. New York: Schocken, 2004.

Rabinovitch, Itamar. *Waging Peace: Israel and the Arabs, 1948–2003*. Princeton, NJ: Princeton University Press, 2004.

Ross, Dennis. *The Missing Peace: The Inside Story of the Fight for Middle East Peace*. New York: Farrar, Straus and Giroux, 2004.

Rubin, Barry. *The Tragedy of the Middle East*. Cambridge: Cambridge University Press, 2002.

Rubin, Barry. *The Truth About Syria*. New York: Palgrave Macmillan, 2007.

Rubin, Barry, ed. *Conflict and Insurgency in the Contemporary Middle East*. New York: Routledge, 2009.

Rubin, Barry, ed. *Lebanon: Liberation, Conflict and Crisis*. New York: Palgrave Macmillan, 2009.

Rubin, Barry, and Judith Colp. *Chronologies of Modern Terrorism*. Armonk, NY: Sharpe, 2008.

Sachar, Howard M. *A History of Israel*. Vol. 2: *From the Aftermath of the Yom Kippur War*. Oxford: Oxford University Press, 1987.

Sachar, Howard M. *A History of Israel from the Rise of Zionism to Our Time*. New York: Alfred A. Knopf, 1998.

Said, Edward. *The Politics of Dispossession*. New York: Random House, 1994.

Segev, Tom. *One Palestine, Complete: Jews and Arabs Under the British Mandate*. New York: Metropolitan Books, 2000.

Shanks, Hershel. *Ancient Israel: From Abraham to the Roman Destruction of the Temple*. Upper Saddle River, NJ: Prentice Hall, 1999.

Sharon, Ariel. *Warrior: An Autobiography*. New York: Simon and Schuster, 2001.

Shepherd, Robin. *A State Beyond the Pale: Europe's Problem with Israel*. London: Weidenfeld and Nicholson, 2009.

Sofer, Sasson. *Zionism and the Foundations of Israeli Diplomacy*. Cambridge: Cambridge University Press, 1998.

Spyer, Jonathan. "The Impact of the Iraq War on Israel's National Security Conception." *MERIA Journal: The Middle East Review of International Affairs* 9, no. 4 (December 2005). http://www.gloria-center.org/meria/2005/12/spyer.html.

Spyer, Jonathan. "Lebanon 2006: Unfinished War." *MERIA Journal: The Middle East Review of International Affairs* 12, no. 1 (March 2008). http://www.gloria-center.org/meria/2008/03/spyer.html.

Spyer, Jonathan. *The Transforming Fire: The Rise of the Israel-Islamist Conflict*. New York: Continuum, 2010.

Sternhell, Ze'ev. *The Founding Myths of Israel*. Princeton, NJ: Princeton University Press, 1998.

Tessler, Mark A. *A History of the Israeli-Palestinian Conflict*. Bloomington: Indiana University Press, 1994.

Wasserstein, Bernard. *Divided Jerusalem: The Struggle for the Holy City*. New Haven: Yale University Press, 2001.

Weizmann, Chaim. *Trial and Error: The Autobiography of Chaim Weizmann*. London: Hamish Hamilton, 1949; New York: Schocken, 1966.

Chapter Three

LAND AND PEOPLE

From Mount Hermon's snow-capped peak in the north to the rocky Negev desert wilderness in the south, from the relatively green Mediterranean coast in the west to the Dead Sea's lunar landscape in the east, Israel has enormous geographical variety despite its small area. At 7,992 square miles (20,700 square kilometers), Israel within its pre-1967 borders ranks 152nd in size among the approximately 200 countries in the world. It is around the same size as Djibouti, Belize, El Salvador, and Slovenia and slightly smaller than the U.S. state of New Jersey. With just fewer than 7.5 million people, Israel ranks ninety-seventh in terms of population, placing it among Serbia, Tajikistan, Bulgaria, and El Salvador. Neighboring Egypt has around twelve times the population.

Not only is Israel a tiny country with a population smaller than that of many large cities—including Tehran and Bangkok, for example—but it has been surrounded by hostile neighbors, a problem diminished only by fragile peace treaties with Egypt and Jordan. The borders with Lebanon and Syria, both formally at war with Israel, are, respectively, 49 and 47 miles (79 and 76 kilometers) in length. The border with the Hamas-ruled Gaza Strip is 32 miles (51 kilometers) long. The frontier with the West Bank, 191 miles (307 kilometers) long, has also been vulnerable to attack by guerrilla and terrorist forces. Two of Israel's borders—with Egypt, 165 miles (266 kilometers), and Jordan, 148 miles (238 kilometers)—have been largely peaceful in recent years but were crossed by terrorists and Arab armies in the past.

More than 80 percent of Israel's land is not usable for agriculture, at least given present technology. The country lacks a large supply of fresh water, and except for phosphates, it has not had much in the way of valuable natural resources, although it might produce significant amounts of natural gas from offshore wells in the future. There are no major rivers—though one overgrown stream, the Jordan River, is among the world's most famous—and there are only two lakes of any size, the Sea of Galilee and the Dead Sea.

By these standards, Israel should be an obscure country of little interest beyond its own frontiers. Why, then, is Israel so prominent in the news and in the minds of people around the world? There are three key reasons: location, historical significance, and contemporary conflict. Israel is at the crossroads of three continents—Europe, Asia, and Africa—as well as two strategic seas: the Red Sea and the Mediterranean. Historically, ideas and cultures came together at this crossroads between civilizations and great powers, there to be developed into

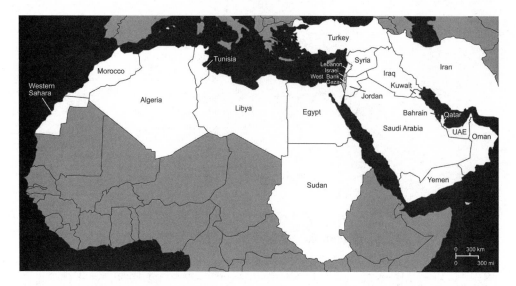

Israel is a tiny part of the Middle East region, shown in white on the map. It has about 5 percent of the people (7 million compared to 150 million) and less than 0.2 percent of the area (8,000 out of 5 million square miles). The Arab League of the Middle East has twenty-two predominantly Arab and Muslim countries as members. (© 2003–2010 Koret Communications Ltd. All rights reserved.)

something new. Hence, too, this territory has always had an important strategic value. Many wars have been fought over these trade routes and this borderland of contending empires over the millennia, from Biblical times through the Crusader-Muslim wars to World War I and the Arab-Israeli wars of modern times.

As the birthplace of Judaism and Christianity and an important site in Islam, the Land of Israel became a focal point in the world's religious and intellectual development. What to the Jews has always been the Promised Land is viewed by Christians as the Holy Land and by Muslims as a holy land. People of all three faiths have claimed the land over the centuries. Details about its history and geography were disseminated throughout the world by way of the Bible and, to a lesser extent, the Quran. Illiterate peasants living thousands of miles away, who had never traveled more than a few miles from their villages, knew of its places and its past. In Jewish life, the Land of Israel has always been overwhelmingly at the center of consciousness, culture, and religious practice; it was the Promised Land from which Jews had been exiled and to which they believed they would eventually return.

Disputes over the territories that make up Israel as well as those captured by Israel in 1967 have brought a half-dozen major wars, several revolts, and some of the most intense, continuing diplomatic efforts of modern history. Israel today is a focus of international attention. A wide variety of new events on almost a daily basis bring into existence continents of passionate debate, rivers of research, mountains of media coverage, and tectonic plates of policy. Great powers have been drawn into all of these conflicts and debates to a tremendous extent.

Israel borders Lebanon to the north, Syria to the northeast, Jordan to the east, and Egypt to the south. To the west is the Mediterranean Sea. The country is about 290 miles

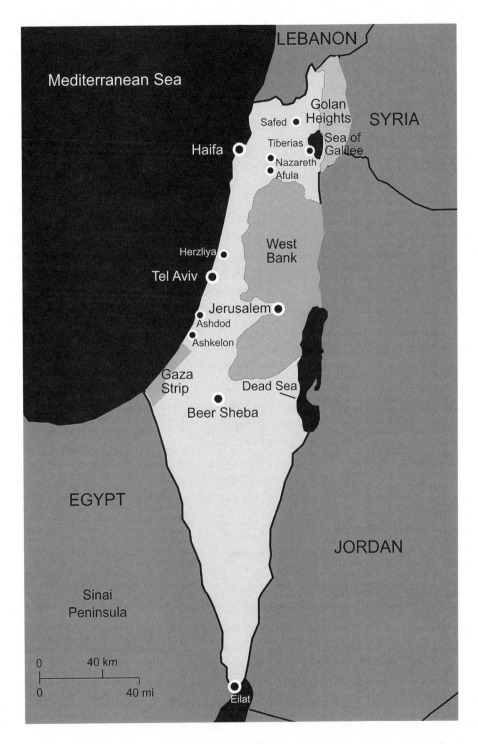

Israel is about 290 miles (470 kilometers) long, and it is 85 miles (135 kilometers) across at its widest point. It administers directly two areas captured in the 1967 war—the Golan Heights and east Jerusalem—along with parts of the West Bank, which is largely governed by the Palestinian Authority. (© 2003–2010 Koret Communications Ltd. All rights reserved.)

(470 kilometers) long, which means that an automobile can travel from the northernmost point to Eilat, a city at the country's southern tip, in about nine hours. The biggest east-west expanse is across the northern Negev desert; a car can travel those 85 miles (135 kilometers) in a speedy ninety minutes. At its narrowest, within the pre-1967 borders, the country is just 9 miles (12 kilometers) across. The narrow corridor connecting Jerusalem to the rest of the country is just 4 miles wide (less than 6 kilometers) north to south, within the pre-1967 borders.

BORDERS

1948–1967

Israel's borders have in practice been the ceasefire lines from 1948, demarcating the territory of Israel when the fighting ended after its War of Independence. Those borders were confirmed by armistice agreements with Egypt, Jordan, Syria, and Lebanon—each of Israel's neighbors. As a result, Israel includes the Galilee hill region in the north, stretching from the Sea of Galilee to the Mediterranean and including the cities of Acre and Haifa. A narrow belt of territory along the coast, including Tel Aviv, links this area to the large but only lightly inhabited Negev desert and then extends southward through Beer Sheba to Eilat, at the end of the Gulf of Eilat, which empties into the Red Sea. In Israel's center, another narrow belt, the Jerusalem Corridor, stretches eastward to connect Jerusalem with the rest of the country.

Other territory from the Palestine Mandate after its dissolution in 1948 was outside Israel. Egypt occupied and governed the Gaza Strip. Jordan captured and annexed the West Bank (the Judea and Samaria of Jewish history) and the eastern part of Jerusalem, including the Old City. This annexation went largely unrecognized internationally.

Under the UN Partition Plan of 1947, which proposed the creation of two states, a Jewish one and an Arab one on the territory of the former Palestine Mandate, Jerusalem was to be under UN control. But neither the Jewish nor the Arab side supported that part of the proposal, and no one ever made any attempt to implement it. As a result, almost all countries have refused to recognize Jerusalem as Israel's capital and have located their embassies in Tel Aviv.

A look at Israel's pre-1967 geography shows the strategic vulnerabilities imposed by its terrain. In the north, the Golan Heights of Syria looked down on a flat Israeli plain that stretched with no natural defensive barriers to the nearby Mediterranean.

To the east, the long, winding border, hilly country, and narrow corridor connecting west Jerusalem to the rest of Israel provided numerous military advantages to Jordan's army and, after 1967, to Palestinian forces. In Jerusalem itself, before 1967, Jordanian snipers could and did fire into the Israeli part of town from the Old City's walls.

To the south, the Sinai Peninsula provided Egypt with a large military operational area separated from its population centers and the Suez Canal while giving Israel a long border that was hard to defend. Egyptian artillery controlling the Gulf of Eilat from its narrowest point at Sharm al-Shaykh could easily cut off ship traffic to Israel's southern port of Eilat.

Guerrilla and terrorist forces could cross Israel's border at many points to reach population centers and sabotage facilities. The country's small size would also make it vulnerable in the future to short-range missile attacks. Indeed, so close was the pre-1967 border that planes

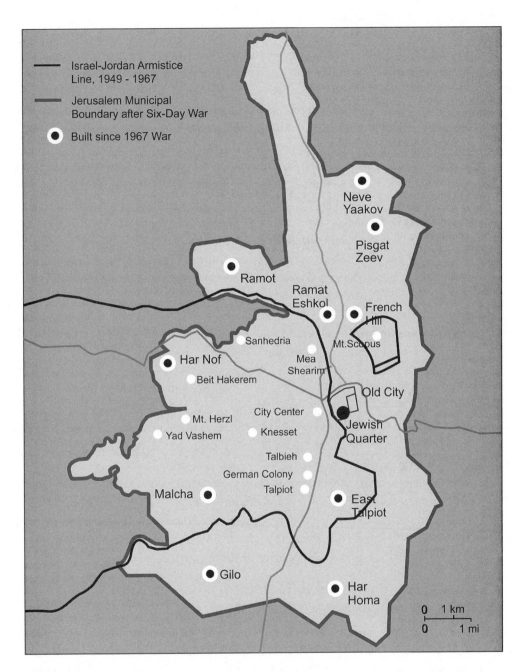

Israel's pre-1967 capital of Jerusalem is the area west of the heavy black line. In 1967, Israel captured the eastern part of the city, which Jordan had annexed in 1950. The city was reunited, and Israel annexed the eastern part. In subsequent negotiations, starting in 1993, Israel indicated a readiness to negotiate the future, and future boundaries, of the eastern part of the city. The plan that Israel put forward during the Camp David talks in 2000 included a suggestion that in return for full peace, Israel would give control over most of east Jerusalem to a Palestinian state. (© 2003–2010 Koret Communications Ltd. All rights reserved.)

leaving Israel's Ben-Gurion Airport could not fly east like aircraft everywhere else in the world, which use the Earth's rotation to assist takeoffs; instead, they had to head west, incurring extra fuel costs, to avoid crossing into Jordanian and later Palestinian Authority territory.

The encirclement by hostile states brought not only strategic challenges for Israel but also commercial ones. Only the Mediterranean was available to Israel as an open frontier. All roads, railroads, and pipelines formerly used for transport into and through neighboring countries were closed in 1948; those through Lebanon and Syria remain closed to this day.

Among other border issues added in the aftermath of the War of Independence was the Syrian occupation of two small areas that had been part of the British Mandate for Palestine. One of them was Hamat Gader, a hot spring dating back to Roman times, near where the borders of Israel, Syria, and Jordan met.

More important was the Syrian takeover of a strip of land near the Sea of Galilee. A 1923 border agreement had given Israel control over the entire sea (actually a lake), including a 164-foot-wide (50-meter-wide) strip on its eastern shore and some other nearby areas. Shortly after the War of Independence, however, the Syrians occupied this zone. That advance made it possible for Syria to control the Jordan River and the sea—and fire at Israeli farmers across the frontier. There were repeated small-scale clashes here during the 1950s and 1960s. Israel took back both of these border areas in the 1967 war.

Another small no-man's-land was created along sectors of the frontier between Israel and Jordanian-ruled territory in the Jerusalem area. An unusual provision of the 1949 armistice gave Israel control of a tiny enclave on Mount Scopus, where Hebrew University had its main campus. Israel was entitled to keep a small police force on the hill, but the university had to move elsewhere in the city. It returned many of its facilities to Mount Scopus after Israel captured all of Jerusalem in the 1967 war.

Despite the temporary nature of the 1949 agreements setting ceasefire lines, within a few years these borders came to be regarded as state frontiers. The geographical situation changed in 1967, but even today the 1949 lines are viewed internationally as Israel's actual boundaries. Informally, these are known as the "Green Line" borders because Israelis plant trees and crops on its side right up to the border and because green designates that line on Israel's maps.

Post-1967

During the 1967 war, Israel defeated the combined forces of Egypt, Jordan, and Syria and captured a large amount of territory. From Egypt, Israel took the Sinai Peninsula (9,650 square miles, or 25,000 square kilometers) and the Gaza Strip (146 square miles, or 378 square kilometers). From Jordan, it took the West Bank (2,270 square miles, or 5,879 square kilometers) and the eastern and other parts of Jerusalem (27 square miles, or 70 square kilometers). From Syria, it took the Golan Heights (444 square miles, or 1,150 square kilometers). The gains in territory improved Israel's strategic situation, but Israel also had to manage the populations of each of these areas—Bedouin tribes in the Sinai; Druze in the Golan Heights; and Palestinian Arabs in the West Bank, Gaza Strip, and east Jerusalem. Equally, it had to decide how it regarded these territories, whether as temporary, long-term, or permanent possessions. The frontiers were known as the "Purple Line" borders because of the color used to show them on maps.

Almost unanimously, Israelis believed that they would remain in control of these territories until a full peace treaty was signed with Arab states and the Palestinians. Some thought that a peace treaty would never be signed, others that reaching a peace agreement would take a very long time. Each group had a different list of what Israel should give up or retain, with east Jerusalem and the Golan Heights at the top of the "keep it" list and the Sinai and the Gaza Strip at the bottom.

Widening the Jerusalem Corridor and then having an Israeli presence in the Jordan Valley—to ensure the security of Jerusalem and the border with Jordan, respectively—were considered the highest priorities at the beginning. By the mid-1990s, a distinction was made between "settlement blocs"—several highly populated settlements very near Israel's border with the West Bank that most Israelis wanted to keep—and the larger number of small settlements deeper inside the West Bank, which they were willing to give up. Among the main large settlements were the Etzion Bloc and Ma'ale Adumim.

In general, there was a consensus among the major Israeli political parties on keeping east Jerusalem, the Golan Heights, and parts of the West Bank and a widespread willingness to give up Sinai, the Gaza Strip, and most of the West Bank. Broadly speaking, most Israelis agreed with Prime Minister Yitzhak Rabin's formula: peace in exchange for territory, with Israel returning more captured territory if it received a more beneficial and secure deal.

CHANGES AFTER PEACE WITH EGYPT

During the Yom Kippur War of 1973, Israel advanced farther into Egypt and Syria but, as part of the ceasefire agreements, returned to the post-1967 lines. Israel's peace treaty with Egypt in 1979 included its full withdrawal from the Sinai Peninsula; it returned that territory to Egypt in 1982, which gave Cairo control over the oilfields in the western part. In exchange, Egypt agreed to limit its military presence in the Sinai and to have an international force there to help ensure peace. The international border between Israel and Egypt became the same as that defined by the British and the Ottomans back in 1906.

There was, however, a dispute regarding a small area called Taba (under half a square mile, or a square kilometer), at the northern tip of the Gulf of Eilat, which Israel claimed had mistakenly been given to Egypt in the 1906 settlement. After several years of dispute, the two countries submitted the issue to an international committee formed for the purpose. The group ruled in Egypt's favor, and in 1989, Israel returned the land, which mainly consisted of a resort hotel. As part of the agreement, it became a zone that Israelis could enter without formally passing into Egypt or needing a visa.

Annexation of the Golan Heights

Israel's border in the July 20, 1949, armistice agreement with Syria deviated slightly from the 1923 border between the Palestine Mandate and Syria because Syria had seized 26 square miles (67 square kilometers) after the 1948 war. According to the pre-1948 border, three small areas, including a 33-foot-wide (10-meter-wide) strip on the northeast shore of the Sea of Galilee, all of the Jordan River, and the Banyas spring belonged to Israel. Israel recaptured these parcels in 1967. After the Yom Kippur War of 1973, Israel released 5 percent of the captured land of

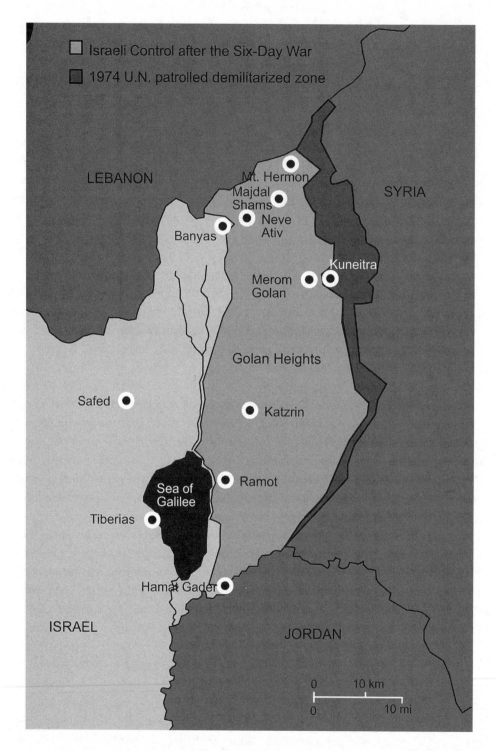

- ☐ Israeli Control after the Six-Day War
- ☐ 1974 U.N. patrolled demilitarized zone

LEBANON

SYRIA

Mt. Hermon

Majdal Shams

Neve Ativ

Banyas

Kuneitra

Merom Golan

Golan Heights

Safed

Katzrin

Ramot

Sea of Galilee

Tiberias

Hamat Gader

ISRAEL

JORDAN

| 0 | 10 km |
| 0 | 10 mi |

The Golan Heights was captured by Israel in the 1967 war, and Israeli law was extended there in 1981. The region overlooks the plain of Israel to the west and also contains the sources for much of Israel's water, making it of great strategic importance. (© 2003–2010 Koret Communications Ltd. All rights reserved.)

the Golan Heights—a strip that runs along the ceasefire line and is now a demilitarized zone patrolled by UN peacekeeping forces. Syria has consistently demanded that all of the land on Israel's side of the international border be turned over to it, in addition to the Golan Heights. This issue is important because possession would give Syria a claim on the Jordan River and the Sea of Galilee waters.

From 1967 until 1981, Israel placed the Golan Heights under military administration. Then, in 1981, several months before it gave the Sinai back to Egypt, Israel's parliament passed the Golan Heights Law, placing the region under Israeli civilian law, jurisdiction, and administration. The Druze and the handful of Alawite inhabitants were offered Israeli citizenship, although only a minority accepted, in part because those living there feared reprisals and the eventual return of the territory to Syria.

The Israel-Palestinian Peace Process and Territorial Shifts, 1993–2000

In 1993, Israel and the PLO signed the Oslo Accords, which established the Palestinian Authority (PA). The plan was for Israel to turn over the Arab-inhabited portions of the Gaza Strip and the West Bank to the PA, with Israel retaining control over parts of the territory, including key roads and Jewish settlements. The final borders between Israel and a Palestinian state, including the one in east Jerusalem, were to be set by bilateral negotiations leading up to a full peace treaty.

In 1994, Israel turned over to the PA control of the Gaza Strip—except for certain roads and Israeli settlements—and the Jericho area in the West Bank. The following year, it turned over to the PA's political control all the West Bank towns—except for Hebron—and villages, although Israel retained the right to exercise security control in the villages. In 1996, Israel turned over 80 percent of Hebron to the PA but kept the other 20 percent, inhabited partly by Jewish settlers, under Israeli administration.

The 1994 peace treaty with Jordan secured Israel's longest frontier with an existing state. Since Jordan had given up its claim to the West Bank and east Jerusalem in 1988, the future of those areas was left to the PA to negotiate. Israel did return to Jordan a small, 116-square-mile (300-square-kilometer) piece of Jordanian territory captured in 1967. Part of this territory was renamed Peace Island, which Israelis could visit, and a small portion of this land was leased by Israeli farmers for their orchards. The two countries also agreed to cooperate on management of the Jordan River, which formed part of their border.

In 2000, Israel offered Syria all the Golan Heights up to the international border in exchange for full peace. Syria rejected the proposal, as it had previously done when Israel had made the offer secretly. At both the Camp David summit in July 2000 and in the December 2000 Clinton plan, Israel offered to negotiate a peace agreement with the PA that would include an independent state of Palestine comprising the entire Gaza Strip, almost all of the West Bank, and part of east Jerusalem. Arafat rejected this as even a framework for further negotiations.

So no further major change in Israel's borders came until August 2005, when Israel unilaterally withdrew all military forces and settlements from the Gaza Strip. The goal was to give the PA a chance to show its ability to govern the territory and move toward peace. Instead, the PA

Israelis boating on the Jordan River, August 2000. Before 1967 much of the eastern bank was part of Jordan. (Getty Images / Image Bank.)

lost the January 2006 elections to Hamas, which seized the territory completely in June 2007 and expelled the PA. Israel also dismantled several settlements in the northern West Bank as part of its August 2005 peace gesture.

Given the failure of negotiations, Israel was left in control of the Golan Heights, east Jerusalem, and part of the West Bank.

Borders in Israeli Life, Politics, and Society

Since the 1967 war, border questions have played an important role in Israeli debates over the Israeli-Arab and Israel-Palestinian conflicts and any possible solutions. The proposals and arguments have shifted over time. Prior to the Egypt-Israel peace treaty, for example, Minister of Defense Moshe Dayan said that control over Sharm al-Shaykh—the area of Egyptian Sinai territory on the Red Sea coast where Egypt had blocked shipping to Eilat—was more important than peace with Egypt. But when Egypt actually offered a deal in 1979, Dayan quickly supported it.

The basic strategic argument was between those from the center to the left, who argued that trading land for peace could end the conflict, and those from the center to the right, who said that the Palestinians would not make peace at all. This exchange remained abstract until the 1993–2000 peace process put it to the test. After the 1967 war and before the 1993 start of the Oslo peace process, east Jerusalem, the Golan Heights, and small parts of the West Bank topped the keep-it list for those left of center; those right of center added much of the West Bank. At the bottom of both lists were the Gaza Strip—from which Israel withdrew partly in 1994 and completely in 2005—and, last of all, the Sinai Peninsula, which Israel left in the 1979 peace agreement with Egypt. Meanwhile, during the 1970s and 1980s, those in the right-wing Gush Emunim movement argued that settling the West Bank would bring religious redemption as well as enhance Israel's security.

A common view was that the 1967 frontiers were inherently indefensible. The Golan Heights gave Syria a huge strategic advantage; the West Bank hill country gave Jordan or any Palestinian state established there a similar advantage. The narrowness of the country meant that it could easily be sliced in two, and the narrowness of the Jerusalem Corridor made it easy to cut off that city from the rest of the country. With full peace and no conflict, these issues would not matter, but what if stability and peace did not prevail? .

Another relevant factor was that virtually all of the largest post-1967 settlements were at strategic locations very close to Israel's Green Line—like the Gush Etzion bloc, a group of reestablished pre-1948 Jewish villages, and Ma'ale Adumim, a large town just outside Jerusalem. This led to the argument for minor border modifications, land swaps, and "settlement blocs"—in short, a solution in which most of the West Bank would become part of a Palestinian state in a comprehensive peace agreement in exchange for which the PA would cede these particular areas of concentrated settlement, around 4 percent of the West Bank. Some even proposed swapping Israeli land in exchange for these parcels.

The overwhelming majority of Israelis, well over 90 percent, live within the Green Line and rarely visit the various disputed areas. These places are not essential for Israel's economy since they have no useful resources. The Palestinian laborers—large numbers of whom worked in

Ma'ale Adumim, among the largest of the post-1967 Israeli settlements, is just east of Jerusalem. September 2009. (Getty Images / Image Bank.)

Israel during the 1990s peace-process era and thus benefited the Palestinian economy—were replaced by foreign workers after 2000.

Israel's final boundaries will be settled only by a peace treaty with Syria and the Palestinians.

REGIONS

Israel has four main geographic regions: the Mediterranean coastal plain to the west, the hilly region of the Upper Galilee that runs southward into the West Bank, the Jordan Rift Valley in the east, and the Negev desert in the south. Within each area are subsections with their own unique features. Israel's location at a meeting point of three continents makes it a pivotal area for weather patterns, animal migrations, plant life, and tectonic plates.

The Coastal Plain

The coastal plain stretches 118 miles (190 kilometers) along or near the Mediterranean, from the white chalk cliffs by the caves of Rosh HaNikra at Israel's northern border with Lebanon to the desert along its southern border with the Gaza Strip and Egypt. Beyond the sand of the coast itself, there is much fertile ground, and the area is famous especially for orange groves. Along the coastal highway and the country's main railroad line lies a string of cities—Nahariya, Acre, Haifa, Netanya, Tel Aviv–Jaffa, Rishon LeZion, Ashdod, and Ashkelon—making the coastal plain Israel's most densely inhabited area. Indeed, half of Israel's entire population lives there.

Around one-fourth of Israel's Mediterranean coast remains in its natural state. There are major ports at Haifa and Ashdod. Eilat, on the southern gulf, has a coastline of 8 miles

(13 kilometers). Many people along the coast obtain their livelihood from the sea directly or indirectly, through shipping, fishing, and especially the tourism drawn to the beaches.

The coastal plain runs along the Mediterranean Sea and inland to a width of between 9 miles (14 kilometers) in the north and 25 miles (40 kilometers) in the south. The region has three subsections. The northern coastal plain includes the western Galilee, Acre, Haifa, and the rocky Carmel region up to Taninim Lake. Many kibbutzim and moshavim, as well as small Druze and Arab villages, sprinkle the area. Acre, with its imposing Crusader buildings and tiny colorful port, is a mixed Jewish-Arab city, once unsuccessfully besieged by Napoleon. Mount Carmel has vineyards, along with caves inhabited during the Stone Age; human remains 80,000 years old have been found there.

Haifa is Israel's third-largest city and a center of industry, with the country's main oil refinery, port, and granary. Of all the cities in the world, it was ranked by *Monocle* magazine as the one with the most business potential in 2011. Its attractions include a Baha'i temple, tomb, and gardens, composing the main shrine of a religion born in Iran whose leader was exiled to Haifa by the Ottomans. The University of Haifa sits atop a mountain that affords spectacular views of the city and Haifa Bay. Nearby is the Technion–Israel Institute of Technology, Israel's most important engineering and scientific university. Historically, Haifa has voted Labor.

To the south of Haifa, the Sharon region's rich red loam grows some of the world's finest oranges, while the sandy shore has many beaches. This is the area of highest population concentration, dominated by Tel Aviv and its suburbs. Hadera with its large power plant, Netanya, and Herzliya line the coast down to Tel Aviv. This region, given the westward bulge of the

Haifa University, with the city of Haifa and Haifa Bay below, September 2007. (Getty Images / Image Bank.)

Samarian region of the West Bank, is also Israel's narrowest, at times extending only 9 miles (14 kilometers) in width.

Tel Aviv itself is very much a Mediterranean and largely secular city of beaches and white concrete buildings, including the world's greatest concentration of Bauhaus (International Style of architecture) structures. This is Israel's cultural, business, and intellectual center, priding itself on an active nightlife and many cafes. It also contains Israel's clothing design industry and stock exchange, as well as the headquarters of all the main newspapers and political parties.

Jaffa, on the southern end of Tel Aviv, is a mixed Jewish-Arab area. It has one of the world's oldest continuously used harbors, although today it is reduced to a small fishing port. Tel Aviv has many other suburbs of varying socioeconomic levels, including Ramat Aviv, Rishon LeZion, Ramat Gan, Holon, and Giva'tayim.

To the south, Ashdod is another major commercial port, as is the smaller city of Ashkelon down the coast. Beyond Ashdod, the southern coastal plain becomes drier, gradually leading into the Sinai desert to the west and the Negev desert to the east and south. Israel's nuclear reactor is in this area. Across from the Gaza Strip, the small town of Sderot and several agricultural villages have become the targets for hundreds of rockets fired from the Gaza Strip.

The Central Hill Country

Parallel to the coastal plain and to its east is a rocky hill region, most of which is in the West Bank. In the central hill country of Israel, on the far northern end, in the Golan Heights and on the border with Lebanon and Syria, is Israel's highest mountain, Mount Hermon (9,232 feet, or 2,814 meters, high). Southward is the Galilee plateau. The Shomron and Judean Hills in the center of this geological region are located mainly in the West Bank. Israel's corridor to Jerusalem runs through these hills. Farther south is the hilly part of the Negev desert.

The rocky terrain is interrupted at its northern end by Israel's fertile Jezreel and Hula Valleys, which are important agricultural areas that also have light industry. In ancient times, the route through the Jezreel Valley connected the Mediterranean with the empires to the east. The valley contains many ancient and Biblical sites. Today, corn, sunflowers, and wheat are grown there, and sheep and cattle graze in the pastures.

The Hula Valley was once a swampy malarial area. Its draining in the 1950s was one of the country's main engineering projects; in more recent years some water has been restored to balance the ecological system. This valley remains an important stop for birds migrating between Europe and Africa.

Although the hills of central Israel appear to be fairly continuous, they were shaped at different periods of time and are not geologically consistent. They were created from the movement of the Euro-Asian and nearby African-Arabian tectonic plates, making them cousins to Europe's Alps, though much lower. The Galilee hills reach a height of 4,000 feet (1,219 meters) and are largely limestone, dolomite, and chalk. Toward the Golan Heights, however, the hills are basalt because of volcanic eruptions.

The region's most famous feature is the historic city of Jerusalem, Israel's capital, an important center for three major religions: Judaism, Christianity, and Islam. In Jerusalem are

Skiers ride a lift to the slopes of Mount Hermon in the northern Golan Heights, February 2009. (Getty Images / Image Bank.)

found the remains of the First and Second Temples and other sites central to Jewish religious and political history, many places associated with the life and death of Jesus, and the Muslim al-Aqsa Mosque and the Dome of the Rock.

East of the Judean Hills and extending to the Jordan Rift Valley is a hilly desert region, the Judean Desert. It was to this desolate area that small religious sects withdrew during the Roman period. One such group wrote the Dead Sea scrolls, an important source of information about early Biblical texts and religious thinking around the beginning of the Common Era.

The Jordan Rift Valley and the Arava

The Jordan Rift Valley, whose western side is in Israel and the West Bank and whose eastern side is in Jordan, is one of the world's most unusual areas, much of it bereft of all but the tiniest amount of rainfall. About 260 miles (418 kilometers) long, this geological feature includes the Jordan River, Jordan Valley, Hula Valley, Sea of Galilee, and Dead Sea. The Dead Sea is the lowest land on the surface of the Earth. The Jordan Rift Valley is part of a great African-Syrian rift, located where two tectonic plates come together. Part of the valley is in the PA-ruled West Bank. The rift continues in Israeli territory southward from there, going from the Dead Sea through the Arava region and along the eastern shoreline of the Gulf of Eilat for another 110 miles (177 kilometers).

The movement of the tectonic plates can set off earthquakes. The biggest in modern times took place in 1837. Between 6.5 and 7.5 on the Richter scale, it hit the northern Galilee hard, including Tiberias and Safed. The most recent major earthquake in what is now Israel, measuring 6.2 on the Richter scale, took place around the northern Dead Sea on July 11, 1927. The largest earthquake in the State of Israel's history occurred near Eilat on February 11, 2004; it measured 5.4 on the Richter scale but caused little damage. Researchers warn that another destructive earthquake may occur, a factor taken into account in Israel's building codes.

The northern end of the Jordan Rift Valley is agriculturally rich and receives water from the Jordan River and a significant amount of rain. Yet southward toward the Dead Sea and the Arava, the climate becomes increasingly arid, and the land is largely unpopulated.

The famous Jordan River flows into the Sea of Galilee from the north and exits it again to the south—a course that makes it virtually unique in the world. Today the Dead Sea is a popular tourist destination, and its mineral-laden mud is considered therapeutic. Another important product of the area is phosphates, Israel's most abundant commercially valuable geological resource.

The Arava Valley has the red Edom Mountains to the east and the brown Negev desert to the west. Temperatures there can exceed 105 degrees Fahrenheit (40 degrees Celsius). Only about 3,000 people live there, mainly Jews in agricultural villages—moshavim, such as Ein Yahav and Faran, and kibbutzim like Yotvata, established in the 1950s—along with Bedouin. Yotvata has its own chain of restaurants and distributes dairy and other products throughout the country.

It was here in the arid, hot Arava that modern drip irrigation was developed, one of Israel's most important technological innovations. Drip irrigation delivers water to plants at a slow rate, minimizing losses through evaporation. Remarkably, more than 40 percent of the country's vegetables are now grown in this area, and fruits and flowers are exported to Europe.

The Negev Desert

The triangular Negev with 4,633 square miles (11,999 square kilometers) stretches over almost 60 percent of Israel's territory. It reaches Egypt (the Sinai Peninsula) to the west, the Arava and the rift valley to the east, and the Gulf of Eilat, an arm of the Red Sea, to the south. At its northern end is Beer Sheba, the largest city of the Negev region, and at its southern tip is Eilat. The region also includes the small towns of Dimona and Yeruham—the poorest in Israel—and Bedouin settlements. There are small quarries for salt, sulfur, marble, and clay, among other resources.

The Negev itself has four main geographical subregions. The northwest consists mostly of sandy dunes with fairly fertile loess soil, making it part of the Mediterranean climatic zone.

The northeast features mountains, streams, canyons, and craters; in the terrain, chalks and dolomite predominate. The towns of Dimona, Yeruham, and Mitzpe Ramon are located in this subregion, as is the Negev's highest mountain, Mount Ramon, which rises 3,395 feet (1,035 meters). Mitzpe Ramon is set on the edge of the Ramon Crater (Makhtesh Ramon), the largest of the five Negev craters, which are actually sinkholes. The dramatic crater—24 miles (39 kilometers) long, 5 1/2 miles (9 kilometers) wide, almost one-third of a mile (half a kilometer) deep—with its colorful rock formations is a national nature reserve.

The main city of the central Negev is Beer Sheba, an important industrial center and the home of Ben-Gurion University, founded in 1965, Israel's fastest-growing institution of higher education.

At the southern tip of the Negev is the fourth subregion: the granite Eilat Mountains and the town of Eilat. Eilat is both a port and a tourist destination for Israelis and Europeans, especially given its warm temperatures throughout the winter months. It offers snorkeling and skin diving, an aquarium, and a submarine ride utilizing the beaches or adjacent waters with their rich coral reefs and sea life.

David Ben-Gurion was an advocate of settling the Negev. After his retirement as prime minister, he lived on Sde Boker, a kibbutz there, where he worked as a laborer until his death; he was buried on the grounds. Nevertheless, the Negev remains only very lightly populated, holding only 8 percent of Israel's population. About 85 percent of the land belongs to the state; the IDF uses much of it for training and bases. The Negev is also the site of experimental agriculture and enterprises such as fish farming, although the Negev's potential is still far from realized.

CLIMATE

Israel's climate can vary widely from geographical area to geographical area. Forested highlands, lush green valleys, barren mountains, stony deserts, long beaches, and a fertile coastal plain, each with its own micro-climate, may be found within a short distance of one another. In general, though, there are two main seasons: a mild winter and a long, hot summer. Southern Israel is subtropical, albeit much affected by aridity; northern Israel is in the eastern Mediterranean temperate zone.

The temperate zone has generally moderate temperatures and sufficient rainfall—though unreliable and varying greatly each year—for agriculture and concentrated human settlement. The average annual rainfall is around 19 to 27 inches (about 50 to 70 centimeters). Summer temperatures range between 71 and 86 degrees Fahrenheit (22 and 30 degrees Celsius). High humidity, which may reach 70 percent on the coastal plain, raises perceptions of temperature five to ten degrees, somewhat less inland.

Israel's winter season is short and usually lasts from December to March, when temperatures remain moderate, though colder in the hill country. Jerusalem occasionally sees light snow. The lowest winter temperatures range from 35 degrees Fahrenheit (2 degrees Celsius) in the mountainous north to 50 degrees Fahrenheit (10 degrees Celsius) in the coastal plain. Around 65 percent of the country's annual rainfall comes in December, January, and February, mainly in the north.

One unusual feature of Israel's climate is the *sharav*, a hot, dry summer wind. Israel's weather usually comes from the west, but during a sharav, the wind blows in from the Arabian Desert to the east. Barometric pressure rises, humidity plummets, and sand and dust damage crops and make people dehydrated and irritable.

Israel's semiarid climate zone, a small area between the temperate north and the subtropical desert in the south, includes the northern Negev and the town of Kiryat Gat, as well as the Gaza

The Mar Saba Monastery amid the desolation of the Judean desert. This Greek Orthodox monastery was built in the fifth century. (Getty Images / Image Bank.)

Strip. It receives roughly 8 to 16 inches (20 to 41 centimeters) of rain a year, compared to less than 7.5 inches (19 centimeters) for the desert. That rainfall, along with the northern Negev's fertile loess soil, permits commercial agriculture.

The subtropical desert climatic zone in Israel's southern Negev, about half the country's land, and in the eastern Judean Desert is characterized by high temperatures and low rainfall. Sandstorms, flash floods, and scorching heat waves can occur in the summer, and frigid temperatures can occur in winter.

Although this area is low in population, a number of creative solutions have been developed to make it arable or economically productive in other ways. These include special greenhouses, indoor fish farming, advanced irrigation systems, and new hybrids of food crops and flowers that can survive the climate.

WATER

Israel faces a tough environment with too much desert and insufficient rainfall or water. It has used technology to help save water and use marginal resources effectively. Now, however, water pollution has become a threat, especially to the underground aquifers where water naturally accumulates.

The Bible speaks about years of plenty and years of famine in the Land of Israel—a record of irregular rainfall. Even today, years of plentiful rain are followed by years of drought.

Archaeologists have found ingenious water collection and irrigation systems going back to pre-Roman times. During the British Mandate period, the perennial water shortage made authorities doubt that the area could hold anywhere near the number of people who live there today. Since 1948, there have been three main periods of drought: 1957–1963, 1989–1991, and 1998–2001. Israel's worst drought to date was in the winter of 1962–1963, when a bit over 8 inches (20.6 centimeters) of rain fell—one-third less than usual in a low-rainfall year.

Prior to the 1990s, Israel's water requirements were met naturally. Since the start of the 1990s, however, water resources have dramatically worsened in quality and supply. At the current level of usage, water resources cannot replenish themselves naturally. As demand for water rises from Israel, the Gaza Strip, and the West Bank, and as agricultural, industrial, and municipal needs grow, the supply is further reduced. High population concentrations, sewage, fertilizers, and poor environmental policies—like the excessive digging of wells in the PA-ruled areas of the West Bank—also lead to salination and pollution of the natural underground reservoirs.

Increasing populations and living standards meant that consumption exceeded Israel's water production in 2000, although water use per capita in Israel is less than half that in southern California, an area with similar climatic conditions. Low rainfall and several years of drought have brought Israel's water deficit at present to an estimated 70.6 billion cubic feet (2 billion cubic meters). What Israel has to do—and in part has done—is to make maximum use of its water resources, increase its agricultural productivity, recirculate waste water, conserve water, and create new usable water from desalination.

Rainwater in Israel accumulates in three main places: the Sea of Galilee, the coastal aquifer, and the mountain aquifer. Streams, underground water tables, and natural springs are also used as freshwater sources, but drawing on them too much increases their salt content, damaging the supply.

Sea of Galilee

The Sea of Galilee, or Kinneret, is a large lake in northern Israel with a surface area of 65 square miles (168 square kilometers). This natural reservoir holds 141 billion cubic feet (4 billion cubic meters) of water. Water is fed into the Sea of Galilee directly from the Jordan River. Other streams from the surrounding mountain areas of Mount Hermon, the Golan Heights, the Naphtali Mountains, and the Galilee Mountains also flow into the sea.

In 1964 an extensive network of pipes, canals, aqueducts, underground tunnels, and pumping stations was put into operation to create Israel's National Water Carrier (NWC). This allowed the Sea of Galilee's water to be used all over Israel, providing 25 percent of the country's needs.

Because of overpumping from the Sea of Galilee in order to meet demand, a major effort was launched to develop alternative water sources, including treated or reclaimed sewage water, for farming and industries. The increase in these sources has gradually decreased Israel's dependence on the Sea of Galilee's water for agricultural use, so the water of the Sea of Galilee is primarily now for consumer use. Currently, Mekorot, the company in charge of the NWC, provides 80 percent of Israel's drinking water from the Sea of Galilee and other sources.

The amount of water in the Sea of Galilee depends on the weather and rainfall. Pumping rates must constantly be adjusted. When the surface of the Kinneret falls to 698 feet (213 meters) below sea level, pumping must stop lest the remaining water become too salty. Drought has at times reduced the level to nearly that low. In recent years, the level has been dangerously low more often than high; the water was as low as 707 feet (215 meters) below sea level in 2001.

The high temperatures generated by the pumping process dissolves salt in the rock formations surrounding the water in the lake or in aquifers, which can also lead to high levels of salinity, thus reducing water quality.

Coastal Aquifer

Another major source of water in Israel is the coastal sand aquifer, which stretches along the western rim of the Judean Mountains and near the Mediterranean coast. Water seeps down through permeable sand, chalk, and gravel but is then stopped by hardened clay to form natural underground reservoirs from which water can be extracted by wells throughout the year, thus alleviating the pressure on the Kinneret when necessary. In recent years, however, the quality of the aquifer water has deteriorated owing to infiltration of salt and other substances from Mediterranean seawater.

Mountain Aquifer

The limestone-dolomite mountain aquifer is a third main source of freshwater in Israel. It stretches from Mount Carmel to Beer Sheba and along the crests of the Judean Mountains. The western part is called the Yarkon-Taninim basin. The mountain aquifer, whose source of water is rainfall, lies at a much deeper level underground than the coastal aquifer, making the water harder to extract, but it is of better quality.

Other Water Sources

Streams and springs also contribute to Israel's overall water resources, although in smaller quantities than other sources do. In general, the water from springs and streams is the best-quality water in Israel and thus is used by bottled water companies. The Dan springs, located on Mount Hermon, are the most productive in the country. The NWC also diverts some streamwater in the north into reservoirs rather than having it flow into the Jordan and the Sea of Galilee.

Water from some alternate sources is wasted owing to lack of infrastructure. For example, in the winter months a large amount of floodwater flows into the Mediterranean. Israel has two large water-collection stations, the Nahal Menashe station in the coastal region and the Ma'agar HaShikma station in the south. There are smaller reservoirs elsewhere, but in the southern Negev—where torrential flooding commonly occurs—the collection of floodwater is still very limited.

Pricing policies are aimed at encouraging conservation by charging more for household use over a certain level, and a number of efforts have been made to produce additional clean water. Seeding clouds to force more rainfall has proven to be too expensive to be practical.

A more cost-effective method is desalination. Four desalination facilities, among the world's largest, along the Mediterranean are providing about 40 percent of Israel's needed drinking water, a proportion that is expected to rise to about half with the opening of two more.

The Dead Sea

At 1,365 feet below sea level (416 meters), the Dead Sea is the lowest point on the Earth's surface. It is about 35 miles (56 kilometers) long and 2 to 12 miles (3 to 19 kilometers) wide. The Hebrew name for this body of water is Yam HaMelach (Salt Sea), since it is about 30 percent salt, ten times saltier than ocean water. The high percentage of salt gives it extra buoyancy—people float easily—but also makes it impossible for any type of life (other than bacteria) to exist there. Several spas are located near the Dead Sea, whose mineral-rich water and mud have long been thought to have healing powers.

Since the Dead Sea has no outlet to any other body of water, much of its liquid is lost by evaporation in the hot climate, a major cause of the increased salt content. But the sea's water level is sinking faster than evaporation accounts for. Over the past fifty years its surface area has shrunk by one-third, and its depth has dropped approximately 82 feet (25 meters). Israel, Jordan, and Syria have all diverted water from the Jordan River in recent years for agricultural and industrial use, reducing the amount flowing into the Dead Sea. Currently, the Dead Sea is dropping by around 3 feet (1 meter) of water per year.

The Dead Sea Works and various Jordanian companies use the sea's natural minerals to make table salt, fertilizers, cosmetics, and medicinal products. They harvest phosphates and minerals by creating evaporation pools at the cost of the sea's water supply, further contributing to the reduction of the water level. Efforts have barely begun to avoid ecological damage.

NATURAL RESOURCES AND ALTERNATIVE ENERGY

Israel is a country of limited commercially viable natural resources and no heavy industry. The main mineral resource is Dead Sea salt, which yields magnesium, salt, calcium citrate, potash, phosphates, and bromine. These are extracted in evaporation pools and exported by rail to the port of Eilat. Other usable items include construction materials, such as sand, marble, plaster, clay for ceramics, and glass. Quartz deposits from the southern Negev are used for the glass. At one time, the Timna mines near Eilat, exploited since the time of the pharaohs, produced copper, but they were closed in 1983.

Although Israel has always been short on natural resources, natural gas has recently been found off the coast near Ashdod and Haifa. In 2010 a gas field estimated to be as large as 16 trillion cubic feet (4.5 trillion cubic meters) was discovered near the northern coast. This amount may be small in global terms, but the income could dramatically boost Israel's economy, especially if it becomes a natural gas exporter.

Israel is also one of the world's leading pioneers in solar and alternative energy technologies. Eighty-five percent of households use solar power for water heating—a system largely developed in Israel—and solar power supplies about 4 percent of the country's overall energy needs. The potential for generating solar power in the Negev is particularly promising.

Kibbutz Reim, located in the western Negev, became one of the first communities in the world to rely exclusively on solar energy.

In addition, Israel has also been in the forefront of research on geothermal energy, biofuels, the use of waste to generate low-cost electricity, improved efficiency for existing fuels, and wind farms. The government has set a goal of producing 10 percent of the nation's electricity from renewable materials by 2020.

Among Israel's most innovative projects is the development of electric cars—not only the vehicles themselves but a national system of battery swap stations and places where the automobiles can be recharged. The effort, in partnership with a Danish company, is intended to reduce both Israel's dependence on imported oil and pollution.

NATURE AND ENVIRONMENTAL ISSUES

There are approximately 100 mammal, 500 bird, 100 reptile, 7 amphibian, and 2,600 plant species in Israel. Protected species include types of vulture, gazelle, ibex, and leopard. The two main wildlife reserves on Mount Carmel in the north and the Hai Bar reserve in the southeast work to save existing species and to rebuild the populations of species that once lived in the country but no longer do. Among the reintroduced species are Persian fallow deer and roe deer in the north and onagers and Arabian oryx in the south. A special feature of Israel's location is that it is on one of the world's major bird migration routes. An estimated 500 million birds cross the country en route to Africa in the autumn and to Asia or Europe in the spring.

Israel has a wide variety of conservation areas, managed by the Nature and Parks Authority, totaling 2,300 square miles (6,000 square kilometers)—about 20 percent of the country's total territory. The 142 nature reserves were established to protect forests, oases, desert areas, and sections of beach and sea. Another 44 national parks preserve archaeological and historic sites.

Large-scale natural disasters are infrequent although they do occur. Earthquakes, flash floods in areas with low rainfall, small floods, freak tornados, and forest fires are all on record. The Land of Israel was hit by devastating earthquakes in 1202, 1546, and 1837: entire cities were destroyed, and thousands died. In 1927, a big earthquake in the central region of the country caused 300 deaths and the destruction of 1,000 buildings. Today construction codes have special provisions to protect buildings in the event of an earthquake. The last major earthquake was in 1995 in Eilat and the Sinai Peninsula, but modern methods of construction and communication minimized the damage.

The worst fire in Israel's history took place in the Carmel region near Haifa in December 2010. A teenage boy accidentally began the blaze, which burned across thousands of acres. When a bus rushing guards to evacuate a prison was caught in the fire, the forty-one passengers died. Several countries and the Palestinian Authority provided aid in extinguishing the fire.

Israel has a reputation for providing swift and effective aid to other countries facing natural disasters. Some of the techniques developed by Israel for dealing with the results of war and terrorism—such as special equipment to detect people trapped under fallen buildings—are useful in these circumstances. Among major efforts in this regard were the search-and-rescue and field hospital teams sent to Turkey and Greece after the 1999 earthquake and to Mexico and Armenia after their earthquakes in 1985 and 1988, respectively. After the devastating earthquake in Haiti in 2010, Israel sent ten tons of medical equipment and more than 200 people, including doctors, nurses, medics, police, and a search-and-rescue team. Israel set up the first field hospital in Haiti, which treated at least 500 victims a day.

Israel was relatively late in beginning to deal with environmental problems compared to Western industrial states, but the country's small size and its ecosystem's delicate balance have forced it to take such problems very seriously. The tendency had been to use the relatively unpopulated Negev as a dumping ground, especially Dudaim and Ramat Hovav, the location of the two main waste disposal sites. The latter opened in 1979 to hold toxic waste. According to studies, leakage has led to higher rates of birth defects and cancer in the local population.

The sharp increase in the number of automobiles—from 1 million in 1990 to 2.5 million less than a decade later—brought a major increase in air pollution and traffic within cities. The contamination of limited water supplies by industry is also a leading concern. Local governments have implemented vehicle and fuel standards to reduce pollution in line with European practices and promoted alternative fuels such as electricity and liquefied petroleum gas.

Israel has been among the world leaders in recycling, however. About 70 percent of waste water is recycled—triple the percentage for any other country. Overall recycling rates of materials rose from 3 percent in the early 1990s to 21 percent in 2008. New facilities have been built and innovative methods have been used. The target for 2020 is a 50 percent recycling rate.

ARCHAEOLOGY

Given Israel's long history and its location at a geographical and cultural crossroads, it is one of the most important and productive areas in the world for archaeology. Archaeology became something of a national hobby, with the participation of many amateurs as well as academic archaeologists from Israel and other countries.

Finds date back to the Stone Age. Archaeologists discovered ancient human remains in the Carmel mountain range and a site in the Jordan Valley where prehistoric hunters killed and butchered an elephant. One of the most spectacular early finds, made in the central hill country, was the city of Megiddo (the Biblical Armageddon).

Many discoveries relate to Biblical history. They date back to the Iron Age and the arrival of the Israelites and continue up through the Roman, Muslim, and Crusader periods. Gezer was the first Biblical-era city excavated, and the material uncovered tended to confirm the main outlines of the history recounted in the Jewish Bible. Two of the most significant finds were Masada, where Jews held out until they committed suicide to avoid capture during the revolt against Rome, and the Dead Sea scrolls, among the earliest known texts of the Bible. Other notable finds date to the Roman and Byzantine periods and include entire cities, beautiful mosaic floors, and synagogues.

The Islamic authorities who control the Temple Mount in Jerusalem, where the al-Aqsa Mosque and the Dome of the Rock are located, have repeatedly discarded materials excavated during construction and repair projects that have been shown to contain important archaeological artifacts. Upon examining this waste, Israeli archaeologists discovered many artifacts

Masada, near the Dead Sea, is the site of a fortress built by King Herod. There Jewish defenders resisted a Roman siege in 73 CE, then committed suicide rather than surrender and be enslaved. (Getty Images / Image Bank.)

from the eighth to the sixth centuries BCE, that is, from the First Temple period, including seal impressions carrying Hebrew names—one of a family mentioned in the Book of Jeremiah.

Several controversies involve archaeology. The PA leadership and other Palestinian institutions all continue to deny any connection between the Jewish people and the area. When Israel made peace with Egypt, all the archaeological finds from the Sinai Peninsula were given to the Egyptians. Within Israel, Haredim often oppose archaeological excavation, saying that digging desecrates ancient Jewish graves, an act forbidden by Jewish law.

INFRASTRUCTURE

Israel does not have major transportation links with any of its neighbors, an unusual situation for any country in the contemporary world. Although in many ways Israel has advanced transportation systems, the country's internal infrastructure is underdeveloped in the peripheral areas and has only recently built up even in densely populated ones. Still, the changes during the past few decades have been dramatic.

In the 1980s, Israel's sole international airport, Ben-Gurion, resembled a facility that might be serving a small Midwestern American city, with only a lunch counter providing meals. After being repeatedly upgraded, the airport was largely replaced by a new, very modern building comparable to those found in major Western capitals.

Despite heavy taxes that make the purchase of an automobile more expensive in Israel than in virtually any other country in the world, the number of cars is high compared to the miles of road. This factor produces commuter traffic jams, especially in the Tel Aviv area, and many accidents.

There are 143 miles (230 kilometers) of freeway-level highways. The main Tel Aviv–Jerusalem road is built very close to the pre-1967 border and at a few points even crosses it, posing a major strategic hazard in the event of a return to those old frontiers. Of special importance is Highway 6, generally called the Cross-Israel Highway although its official name is the Yitzhak Rabin Highway. It is a north-south state-of-the-art toll road that was mainly completed by 2009.

For decades, before widespread automobile ownership, the well-organized bus system was dominant. The Egged cooperative is Israel's largest bus company and operates throughout the country. The main cities have local bus systems as well as many taxis.

The need for an effective commuter rail system has led to expansion of the state-operated railroad, including double-tracking of the main line along the coast, importing of modern equipment, opening of new stations, and extension of service between Ben-Gurion Airport and the Tel Aviv area. Light commuter rail is planned for the Jerusalem area, and a Tel Aviv subway is also slated, both expensive, very long-term projects.

The Israeli cargo ship line Zim and the El Al airline serve international traffic needs. The popularity of foreign travel among Israelis has led El Al to establish a charter subsidiary, Sun d'Or. Because El Al, as Israel's airline, faces special threats of attack and sabotage, it insists on providing its own security at foreign airports; in fact, it stopped flying to several cities that did not comply.

It has compiled an outstanding safety and security record, and the security and maintenance practices that it has developed have been a model for other airlines. El Al's inability, as a state carrier, to fly on Shabbat (the Jewish Sabbath) and major Jewish holidays leads to a significant loss of revenue. Moreover, the airline must skirt countries at war with Israel, lengthening several routes.

Despite security and other issues, including sporadic violence and attempts at boycotts, Israel's tourism industry has grown rapidly. To support it, a substantial infrastructure of hotels and other services has developed. During 2010 more than 3.1 million people visited the country, 18 percent above the number in 2009 and 10 percent more than in 2008. Not including airfare, the amount spent in Israel by tourists is over $3 billion annually.

POPULATION AND DEMOGRAPHIC TRENDS

Israel has a population of more than 7.5 million people. For an advanced Western society, it has a relatively youthful profile, with almost 28 percent of its citizens under the age of fourteen; more than 62 percent between fifteen and sixty-four; and almost 10 percent over age sixty-five.

Its population growth rate is 1.8 percent annually, placing it alongside such countries as Malaysia and El Salvador. In comparison, the U.S. rate is only 0.97 percent, and that of the United Kingdom is 0.28 percent. Israel's birthrate is about 19.8 per 1,000 people, which is much higher than those of the United States (13.8) and the United Kingdom (10.6). The fertility rate in Israel in 2009 was 2.96 children per woman: 2.9 for Jews; 3.73 for Muslims; 2.2 for Christians; and

2.49 for Druze. Collectively and individually, these rates are sharply above the 1.66 children per woman in the United Kingdom and the 2.05 children per woman in the United States.

Israelis can expect to live nearly eighty-one years, a life expectancy rate that is very high, ranking thirteenth in the world, higher than that of the United Kingdom (seventy-nine) or the United States (seventy-eight), despite the number of Israeli casualties from war and terrorism. Ninety-two percent of the population of Israel is urban, and more than 97 percent of the people are literate.

Birthrates tend to decline as living standards rise and women achieve more equality. For example, the fertility rate of Muslim Arab citizens of Israel dropped from 4.67 throughout the 1990s to 3.73 percent in 2009. But for religious and cultural reasons, the relatively higher birthrate for Jewish Israelis than for Europeans or North Americans will probably continue.

Although 75.4 percent of Israel's population is officially classified as Jewish, most of the almost 4 percent whose religion is unspecified are Russian immigrants who identify themselves as Jewish even though not being considered Jewish by the rabbinical authorities. A small number of Russian immigrants consider themselves Russian Orthodox Christian.

In 2009, the Arabs accounted for 20.3 percent of the total population; 16 percent of Israelis were Muslim, 1.7 percent were Christian, and 1.6 percent were Druze. The Muslim population is about 1.25 million, including east Jerusalem residents.

Much of Israel's rapid population growth after 1948 was due to Jewish immigration. The first census showed a population of 872,000, but by 1958, the population had risen to just under 3 million. Augmented by immigrants from the former Soviet Union, Israel's population stood at around 6 million in 1998 and 7.24 million in 2007. It showed one of the fastest growth rates in the world.

An ever-larger proportion of the population is native-born, rising from only 8.4 percent of the population in 1972 to more than 67 percent of the population in 2004 to 76 percent in 2009. Israel's total population has been growing at a rate of 1.8 percent every year since 2003, the Jewish population at a rate of 1.6 percent and the Arab population at a rate of 2.6 percent, although this gap has narrowed.

Population growth together with Israel's small size have contributed to high population density, which increased by more than 125 percent between 1995 and 2007. Israel is one of the most densely populated countries in the West, with an average of 883 people per square mile (341 people per square kilometer). Even this statistic understates the crowdedness of the urban areas because more than half the country is sparsely populated desert and rocky hills. Slovenia, a country of similar size and topography, has a population density of only 256 people per square mile (99 people per square kilometer).

After the War of Independence, half of Israel's population resided in Tel Aviv and the central region along the coast and in Jerusalem; only 13 percent lived in the north and the south. The second most populated area during the early years was Haifa, in the north. Over the years, the population in Tel Aviv and central Israel has declined in relative terms while the population of the periphery has increased to approximately 30 percent of the entire population.

These trends were a result of individual residential preferences. Today, almost half of Israel's Jewish population resides in the central region, where Jews make up 90 percent of the population; in Tel Aviv, Jews make up 93 percent of the population. Less than a quarter of

Israel's Jews live in the north and the south, where, in contrast, the majority of the Arab population resides. Jerusalem is home to approximately 10 percent of the total Jewish population, and about 5 percent of Israeli Jews live in the West Bank.

Arabs make up slightly more than half of the population in the north; Jewish and Arab households balanced in relative number there by 1980. Following the Six-Day War in 1967, the Arab population began moving out of the northern region and settling in east Jerusalem; today, nearly one-fifth of the total Arab population in Israel resides in east Jerusalem. Jerusalem has seen a decline in the relative number of Jews since 1948; it has gone from 97 percent Jewish to 70 percent Jewish, although the change is due largely to the addition of east Jerusalem—there has been little change in the western part of the city.

Whereas an average-sized household in Israel consists of 3.73 family members, Arab households tend to be larger, with 4.87 family members, and Jewish households tend to be smaller, with 3.53. Average household size also varies between cities. For example, an average household in Jerusalem—with its larger portion of Orthodox (Haredi and Dati) Jews, who tend to have more children—has 4.26 family members, whereas an average household in Tel Aviv has 2.98 members. Haifa has an average household size of 3.05; Rishon LeZion, 3.35; and Ashdod, 3.56.

While the rise in Jewish population in past years was primarily due to the immigration surge, the population rise of the Arab population resulted from a high fertility rate. Both factors have declined. Religious piety has been more consistent in influencing the Jewish fertility rate. The Haredim have the highest fertility rates within the Jewish population, especially compared to secular Jews.

In the Arab population, the Muslim community tends to have a higher fertility rate than the Christian community. Aside from religion, factors that contribute to a high fertility rate include professional opportunities, education level, and cultural background. In the early years of statehood, the Arab population had three times the fertility rate of the Jewish population.

Today, the Israeli Arab population has only a 33 percent higher fertility rate than the Jewish population, and the gap is quickly closing.

Life spans for Israelis have increased dramatically across the board. The decline in mortality rate can be credited to improved health services and better living conditions. Nevertheless, the Muslim and Druze communities have higher mortality rates than Jews.

Since the 1950s, average Jewish life expectancy has increased by 12 years while the average life expectancy of the entire population of Israel has increased by approximately 8.5 years. Among Israelis as a whole, male life expectancy stood at 70.1 years of age between 1971 and 1974, while female life expectancy stood at 73.4 years. By 2005, male life expectancy had increased to 78.3 years, and female life expectancy had increased to 82.2 years.

Educational level is also increasing dramatically. In the early years of statehood, most Arab women did not even attend high school. In 1961, a national census recorded that 70 percent of Arab women were uneducated (that is, did not go to school at all or had only minimal schooling). Three decades later, this had fallen to 10 percent.

Other statistics show a similarly significant change. Twenty-one percent of females and 23 percent of males pursued a college education in 1985. These percentages increased to 40 and 42 percent, respectively, by 2005, with females surpassing males thereafter. In 2005 the number of students in higher education institutions showed a corresponding increase: 91,000 male students were enrolled compared to 113,000 female students. Women made up 56 percent of the entire student population: 55 percent in bachelor's degree programs, 57 percent in master's degree programs, and 52 percent in doctorate degree programs were female.

Employment has risen along with the population, with women accounting for an ever larger percentage of the workforce. In 1955 approximately 631,000 people were employed. By 2007 this number had grown to 2.9 million. The number of women in the workforce rose from 25 percent in 1955 to 47 percent in 2007. The sector with the biggest decline is agriculture, which involved 10 percent of the work force in 1968 but only 2 percent in 2007. The professions and business grew during this period from 56 to 76 percent of the workforce.

CITIES AND COMMUNITIES

Israel has 214 urban locales, defined as places with more than 20,000 residents: cities, suburbs, and larger towns. About 130 are mainly or all Jewish, and about 90 are mostly or all Arab. The urban population is 5,830,000, or more than 90 percent of Israel's total population. There are almost 1,000 villages, kibbutzim, moshavim, and small towns, whose population totals about 540,000 people, just 8.5 percent of Israel's population; about 950 are Jewish, 33 are Arab, and the rest have a mixed population.

By definition, cities have more than 200,000 residents in the incorporated area. The largest cities are Jerusalem, with 747,000 residents; Tel Aviv, with 384,400; Haifa, with 266,300; Rishon LeZion, with 222,000; Ashdod, with 204,200; and Beer Sheba, with 185,000. These figures are misleading, however. The Tel Aviv metropolitan area is the most highly populated in Israel with more than 1.2 million people; the central region has about 1.7 million in addition to those living in Tel Aviv.

The reason for this disparity is that Jerusalem has virtually no incorporated suburbs but has been able to expand its boundaries outwards, while Tel Aviv is surrounded by separately governed suburban towns. It is also the most densely populated city in Israel with 18,388 people per square mile (7,100 people per square kilometer). The Jerusalem metropolitan area has almost 900,000, followed by Haifa's metropolitan area with about 870,000. Israel's northern and southern regions are fairly evenly balanced, with more than 1.2 million people and a bit over 1 million, respectively.

Despite the statistically high population density, there are many open areas in all parts of the country. One reason is the relative lateness of suburban development, which relates to people having automobiles and the ability to buy private homes. In Israel, houses (villas) or row houses (cottages) are uncommon in built-up areas, where most people live in apartment buildings. In addition, the Jewish National Fund, which owns a great deal of land outside the cities, has traditionally been reluctant to hand over real estate for housing developments given its historic priority to agriculture.

Small towns, defined as those with fewer than 2,000 residents, include the kibbutz (collective), the moshav (cooperative), and the Arab village. In the past, these settlements were agriculture based, but today they often furnish suburban or residential housing for people who work in larger places nearby. If they are too far from centers of population or not in good farming areas, they may be quite impoverished, especially since the transportation infrastructure in Israel remains weak in the north and south.

Cities

A well-known saying describes the trio of main cities: "In Jerusalem we pray, in Tel Aviv we play, in Haifa we work." However exaggerated, it does give a sense of the distinctive identities of each of these places.

Jerusalem

Jerusalem is Israel's capital, its most famous city, and one of the country's most important features. It contains many holy sites—the Temple Mount, which includes the Western Wall of the Jewish Temple compound and which is associated with the kings of ancient Israel; the Dome of the Rock and al-Aqsa Mosque; and Christian churches and sites associated with the life and death of Jesus of Nazareth, including the Church of the Holy Sepulchre. Many of the holy sites are clustered in and around the Old City.

Yet Jerusalem is not merely a religious center and cultural symbol but an actual living city, home to three-quarters of a million people, about one-third of them Arab and two-thirds of them Jewish. The Arabs mainly live in the eastern part of the city, the Jews mostly in the western part.

The mosque of the Dome of the Rock with its golden dome is visible in the background on top of the Temple Mount. In the foreground is the Western Wall, the western retaining wall of the Second Temple, the last remaining portion of that structure and the holiest site in Judaism. (Getty Images / Image Bank.)

In the War of Independence, the Jordanian army took the eastern part of the city and expelled all of the Jews living there. For the next two decades, Jerusalem was divided between Israeli and Jordanian rule. The two halves were reunited in the 1967 war, when Israel recaptured the eastern part. Today, the populations still largely follow that division, although Jews have built additional residential neighborhoods, especially Ramot to the west and a number of places on the city's north side, on previously empty land as well as in the Old City's Jewish Quarter. Haredim, who form a large portion of the Jewish population, live in several west Jerusalem areas, notably Mea Shearim and Geula, both near Jerusalem's current center. Many new neighborhoods have been built on Jerusalem's east side, too, and large numbers of Arabs have moved from the West Bank to east Jerusalem.

During most of a 3,000-year-long history, until the mid-nineteenth century, Jerusalem largely consisted of the small area now inside the walled district called the Old City, which comprises four quarters—Jewish, Arab, Christian, and Armenian. Almost all of its streets are still narrow, pedestrian-only lanes. The relatively traditional appearance of other parts of the city is kept by a ban on high-rises, and all buildings must have fronts of white Jerusalem stone.

But the status of Jerusalem is very much in dispute. The future of Jerusalem has long been and will continue to be one of the most passionately and hotly contested issues in any Israel-Palestinian negotiation. For Israel, Jerusalem is its capital. That is where the prime minister and the president reside, it is the location of the Knesset and the Supreme Court, the place where government ministries are headquartered, and the home of such key cultural institutions as the Israel Museum and the Hebrew University.

For the Palestinians, Jerusalem is its future capital, whether just east Jerusalem or the entire city after the State of Israel has been destroyed. The PA sees Ramallah, in the central West Bank, as just a temporary capital. Although most Israelis want to keep the city united, Israeli governments have offered—most notably at the Camp David summit and in the Clinton plan—to repartition the city, giving most of east Jerusalem to the PA while keeping the Jewish and Armenian Quarters of the Old City and some other neighborhoods as part of Israel. The PA rejected both of these proposals.

Despite both Israeli and Palestinian opposition to partition, most countries in the world still officially accept the 1947 plan to have Jerusalem under international control. They not only reject the idea that a united Jerusalem is Israel's capital but refuse to recognize that pre-1967 west Jerusalem has that status. Neither side wants the city to be internationalized. It is unlikely that anything other than a repartition of the city along some agreed-upon line would produce a comprehensive peace agreement.

Palestinians have made sporadic terrorist attacks on Israelis in Jerusalem, and at times—especially from 2000 to 2005—the security situation has deteriorated badly. With rising tension, there have been Palestinian riots near the al-Aqsa Mosque, and the city has been closed to those entering from the West Bank. Yet the amount of unrest in the city should not be overestimated, since the level of political violence is usually limited in time and space. Jerusalem almost always functions in a normal manner.

A second division in Jerusalem is between secular and religious Jews. About half the Jewish population in the city is highly religious—Datim or Haredim—and one-third of those are

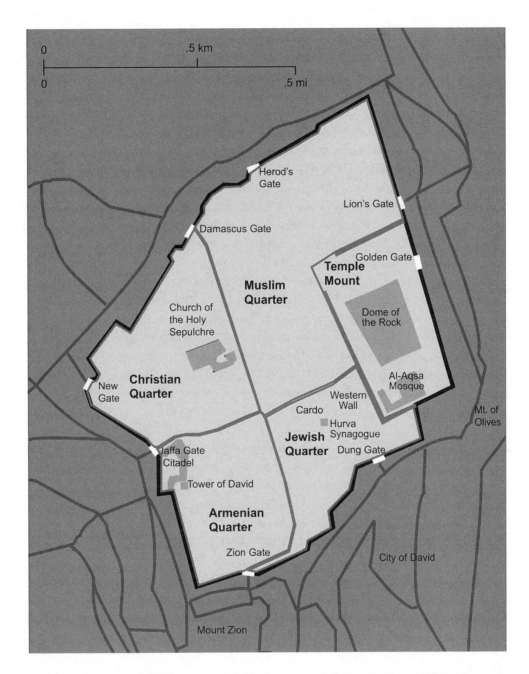

The walled Old City of Jerusalem is located in the eastern part of the city. Less than a quarter of a square mile (about one square kilometer) in size, the area is historically defined as having four sections—the Muslim Quarter, the Christian Quarter, the Jewish Quarter, and the Armenian Quarter—plus the Temple Mount. (© 2003–2010 Koret Communications Ltd. All rights reserved.)

Haredim. The birthrate of religious Jews is higher than that of secular Jews, and the latter have tended to move out of town. The Haredi community is more united than its secular counterpart, so religious, especially Haredi, political power has grown in the city. Many secular residents feel that the city is undergoing Haredization, as reflected by the composition of the city government. There is no public transportation in Jerusalem on Shabbat, and cars cannot enter religious neighborhoods on that day. Most businesses and restaurants in Jewish neighborhoods are closed on Shabbat, and most restaurants are kosher.

Contemporary Jerusalem was largely shaped by the almost-three-decade term—1965 to 1993—of Mayor Teddy Kollek, who helped create many new facilities and gave the city a modernizing face-lift. The elderly Kollek was finally defeated by Ehud Olmert in 1993. A decade later, Jerusalem elected its first Haredi mayor, Uri Lupolianski. In 2008, the secular businessman Nir Barkat defeated another Haredi candidate. On a national political level, Jerusalem is conservative, and a majority of its inhabitants support the Likud Party.

East Jerusalem Arabs have been offered Israeli citizenship, but because of PA pressure and their support for partition of the city or its assimilation to a Palestinian state, only a minority have accepted. Still, polls have shown a high proportion of Arab Jerusalemites who wish to remain under Israeli rule rather than become part of a Palestinian state. All Arab residents are entitled to vote in municipal elections, but few do so, following the PA boycott to protest the annexation and unification of the city by Israel. Consequently, since they are not represented in city hall, they have little political leverage.

Tel Aviv

When Tel Aviv was founded in the sand dunes north of Jaffa in 1909, it became the first Jewish city in the modern world. By the 1930s, it had become larger than Jerusalem and acquired its own small port. Architects trained in Europe returned to build three- or four-story, flat-roofed Bauhaus (International Style) concrete buildings, designed to provide airy, comfortable living spaces for working-class people. Because of this distinctive housing, Tel Aviv was nicknamed the White City. After Jaffa's capture in the War of Independence, Jaffa was merged with Tel Aviv.

Not until the 1960s did high-rise construction begin. The first skyscraper built, in 1965, was the thirty-story Shalom Meir Tower, which rises over 466 feet (142 meters). Since then, the Tel Aviv area has acquired more skyscrapers, such as the diamond exchange in Ramat Gan and the three-building Azrieli Towers. Tel Aviv is also the site of the Ministry of Defense, located there owing to Jerusalem's vulnerability to attack, and almost all foreign embassies. A string of beaches and high-rise hotels draws tourists as well as locals, especially for strolls along the promenade (*tayelet*), which extends all the way to Jaffa.

Remarkably, Tel Aviv and the towns around it within commuting distance are the home of 40 percent of all Israelis. Though lacking historical and religious significance like Jerusalem, Tel Aviv has come to represent the modernity of Israel. Certainly, it is the center of cultural, intellectual, financial, and much commercial life—the diamond and fashion industries in particular—with hundreds of cafes and a lively nightlife. The city's cultural assets include the Helena Rubinstein Pavilion for Contemporary Art, Tel Aviv Museum of Art, Golda Meir Center for performing arts, Cameri and HaBima theaters, Mann Auditorium (home of the

Tel Aviv's skyline as aircraft fly overhead during festivities marking Israel's sixtieth Independence Day, May 2008. (Getty Images / Image Bank.)

Israel Philharmonic Orchestra), Tel Aviv Performing Arts Center, and Suzanne Dalal Center for dance and theater.

Tel Aviv's business life has gone through a transformation. Small, old-fashioned stores along Herzl and Allenby Streets have given way to air-conditioned shopping malls (*kanyonim*). Although the outdoor markets and small grocery stores face competition from large supermarkets, the replacement of local family businesses by big chain stores has been far less extensive than in North America. With the waning of the Arab boycott, large Western retail and food outlets have moved into Israel, but loyalty to traditional brands and businesses remains strong.

Despite the presence of cars and commuters, Tel Aviv is still a largely pedestrian city. From the 1930s to the 1960s, Dizengoff Street, with its fashionable cafes, was the place to stroll, but the city has become decentralized. Sheinkin Street has become the main focus for bohemian life, yet it also has the greatest concentration of the city's religious population. The city's districts include the Greenwich Village–type Neve Tzedek district and the Yemenite Quarter, as well as poorer neighborhoods like HaTikva to the east, the south Tel Aviv area, and the run-down area near the Old Central Bus Station, which is frequented by foreign workers. To the north is the wealthy neighborhood of Ramat Aviv; to its east are the middle-class suburbs of Ramat Gan and Giva'tayim; a bit farther away are Petah Tikva and the largely Orthodox Bnei Brak; and to the south is Holon.

Tel Aviv sees itself as a hedonistic Mediterranean city and promotes itself as the Big Orange and the City That Never Sleeps. In political terms, Tel Aviv has historically been split almost evenly between supporters of the Labor and the Likud parties.

Haifa

As Tel Aviv serves as the financial and commercial hub of the country, Haifa is the principal port and industrial center. The modern port opened in 1933 under British auspices. Food processing, textiles, cement, and chemical industries developed there, along with petroleum refineries. The de facto capital of northern Israel, Haifa stretches across the hills between Mount Carmel's northern slopes and the port on Haifa Bay. At the port are its giant grain silo, railroad station, and other industries. On the mountainside are residential and commercial areas. Near the top of the mountain are the Technion—Israel's institute of technology, founded in 1912— and the University of Haifa, which opened in 1964. Haifa is also world headquarters of the Baha'i religion, which originated in Iran.

The Kibbutz and the Moshav

The kibbutz, a communal settlement unique to Israel, was established as a socialist utopian scheme but has been adapted—with varying degrees of success—to changing conditions. The first kibbutz, Degania, was established in 1910 near the Sea of Galilee. Twelve young adults pooled their property and divided jobs and income equally. In total, 268 kibbutzim have been established since then, mainly in the north and in border areas.

In a kibbutz, all members work at collectively owned enterprises—usually mainly agriculture though the work is increasingly diversified—and receive in exchange the goods and services that they need. Traditionally, the kibbutz employed no outside help. Members are

A kibbutz on the shores of the Sea of Galilee in 1958. The Golan Heights, then held by Syria, loomed over the flat land on Israel's side of the border. (Getty Images / Image Bank.)

equal in income and privileges. There is no such thing as private property; everything belongs equally to all members. All decisions are made democratically in meetings by majority vote. In most kibbutzim in earlier years, children lived together in crèches, and jobs rotated on a regular basis. But these practices were abandoned long ago.

Many kibbutzim were profitable agricultural enterprises during Israel's early years. A significant proportion of Israel's top military officers have come from kibbutz backgrounds. In the 1980s, however, Israel suffered from massive inflation and an economic slowdown. Many kibbutzim went deeply into debt, and government bailouts did not prevent a crisis. A combination of factors—materialism and individual ambition—facilitated their decline.

Since the 1990s, many kibbutzim have made major changes to let members take outside jobs, to permit private property (including automobiles), to engage professional managers for their enterprises, to rent out housing to nonmembers, to charge members for food and services, to offer varying pay levels for different jobs, and/or to use outside workers in kibbutz industries. These innovations have been successful for some kibbutzim, which have gone into light industry, tourism, and retail enterprises. Others, often with locations on the country's periphery, continue to be swamped by debt.

One of the biggest success stories is Ma'agan Michael, the largest kibbutz in the country, with more than 1,400 residents. Founded in August 1949, its diversified economy now includes field crops (cotton, avocados, and papayas), banana orchards, poultry, dairy cows, and fish farming; the fish are either edible carp, gray mullet, and striped bass, or ornamental goldfish, sold to Japanese collectors. The main source of income and employment is a plastics factory that makes pipe fittings, animal feeding systems, and toilet parts. A second factory produces metal parts and plating.

A number of experiments with new types of kibbutz have been conducted. In 1987, a group of young people established the Tamuz kibbutz in the town of Beit Shemesh, with seventeen families sharing their property and work. In 1980, Hararit was founded in the southern Galilee; fifty families live there in a community built around transcendental meditation. One kibbutz produces and markets vegetarian food products; another raises pigs. Still another, formerly a poor fishing village, has opened a hugely successful shopping mall. The kibbutz sector has become less important in Israel over time, but it still plays a disproportionate role in shaping the country.

Moshavim are agriculture-based communities, usually of sixty to a hundred families, whose members farm their own land and own their own houses but cooperate over some elements of equipment ownership and marketing. The first two moshavim, established in 1921, were Nahalal and Kfar Yehezkel.

In the 1980s, moshavim were affected by the economic recession, which brought down the prices they received for their products. On many moshavim, people who held other jobs bought houses and turned over the farmland to professional managers. Many moshavim expanded and allowed new neighborhoods to be built on their land.

Arab Towns and Villages

Arab citizens of Israel form either the majority or totality of residents in 122 towns and villages, 89 of which have more than 2,000 people. About half live in the north, including the mixed

The Church of the Annunciation in Nazareth, a town with a Muslim Arab majority. (Getty Images/Image Bank.)

cities of Haifa and Acre, the Arab city of Nazareth (the largest Arab city, with a population of 60,000), and the large Arab town of Umm al-Fahm. Twenty percent live in the Jerusalem area. The remaining 30 percent, including large numbers of Bedouin, live in the south; the largest town there is Rahat.

During the 1980s, Arab villages with growing populations began building upward by adding stories to existing buildings. The architectural styles of buildings in those villages have more in common with those in neighboring Arabic-speaking countries than in the rest of Israel. Arabic is used in these villages, including in the school system.

There is still a distinct gap between these villages and the generally larger Jewish towns. In 2003, the average salary of Arab workers was 29 percent lower than the salary for Jewish workers, although the level correlates to educational level and residential location, not to ethnicity. Arab employment is concentrated in agriculture, construction, and industry. Arab women have an extremely low rate of participation in the economy. One response to this situation is migration to bigger places, like Acre, Nazareth and its surrounding villages, and Haifa. About 7 percent of college students—constituting roughly one-quarter of Arab high school graduates—are Arab.

Settlements in the West Bank, the Gaza Strip, and the Golan Heights

Since 1967, Israeli Jews have established 121 settlements in the West Bank. In the 1993 agreement with the PLO, Israel's government promised not to allow the creation of new settlements or the geographic expansion of existing ones. At times, especially in 2005, small groups of activists established outposts, called "illegal settlements," which were often but not always dismantled by the government.

Settlements were established for several reasons. The government constructed a few for security purposes soon after the 1967 war—for example, in the Jordan Valley and the Golan Heights. By 1977, Jews had established twenty kibbutzim and moshavim in the Golan Heights; today thirty-three settlements are there, with a total Jewish population of 18,000. The largest settlements in the West Bank were commercial residential bedroom communities just across the pre-1967 border, allowing the Palestinians and Jordanians working in Israel to enjoy decent housing. Gush Etzion was a special case, rebuilt to replace Jewish towns captured by Jordan whose residents were expelled in the War of Independence.

Most of the smaller settlements, both in the Gaza Strip and farther from the pre-1967 border in the West Bank, were, however, built as political acts by those who wanted to ensure that Israel retained that land. In the case of some Dati communities, they were also built in the belief that settling the land would bring the Messiah.

The West Bank—which many Israelis call by its historic Jewish name, Judea and Samaria— was captured from Jordan in the 1967 war. Once no speedy peace settlement was forthcoming, one involving return of the territories, Israelis began to establish settlements there, more than twenty-five by 1977. Today, an estimated 187,000 Israelis live in the West Bank, 20,000 in the Golan Heights and 175,000 in areas of Jerusalem beyond the 1967 borders. About 4,500 settlers lived in the Gaza Strip before Israel removed them in withdrawing from that territory in 2005.

The settlement in Hebron is unique in being located in the middle of a Palestinian city, which is why the Israel-PA agreement in 1996 gave Israel's forces control over 20 percent of the town, with the rest under PA rule. Massacres in 1929 prompted the original Jewish population there to flee. The current settlement was established in Hebron in April 1968, and the nearby village of Kiryat Arba was created two years later. The former has 600 residents; the latter, 7,000. Hebron is also the location of the Tomb (or Cave) of the Patriarchs and Matriarchs, a holy site for Jews, Muslims, and Christians, where Jews were not allowed to pray before 1967. A Jewish settler massacred Muslim worshippers there in 1994; much of the building is now maintained as a Muslim endowment.

The international community has often criticized the settlements, declaring them to be not only illegal but roadblocks to peace. Within Israel, opponents say that the settlements tie down military forces, their defense risks soldiers' lives, and their maintenance takes away funds that could be better used for domestic needs. In 1993, however, the PLO—and in subsequent agreements, the PA—agreed that the settlements would remain until a comprehensive peace treaty was signed.

Within Israel, even most critics agree on removing the settlements from all places to be under Palestinian rule if a peace agreement is reached. The Palestinian side, by failing to agree to peace, is thus ensuring that they remain in existence, which brings into question the criticism that the settlements themselves are blocking the road to peace.

Israel has in fact dismantled settlements on two occasions related to its withdrawals from captured territory. The first occasion was in 1982, when it removed all fifteen settlements in

The West Bank settlement of Shilo, north of Ramallah, near the Palestinian Arab villages of Turmus Aiya and Senjil. (Getty Images / Image Bank.)

the Sinai during implementation of the Egypt-Israel peace agreement. The second time was when Israel withdrew from the Gaza Strip in 2005, when it removed twenty-one settlements, along with several in the northern West Bank, as a signal to the Palestinians of the benefits they would obtain by making peace.

PROGRESS DESPITE LIMITED RESOURCES

Israel has a tiny, mostly desert, or at least arid, territory; a small population; few natural resources of commercial value; limited rainfall; larger, hostile neighbors; and massive defense costs.

Having succeeded in what might be called Phase One, the securing and survival of the state, and Phase Two, achieving general prosperity, Israel now faces Phase Three tasks. Aside from continuing security and development, these include such post-development missions as strengthening sometimes neglected areas of social concern: the environment, health, social welfare, and education—in short, the quality of life and living standards.

The tasks involve better integrating areas of the country and sectors of the population—more recent immigrants, Arabs (especially Bedouin), Haredim—as well as dealing with gender gaps, gaps related to national origin (Mizrahim), and other matters. The ability to address this agenda, however, requires that threats and security problems remain manageable, for these always must take priority in directing the nation's attention, resources, and activities.

BIBLIOGRAPHY

Bronner, Ethan, and Sebnem C. Arsu. "Facing Its Worst Natural Disaster, Israel Appeals for Help." *New York Times*, December 4, 2010.

Central Bureau of Statistics, State of Israel. "Men and Women in Israel, 1985–2005," February 1, 2007.

Central Bureau of Statistics, State of Israel. "Population and Demography," January 1, 2007. http://www.cbs.gov.il/reader/?MIval=cw_usr_view_SHTML&ID=389. [In Hebrew.]

Central Bureau of Statistics, State of Israel. "Sixty Years of Statistics," May 1, 2008. http://www.cbs.gov.il/reader/publications/statistical_new.htm#901. [In Hebrew.]

Central Intelligence Agency, United States. "Israel." *CIA World Factbook.* https://www.cia.gov/library/publications/the-world-factbook/geos/is.html.

Consulate General of Israel to the Pacific Northwest. "Electric Cars Soon to Charge in Israel," May 3, 2010. http://www.israeliconsulate.org/index.php?option=com_content&view=article&id=167:electric-cars-soon-to-charge-through-israel&catid=49:economy&Itemid=240&lang=en.

Dever, William G. "Gezer Revisited: New Excavations of the Solomonic and Assyrian Period Defenses." *Biblical Archaeologist* 47, no. 4 (December 1984): 206–218.

Faiman, David. "Solar Energy in Israel," November 2, 2002. Israel Ministry of Foreign Affairs, http://www.mfa.gov.il/MFA/Facts%20About%20Israel/Science%20-%20Technology/Solar%20Energy%20in%20Israel.

Gabbay, Shoshana. "The Environment in Israel," August 2002. Israel Ministry of Foreign Affairs, http://www.mfa.gov.il/MFA/MFAArchive/2000_2009/2002/8/The%20Environment%20in%20Israel.

Goldreich, Yair. *The Climate of Israel: Observation, Research and Application.* New York: Kluwer Academic/Plenum Publishers, 2003.

Henderson, Simon. "Seismic Shift: Israel's Natural Gas Discoveries." *PolicyWatch*, no. 1736, January 4, 2011. https://www.washingtoninstitute.org/templateC05.php?CID=3286.

Invest in Israel. "Israel: Global Center for Breakthrough Innovation: Climate Change," 2009. http://www.investinisrael.gov.il/.

Israel Land Administration, State of Israel. March 11, 2007. http://www.mmi.gov.il/Envelope/indexeng.asp?page=/static/eng/f_project.html.

Kloosterman, Karin. "Quenching Your Thirst with the Sea." *Israel 21C*, July 1, 2010. http://www.israel21c.org/201007018072/environment/quenching-your-thirst-with-the-sea.

Knesset, State of Israel. "Bedouins in the State of Israel," 2010. http://www.knesset.gov.il/lexicon/eng/bedouim_eng.htm.

Medzini, Aaron. *The River Jordan: Frontiers and Water.* London: Water Research Group of the School of Oriental and African Studies, University of London, 2001.

Milstein, Mati. "Solomon's Temple Artifacts Found by Muslim Workers." *National Geographic*, October 23, 2007. http://news.nationalgeographic.com/news/2007/10/071023-jerusalem-artifacts.html.

Ministry of Environmental Protection, State of Israel. Official website: http://www.sviva.gov.il/bin/en.jsp?enPage=e_homePage&enDisplay=view&enDispWhat=Zone&.

Ministry of Environmental Protection, State of Israel. "Contaminated Land and Fuel Pollution," December 13, 2010. http://www.sviva.gov.il/bin/en.jsp?enPage=e_BlankPage&enDisplay=view&enDispWhat=Zone&enDispWho=contaminated_land&enZone=contaminated_land.

Ministry of Environmental Protection, State of Israel. "Recycling," December 24, 2009. http://www.sviva.gov.il/bin/en.jsp?enPage=e_BlankPage&enDisplay=view&enDispWhat=Zone&enDispWho=recycling&enZone=recycling.m.

Ministry of Envirional Protection, State of Israel. "Vehicular Pollution," June 30, 2010. http://www.sviva.gov.il/bin/en.jsp?enPage=e_BlankPage&enDisplay=view&enDispWhat=Zone&enDispWho=Vehicular_Pollution&enZone=Vehicular_Pollution.

Ministry of Foreign Affairs, State of Israel. "Israeli Settlements and International Law," May 20, 2001. http://www.mfa.gov.il/MFA/Peace+Process/Guide+to+the+Peace+Process/Israeli+Settlements+and+International+Law.htm.

Ministry of Foreign Affairs, State of Israel. "Israel's Story in Maps," 2008. http://www.mfa.gov.il/MFA/Facts+About+Israel/Israel+in+Maps/.

Mor, Amit, Shimon Seroussi, and Malcolm Ainspan. *Large Scale Utilization of Solar Energy in Israel: Economic and Social Impacts*, June 16, 2005. Eco Energy, http://www.ecoenergy.co.il/Portals/0/Solar%20Energy%20in%20Israel%20-%20a%20cost-benefit%20analysis.pdf.

National Campus for the Archaeology of Israel. "Temple Mount First Temple Period Discoveries." Friends of the Israel Antiquities Authority, http://www.archaeology.org.il/.

Nature and National Parks Protection Authority, State of Israel. http://www.parks.org.il/BuildaGate5/general2/company_search_tree.php?mc=378~All.

"The Place Race: Global." *Monocle* 4, no. 39 (December–January 2010). http://www.monocle.com/sections/business/Magazine-Articles/The-Place-Race/.

Rebhun, Uzi, and Gilad Malach. *Demographic Trends in Israel.* Jerusalem: Metzilah Center for Zionist, Jewish, Liberal and Humanist Thought, 2009. http://www.metzilah.org.il/webfiles/fck/Demo%20eng%20final.pdf(1).pdf.

Shragai, Nadav. "Temple Mount Dirt Uncovers First Temple Artifacts." *Ha'aretz*, October 19, 2006. http://www.haaretz.com/hasen/pages/ShArt.jhtml?itemNo=776621.

Stypińska, Justyna. "Jewish Majority and Arab Minority in Israel Demographic Struggle." *Central and Eastern European Online Library* 1, no. 157 (2007): 105–120.

Tal, Alon. *Pollution in a Promised Land: An Environmental History of Israel.* Berkeley: University of California Press, 2002.

Tidhar, David. *Encyclopedia of the Founders and Builders of Israel*, 1971. http://www.tidhar.tourolib.org/.

Chapter Four

SOCIETY

I
n Israel are blended East and West, ancient and modern, religious and secular, traditional
and highly innovative. And although Israel's society is extraordinarily diverse, its sense of
community is also extraordinarily strong.

The Jewish population sets the predominant tone in the country. Jews have arrived with
distinct customs, languages, and religious practices flavored by the places they lived for centuries. Yet they have had a huge amount in common, and in Israel the emphasis has been on
building a united community in which such differences, though preserved to varying degrees,
are distinctly secondary.

While schisms within the Jewish population are significant, it would be a mistake to characterize Israeli society by religious and ethnic differences. As in other countries, habitat (agricultural village, small town, big city); region of residence; age; class; profession, and so on,
define other differences. Many factors mitigate each of these distinctions. For example, there
are religious and secular people, but there are many somewhere in between, just as there are
important subgroups among the religious: Ashkenazim and Sephardim; Haredim and Datim;
Mitnagdim and *Hasidim* within the Haredim.

Similarly, there are historical, political, and cultural distinctions between Mizrahim (Jews
of Middle Eastern origin) and Ashkenazim (Jews of European origin). Distinctions are also
reflected in the variations of religious practice between Sephardic (largely Mizrahi) and Ashkenazic Jewish religious traditions. Yet a growing number of Israelis are descendants of multiple
groups owing to the increasing frequency of intermarriages.

Political loyalties, to the left or the right—in a specific Israeli meaning of these terms—have
been important indicators of differences in worldview. At one time, support for a specific political party would indicate which soccer team someone cheered, which publications someone
read, and which health fund someone joined. Much of this deeper cultural-ideological split
has filled in; the trend is toward a national consensus, pragmatism, and the political center.

All of these ideological, political, "ethnic," and, to a lesser extent, religious-secular disputes are not as salient now as in the past. While Israelis are well aware of some decline in
community-mindedness, along with a growth in individualism and materialism, reduced differences have somewhat balanced out those trends. Israelis still have a strong sense of national
cohesiveness.

One of the most prevalent myths about Israel is that it is organized on the basis of religion. Yet the principle on which the state is founded is that the basis of Jewish identity is purely, or even mainly, a matter of peoplehood. True, the primary indicator of that identity is religion—at least in terms of the historic background of its individual members—but identity is not based on a theological viewpoint or a theocratic worldview. For example, Spain, Poland, and Italy are historically Catholic countries, yet their basis for national identity is primarily one of peoplehood and common history, not religion.

In contrast to other modern religions, Judaism is a faith related to only a single people. Yet what appears to be a religious word—"Jewish"—actually refers to religion and national identity simultaneously. This extended meaning is made instantly clear by substituting words historically used to describe Jews that have a clear national reference, such as "Israelite" or "Hebrew." Of course, like a Spanish, Polish, or Italian Catholic immigrant to other lands, a Jew can choose to assimilate into a different national culture whether or not he or she retains the original Jewish religion.

Even the most punctiliously religious Haredi Jews recognize as Jewish those who are non-observant or atheist if they are also of Jewish descent, meaning at minimum that they have a mother who is Jewish. Israeli law recognizes as Jewish, for purposes of immigration, anyone who has at least one Jewish grandparent—a grandparent who identifies himself or herself as Jewish. Although Israelis recognize Judaism as their national religion, as a central element in their history and culture, most are not religiously observant. Thus, Israel is a state based on nationalism; it is not a theocracy.

At the same time, though, given the interlacing of Jewish history and religion, many officially sanctioned practices in Israel do originate in religious structures and traditions, often quite secularized in the process of being adapted. For example, the cycle of the holidays arises directly from Jewish religious observances. But that religious system, in turn, arose from the cycle of the mainly agricultural year in the ancient Land of Israel. Thus, one can argue that religious Judaism is an aspect of "Israelite" society and history just as easily as that Israel is a "Jewish state."

Hanukkah, for instance, is a religious holiday, but it marks a political historical event: the reestablishment of Jewish independence after the Maccabean revolt. While most Israeli Jews light Hanukkah candles, many do not accept or adopt the associated religious laws. Sukkot is a religious festival, but it is based largely on harvest time. To put it a different way, with some exceptions—mainly marriage, divorce, and burial—there is not much conflict between religiosity and secularism when they are seen through their common historical/national background.

Although Israel incorporates religion into the state and governance to a greater extent than in other contemporary Western democratic societies, it does so in a far different way than they did historically, too. As a result, the close relationship between Israeli society and religion has not inhibited an emphasis on modernism, innovation, and pragmatism—which makes Israel quite different from tradition-bound, religiously guided societies. This paradox is often expressed in kitschy photographs contrasting black-coated religious Jewish men walking down a street near miniskirted women or showing diners at a secular kibbutz sitting down to a seder, a traditional Passover meal.

As the examples may suggest, Israeli society is characterized by a nonconformist, rebellious streak. The society was born in revolt against the Jewish Diaspora past. The Zionist movement—and most of Israel's founders—opposed religious authorities and community leadership by defining Jewish identity largely in national and modern, rather than religious, traditional, or assimilationist, terms. Jewish religious tradition also values critical questioning up to a point.

Each sector of Israel has expressed the rebellious impulses differently, but the overall tendency has been to intensify individualism and pluralism. Socialist Zionism was especially iconoclastic in rejecting religion and class distinction; liberal Zionism stressed modernism; conservative Zionism emphasized nationalism. In addition, Israeli society is undergirded by a strong tradition of voluntarism, its military system offering a prime example. All these nonconformist, individualistic forces make a powerful mix that rejects any sort of social authoritarianism.

COMMUNITY AND IDENTITY

Israeli attitudes toward community and identity, which are central to its unique society, include tensions between rebellion and tradition, often within the same individual or group; high levels of solidarity and communal identity coexisting with strong individualism and contentiousness; solidarity derived from war and trauma as well as a great deal of diversity; a relative lack of class identity but also real—perhaps growing—differences in that regard; contemporary skepticism toward national symbols combined with a higher respect for them than in Western democratic states in this era; the strong influence of the military coupled with anti-militaristic attitudes; high personal satisfaction levels alongside high complaint levels; low crime and high terrorist threats; and acceptance of the importance of the Hebrew language and local culture in shaping society juxtaposed with a high degree of acceptance of foreign ideas and cultural products.

Rebellion against the real and perceived Jewish Diaspora society is a dominant feature of Israeli society. The two millennia of the Diaspora, when Jews were in exile from the Land of Israel, is viewed as a time when tradition was frozen and life was slow, limited by tradition, and unchanging except for periods of persecution. The Jews of those times and places are thought of as conformist within their own communities and fearfully subservient to the surrounding, non-Jewish world. In contrast, most Israelis today operate at a rapid pace and take pride in innovation and improvisation. They see themselves as confident, empowered, and able to control their environment and achieve their goals even when opposed by powerful foes.

The stereotypes of historic Diaspora society have declined somewhat among Israelis with increased knowledge, especially of the Holocaust era, but are still potent and have some influence on Israel's relations with modern-day Diaspora Jewish communities. To some extent, the Haredim continue to embody the Diaspora characteristics and, as a result, are viewed negatively among some secular and sometimes Datim (Modern Orthodox) segments of society.

In a real sense, too, despite this self-conscious rejection of the Diaspora past, Israel does represent a continuation of traditional Jewish society in its various European, Middle Eastern, and North African versions. Jewish communities still in Diaspora are heavily influenced by the host societies and thus have discontinuities from their predecessors in re-assimilationist times. But since they also still embody many longer-term Jewish religious, cultural, and political characteristics, they still have a great deal in common—notwithstanding real differences—with Israeli Jewish society.

The tensions between tradition and rebellion in Israeli society are mediated by a general respect for Jewish tradition and historic experience even by those who are religiously nonobservant and critical of that past. When Israelis circumvent rules—including religious ones—they still know the rules exist and may respect them in other circumstances. Indeed, although it seems paradoxical, acting in this "antitraditional" manner does have its traditional aspect. After all, in Jewish law and society, finding a proper way to circumvent a regulation without breaking it was always viewed as legitimate. For example, a religiously observant man could use an automatic timer to turn lights on or off on the Sabbath, though he would never dream of switching them on or off directly, which is forbidden on that day.

With no history of an oppressed peasantry or a working class that "knew its place," Israelis are notoriously obstinate, egalitarian, and insistent on their personal rights. The lack of a well-developed system of etiquette derives from the lack of a subservient or class-conscious past. But individualism and contentiousness are mitigated by the strong sense of solidarity that pervades Israeli society.

The Israeli concepts of *rosh gadol* (literally "big head," referring to a person who puts the needs of the larger community first) and *rosh katan* (literally "small head," referring to a person who puts his or her own individual needs first) express this dichotomy between community consciousness and selfish individualism. The expectation is that the needs of society and nation will ultimately prevail and that people exhibiting excessive greed or showing off their material advantages will be shamed into more acceptable behavior.

Another concept expressing how aggressive individualism is generally tempered is the term *Sabra*, used to describe a native-born Israeli Jew. In Hebrew, a sabra is the fruit of the prickly pear cactus—thorny on the outside, soft on the inside. Applied to Israelis, the word contrasts their rough, touchy, individualistic behavior with their underlying sentimentalized sensitivity, the product of group solidarity, close-knit families, and a tradition-oriented, small-town sensibility. While this description has become a cliché, it is nonetheless largely accurate.

Israel is, after all, a small society. There may be just two—not five or six—degrees of separation, as in a large family. People know each other or have acquaintances and experiences in common. Service in the military is one of the bonding experiences that bring people together who would never otherwise mix. Kindergarten classes have reunions decades later.

To use the analogy of a family is not merely sentimental, since one does not have to be as nice to family members as one would be to strangers. A parable often used to explain Israel's social style is of a reckless driver who runs you down, then drives you to the hospital and nurses you back to health. Civility is not a high priority. Yet, when necessary, the sense that everyone has a great deal in common and belongs in the same boat provides a major cushion for social stability.

Having a national language that is not shared with any other countries also enhances national and social cohesion. The revival of Hebrew was in itself an achievement since it had not been in daily conversational use for well over 2,000 years. Israelis have endowed Hebrew with a modern vocabulary that expresses their experiences and worldview.

But use of Hebrew is not exclusionist. The knowledge of foreign languages, especially English, is widespread. There is no stigma to using English. On the contrary, it has social prestige value and is much used at the higher levels of the educational system since many necessary texts are not available in Hebrew. More generally, far from erecting protectionist measures against foreign influences, Israelis remain very much open to them, and if the imports do not contradict core values, people are quick to incorporate them into their society.

Another result of having a small, mostly coherent society is the importance of informal connections for getting things done, from finding jobs to buying goods at a discount, cutting through government bureaucracy, or obtaining inside information. This networking technique is identified by an Israeli word, *protectzia*, meaning a personal contact—either direct or through a friend, relative, or string of people—with someone who can get things done to one's benefit.

This contact is not necessarily someone who is powerful, and the use of protectzia certainly does not imply bribery but rather personal favors. Often a low-level connection, a clerk for example, can be more valuable than a high-level manager. Government bureaucracy can be as maddening in Israel as anywhere—often more so—but there is always a way around it by using the close-knit human networks.

Israelis' highly vocal conflicts, rebellious tendencies, and relentless self-criticism often lead outside observers to underestimate Israel's strength and solidity. Yet the flip side of these dynamics—a strong sense of common identity and unity—permits such apparent friction to exist without a deep threat to the social fabric. Although Israel does not lack crime, injustice, and mistreatment, there is a clear sense of limits, especially regarding public issues. Truly serious national quarrels—the Ashkenazic-Sephardic discord of the 1970s; the responses to Prime Minister Yitzhak Rabin's assassination in 1995; the passionate debate over the 1990s peace process—triggered powerful popular efforts to resolve them.

Given that Israel is a Jewish state, a nation-state in the sense that most countries have been for the past couple of centuries or more, its citizens have a bond stronger than merely living in the same geographic area and under the same government would create. Living in a country that has been under attack and knowing the cost of oppression historically also binds Israelis together.

Beyond these points, however, is the factor of choice. In general, Israel's Jewish citizens have chosen to live there, despite historic and present-day opportunities to go elsewhere. The following lines from Gilbert and Sullivan's *HMS Pinafore* capture this sense of choice.

> For he might have been a Russian,
> A French, or Turk, or Prussian,
> Or perhaps Italian!
> But in spite of all temptations
> To belong to other nations,
> He remains an Englishman!

In the original context, the song is a comical one. After all, the authors were saying—and their audiences took for granted—that it would be unimaginable for someone born in England not to be English. But many of Israel's Jews could have decided to be French, Turkish, or English, along with lots of other possibilities; they could have stayed in their Diaspora communities or migrated elsewhere. Therefore, their identity is based on a conscious rejection of such assimilation and an acceptance of the risk of living in a country that, in effect, is at war, often unpopular internationally, and situated among hostile neighbors.

Israeli society's pioneer ethos, familial aspect, and contempt for snobbishness or class distinctions is reflected in its high levels of informality. With the exception of the Haredim, most Israelis wear casual clothing. The ubiquitous Western suit and tie stay in the closet, even for weddings and funerals. Students interact on a first-name basis with their teachers, and business dealings are often managed on the same level as social conversation. Punctuality is not a high priority. It is not unusual for events and even television programming to start later than scheduled.

Unpredictability, ingenuity, and thinking outside the box are highly valued. As the American investor, businessman, and philanthropist Warren Buffett said, "Israel possesses a disproportionate quantity of brains and ideas." This is reflected in the proportionately large number of Israelis who have won Nobel Prizes. Such a flexible, somewhat freewheeling approach has advantages and disadvantages. A strong sense of innovation fosters creativity, as seen in the Israelis' propensity for innovation and adaptation and their advances in science, medicine, and high technology. There is also, however, an equal tendency toward disorganization, delay, and lack of responsibility. This unsystematic approach to solving problems may mean that they linger for a long time.

Two other patterns central to Israeli society are its historically not-so-rigid class identity and the seesawing between an emotional attachment to country and a strong skepticism toward national symbols and government. The patterns are historically interrelated.

During the pre-state era and in Israel's early years, necessary national projects involved high risks, limited profits, and little individual financial capital. Establishing a state required a state-oriented, mildly paternalistic socialism, albeit with full freedom for generally smaller-scale, private enterprises. Given the strong connection between the building of the state and various public enterprises and the security and well-being of each individual, the ruling elite emphasized the values of sacrifice and communal service, and the general public responded strongly to this appeal. A typical member of this elite was born in Russia or Poland, came from a religious family but had become secular, spent the early years as a manual laborer or an official in a Yishuv institution, supported the Labor Party, and wore a white shirt but no tie or jacket. They were not interested, and did not attain, wealth or luxury. They extolled manual labor, hard work, and—especially in the early period—rural life and agriculture.

Immigrants from German-speaking countries, who usually came in the 1920s and 1930s—that is, after the East European–origin leadership of the Yishuv took hold—tended to be centrist in politics, involved in the professions or business, more formal, more highly educated, and more assimilated to their previous host communities. One lasting joke was to call them *Yekkes*, from the Yiddish word for "jacket," a reference to their tendency to wear sports jackets

ISRAELI NOBEL PRIZE WINNERS

Dan Shechtman (Chemistry, 2011) won the prize for his discovery of quasicrystals with mathematical non-repeating patterns.

Ada Yonath (Chemistry, 2009) received the prize for her studies on the structure and function of ribosomes (which make proteins from amino acids in cells).

Robert Aumann (Economics, 2005) received the Nobel Memorial Prize in Economics for his work on conflict and cooperation through game-theory analysis.

Aaron Ciechanover and Avram Hershko (Chemistry, 2004) discovered ubiquitin-mediated protein degradation, associated with the potential treatment of several diseases, including cancer, Alzheimer's, and Parkinson's.

Daniel Kahneman (Economics, 2002), a research psychologist, won the prize in economics for his work in prospect theory (describing decisions between alternatives with uncertain outcomes).

Yitzhak Rabin and Shimon Peres (Peace, 1994) won the prize when Rabin was prime minister and Peres was foreign minister for their diplomacy resulting in the Oslo Accords.

Menahem Begin (Peace, 1978) was prime minister when he and Egyptian President Anwar al-Sadat won the prize for achieving the Camp David peace agreement between Egypt and Israel.

Shmuel Yosef Agnon (Literature, 1966), a novelist, wrote about Jewish life in Europe and Israel, developing his own style of Hebrew that drew on both Biblical and modern usage.

---

or suits and ties. They usually did not enter politics or attain leading positions, but they did form a solid middle class.

Over time, the governing establishment was challenged by the next generation. These native-born Israelis were far more often the product of secular backgrounds, and a disproportionately large number grew up on kibbutzim. Their formative experience was often military since they came of age during World War II and the War of Independence. Such people—examples include Yitzhak Rabin and Moshe Dayan—embodied the Sabra character that the founders had tried to instill. They dominated the army from its beginning and the political scene from the 1970s on.

The 1977 electoral earthquake marked an alternative elite's arrival in power. Its leader, Menahem Begin, had a great deal in common with the first generation in his character but had quite dissimilar views and appealed to a very different constituency.

The new group arose from the nationalist opposition to the Labor Party from the Herut (later the Likud) Party—and was also rooted in the Irgun rather than the Labor-dominated Haganah militia in the pre-state period. During the three-decade-long era of Labor rule, this opposition had the character of a subculture and produced its own second generation, the "princes," from the sons of its leaders.

But it was Mizrahi support that changed this group from a small opposition to a ruling bloc. The group also gained support among more religious Jews—both Ashkenazic Datim and traditionalist Sephardim—because of its nationalist stance, although Herut was a secularly oriented party.

Once in power, however, the Herut and its center-right coalition partners did not dismantle socialist institutions built up by Labor. Such economic issues were not an Israeli priority. Rather, socialism declined slowly, finally to be largely replaced by the privatization of the 1990s. Given the country's lack of heavy industry or interests entrenched enough to block change— and given the strong inclination toward flexibility and innovation—Israel was well poised to become a postindustrial society.

The durability of Israeli society has also been strengthened by the experiences of war, terrorism, and other outside threats, which inevitably bind people together. In the wake of trauma, a number of seemingly contradictory reactions—familial and national solidarity; hedonism or living for the moment; and religious faith—offer refuge. All of these impulses coexist strongly in Israeli society.

So does another characteristic, highly identified with Jewish history: a strong sense of humor. Israeli humor is not the same as the historic, Yiddish- and Diaspora-oriented Jewish humor. It is far more literal and linear, based less on wordplay and possessing a strong streak of political and social satire.

One of the most remarkable examples of this use of humor was an unannounced, unscheduled television program broadcast by what was then Israel's only channel on the evening of January 14, 1991. Israel faced an imminent Iraqi assault in response to the U.S.-led attack on Iraqi-occupied Kuwait. At the time, many thought chemical and biological weapons would rain down on Israel within hours. Citizens were glued to their televisions.

With no introduction, a comedian who strongly resembled the Iraqi dictator, Saddam Hussein, appeared on the screen. Speaking Arabic-accented Hebrew, he described how he was about to destroy Israel. At first, the tone was serious, but then it became increasingly hysterical and silly. Pulling out vegetables, as in some cooking demonstration, the Saddam look-alike started jamming them into a food processor to show what he was going to do to Israel. As realization dawned on the massive audience, horror turned to laughter, and Israel's population became ready to face a barrage of Iraqi rockets.

This approach to life and politics ensures that the military's strong role in the country does not turn its citizens toward militarism. Other factors that keep the military from holding undue power are the lack of a military caste or tradition, the army's relaxed discipline, and the high level of individualism. The great majority of people serve temporarily through their mandatory service and then in the reserves, and even full-time officers retire early to pursue second careers. Thus, Israel has no military caste or even a military lobby, in contrast to other countries.

The army itself operates in a specific Israeli style, with its successes owed in no small part to values that are the opposites of the usual military virtues. The Israel Defense Forces are characterized by informality, anti-hierarchical sentiments, continual self-criticism, and close, constant contact with civilian society. The preference for improvisation over systematic planning has at times led to serious shortcomings, as in the war against Hizballah in Lebanon in 2006. But, by the same token, these problems were quickly identified and were resolved soon afterward.

Overall, Israel lacks an aggressive nationalism in the sense understood in other countries. There has never been any significant expression of a desire to dominate the region or to rule over other people except in pursuit of limited, defensive-oriented aims, beyond the borders of the pre-1948 Palestine Mandate.

Due to the trajectory of Jewish history, there is no word in Hebrew for "patriotism." Anti-semitic conspiracy theories notwithstanding, the Jewish nation does not have global ambitions. The maximum goal, and the objective of the more militant nationalists, has been to rule the full territory of the historic Land of Israel, and even this aim has never received anything close to consensus support.

Given the powerful tendency of Israelis toward complaint, self-criticism, and endless re-evaluation of even the most basic assumptions, one might assume that Israeli society is full of dissatisfaction, pessimism, and low morale. Yet expectations to that effect are shattered by public opinion polls conducted regularly since the 1990s. These show that a sizable majority of all Israelis have a positive view of their country and personal circumstances.

In 2007, for example, according to the Israel Central Bureau of Statistics Social Survey, almost 85 percent of Israeli adults were happy and almost 54 percent believed their lives would continue to improve. Equally, 53 percent said they were satisfied or very satisfied with their financial situation, and 45 percent said they believed their financial situation would improve. This annual poll has shown very similar results every year.

Israeli Jews are more satisfied but less optimistic than Israeli Arabs, although even the Arabs have quite positive views: 86 percent of Jews, compared to 79 percent of Arabs, are satisfied with their lives. Even more remarkably, although a high percentage of Jews think their lives will improve, an even higher percentage — 61 percent — of Arabs have that expectation. Among Jews, Haredim are the most satisfied, with 95 percent expressing satisfaction, compared to 89 percent of those identifying themselves as Datim, 84 percent of those identifying themselves as "traditional," and 86 percent of those identifying themselves as "secular or not religious."

Women and men report similar rates of general satisfaction (86 percent of men compared to 84 percent of women), but men report slightly higher financial satisfaction levels, with 56 percent of men satisfied or very satisfied as opposed to 51 percent of women.

A 2006 survey taken by the Institute for Policy and Strategy found that 85 percent of the population would fight to defend Israel, a percentage significantly higher than is found among the citizens of any other Western democracy regarding their own countries. Both Jews, 87 percent, and Arabs, 82 percent, said they wished to continue living in Israel despite security, economic, and social challenges. Remarkably, more Israeli Arabs than Israeli Jews (77 percent compared to 66 percent) believe Israel to be better than other countries, especially with regard to social welfare, presumably because they are comparing Israel to Arab and Muslim-majority countries.

ZIONISM

Zionism describes the belief that the Jews are a people and a nation that need a country of their own in order to survive and flourish. As such, it is comparable to other national liberation movements. But three elements of Zionism make it different from other nationalisms, and each has had important ramifications in Israeli society.

First, Zionism began at a time when there was no Jewish-populated homeland in existence. People had to be transported to the Land of Israel and the territory built up. Diplomatic efforts were required even to allow immigration, to mobilize popular support, and to create new institutions and approaches to state building.

Second, at the time of its formation and development, Zionism was only one of several competing visions for the Jewish future. Its advocates had to compete for supporters and funds. Others wanted an exclusively religious Jewish identity, or assimilation to other countries' cultures, or immigration to North America, or autonomy in the East European countries where they lived (the Jewish Socialist Bund), or affiliation with Communist or socialist movements. Zionism's basic success arose from the Yishuv's ability to build up the country and defend itself. Having a Jewish state thus became seen as a viable possibility before 1948 and a reality once Israel was established.

Although the Holocaust destroyed Jewish communities in Europe—killing many, uprooting survivors, and eliminating some alternatives to the creation of a Jewish state—the triumph of Zionism within the wider Jewish community was not a result of that event. After all, World War II also enabled the spread of Communist governments, which led to the breaking up of Jewish communities in central Europe, and prompted many Jews to assimilate in Western Europe or to immigrate to other places.

Moreover, Jewish communities in the West enjoyed more security after the war, with reduced antisemitism and greater prosperity, which encouraged them to consider supporting the establishment of the State of Israel: they could do so and still be visibly loyal to their countries of residence. Ironically, the expulsion of Jews from Arabic-speaking countries—a result not only of opposition to Zionism there but also of growing nationalism, Islamism, and anti-Western feeling (North African Jews being French citizens)—also increased Jewish immigration and support for Israel.

Third, Zionism was a broad umbrella movement that included a wide variety of views ranging from near-Communist to piously religious, from social democratic to liberal to conservative. On the religious plane alone the variations in viewpoint went from militant secularism to Haredi religiosity.

Each of these distinguishing aspects of Zionism contributed to the eventual shape of Israeli society. The socialist Zionists played a central role in establishing the labor unions, marketing cooperatives, farms, and national institutions. They believed that manual labor was a virtuous act and contrasted it with what they considered the mercantile economy of the European ghetto. Jews in Eastern Europe were generally not allowed to own land and had to support themselves in nonagricultural occupations.

Although the bulk of the socialist Zionists constituted Mapai (the organizational ancestor of the Labor Party), the further left formed HaShomer HaTzair, which advocated the kibbutz as a way of life. Just a small portion of the Yishuv lived on a kibbutz—only 15 percent dwelt on any agricultural settlement before 1948—but it emerged as a symbol and prime example of Zionist goals. On the kibbutz, everyone worked for the good of the collective group. All activities, including meals, education, and even sleeping arrangements for children, were communal; all tasks were considered equal and received equal compensation.

The ascendancy of socialism in the Zionist movement starting in the 1920s arose from the convergence of three factors. First, in Eastern Europe, most Jews were poor, and right-wing movements were hostile to Jews. Therefore, Jewish politics, both non-Zionist and Zionist, were skewed to the left. Second, the socialists had the best-organized movement with the most effective and charismatic leaders. Socialist Zionism with its near-utopian vision and emphasis on the collective good inspired the young founding generation to make difficult sacrifices.

Third, Jews saw that the institutions created by the socialist-Zionists—agricultural settlements, the trade union federation (Histadrut), self-defense forces, manufacturing and marketing enterprises, plus medical and educational systems—would continue to play central roles in Israeli society long after the state was established. The socialist orientation of Zionists derived, therefore, from both preference and necessity.

Because the socialist wing, especially the Labor Party, was so powerful and ruled the state so long, the contributions of centrist bourgeois and conservative nationalist forces have often been understated. Nevertheless, these centrist and conservative groups made vital contributions to building commercial and state institutions and especially to shaping life in the cities. The socialist movement, meanwhile, looked down on private farmers and shopkeepers. Still, the kind of class system that existed virtually everywhere else in the world was turned on its head to some extent in Israel's political culture.

Religious Zionism, the ideology of most Datim, also had its part to play in this process of social formation that included tensions but also promoted stability and diversity. It prevented too severe a break with tradition and avoided a major schism among the Jewish people. The religious Zionists (the Mizrahi movement, not to be confused with the Mizrahim—the Middle Eastern Jews) had to compete with the anti-Zionist rabbis among the Haredim, who had tremendous influence over a large portion of the Jews, especially in Eastern Europe, for whom religious piety was the main priority. Winning many of these people over for Zionism would have been impossible without the Mizrahi movement.

In Europe, normative Judaism had been what is today called Orthodox, that is, observant of Jewish traditions. Yet a split had been developing between the Datim (Modern Orthodox) and the Haredim (often referred to in English by the misnomer "ultra-Orthodox"). The Datim, who stressed acceptance of modern ways coupled with a full observance of Jewish law, were, of the two groups, far more supportive of Zionism, so much so that today in Israel they are called the "national religious" camp, and their main voice for decades was the National Religious Party.

Following the teachings of Rabbi Abraham Isaac Kook, the first chief rabbi of modern Israel, the Datim justified their view with religious injunctions: to live in the Land of Israel was the highest honor, certain commandments could be fulfilled only there, and settling the land would further the divine plan. They saw their mission as ensuring that the state protected not only the material life of its citizens but also Jewish life. To achieve these goals, the Datim were willing to become partners with secular Jews. Aware that they would not dominate the homeland, they still wanted to maximize religious observance there and ensure Israel's links to religious Judaism.

Haredi Jews generally opposed Zionism on two main grounds. First, they insisted that only the coming of the Messiah would signal the time for Jews to return to the Land of Israel and that humanity should not try to hurry the process. Second, they feared that secular Zionists and the state would undermine religion whether or not that was their deliberate intention.

The Haredi view of Jewish survival was to "build a fence around the Torah": to withdraw from the secular world as much as possible and to resist change. The Torah, the holiest Jewish religious text, consisted of the first five books of the Bible. They even opposed the use of Hebrew except in religious matters and instead spoke Yiddish among themselves. This group formed the Aguda movement, which continues today.

After 1948, Haredi Jews made a series of compromises with the state. A few groups maintained their anti-Zionism, more moved toward a neutral position, while others (most notably the Chabad or Lubavitcher movement) became enthusiastically Zionist. The tendency of Haredi groups to become more integrated into Israeli society and more accepting toward Zionism is one of the most subtle trends in the country today.

The main group challenging socialist dominance was Revisionist Zionism. Starting in the 1920s, the movement was led by Ze'ev Jabotinsky, a skilled writer and charismatic orator. The movement demanded organized mass immigration right away since Jabotinsky, predicting the impending Holocaust, argued that time was running out for Jews to leave Europe. It also advocated a tough stance toward the British authorities of the Palestine Mandate. Yet it did not take a strong pro-capitalist stance, because class and economic issues were not central in Zionist debates and agendas.

IMMIGRATION: INGATHERING OF THE EXILES

Israel's Zionist founder's took the religious Messianic idea of *kibbutz galuyot*—"ingathering of the exiles"—and transformed it into a nationalist tenet. During the pre-state period, the British strictly limited immigration. The Zionist movement circumvented their controls whenever possible, smuggling in refugees from fascism who otherwise would probably have perished.

Not until 1948 did things change. As the country's Declaration of Independence declares, "The State of Israel will be open to Jewish immigration." Two years later, in 1950, the Knesset passed the Law of Return, proclaiming that every Jew has the right to immigrate to Israel as long as the potential immigrant is not deemed a security or public health risk. Between 1948 and 2000, more than 2.9 million people immigrated to Israel under this law. Every wave of immigration, before and after Israel became a state, shaped Israeli society by contributing ethnic and other characteristics and by widening its horizons.

During the 1930s, 1940s, and 1950s, Israel became a haven first for Holocaust refugees from Europe and then for Jewish refugees fleeing Arabic-speaking lands. In 1948, about 650,000 Jews resided in Israel, 85 percent of whom were Ashkenazim, with 110,000 living on agricultural settlements. The largest concentration of Jews from Asia and Africa—and also of highly religious Jews—lived in cities, particularly Jerusalem and Safed. Thus, in the pre-state years, society was dominated by European influences and ideas. And this influence continued after the state was established, even after a higher proportion of Sephardic and religiously observant European Jews arrived. By 1965, Sephardic Jews outnumbered Ashkenazic Jews.

Once Israel was established, however, Jews could immigrate freely. Within the first three and a half years of statehood, 680,000 Jews immigrated to Israel, doubling the size of the population. These included both Holocaust survivors and Middle Eastern and North African Jews, two very distinct groups with somewhat different needs, cultures, expectations, and skills.

A Jewish family look out from their tent in a new immigrants' camp, or ma'abara, Beit Lid, December 1949. (Getty Images / Image Bank.)

Among each of these groups, there was a great deal of variety. For example, Iraqi and Syrian immigrants were largely urban and modern in Middle Eastern terms, with relatively more formal education. Jews from Yemen and Morocco usually came from more rural backgrounds and were traditionally religious; some of the Yemeni Jews still practiced polygamy. The average educational and economic status of North African Jews arriving in Israel was lower since much of those countries' Jewish elite immigrated to France.

Variation among European Jews was equally extensive—including degree of education, religiosity, and assimilation to non-Jewish society—depending on country of origin and, especially for those from Eastern Europe, whether they had lived in cities or in small towns or villages. Managing the integration of these different groups during the wave of immigration extending from 1948 until the mid-1960s presented numerous social challenges.

A much smaller wave of immigration occurred after the Six-Day War, when the seemingly miraculous victory brought a number of North American Jews and other English-speakers; a high proportion were Modern Orthodox Jews who had dreamed of living in Jerusalem. In some Jerusalem neighborhoods, the English language continues to be widely used.

Far more numerically significant was the influx of what would eventually be over a million Soviet Jews, who started arriving with the partial opening of emigration from the Soviet Union in the mid-1970s and who emigrated freely after that country's collapse in 1991.

Finally, starting in the 1980s and continuing for the next two decades, came the Ethiopian Jews, the poorest group of all. They had been largely cut off from the rest of the Jewish world for centuries. War and political turmoil in Ethiopia had worsened their position, so Israel undertook their rescue in a covert operation. A steady flow of immigrants also came later from a displaced persons' camp near Addis Ababa. Given the unique background of the Ethiopian Jews and some debate over whether Ethiopian Jews were really Jews and how their religion varied from mainstream Judaism, they were remarkably well accepted. Within a generation, education had brought some of those born in Israel or who had arrived as children to the point where they were able to move into skilled and professional jobs.

By the year 2000, Jewish immigration slowed considerably, with most of those from the former Soviet Union who wished to emigrate to Israel already having done so. With the collapse of some economies and a growth in antisemitic incidents, there were small increases of immigration from Argentina, Turkey, and France. But since about half of the world's Jews were already Israeli citizens, it was not clear whether Israel would ever again see a large immigration wave like the ones in the past.

Israel devoted extensive resources to supporting new immigrants as each wave arrived, since providing a home for Jews was its most basic reason for being. The term "Jew" was not defined in the original 1950 law, but the omission did not have practical implications, for all those who wished to immigrate to the national homeland of Jews were allowed to do so. In 1970 the Knesset amended the 1950 law to define a Jew, in accordance with Jewish law, as anyone "born of a Jewish mother or [who] has become converted to Judaism and who is not a member of another religion." An additional article granted eligibility to a "child and a grandchild of a Jew, the spouse of a Jew, the spouse of a child of a Jew and the spouse of a grandchild of a Jew, except for a person who has been a Jew and has voluntarily changed his religion."

This addendum was necessary to continue accepting those family members of Jews who did not meet the stricter definition.

The problem of defining a legitimate conversion to Judaism has given rise to a series of controversies. In Israel, the Orthodox interpretation of Judaism has usually dominated when addressing this issue, but there have been individual exceptions and complex cases. Generally speaking, those who have converted through Reform and Conservative rabbis abroad can meet the immigration requirements by finding a clerk who interprets the law flexibly. Sometimes, however, converts do not know how to handle the system, or they ask to have non-Orthodox conversions recognized. Various plans have been put forward to deal with this. Some cases have been settled by granting citizenship, but other applicants have been refused, or their cases have become wrapped in red tape.

The Orthodox Rabbinate is determined to maintain its monopoly on determining who qualifies as a Jew. A large majority of Israelis, having no direct experience with other forms of Judaism, do not care very much about the issues. There is a consensus, though, that so-called Messianic Jews—Jews who have become Christians or Christians who incorporate aspects of Jewish terminology and ritual—do not qualify, and a few Western immigrants from this group have been refused citizenship.

Immigration continues to hold an exalted place in the Israeli national consciousness. The Hebrew term for Jewish immigration, *aliya*, which literally means "ascension," symbolizes the positive connotations of coming to Israel to live. Israeli society has at times experienced tensions between new and veteran and between new and native-born Israelis. Yet given the sacrifices that Israelis have collectively made on behalf of immigrants—the costs of absorption, competition for jobs and housing, the privileges accorded to immigrants, and adjustments to cultural differences—the level of friction, protest, and public criticism has remained remarkably low.

Among the institutions created to ease the transition of immigrants is the *ulpan*, an intensive Hebrew language class. Besides learning basic Hebrew, new immigrants are taught about national identity, mix with others from different countries, and are introduced to important facets of Israeli culture. In addition to free instruction, immigrants receive other benefits from the government to help them adjust. These have varied greatly over time but often include subsidized housing, tax breaks when they buy items, including automobiles, and cash payments.

By 2005, for the first time, Israel had more Jewish citizens than any other country in the world: 5.5 million, compared to about 5.3 million in the United States and a total of around 13.2 million Jews worldwide. By 2020, when the worldwide total is projected to be 13.6 million, Israel will have an estimated 6.3 million Jewish citizens (though not all of them reside in the country), and not long after that, the majority of the world's Jews will hold Israeli citizenship. The population increase in Israel is due mainly to higher birthrates there than among Jews in the Diaspora, who also tend to assimilate into the local population, particularly through intermarriage.

According to the Central Bureau of Statistics, the population of Israel in 2030 will be an estimated 10 million people or so, with a Jewish population of around 7.2 million, or 72 percent (compared to 76 percent in 2010), and an Arab population of around 2.4 million, or 24 percent (compared to 20 percent in 2010). The Jewish population would be proportionately larger if there were a major wave of immigration or if east Jerusalem were to become part of a Palestinian state.

EMIGRATION

Although immigration outpaces emigration, some Israelis do choose to leave the country. Emigrating from Israel is known as *yerida*, or "descent." During the early years after independence, emigration was considered so shameful that families left in virtual secrecy. With the gradual normalization of society and the setting in of some cynicism, emigration was no longer classed as a social sin.

Those emigrating can be divided into two basic categories. Some short-term immigrants who fled Europe or, later, the Soviet Union ultimately did not want to remain in Israel. Many immigrants from the North America also find adjustment to be difficult or cannot find appropriate jobs. In addition, there have been economic emigrants, often professionals who can procure high-paying jobs in the West (especially the United States) in their fields of specialization.

The estimated number of Israelis living abroad is reported to be as high as 700,000, about 450,000 of whom may live in North America. The Central Bureau of Statistics estimated that in 2010 about 6,600 Jewish Israelis per year would leave the country for a protracted period of time. The main reasons include a desire for a higher living standard, professional opportunities, and pursuit of advanced education. The security situation and the desire to escape the tension of living in Israel are cited as secondary motives.

Many emigrants maintain close ties to Israel. From time to time, Israel has set up campaigns to encourage those living abroad to return. In 2008, for example, the Ministry of Immigration and Absorption launched an initiative offering returning residents financial incentives, including tax breaks. These programs have enjoyed some success.

FROM MELTING POT TO PLURALISM: SOCIOCULTURAL MINORITIES

Like other immigrant nations, Israel has struggled over how best to develop a cohesive society with regard to assimilation alongside some preservation of subcultures. During the early years, a systematic effort was made to encourage homogeneity among Jews. To become a normative Israeli then, a citizen discarded ties to his or her country of origin and adopted an overall European-oriented culture. Immigrants should come to the Land of Israel to "build and be rebuilt"; they should shed such characteristics as fearfulness, lack of contact with nature, and preference for commerce rather than manual labor—all perceived as typical of Diaspora Jews. To be born as a new Israeli, newcomers, or at least their children, had to give up old customs. Indeed, Ashkenazic immigrants underwent almost as much of a transformation as Mizrahi immigrants; they changed from Russian, Polish, or German Jews into Israelis.

By the 1980s, Israeli society had developed distinct characteristics, a nation had been built, and a cohesive people had been formed. In the relaxed, self-confident atmosphere of a maturing state, differences in national origin were more accepted and were even woven into the national culture. But pluralism was accepted within a very strong framework of national homogeneity. Most Israelis have not been very interested in where their ancestors came from;

Prime Minister Benjamin Netanyahu (left of the man with the microphone) and his wife, Sara, attend a ban-quet to celebrate the traditional Moroccan holiday Mimouna with leading members of the Moroccan-origin community. Mimouna has become a national holiday in Israel. (Getty Images / Image Bank.)

"ethnic" consciousness or adherence to ethnic subcultures has been very limited. Perhaps the single most significant ethnic subculture among Israeli Jews is that of those originally from Morocco; members of that group came relatively late, they were usually impoverished upon arrival, and some, in response, reacted to the mainstream society with resentment. The Shas political party is to some extent a product of that subcultural consciousness. The most visible "ethnic" holiday in Israel is the Moroccan Jewish holiday of Mimouna, celebrating the end of Passover.

Starting in the 1970s and accelerating in the 1990s, Israel faced mass immigration again, especially from the former Soviet Union and Ethiopia, but managed it more easily. The country was wealthier, more secure, and more established than when it was trying to deal with the post-independence wave of immigrants, and the size of the wave, though large, was propor-tionately smaller than the previous one. Israeli society had also grown more individualistic, less ideological, and more diverse.

There was no official pressure on the immigrants from the former Soviet Union to be a certain type of Israeli. In addition, these immigrants were generally more educated than the earlier ones and used to a modern technological society. Indeed, some thought Israel was not sufficiently sophisticated and developed important supplemental educational programs for their children. Assimilation became a natural process, with the next, native-born generation having a primarily Israeli identity.

The Ethiopian immigrants were unlike any earlier immigrants, although their small number minimized any resulting challenges for Israeli society as a whole. They also had their own religious clerics and quite divergent customs, developed during their long isolation from the main body of Jews. But they had no sentimental attachment to Ethiopia, a country that had treated them badly, and were eager for acceptance. Most distinctions quickly declined, and basic assimilation took place with surprising speed.

After years during which Israeli society promoted homogeneity to build a successful society while facing military threats, absorbing immigrants, and facing economic challenges, it moved toward greater pluralism. The general attitude shifted toward accepting subcultural traditions, and the general society even adopted elements of the subcultures, mostly food and music.

Mizrahim/Sephardim

Mizrahi Jews are those who lived for centuries in North Africa or the Middle East before immigrating to Israel. The term *Mizrahi* is also used to refer to their descendants. The word *Sephardic*, which literally means "Spanish," properly refers to Jews expelled from Spain in 1492. It has come to refer more generally to the Judaism that Jews in the Middle East, North Africa, Turkey, and the Balkans practiced; the variants were slight. Each synagogue follows either the Ashkenazic or the Sephardic rite, although the differences between them are also limited.

Ashkenazic Jews dominated all aspects of Israeli society because they arrived first and because they led the pre-state Zionist movement. In general, Mizrahi immigrants were at a disadvantage, not only arriving later, but also coming without capital, with less education on average, and sometimes without some of the skills needed for modern society.

The two groups have their own narratives about that early period of the state. In the collective memory of Ashkenazim, the 1950s were a difficult time of austerity and deprivation for everybody. The immigrants from Europe and the Middle East arriving during the country's first decade often had poor health and brought few or no possessions with them. They all needed housing, and living spaces were scarce during this immigration surge. The mass immigration also led to serious unemployment and food rationing. Despite economic hardships and the immigrants' lack of education and capital, Israelis of the time accepted as a very high priority the need to help hundreds of thousands of Mizrahi immigrants seeking refuge in the struggling state.

Many, though by no means all, Mizrahim remember the 1950s as a time of difficulty and deprivation when they were also stripped of their traditions and cultures. They recall facing discrimination and marginalization. These different perceptions account for the political leanings of both groups to this day. Ashkenazim still dominate Labor and other left-wing parties; Mizrahim tend to favor nonreligious rightist parties and Shas, a kind of religious-communal party expressing Mizrahi identity. Still, these tendencies do not create full-scale voting blocs.

Indeed, the differences and frictions between these two groups, which reached a peak in the 1980s, have declined. Although Mizrahi Jews are generally poorer and hold fewer positions of social or economic power than Ashkenazim, the gap has narrowed. Significantly, around 25 percent of marriages are between members of these groups. Many Israelis—including the offspring of such marriages—have so assimilated to the general culture that they could not be put into either category without knowing their families' geographical past. In physical appearance, most Israelis are not easily identifiable as either Ashkenazic or Mizrahi.

The most salient area of Mizrahi consciousness and, to some extent, identity is in poorer towns and some city neighborhoods in Jerusalem and Tel Aviv. Overall, Mizrahi Jews tend to be more conservative in social behavior and more traditional in religious observance. Whereas Ashkenazim tend to be either highly religious (Dati and Haredi) or secular, many Mizrahi Jews are somewhere in between.

One of the prominent differences between Ashkenazim and Mizrahim, especially in the 1950s and 1960s, was family structure. Mizrahi families tended to have a larger number of children; women married at a younger age and participated less in the labor force; and women and men followed traditional gender roles more rigorously. When Mizrahim arrived in Israel, the dominant culture expected that Mizrahi family structure would come to resemble Ashkenazic family structure. Over time, this did in fact happen. By the 1970s, the average age of marriage in each sector was identical. And by the 1990s, second- and third-generation Israelis of both groups had nearly the same birthrate. The same narrowing of gaps happened with women's participation in the workforce and with overall income levels.

Patterns of religiosity also became more similar, with Mizrahim becoming relatively more secular. An exception was the development of what might be called a Mizrahi Haredi movement. This kind of approach to religion had not existed in the immigrants' pre-Israel places of residence. When the most religious Mizrahi arrived in Israel, they began studying at the yeshivot (religious academies) of Ashkenazic Haredim, where they were at times treated in a patronizing manner. Under the spiritual guidance of the Iraqi-born rabbi Ovadia Yosef, a large group of Mizrahim, most with roots in Morocco, developed their own interpretation of Haredi Judaism. Ironically, this movement adapted many historically non-Mizrahi traditions, including the eighteenth-century European-style clothing for yeshiva students and rabbis worn by Ashkenazic Haredim.

The Shas Party, founded in 1984, set up its own social welfare institutions and state-supported school system, cementing the loyalty of its constituency by providing jobs and services to them. When party leaders were accused, and sometimes convicted, of corruption, they and their supporters often attributed this to anti-Mizrahi bias, although most Mizrahim did not accept this shifting of blame. The party usually polls about 10 percent of the national vote, corresponding with roughly one-fifth of all Mizrahim, mostly originating in North Africa.

Mizrahim as a whole tend to be more politically conservative than Ashkenazim. Mizrahi support was especially important for the Herut Party (later called the Likud). There are a number of reasons for these political leanings: their more conservative social and religious backgrounds; their view of those on the left as members of a privileged caste who looked down on them; and their more skeptical view of Israel's Arab neighbors, derived from the oppression they (or their parents) suffered in the Arabic-speaking societies of their Diaspora.

Mizrahim are still underrepresented in certain areas, notably academia. But as the decades have passed, they have achieved upward social mobility and greater social integration. Although Israel has still not had a Mizrahi prime minister, almost every other high political post—president, chief of staff of the armed forces, and cabinet positions—has been filled by a Mizrahi.

To a large extent, then, the frictions of the 1970s and 1980s have dissipated. By the turn of the millennium, more than 50 percent of Mizrahim belonged to the middle class; only some income disparity between Ashkenazim and Mizrahim remains. The high levels of marriage between Ashkenazim and Mizrahim is often cited as proof of their integration, as is the Mizrahi presence at the upper echelons of the government, the military, and the business world.

Overall, the Mizrahim are integrated into Israeli society. Polls show that allegiance to groups based on pre-immigration residence declines in importance with every generation, and members of both groups rank being Israeli as their primary identity, far above any particular "ethnicity." Primary identification of oneself as Israeli also increases with level of education.

Immigrants from Russia and the Former Soviet Union

As late as the 1920s, the Jews of the Soviet Union were much like nineteenth-century Eastern European Jews. Highly traditional, with a strong sense of community and religion, they were concentrated in shtetls—small Jewish towns and villages, where their families had lived for centuries—in such places as today's Belarus and Ukraine. The more modernized, secularized Jews of the cities spoke Russian rather than Yiddish.

The Communist system Russianized both the rural and the urban groups, however, especially for later generations. Their communal, cultural, and religious institutions were destroyed, their language was largely eliminated, and their group loyalty was badly eroded. They had absorbed Russian culture and forgotten most or even all of their own. These Jews were highly secularized, and there was a high degree of intermarriage with Russian Christians.

Their cousins had immigrated earlier to the Land of Israel from societies in Eastern Europe—Bulgaria, Czechoslovakia, Hungary, Poland, and Romania—before those societies were fully taken over by Communist regimes after 1945. These pre-Communist Eastern European Jews, compared with the post-Communist Jews from the Soviet Union, had ways of life closer to traditional Jewish life. The Communist-era Jews who went to Israel had, in contrast, undergone intensive forced assimilation for many decades. They were certainly used to modern society, and life under Communism made them eager to enjoy freedom, but Lenin and Stalin had more influence on their lives than rabbis or shtetls did. Most of them did not identify themselves as Zionists, and many found it a novelty even to think of themselves as primarily Jews.

By 2000, a total of 1.1 million people from all the former republics of the Soviet Union had immigrated to Israel, increasing Israel's Jewish population by around 20 percent and the overall national population by about 15 percent. The vast majority, about 880,000, arrived in the decade after 1989. Although there is significant diversity among these groups, in Israeli society they are collectively referred to as Russian because they hail from the former Soviet Union and all speak Russian. The new immigrants settled mostly in the cities. In some places, like Beer Sheba, Ashdod, and Ashkelon—all in the south—they form one-quarter of the entire population.

Soviet Jewish immigrants at a welcome reception outside their airplane after arriving in Israel, December 1990. (Getty Images/Image Bank.)

Many Soviet immigrants had belonged to the Russian middle class and held high-status jobs as doctors, engineers, scientists, and artists. Immigration from Russia gave Israel the highest proportion of classical musicians of any country in the world. In some cases, immigrants had trouble finding work in their professions because those fields were already full; their specific specialties were not needed. A few immigrants were mining engineers, for example, and Israel has no mines. Sometimes their education was deemed insufficient—fairly or otherwise—to qualify them for their old professions. Many had a difficult adjustment period. A joke of the time concerned an office employee who had a heart attack and was saved by the cleaning woman, who had been a medical doctor in the Soviet Union.

How did Israelis receive this huge new population group? A number of potential problems could have caused friction. The question of the immigrants' religious affiliation provoked a few controversies in the Rabbinate but produced no major difficulties in practice. But there was some transitional ethnic bias. Prior to the peak of immigration from the former Soviet Union, only 4 percent of non-immigrant Israelis said they would not want to live in the same building as Russian immigrants, but by 1994 a full one-quarter of the non-immigrant population expressed this sentiment and reported that they viewed these immigrants as "a social problem." The most tolerant group consisted of the secular Ashkenazim, and the least tolerant groups, Mizrahim and Arabs.

This attitude declined steeply. In the years immediately after arriving, Russian immigrants posed a threat in the labor market, competing for jobs with upwardly mobile Mizrahim and Arabs, as well as diverting resources away from their sectors of the population. In practice, however, the cost of immigration was low, and the overall balance in expenditures was quite positive. The immigrants not only earned their own living but added a large productive population and new consumer group, which helped Israel's economy grow. Everyone benefited from this development. Although a small proportion of these immigrants proved transient, as a group they seemed to assimilate remarkably well into Israeli society.

In contrast to most previous immigrants, arrivals from the former Soviet Union often expressed the feeling that Israeli society was less cultured than their old one. They also had the sophistication to create their own institutions. Soon there were fifty Russian-language periodicals, dozens of social welfare, cultural, and other organizations, and even sports clubs and enrichment classes for students.

At times, these immigrants also created largely ethnic political parties. Natan Sharansky, who had been imprisoned in the Soviet Union for his Zionist beliefs before being released to immigrate, emerged as a major leader, although he eventually quit electoral politics. The Yisrael Beiteinu (Israel Is Our Home) Party, led by another immigrant from the former Soviet Union, Avigdor Lieberman, is largely—though not explicitly—an "ethnic" party of Russian-speaking immigrants and their descendants. While only a minority of the immigrants support the party, they form a significant proportion of the community.

These institutions simultaneously eased the integration of the immigrants, represented their interests, and preserved a subculture. The longer immigrants are in Israel, however, the more Israeli they feel. Generational transition and cross-group marriage further dilute group identity.

Just as Israeli society affected the immigrants, the Russian immigration wave affected Israeli society, moving the country toward more secular positions on various issues. Economic advantage and consumer convenience had already led more restaurants and stores to stay open on the Sabbath (from sundown on Friday night until sunset on Saturday night), and this tendency was increased.

Two holidays celebrated in Russia—Victory Day, marking the end of World War II, and New Year's Eve (called Sylvester in Israel)—became increasingly popular events in Israel. Non-kosher food (food not following Jewish dietary laws), especially pork products that Soviet Jews had eaten in the old country, also became more common. Other effects included a higher average consumption of alcohol—traditionally lower in Israel than in comparable European countries. And a few immigrants, with associations in the highly structured Russian underworld, brought their wealth to Israel and laundered money there.

In the beginning of the wave of immigration, the vast majority of the immigrants from the former Soviet Union were Jewish according to Jewish law. But by the late 1990s, many were technically not Jewish according to Jewish religious law—that is, they were the children of

Jewish fathers and non-Jewish mothers—or were non-Jewish spouses of Jews. The number of such people eventually reached 300,000. A few saw themselves as Christians, but the great majority of them chose to identify as Jews and easily function as Jewish Israelis on a daily basis. For the secular or non-Orthodox majority of Israelis, such distinctions are unimportant.

In addition, Israeli society is very much attuned to bypassing laws and formal procedures, so in some individual cases theoretical restrictions are simply ignored, although this is hard to do with marriage. Formally converting to Judaism would make the situation easier for those from the former Soviet Union whose status is technically non-Jewish, but only about 5 percent are interested in converting, since they already regard themselves as Jewish. They attend Jewish schools, speak Hebrew, live according to the Jewish calendar, and celebrate Jewish holidays.

The debate over conversion also involves a sub-debate between the dominant Orthodox rabbinical establishment and minority Reform and Conservative Jewish rabbis who are not allowed to supervise conversions in Israel. Many Orthodox rabbis have conditioned their approval for conversion on the candidates' willingness to pledge that they would continue a religious lifestyle. Almost all the Russian immigrants applying, however, are doing so in order to live as fully Jewish secular citizens. More recently, a conversion process with far more lenient guidelines than in the past has been set up and includes non-Orthodox rabbis among the supervisors. All of these complex issues involve more theoretical discussion than practical impact. But the debate on precisely how to handle these problems continues. They will probably be resolved normally over time as the children and grandchildren of these immigrants become fully integrated into Israeli society.

Immigrants from Ethiopia

Ethiopian immigrants are the newest group in Israeli society. Although they look different, and they come from a very different society and culture, Israeli society has accepted them as equal citizens with full rights. Israel recognized Ethiopian Jews—also known as Beta Israel, their preferred term, or Falashas—as Jews in 1975. Threatened by political violence in their isolated region of Ethiopia, Beta Israel began to migrate to refugee camps in Sudan in 1980. Many died along the way. Then, secretly, Israel brought them from the camps to Israel. Sudan was at war with Israel at the time, and any leak would have brought enormous Arab pressure on the Sudanese government to stop the immigration.

By 1983, as many as 4,000 Ethiopian immigrants had arrived in Israel. With conditions growing worse in Sudan and Ethiopia, Israel's government decided to speed up the immigration. Between November 1984 and January 1985, nearly 7,000 Ethiopian Jews were airlifted to Israel in what became known as Operation Moses. After an agreement was reached with Ethiopia, on May 24–25, 1990, Israel arranged another airlift. In Operation Solomon, Israel flew in 14,323 more. El Al passenger planes, C130 air force transports, and rented airliners from other countries had their seats ripped out to maximize the number of passengers each flight could bring. The excitement generated by the operation's size and smooth operation—seen as an example of Zionism in action—and the thrill of providing a safe haven for endangered Jews built strongly positive feelings toward the immigration.

A member of the IDF's Golani Brigade embraces a relative airlifted from Ethiopia to Israel during Operation Solomon, 1991. (Getty Images / Image Bank.)

Immigration continued thereafter at a slow but steady pace. There was a further problem, however. A group known as the Falash Mura had been converted to Christianity, reportedly under duress. It had not been included in the earlier operations. Some Ethiopian immigrants, who had relatives among them, lobbied for their inclusion, while others opposed it. In 1996, the chief rabbis expressed their view that the Falash Mura were Christians who preferred to remain so. With typical Israeli flexibility, though, about 10,000 were eventually brought to Israel anyway.

By 2009, about 85,000 Jews of Ethiopian origin were residing in Israel. About 25,000, or 30 percent, had been born in the country. As the immigrants arrived, they were placed in absorption centers because of their unfamiliarity with modern society; Russian newcomers, in contrast, were sent directly to permanent housing. The centers made it easier to provide such necessary services as Hebrew classes, health care, job training, and general instructions on living in Israeli society. On the other hand, the absorption centers tended to isolate the recent immigrants from the rest of society and could create long-term dependency on the government. The government eventually created a special mortgage program to help immigrants in poorer towns buy permanent housing.

Like the Russian immigrants, the first generation of newcomers from Ethiopia tended to stick together, to speak their own language (Amharic) among themselves, and to create organizations to help immigrants acclimatize. In the usual pattern, those who arrived as children or who were born in Israel have been able to integrate far better than their parents. But about

50 percent of the entire group remain classified as poor. They have above-average unemployment and below-average numbers of high school graduates.

As often happened with the Mizrahi immigrants and others with a highly traditional background, family patterns underwent stress and change in Israel. Ethiopian women gained greater independence through education and employment. By 2009, one-third of Ethiopian women worked outside the home compared to about half of women in Israel overall. Family strife and divorce rates among this group have increased.

As with the Russian immigration, a specific religious issue arose. Cut off from Jewish communities elsewhere in the world, Ethiopian Jews followed somewhat different traditions. At first, the credentials of their rabbis (*qessim*) were not recognized. But beginning in the 1990s, these leaders were seated as full members of local religious councils.

Like previous groups, Ethiopian immigrants focused on integrating. They did not establish their own synagogues, and the rabbis of the next generation will achieve ordination through existing institutions. Their annual festival of Sigd, which commemorates their return from exile to Israel, became an official Israeli holiday in 2008. This step was explicitly taken to show the country's desire to show acceptance of the Ethiopian immigrants.

At other times, cultural misunderstandings caused friction. The biggest incident came in the mid-1990s when it was revealed that the country's main blood bank did not use blood donated by Ethiopians for fear of HIV infection, a problem common in Ethiopia. Indeed, the majority of new HIV cases in Israel were among the Ethiopian newcomers. But the immigrants protested this as an insult, and blood bank policy was changed. Now the health of each donor is examined on an individual basis.

Although Ethiopian immigrants occasionally raise the issue of racism and other forms of discrimination—as with the blood bank policy, the debates over accepting the Falash Mura, and religious traditions—by and large, their acceptance into Israeli society proceeds smoothly. Affirmative action programs, when they were established, encountered little opposition. The integration of the Beta Israel remains a work in progress.

Anglo-Saxon Immigrants

English-speaking immigrants—known in Israeli parlance as "Anglo-Saxons" and including those from the United States, the United Kingdom, Canada, South Africa, Australia, and New Zealand—have been fewer in number than those from many other countries, but they have often brought new ideas and enterprises. The number of immigrants and their children from the United States is an estimated 180,000; from the United Kingdom, Australia, and South Africa, 85,000; and from Canada, 35,000. In general, they have left lives of material comfort, and often they find life in Israel more difficult than they had imagined; about one-third return to their home countries. Finding a suitable job is the biggest difficulty. Still, high levels of education and employable skills make their integration into Israeli society relatively easy if this problem can be solved.

This group has produced a large number of Israeli academics and scientists as well as innovative businessmen. Among the many English-speaking immigrants who have shaped Israel politically are Prime Minister Golda Meir, Chief Justice of the Supreme Court Shimon

Agranat, Foreign Minister Moshe Arens, Stanley Fischer, governor of the Bank of Israel, and important figures in media, music, academia, sports, and religion. A large portion of the immigrants are religious Jews, who mostly live in Jerusalem. Several towns, notably Ra'anana and Beit Shemesh, also have concentrations of English-speakers. Immigrants from the United States constitute a disproportionately high number of settlers in the territories captured in 1967.

Motivated by idealism and coming from countries where nongovernmental organizations are common, the Anglo-Saxons are also often involved in social-welfare, reform, and environmental groups. They have also played a leading role in Reform and Conservative Jewish circles, which account for the majority of Jews in North America but a small minority in Israel. As activists, U.S. immigrants are frequently found in right-wing (as with Jewish Defense League leader Meir Kahane) and left-wing organizations.

Arabs

When the State of Israel became independent in 1948, about 150,000 Arabs found themselves living within its borders and classified as citizens. Today, more than 1.2 million Arabs are citizens of Israel—20 percent of the total population. Over 90 percent of the Arabs are Muslim; fewer than 10 percent are Christian. Since statehood, the percentage of Muslims has increased, and the percentage of Christians has decreased; their relative numbers at the end of the 1950s were 70 percent and 21 percent. With the immigration of Jews from the Middle East and North Africa, the percentage of Arabs in the overall population decreased to just 11 percent in the 1950s, but their much higher birthrate increased their numbers, which were further boosted by the annexation of east Jerusalem in 1967, as well as by a small number of immigrants (accounting for 3 percent of the increase), mainly for purposes of family reunification.

Israeli Arabs have a natural growth rate of approximately 2.6 percent per year, as of 2009. The birthrate is much higher among Muslim Arabs than among Christian Arabs, but overall, the Arab birthrate is falling significantly. In 2000, the birthrate among Israeli Arabs was 3.8, compared with 2.8 percent in neighboring Syria and Jordan and 2.1 percent in Egypt. Nearly a decade later, in 2008, the average number of people in an Arab family was 4.8, compared to 3.5 for Jews.

The more than 110 Arab municipalities scattered throughout the country, including nine cities, thirty-three rural villages, and thirteen Druze towns, are home to about 70 percent of Israel's Arabs. An additional 24 percent of Arabs live in the "mixed" cities of the Jerusalem area. In Jerusalem proper, Arabs make up over 30 percent of the population, and in Acre, Ramla, Lod, and Ma'alot-Tarshisha, about 20 percent. In Tel Aviv, Haifa, and Nazareth Illit, Arabs are less than 10 percent of the population. Another 1 percent of Israel's Arabs live in predominantly Jewish cities, and the remainder, mostly Bedouin, live in unrecognized villages in the southern part of the country.

Most Arab localities are homogeneous, with eighty-one of them being 90 percent or more Muslim. Overall, about 46 percent of Israeli Arabs live in the north, another 18 percent in the Jerusalem area, 15 percent in Haifa, and 1 percent in the Tel Aviv area; the rest are split between the center and the south. The majority are Sunni Muslims, who live mainly in Jerusalem, the

Jaffa section of Tel Aviv, Haifa, Acre, Nazareth, Umm-al-Fahm, the Bedouin town of Rahat, and a number of largely Arab small towns and villages.

Muslim Arabs, with their relatively high birthrates, have a low median age: around eighteen. Religious practices among Muslim Arabs vary widely, ranging from completely secular to very religious. Since the 1980s, there has been a rise in the number of adherents to the Islamic Movement, which seeks to replace Israel with an Islamist state.

Christian Arabs live mostly in cities and villages in the northern part of the country; Nazareth is an important center for them. Their birthrate is lower than that of both Muslims and Jews. They tend to be more modernized and westernized than the Muslims are. Although some have taken up the causes of Communism or Arab nationalism, they tend to be politically moderate. Their Christianity, like the Islam of Muslim Arabs, is extremely varied; Eastern Orthodox, Roman Catholic, Greek Catholic, and Protestant faiths are all represented. At times, there are frictions between Christian and Muslim Arabs, notably in recent years over the expansion of a mosque in Nazareth into a Christian-owned area.

Arabic is an official language of Israel; government forms and documents are published in both Hebrew and Arabic. The most important internal issue among Israeli Arabs has been over their identity in a Jewish state. One choice, which up to 50 percent have made, judging by voting patterns, is to affirm the basic social framework in either a traditionalist or a pragmatic mode.

Traditionalists give their primary loyalty to clan (*hamula*) and family, whereas pragmatists make accommodations with the state as they try to maximize benefits for the Arab sector, with the association of Arab mayors being the key leadership group lobbying for Arab interests. These groups are not necessarily satisfied with Israel's status as a Jewish state, but they judge the situation unlikely to change and are aware of the relative benefits they enjoy—including democracy, higher living standards, and a more stable society—compared to Arabs in other countries or those living under PA or Hamas rule.

The other basic choice is to support a political course intended to change the structure of society and produce an Arab-dominated country. Since three contending movements—Communist, Arab nationalist, and Islamist—seek that solution, Arab power has been divided even further. Earlier in Israel's history, the Communist Party—originally a Jewish-Arab organization that supported the 1947 Partition Plan—was the most influential. Over time, however, the party became overwhelmingly Arab, and after the breakup of the Soviet Union, the Marxist-Leninist ideology faded. The party is now a vaguely leftist factor in the Arab community.

By the late 1960s, Pan-Arab nationalism had gained a foothold among Israeli Arabs. Those who supported this doctrine might also back Palestinian nationalism—supporting the PLO and especially Fatah—but they might also see themselves as Arabs first and foremost. Most Israeli Arabs never accepted subordination to the PLO directly, nor did they join in its armed struggle, except for a small number who mostly left Israel for that purpose.

The third choice for Israeli Arabs who seek Israel's destruction is Islamism. That movement, which arose within Israel during the 1980s, has a dual appeal for those who not only espouse traditional religious practices but oppose modern social change and the kind of corruption that has sometimes tainted its competitors. This movement is split into two groups, one of which participates in electoral politics and the other of which views even that step as recognition of the Israeli state, which it considers to be heresy.

Traditionalist/pragmatist, Arab nationalist, or Islamist, these groups all identify with the Palestinians of the West Bank and the Gaza Strip, but not necessarily in the same way. Traditionalists and pragmatists see them in a fraternal matter; the nationalists see them as another part of the same Palestinian nation with whom they should be united; and the Islamists see them as part of the world Muslim community (*umma*). The nationalists support Fatah, the Communists back the Palestinian Communists, and the Islamists endorse Hamas.

However Israeli Arabs define their goals and allies, they do not seek to integrate fully into mainstream Israeli society. They do not want a Western-style state based purely on citizenship but either the status quo, involving a large degree of communal independence, or an Arab or Islamic state.

Unless Israeli Arabs become involved in actual espionage or violence, they can express their views without interference. But the potential outcome of this liberality was demonstrated by the fate of the Arab nationalist party leader Azmi Bishara, a Christian, credibly accused of collaboration with Hizballah, who fled Israel for Syria in 2007.

The large Arab population in and around Jerusalem deals with an especially complex situation. The part of the city ruled by Jordan until 1967 and annexed by Israel when the city was reunified in 1967 was then home to Arab residents. By 2007, that number had increased to 260,500. Much of this increase was due to immigrants from West Bank towns and villages rather than from natural population growth. When the city was annexed and all residents were offered Israeli citizenship, most opted for permanent resident status instead. They are eligible to vote in municipal elections and have the rights of city residents, but they may also vote in PA elections. Despite threats from Palestinian organizations, some take Israeli citizenship, since it provides them with benefits. In 2005, only about 5 percent of Jerusalem's Arabs were Israeli citizens.

Israel recognizes the Arab community as a religious, linguistic, and cultural minority. Arabs have their own schools where classes are taught in Arabic. State radio and television stations broadcast in Arabic, and there are independent Arabic publications. Muslims, Christians, and Druze enjoy freedom of religion and receive state funding for religious institutions. Each religious community is responsible for matters of personal status—marriage, divorce, burial—for its constituents, just as the Rabbinate administers all matters of personal status for Jews.

Officially, Israel grants equal rights to all its citizens regardless of ethnicity or religion, as stated in the Declaration of Independence. The only major legal difference is that Jews and Druze are drafted for military service. Some Bedouin volunteer, but very few Christian and Muslim Arabs do, and those that do volunteer are stigmatized by their communities.

Still, there are disparities between the groups.

One reason for economic disparities between the Jewish and Arab communities is that most of the educated and urban elite in the Palestinian community fled to Jordan or Lebanon in 1948. Now, half of the families living below the poverty line in Israel are Arab, and the majority of the towns with the highest unemployment rates are Arab towns, even though the overall economic situation of Arabs in Israel is better than it is in most Arab countries. The high rate of unemployment among Arabs in Israel is attributed to their lower level of education, their tradition of keeping women out of the workforce, their continuing concentration in the agricultural sector, and competition from new immigrants and, recently, from foreign workers.

Educational disparities persist, too. On average, Israeli Jews receive three years more education than do Israeli Arabs, down from a difference of more than four years in the 1970s. Within the Arab community, there are also differences. Christians are the best educated, with 27 percent completing twelve years of school, compared to only 14 percent among Muslims and Druze. Among Christians, education rates are the same for men and women; among Muslims, the rates are higher for men (16 percent, compared to 11 percent of women). But more and more Arabs are attending school for longer: 79 percent of Arabs aged fourteen to seventeen attend or have attended school (compared to 29 percent in 1970), and 96 percent of Jews; and dropout rates in the Arab schools (12 percent) are double those in the Hebrew schools (6 percent). In 2008, roughly 39 percent of Arab Muslims took the matriculation exams compared with approximately 57 percent of Christians, 48 percent of Druze, and 54 percent of Jews who were eligible. The discrepancy in education is most visible at the university level, with Arabs representing less than 10 percent of all students in the universities.

Budget allocations to Jewish schools are significantly higher than those to Arab schools. Part of the problem with resource allocation is that Arab municipalities are notoriously negligent in collecting property taxes from residents, which means that they lack money to finance services and projects. Arabs also have fewer voluntary organizations to raise money. Divisions

Israeli Arab students sit and rest by the gate of the Ben-Gurion University in the southern Israeli town of Beer Sheba. Over 17,000 students are enrolled at the university. (Photo by Serge Attal/Flash90. Serge Attal/Flash90.)

along kinship and political lines have also reduced the Arab leverage in lobbying for more funding.

Another reason for differential allocations, however, is unequal treatment by the state. The government-appointed Or Commission Report of 2003 states, "The Arab citizens of Israel live in a reality in which they experience discrimination as Arabs. . . . Although the Jewish majority's awareness of this discrimination is often quite low, it plays a central role in the sensibilities and attitudes of Arab citizens." The report cites examples of the types of discrimination against Arabs, including government failure to move toward equal allocation of state resources, toward confirming the equality of Arab citizens, and toward uprooting discriminatory policies and actions. Nor does the state supply equal law enforcement in the Arab sector.

Many Israeli Jews admit that they condone preferential treatment for Jews. They tend to view Arabs as a security risk—a view that has a basis in reality—and this reduces the availability of some jobs. Even so, disparities and discrimination have been declining since the 1990s. The gap in the money allocated to Jewish and Arab local municipal councils and education systems has also narrowed.

Generally speaking, although intercommunal relations are not warm, they are quite stable and not usually tense. Yet communal attitudes cannot be easily stereotyped. According to a 2003 poll, 70 percent of Israeli Arabs accept a definition of Israel as a "Jewish and democratic state, in which Jews and Arabs live together," whereas 38 percent accept the Zionist principle of Israel's right to preserve a Jewish majority. Since 2000, however, a majority of Israeli Jews and Arabs have consistently viewed relations between the two groups as "not good."

Indices that measure coexistence have also declined. In 2007, for example, the percentage of those who felt that both sides had historic rights to the land fell from 68.5 percent to 54 percent for Jews and from 67.5 percent to 49 percent for Arabs. Jews supporting full equality between Jews and Arabs in Israel fell from 73 percent in 1999 to 56 percent in 2007, evidently in response to their identification of Israeli Arabs with Israel's enemies.

Differences in geographical location, language, and worldview limit interactions between the communities. Yet neither side evinces eagerness to draw closer. Thus, most Arab Israelis are not enthusiastic about the nature of the state in which they live, and they also have to deal with the conflict between their country of citizenship and members of their ethnic group and religion. Yet they know that the democratic rights and living standards they have in Israel are better than they would enjoy in an Arab or Palestinian state.

The key point is that the majority of Israeli Arabs accept the fact that Israel is a Jewish state and that they benefit materially from the status quo—they are not sufficiently motivated to battle to change this or to move elsewhere, even to a Palestinian state—but they do not believe Israel has a right to be a Jewish state in theory. Their political and worldview choices appear to be deadlocked. Whether increasing modernization of the Arab sector or events elsewhere in the region will change this remains to be seen.

Bedouin

Bedouin number about 170,000. There are approximately 110,000 in the Negev and 50,000 in the Galilee, and the remaining 10,000 are in central Israel. Although Bedouin are Arabs, they are historically nomadic and give primary loyalty to their tribe and clan rather than to Arabs or Muslims as a group. In Israel they have usually been resettled in permanent communities, but a small portion of them continue to be traveling herders for part of the year, living in black tents where they pasture their sheep and goats.

The Bedouin are poorer and less educated than the agriculturalist and town-dwelling Arabs. They have the highest childbirth rate in the country—almost double that of other groups. Health problems arise from unsanitary living conditions and lack of access to clean, potable water, and the frequency of traditional first cousin marriage causes a high rate of congenital disease.

The permanent settlement of Bedouin into towns and villages in the south has been a major project. At times, the green (environmental) police and Bedouin have clashed over use of land for pasture. But the main problems in recent years have been poverty and the organization of government services—like health and education facilities—for those living in unrecognized villages. The law requiring children to go to school is now strictly enforced among elementary-school-age Bedouin children, so disparities in education are decreasing, and literacy is on the rise.

Unlike the rest of the Muslim Arabs in Israel, a small percentage of Bedouin serve in the IDF. This is truer of the northern Bedouin, who in general feel a greater affinity for the state than do their southern counterparts.

Tensions between Arab and Jewish Israelis

Until 1966, Arabs in the north lived under martial law, and regulations facilitated the expropriation of Arab-owned lands. The worst incident during this period came during the 1956 war with Egypt. Arab villages in Israel near the Jordanian-ruled West Bank were put under curfew after 5:00 p.m., under penalty of death, because of fears that Jordanian forces might infiltrate and attack Israel. On October 29, 1956, in Kafr Qasim, forty-eight villagers returning from work in the fields at night were killed. Eleven Border Police were charged with murder, and the two officers were sentenced to seventeen and fifteen years imprisonment, respectively, sentences later reduced on appeal. Judge Benjamin Halevy, presiding over the trial, issued an important ruling—since then accepted as precedent—that Israeli security personnel are required to disobey orders if necessary to avoid breaking the law.

In 1966, martial law was lifted completely in the north, and discriminatory laws were nullified. The incident that brought the greatest friction after that came in 1976, when the government published a plan to take 5,250 acres (12,973 hectares) of land in the Galilee for its use. About 30 percent of this land was Arab-owned. In response, Arab leaders called a general strike on March 30, 1976. Police units opened fire—the police say in self-defense, Arab critics say unnecessarily. In the resulting clashes, six Arabs were killed, and many Arabs and police were injured. The Arab community commemorates this event every year as Land Day.

In another incident, in October 2000, the outbreak of an intifada among Palestinians in the West Bank and the Gaza Strip sparked brief, large-scale protests within Israel. Some turned violent. Police killed twelve Israeli Arabs in clashes. The government commissioned an independent investigation into the police reaction, as well as the conditions that existed in the Arab sector leading up to the clashes.

The findings of the State Investigative Commission on the October 2000 Events, the Or Commission Report, named after the justice who headed the commission, were released in 2003. The report blamed the police for being unprepared to deal with riots and thus having to resort to excessive use of force. It placed responsibility on the internal security minister, Shlomo Ben-Ami, and recommended his removal. The commission also found two Arab members of the Knesset and the Arab leaders of the northern branch of the Islamic Movement in Israel to be responsible for inciting the riots. In this report the government officially recognized discrimination against Arab citizens for the first time.

Through all these years since Israel's independence, Arab society has been undergoing two contradictory but simultaneous changes: Israelization and Palestinization. It has become Israeli as a result of isolation from Palestinian communities in the West Bank and the Gaza Strip—especially before 1967 but even after that—and the influence of Jewish Israeli society. Israelization is expressed through political participation and other forms of integration. A main arena of integration is education. Arabic-language schools teach Hebrew as a second language, as well as Israeli history, literature, and culture, alongside the equivalent Arab topics. Jewish state schools have reciprocal classes in the Arabic language and classes about other religions and cultures.

With the increase in educational levels and the decline in farming, some Arabs have sought employment outside the Arab economic sector. With education and contact with Jewish Israelis in the workplace and elsewhere, Arabs generally have become fluent in Hebrew and more integrated into the larger Israeli society.

At the same time, contacts or identification with the Palestinians, as well as frustration with Arab status within Israel, have led to Palestinization. Israeli Arabs have expressed solidarity with Palestinians with financial donations, food shipments, demonstrations, and strikes. Occasionally, demonstrations have turned violent. A few Israeli Arabs have gathered intelligence for Fatah, Hamas, or Hizballah, and a small number have participated in terrorist attacks. For this reason, some Israelis view Israeli Arabs as a fifth column, which exacerbates tensions. Many Israeli Arabs, but not a majority, support Israel's replacement by a Palestinian, Arab, or Islamic state.

Druze

While they are Arabs in ethnic terms, the Druze have a separate identity and function as an independent community with a distinct worldview and political orientation. The Druze religion developed in the tenth century, based on a blend of mysticism, monotheism, earlier beliefs, and a reverence for historical figures said to have promoted justice. Its tenets are secret except to the more senior members; followers are divided between "knowers" (*uqqal*) and "the ignorant" (*juhal*). Only the former have access to higher religious texts. The men among them wear a white turban, the women a white headscarf. Druze women have equal personal rights with men.

While technically a religious group, the Druze have become a separate people. Conversions to the Druze religion are prohibited. Both their secrecy and their bar on conversions are for protection. As adherents to a post-Islam religion in a Muslim-majority region and a people whose ancestors were Muslims centuries ago, the Druze could fall prey to Islamic provisions condemning to death those who convert to another religion. The Druze have several holy sites in Israel, notably tombs of important prophets, such as Jethro's Tomb (Nebi Shuaib) on the edge of the Sea of Galilee, where the Druze gather annually on April 25 to discuss community affairs.

Israel recognizes the Druze as a distinct religious minority, which means that they have their own court system for matters of personal status like marriage and divorce, as well as their own state-recognized spiritual leadership. They speak Arabic but often intersperse Hebrew words.

Numbering about 124,300 people in 2010, the Druze represent over 1.6 percent of Israel's total population and roughly one-tenth of its Arabic speakers. About 100,000 of them live either in exclusively Druze towns and villages or in towns and villages together with Christian and Muslim Arabs; these settlements are located throughout the Mount Carmel and Galilee regions in the northern part of the country. Another 20,000 Druze live in the Golan Heights.

The biggest Druze town in Israel is Daliyat al-Karmel, located on Mount Carmel. Mixed-population towns with Druze and Muslim Arab residents include Isfiya and Shfar'am. Other Druze villages include Peki'in and Beit Jann.

In the Golan Heights, which Israel captured from Syria in 1967, there are four main Druze communities. Majdal Shams, the largest, has a population of 8,000. Golan Druze are Syrian citizens but were offered Israeli citizenship when Israel annexed the Golan Heights in 1981.

Only about 1,500 Golan Druze—fewer than 10 percent—hold Israeli citizenship. The rest have permanent resident status; they maintain their Syrian citizenship and at least a nominal loyalty to Damascus. Most refused Israeli citizenship, explicitly due to Syrian patriotism but largely from fear of Syrian retribution should that regime ever again control the area. A few have left the area to settle elsewhere in Israel, notably in Eilat.

After the 1967 war, Israel's capture of the Golan Heights separated the Druze communities in the Golan from the Druze in Syria. The state of war between Israel and Syria meant that the border was closed, so Druze on the two sides communicate at a place called Shouting Hill, where they can see and talk to one another, often with the aid of a megaphone or, recently, mobile phones. Druze students and pilgrims to the shrine of Abel, one of their prophets, are permitted to cross over into Syria, and brides are allowed to make a one-way trip.

Neither Islamism nor Arab nationalism appeals to the Israeli Druze, although a few became Communists, and they look to fellow Druze in Lebanon and Syria rather than Arabs or Muslims as part of their wider community. Although the Druze at first supported the Arabs in the 1948 war with Israel, they changed sides—perhaps having concluded that Israel would win—in what was called the Pact of Blood.

Since 1956, the Druze living in Israel have been conscripted into the IDF and have reached high-level positions in the military, the Border Police, and the government. In 1974, a special, mainly Druze unit was formed; this Battalion of the Sword is usually known as the Druze Battalion. Druze serve in all sections of the IDF. Unlike the Druze citizens of Israel, however, the Druze of the Golan are not drafted to the IDF, although a small number serve voluntarily.

There is also a Druze Zionist Organization. Four Druze were elected to the Knesset in the 2009 elections, a number representing double their percentage in the population as a whole.

A Druze woman greets her daughter, who is crossing over from Syria, at the Quneitra Crossing, Golan Heights, September 2007. (Getty Images / Image Bank.)

Druze do not vote as a bloc, and an array of parties have elected them to the Knesset, including the Arab Balad, the centrist Kadima, and the nationalist Likud and Yisrael Beiteinu parties.

Circassians

Muslim Circassians fled the Caucasus region when it came under Russian rule in the late nineteenth century. Today about 3,000 Circassians live in Israel, mainly in Kfar Kama and Rehaniya in the Galilee. They attend elementary schools that focus on their culture and language and can go to either Jewish or Arab schools thereafter, depending on where they live. Circassians have a good relationship with Israel and the Jewish majority. In 1948, the community's leaders requested, as proof of Circassian allegiance, that Israel draft Circassian men into the IDF. Circassians have their own court system for dealing with personal status issues, which is based on their historic law known as *Khabza*.

African Hebrew Israelites

Another minority group numbers in the thousands: the African Hebrew Israelites, commonly known as Black Hebrews. This group of African Americans came to Israel in 1969, mainly from Chicago. The cult's charismatic leader, Ben Ammi Ben Israel, led what he said was a return of Africans descended from the Israelites to the Promised Land. They were permitted to enter Israel and live in the southern town of Dimona.

A debate over this group's status lasted for years, until 2003, when its members were granted permanent resident status and some obtained citizenship. Since 2004, they have served in the

IDF. The community is mostly self-sufficient; members live communally, and children attend a community school supervised by the Ministry of Education. They are vegan in diet and produce food, perfume, and other craft products. The group practiced polygamy until the 1990s.

Foreign Workers

Since the late 1990s, a large number of foreign workers have come to the country to replace the Palestinian workers from the territories. Israel closed the borders to workers from the West Bank and the Gaza Strip in the face of rising Palestinian terrorism. With the continuing development of Israel's economy and heightened prosperity, many Israelis themselves were no longer willing to work in unskilled, low-paying, labor-intensive jobs.

Three main sectors of the economy employ foreign workers, each drawing people from different countries. Construction is mainly done by workers from Turkey, Bulgaria, and Romania. Agricultural workers are usually Thai or Chinese. Nursing of senior citizens and housekeeping are generally the province of workers from the Philippines. In addition, economic refugees from sub-Saharan Africa have entered the country illegally.

It is difficult to estimate the number of foreign workers. Those on fixed contracts are supposed to remain in the country for only a certain period of time, although many leave their jobs or stay on after their contracts expire in order to work illegally. Sections of Tel Aviv, notably around the Old Central Bus Station, have a high population of such people. Many of those employed send money home to families left behind, although in some cases entire families are living in Israel. There are small periodic deportation campaigns.

A Chinese foreign worker outside a grocery store, Tel Aviv, July 2008. (Getty Images / Image Bank.)

Foreign workers are paid low wages, live in poor conditions, and may be mistreated by labor contractors or unscrupulous employers. They live in slums and keep a low profile to avoid expulsion. Still, since foreign workers make far more money in Israel than at home, entry into the country is easier than it is into many other places, and their treatment is better than in some countries, Israel remains a popular destination. Within the country, these workers have created ethnic communities with social clubs and support organizations. Those who have obtained permanent resident status are the best off.

Although there has been some discussion of foreign workers taking jobs away from Israelis, campaigns to fill the positions with citizens have generally failed. A minor scandal erupted in the 1990s, when Prime Minister Benjamin Netanyahu's family was found to be employing an illegal Dutch immigrant as a nanny. A similar incident occurred in 2010, when it was discovered that the wife of Defense Minister Ehud Barak had been employing an illegal worker from the Philippines as a housekeeper. Overall, Israelis are willing to let foreign workers stay.

Diaspora Jewry: The External Jewish Society

The idea of kibbutz galuyot, drawing all Diaspora Jews together in the Land of Israel, was a central motif in Zionist thinking. According to common perception, Jews not resident in the Land of Israel were in exile (*galut*). From the outset, however, many Zionist leaders realized that many or most Jews would continue to live in Diaspora—outside the Land of Israel.

Israel's relations with Diaspora Jewish communities have shaped its relations with the outside world more generally. In the early years of statehood, most Israelis thought Diaspora life was doomed in the long run. Diaspora Jews, they thought, should immigrate to Israel, where the new paradigm of Jewish life was being created, and it was incumbent on Israel to persuade them to do so. This view was known as *shlilat hagalut*, or "negation of the exile."

In later years, this view became more nuanced and complex. The survival and prospering of Diaspora Jewish communities, above all in the United States, as well as the decline of ideological fervor in Israel, has contributed to the change. The Diaspora Jews also became an important source of tourism, investment, and political support.

Today, among the Israeli public, the Jewish Diaspora plays only a very minor role in discussion, although foreign Jewish news and contacts remain of interest. While Israeli Jews certainly remain strongly committed to Jewish peoplehood, the practical focus is on events in Israel itself. The relationship between the State of Israel and the Diaspora sometimes comes into focus as a result of differences—for example, the Orthodox Rabbinate has a monoply in Israel, whereas the Reform and the Conservative movements are important in the Diaspora.

For a large portion of Jews in Diaspora communities, Israel remains a focus of interest and loyalty, one of the defining aspects of their Jewish identity. At the same time, the old debate between Zionism and other alternatives—particularly the leftist and the assimilationist options—has broken out again. Some Jews who have come to oppose Israel's policies or even existence support anti-Israel efforts in various Western countries. Though few in number and small as a percentage of the total number of Jews, they are disproportionately heard, given their passion on the issue and the fact that many have positions in academia, journalism, or other high-profile occupations.

Israel and Israeli groups send emissaries abroad to encourage immigration, teach Hebrew, and do other things to strengthen the relationship with Israel. Diaspora Jews come to Israel to study or visit in groups to gain understanding. A particularly interesting and successful program is Operation Birthright, which brings to Israel young Jews who have never been there before to develop stronger links to the country. Migration as such has become less important than maintaining the continuity of the Diaspora communities and their links with Israel. A complementary program has given Israeli youth more knowledge about the Diaspora by sending them on organized tours of historic Jewish sites in Europe and Holocaust-era concentration camps.

RELIGION IN SOCIETY

What role should religion play in the Jewish state? Zionists had differing ideas. Zionism itself was overwhelmingly secular but never antireligious. There was respect for believers and a readiness to accommodate their needs. Even groups on the left that were explicitly antireligious neither sought to deny others the right to worship nor sought to impose their antireligious views on the state.

Jewish national identity is so entwined with Judaism that the question of religion in the state remains complex. For example, the holiday of Hanukkah celebrates the Jewish national victory over a Greek-Syrian dynasty and the reestablishment of ancient Israel's independence, but religious observance centers on divine intervention: a menorah (candelabrum) in the Temple burned for eight days on one day's worth of oil.

Thereafter, the menorah became a central Jewish symbol and is indeed a symbol for the State of Israel. So while Hanukkah was given religious significance by the pious, it is viewed more in terms of its historical national significance in state schools and in the society in general.

The story of Purim, recalling the survival of the Jews in the face of a planned genocide in ancient Iran, never mentions the existence or intervention of a divine being; yet this, too, is a "religious" holiday celebrated by Orthodox and secular Jews alike.

Other holidays commemorate events of national significance—the exodus from Egypt, spring planting time, the harvest of the first tree fruits each autumn, the main harvest—in tandem with religious occurrences: the granting of the Torah and pilgrimages to the Temple. The historical and cultural experience of Jews stands in sharp contrast to that of Western European and North American societies, in which religion and nationality have often been at odds and have led to organized anticlerical movements and separation of church and state. For Jews, like most people in the Middle East, religious background is the main marker of national-ethnic identity.

Given the central interrelationship between Jewish nationhood and Jewish religion, David Ben-Gurion, one of Israel's founders, and leading rabbis worked out an agreement shortly after independence. According to this "status quo" arrangement, existing conditions governing state-religious and religious-secular affairs stay the same; they do not change. The plan also aimed to ensure that the religiously observant were not discriminated against in the new state.

The status quo structure defines both the authority of the religious sphere, headed by the two chief rabbis—one Ashkenazic and one Sephardic—and the procedures of the state. The

Rabbinate has authority over public religious affairs, including supervision of ritual slaughter of animals, designation of eating establishments as kosher (adhering to Jewish dietary laws), and control of courts dealing with matters of personal status and family law, such as marriage and divorce—a system inherited from the Ottomans and adopted by the British rulers.

The national rabbinic authority is run by the pro-Zionist Datim and not the Haredim, which enhances religious-state cooperation. The Haredim maintain their own, more stringent standards and limit their involvement with the state. In addition, the system excludes Reform and Conservative Jews, who did not exist in Israel at the time of the agreement. Struggles by the small Reform and Conservative groups have led to some official role for them, although the Rabbinate has opposed their involvement for religious reasons and out of self-interest.

For its part, the state sees that all public institutions serve only kosher food and keeps them closed on the Sabbath and on Jewish holidays. In areas with many religious residents—mainly parts of Jerusalem and Bnei Brak—some streets are closed to vehicular traffic on the Sabbath. The Ministry of Religious Affairs, which is always led by a member of the Knesset from a religious party, oversees matters affecting religion.

Yet those who want to circumvent religious rituals and observances can do so easily. All marriage is religious, but since any marriage abroad is recognized, those who want a civil marriage often take the short trip to Cyprus to get married. Stores selling non-kosher items are found in many places, and more and more stores are open on the Sabbath. There is no real state pressure to observe religious practices.

The precise balance of power on religious-secular questions shifts somewhat depending on the composition of government coalitions. In recent years, partly because of the large-scale immigration from the former Soviet Union, secular forces have gained in strength. An important exception is Jerusalem: secular inhabitants have tended to move away, and the religious population has grown proportionately larger.

The majority of Israelis, even those who are secular, consider the Jewish religion a necessary aspect of Israeli society. A small flow of individuals are always changing groups: secular to religious, religious to secular. All sides and subgroups know they will never gain every Jew's allegiance. The religious parties do not seek total power nor try to impose religious observances on the entire country; rather, they act as interest groups, defending their constituencies and obtaining jobs and funding for them.

Among one of the few elements of change has been the ability of Shas, as both a religious and a Sephardic party, to attract large numbers of adherents for its religiously flavored social institutions. Another trend has been the gradual acceptance of Zionism by those in the Haredi community who—depending on their specific group and leader—have undergone Israelization.

In any case, religion is an integral part of Israeli life, even in supposedly secular sectors of society. Not only does the arrangement between the Rabbinate and the state shape society, so does the fact that Israel is a Jewish state built on the foundation of 2,000 years of Jewish history. Zionism has further transformed traditional Jewish tenets into national values. Israelis who are secular may complain about Haredi power as excessive, but they have their own relationship to the historic belief system of the Jewish people.

Jewish Religious Life

The public's understanding of Israeli religiosity has been informed by a series of major studies, most significantly the 1997 Guttman Report, a comprehensive examination of Israeli religious attitudes and practices. Historically, religiosity was seen in terms of two mutually exclusive camps—religious and secular—with a sharply defined boundary between them. But surveys have found a wide variety in attitudes toward religion, ranging from totally nonobservant to very strictly observant.

The idea of a spectrum rather than two separate camps is now accepted as accurate. Aside from highly secular and fully observant, there are two other broad attitudes: predominantly secular people who observe some religious rituals—for example, they celebrate bar and bat mitzvahs; fast on the Day of Atonement, Yom Kippur; and hold a Passover seder—and traditionalists, often Mizrahim, who observe the religious laws selectively. Here, the classic example is to conduct the religious service at home for starting the Sabbath but then to watch television, thereby contravening the religious law that bars the turning on of electrical appliances. Such hybrid attitudes have become common.

The Guttman Report found that a majority of Israeli Jews expressed a commitment to Jewish continuity, celebrate major holidays in some manner, and perform lifecycle rituals to some degree. Such behavior owes as much or more to "identification with the Jewish people"—that is, the motivation is what might be called ethnic-national rather than theological. The report concludes that 93 percent of Israeli Jews observe at least Shabbat, *kashrut* (Jewish dietary laws), or Jewish holidays to some extent, even though one-fifth define themselves as completely nonreligious.

Although the largest group in Israel used to be described as secular, the report found that only 20 percent, mostly Ashkenazim, described themselves that way. The largest group, around 40 percent, saw themselves as "somewhat observant." Of this group, 70 percent were Mizrahi. Fourteen percent of Israeli Jews, mostly Ashkenazim, reported that they were "strictly observant," and an additional 24 percent said they were "observant to some extent."

The Guttman Report found that 70 to 80 percent of the Jewish population marks the Sabbath in some way, perhaps simply by lighting candles, saying the blessing over wine, or having a family meal. The percentage of the population that adheres to the prescriptions for that day—such as not driving a car, cooking, or using electricity—is much smaller. Shabbat observance is marked most often by carrying out rituals at home on Friday evening, by refraining from salaried work, by relaxing, and by spending Saturday with family, although the activities are not necessarily done in strict accordance with Jewish law.

Ashkenazic Jews are more likely to have an all-or-nothing approach toward ritual observance than are Mizrahi Jews, many of whom do not see a contradiction or hypocrisy in attending an Orthodox synagogue Saturday morning and a soccer match Saturday afternoon. But the new Israeli approach is to pick and choose which religious traditions to observe. This is not normative Judaism as it has existed historically. It is the transformation of religion into ethnic-national custom.

High numbers of Israeli Jews not only mark the Sabbath but observe the major holidays in some way. Nearly four-fifths of the population participates in a Passover seder, and over

70 percent light candles on Hanukkah and fast on Yom Kippur. Other holidays, such as Sukkot and Purim, are observed by a much smaller percentage as religious occasions, although Purim is a popular time for parties and costume wearing. Still, most Israeli Jews, even those who are totally nonobservant, indicate that participation in religious ceremonies related to lifecycle events (birth, coming of age, marriage, death) is important to them.

Sixty percent of Israeli Jews report belief in a divine being, including one-fifth of the nonobservant. About one-half of the Jewish population believes that God gave the Torah to Moses on Mount Sinai. One-third believe in the existence of life after death, an issue less defined and important in Jewish than in Christian theology. A large majority of Israeli Jews keep kosher to some degree, with 40 percent reporting that they observe these dietary laws strictly all the time.

In general, Mizrahi offspring tend to be less observant than their parents, whereas Ashkenazi offspring do not report a significant difference from their parents in degree of religious observance. Those going through each school system tend to remain loyal to views taught in the system in which they studied. Higher educational level correlates with less religiosity, a point reinforced by the fact that Haredim almost never seek a university education.

A telling anecdote about religion in Israel involves Yael Dayan, daughter of the former minister of defense, Moshe Dayan. A left-wing member of the Knesset, she was once photographed in a bathing suit on a beach on Yom Kippur, the holiest day of the Jewish year. For a few days, the photograph was the subject of a great deal of public discussion. The consensus was a national-ethnic interpretation: she was neither mocking religion nor making a secularist statement but simply marking the holiday in her own way.

Yet on Yom Kippur, Israel has its own secular customs, too. The country literally shuts down. Many people fast, although they do not necessarily spend the day in a synagogue. With no cars on the streets, tens of thousands of children take to skateboards and bicycles. By so doing, they are violating religious law and, at the same time, marking the day as special. Huge numbers of adults promenade down the middle of the main streets. Thus, for many Israelis, Yom Kippur is a unique national observance as well as a holiday celebrated in traditional ways. For those not fully observant, the Jewish religion has been transformed: it is partly about the human relationship to the divine but also partly about national custom and culture.

Jewish Intra-Religious Tensions

Tensions between those with different levels of religiosity are generally minimal. Still, a number of fault lines exist, mainly between the most secular and the most Orthodox, the Haredim. Secular Jews stereotype those most religious, saying that they shirk their duties as citizens by not serving in the military, that they depend on welfare rather than work, and that they constantly seek to increase their power and restrict the rights of the secular. A further charge by left-wing Ashkenazim against both Datim (the Modern Orthodox) and the Haredim is that they are right-wing and advocate policies damaging to the country. For the religious, to identify the secular as secular, and thus not faithful to religious tradition, is a sufficient criticism.

An interesting finding of the Guttman Report was that the more observant express a greater preference for a socially homogeneous environment than the secular do, but in reality, the more observant—composing the smaller group—must interact more with less observant people than do secular people, who have less contact with those different from themselves. In fact, the most isolated group, religiously speaking, consists of Ashkenazic nonobservant Jews, not Haredi Jews.

A surprisingly high number of Israeli Jews, 67 percent of the total Jewish population, say they tend to favor or definitely favor separation of religion and state. Thirty-nine percent support establishing civil marriage, although half of these report that they themselves would still opt for a religious ceremony. On the other side, 40 percent of the population oppose civil marriage. Support divides somewhat along ethnic lines: Mizrahim are more likely than Ashkenazim to want to maintain the status quo, and immigrants from the former Soviet Union prefer to reduce the current level of religion in public life.

Two-thirds of Israeli Jews believe that shopping malls and places of entertainment should be permitted to be open on the Sabbath. Haredim and most Datim believe they should remain closed. A large majority, including the totally nonobservant, agree, however, that food in public places should be kosher. But they object to giving kashrut certificates only to places that are closed on the Sabbath. Thus, the preference is for a moderate level of public observance of Sabbath laws.

This attitude would seem to indicate support for the Reform and Conservative religious movements. Yet few would consider joining them. While Israelis generally favor equal status for non-Orthodox and Orthodox rabbis, most relatively secular Israeli Jews prefer individual observance to institutionalization of religious practices.

The most emotional issue causing secular-religious (or, more accurately, secular-Haredi) tension has been army service. Haredi men studying full-time in religious seminaries are exempt from military duty, a provision originally set up after the Holocaust, when so many rabbis and religious teachers had been murdered in Europe that few remained alive. Over the decades, however, this privilege of military exemption has been extended to almost all Haredi men.

Many non-Haredim feel this is unfair, though they also admit that most Haredim do not have the skills to make a valuable contribution to the army. Still, 90 percent of Israeli Jews— and 59 percent of the most observant polled—believe that Haredi men should be required to serve, and 70–80 percent support the recruitment of religious women to the army or to national service. In contrast, all Dati men tend to serve, and they often volunteer for combat units.

Despite controversies over the role of religion in public life, the frustration that many feel with Orthodox domination of the Rabbinate, Haredi demands, and the conflict over political power in Jerusalem, Israeli society is not at present polarized between religious and secular. Given the lack of emphasis on making changes and the lack of movements on either side dedicated to doing so, the status quo is likely to remain in place.

Haredim ("Ultra-Orthodox")

The word *Haredim* means "those in awe or fear of divine power." Haredim are often misleadingly called "ultra-Orthodox" in English, even though in Judaism a person either is or is not Orthodox; no extra activities make one Jew more religiously observant than another Jew. In other words, Haredim cannot claim more religious legitimacy than other Orthodox groups, and, equally, their religious practices cannot be defined as excessive. They merely express a specific interpretation of Jewish law and life.

The Haredi response to modernity, as mentioned earlier, was based on the Talmudic concept of "building a fence" around the Torah—that is, permitting the minimum possible intrusion of change. Haredim are characterized by a strict interpretation of Jewish law and a rejection of secular culture.

It is easy to believe—and the Haredim themselves say—that they are a totally static community. But this image is by no means completely true. They use modern technology—computers, cell phones, and radios—albeit with restrictions (for example, avoiding television and never going to see films in theaters). Viewing Hebrew as a holy language, many groups have in the past preferred to use Yiddish among themselves for everyday use. Yet Haredim in Israel increasingly speak Hebrew.

Originally, most Haredim rejected the idea of a Jewish state, believing that Jews should not have sovereignty until the Messiah arrives. Yet they consider it a major *mitzvah* (good deed) to live in the Land of Israel. In addition, some religious commandments can be fulfilled only by those dwelling there. Nonobservant Israeli Jews widely believe that all Haredim share this rejection of Zionism, but in fact many in Haredi society do support the state, and their number has increased over time.

Haredim represent about 7 percent of Israel's population and have an average of 6.5 children per family—they follow the commandment to be fruitful and multiply. They tend to live in concentrated communities, many in the Jerusalem neighborhoods of Mea Shearim, Geula, and Sanhedria, as well as in the cities of Bnei Brak and Kiryat Sefer. Wealthy Haredim, including many immigrants from North America and France, live in Ramat Bet Shemesh and Har Nof, among other select places. Haredi communities produce many specialized products, from publications to food and religious items.

They also wear distinctive clothing. Men wear black to mourn the destruction of the Temple: black suits with white shirts, black hats, and *tzitzit* (religiously mandated fringes worn on a vest or another garment). Many wear long sidelocks in accordance with an interpretation of the commandment not to harvest the corners of fields, originally an injunction to charity. The women wear long skirts and long-sleeved blouses in muted colors, and married women cover their hair with hats or headscarves or wear wigs.

Women's place in Haredi society is complicated. On one hand, the community takes very seriously the notion of gender segregation and different gender roles. The traditional role for Haredi women is as wife and mother. They do not have public religious roles and are excluded from yeshivot, which limits their religious education. But women are often the main breadwinners in Haredi society and may achieve a level of practical education and vocational training that men, who focus on religious education, do not. Since the 1990s, vocational schools specifically geared to Haredim have proliferated, some for women and some for men who cannot or do not want to spend years studying in a yeshiva.

The precise cut of a Haredi person's clothing, especially men's, identifies the group to which he or she belongs. There are two main groupings: the Hasidim, who often take a more mystical approach to religion and who follow a rebbe—a rabbi who is the community's charismatic

The Haredi neighborhood of Mea Shearim, Jerusalem. (Getty Images / Image Bank.)

leader, a position attained by inheritance—and the Mitnagdim ("opponents" of Hasidism), who stress a scholarly approach to the law.

Each Hasidic group has a somewhat different set of customs and views. For example, the Habad (Lubavitcher) movement is Zionist and is the only Hasidic group that devotes a great deal of effort to encouraging greater religiosity among non-Orthodox Jews. The Satmar are anti-Zionist because they believe that only the Messiah can return the Jews to Israel, and they object to the country's not being governed by religious law. The overall trend, however, is toward a greater degree of identification and legitimacy being accorded to the State of Israel, with most groups moving from anti-Zionism to non-Zionism and from non-Zionism to Zionism.

Indeed, the Guttman Report found that more Haredim define themselves as Zionist than as non-Zionist. Only a tiny fringe group actively campaigns against Israel's existence as a Jewish state. The best-known Orthodox anti-Zionist organization is the Neturei Karta.

The course of the main Haredi political party, Agudat Israel, reflects these trends. Before 1948, its leaders spoke out against establishing a Jewish state. Once Israel was established, the speeches discontinued, but not until the 1970s did Aguda Israel become willing to join the government. Today its members take government posts and extend de facto recognition to the state. Incentives for cooperation are obtaining jobs and funds from the government. Besides, Haredim have no illusions as to what their fate would be if Israel were to be destroyed by its enemies.

Historically, Haredim were distinctly Ashkenazim with a European background. Then very religious Mizrahim—Jews from the Middle East and North Africa—joined Haredi (Mitnagdim) yeshivot and copied their teachers' clothing and ideas. With the rise of the Shas movement, Mizrahim developed their own distinct interpretation of the Haredi lifestyle and views. The Mizrahi Haredi community is strongly Zionist.

In Europe, Haredi men followed a full range of vocations, specializing in unskilled and semi-skilled work and craftwork because of their rejection of secular education. After the destruction of the great European yeshivot during the Holocaust, the new State of Israel agreed to subsidize those Haredi men studying to receive rabbinical ordination. The number of such students grew to unexpected levels over the years. Continued study brings higher status within the community, along with exemption from military service, although a few Haredim have always entered the army.

Haredim have accepted lower living standards for their larger families as the price of spiritual elevation. Thus, Haredim, both women and men, are underemployed in the labor force. All families with children receive allowances from the National Insurance Institute. For many years, the addition of each child brought the family an ever-higher allowance, a policy especially benefiting the Haredim, but in 2009 this policy ended; instead, the family receives an equal payment per child regardless of family size.

Since the community has outgrown both welfare payments and contributions from wealthy Haredim, more have to engage in paid work, and the community has slowly accepted the necessity. The increase in vocational schools catering to Haredim is a response. In 2006, more than half of Haredi men were gainfully employed—60 percent—as were 65 percent of Haredi women, mainly in the fields of sales, technology, diamonds, and education.

With employment, Haredim are becoming more involved in transportation, real estate, food, technology, sales, and education. Their overall living standard is on the rise. Increased contact with the world of work has not led to secularization, but it has produced more interaction with mainstream society and thus, for many, a stronger sense of having an Israeli identity.

Israelis do not question the right of Haredim to live as they please—except for the matter of army service. Some Israelis do, however, claim that the Haredim are trying to extend their influence to dictate how others must act. This is sometimes true, sometimes not. To charges of "religious coercion," the Haredim generally give the same response: that they have no serious ambition to transform Israeli society but are concerned—sometimes to a degree bordering on paranoia, fueled by false rumors—that Israeli society seeks to transform them. For example, everyone in Haredi neighborhoods follows a dress code, which emphasizes modesty for women. Billboards implore women to dress appropriately. But can Haredim demand that those passing through their neighborhoods follow the same standards? In Mea Shearim, a stronghold of the most extreme Haredi groups, there is sporadic harassment of non-Haredi women who pass through wearing "immodest" clothing. And Haredim periodically throw rocks at cars passing through their neighborhoods on Shabbat.

Although Haredim have sometimes become involved in broader questions—including those relating to peace, conflict, and the territories captured in 1967—they usually focus on issues closer to home. Should a parking lot or road near their neighborhood be open on Shabbat? Is an archaeological dig disturbing an ancient Jewish graveyard? Should some gender-segregated buses run to and through their neighborhoods?

The single most contentious issue has been military service, since Haredi behavior in this matter directly affects the lives of other Israelis. Haredi refusal to serve the mandatory three years (for men), now reduced to twenty-eight months, or the mandatory two years (for women), now reduced to eighteen months, directly increases the burden on everyone else. After all, when David Ben-Gurion gave an exemption for those learning in yeshivot, only 400 Haredi men were affected. Today, this regulation provides more than 30,000 such exemptions. In theory, these can be obtained only by full-time students who are not earning money, but it is not difficult for individuals to ask schools to provide them with false certification, which also makes them qualified for special stipends.

At the same time, this regulation is in some ways counterproductive for Haredim, because it forces the men not to work in order to keep their exemption. The rationale often used by Haredim is that by praying and maintaining the community of scholars, the students are preserving Israel by pleasing the divine being. Another reason given is their genuine fear that military service would corrupt those enlisted, drawing them away from their religious lifestyle. Army standards of religious observance and kashrut are set for Datim, at a level that does not satisfy Haredi demands.

Numerous commissions have examined ways to reform conscription, and many proposals have been made. In 1999, a special IDF unit, Netzah Yehuda, was created to conform to the demands of a Haredi lifestyle; between 1999 and 2007, about 2,000 men participated. In 2002, the Knesset passed the Tal Law to change the status quo. The law demands that Haredi men decide at age twenty-three whether to stay in the yeshiva—in which case they would receive a formal exemption and would be obliged to continue learning for a long period of time—or to perform a truncated military or national service. This law was never implemented.

Studies show that the younger generation of Haredim are less opposed to military service than their elders, although there is still social pressure against enlisting. Haredim will probably not enter the IDF en masse as long as their rabbis do not approve, and the rabbis' attitude, and their followers' respect for their rabbis' opinion, is unlikely to change. The issue became less pressing when immigration from the former Soviet Union augmented the draft pool. The IDF could be pickier about whom it accepted, and its need for highly trained technical personnel also reduced its interest in drafting soldiers who could not make this contribution.

Over the years, a number of small parties have advocated opposing the religious parties and increasing the secular space in society. Most prominent among them was the former Shinui Party, headed by the late Tommy Lapid, and the Yisrael Beiteinu, led by Avigdor Lieberman, which, not by coincidence, has Russian immigrants as its main constituents. Neither has made much difference in the status quo.

Datim (Modern Orthodox)

When European Jews faced the onset of modernity in the nineteenth century, a large group remained religiously observant but took up the challenge of combining a largely traditional practice of Judaism with secular education, clothing, and ideas. This movement coalesced into a pro-Zionist movement, which, after Israel was established, became the National Religious Party. These adaptive traditional Jews are called Datim ("religious"), or, in the English-speaking world, Modern Orthodox.

Unlike Haredim, the Datim participate fully in mainstream culture and Israeli national identity. This group makes up roughly 11 percent of Israel's Jewish population. Datim, like Haredim, accept the primacy of the Torah but are open to more flexible interpretations, a stance very much in line with the Jewish religion in past centuries. As both Zionist and religious, Datim view Israel as the fulfillment of the deity's plan, an idea increasingly influenced after the 1967 war by the ideas of Rabbi Abraham Isaac Kook, Israel's first chief rabbi.

Most Datim live in cities, in their own or mixed-religious neighborhoods, or in one of a few Dati kibbutzim. Dati men combine religious with secular study. Dati children are educated in the national-religious school system, participate in the Bnei Akiva youth movement, and attend the Dati-run Bar-Ilan University. Datim dress like nonreligious Israelis for the most part, but some women, among Datim whose beliefs are closer to Haredi beliefs, wear long skirts, and married Dati women may cover their hair with hats or scarves (but typically not wigs). Dati men wear a knitted *kippa* (skullcap), usually with a colorful design.

Another key difference from the Haredim is that Dati men go into the army to perform their mandatory military service, and the women often perform their regular military service or national service of another sort. There are also special programs, called *hesder yeshivot*, in which young men combine Torah study with army service.

The National Religious Party participated in every coalition government from 1948 to 1992. Until 1981, the party held twelve Knesset seats, but with the establishment of other parties that appealed to Mizrahi voters—mainly conservative ones—their representation shrank that year to just six seats, and it fell further until in 2006 it won only three seats, and it won those only by forming a joint list with the National Union Party. In 2009, when the party joined other factions and was renamed the Jewish Home Party, it still won only three seats.

A key reason for party's decline was its turn toward single-issue politics rather than focusing on broader communal interests. In the 1970s, it became involved, in particular, with the establishment of Jewish settlements in the West Bank. Gush Emunim (literally, "bloc of the believers") was founded in 1974. Extrapolating from previously held ideas, its members—many of them Datim—believed that keeping control over the territories that Israel captured in 1967 and settling them would accelerate the coming of the Messiah.

Many Israelis came to associate the Dati community politically with right-wing extremists, including such figures as Baruch Goldstein, who murdered Muslims in a Hebron mosque in 1994, and Yigal Amir, who assassinated Prime Minister Yitzhak Rabin in 1995. The Israeli government's decision in 2004 to withdraw unilaterally from the Gaza Strip required the removal of the 8,000 Jews who had settled there, many of them Datim. Dati activists organized protests, with the color orange as their symbol.

Although many Datim were not militant supporters of the settlement movement, or at least did not focus on settlement, this single-issue obsession destroyed the National Religious Party and seriously damaged the Dati community's interests. The group's votes fragmented and the

A rally held in the western Negev town of Sderot against the Israeli government's plan for unilateral withdrawal from the Gaza Strip, August 2005. (Getty Images / Image Bank.)

party collapsed. Dati voters signed on with a variety of parties across the spectrum. The more dovish supported the tiny Meimad Party, while many of the leaders joined with right-wing secularists to form the small National Union and Jewish Home parties.

All these political passions and splits notwithstanding the Datim continued to make up a community with a full range of social needs and multiple interests. Many make a conscious attempt to show their dedication to the country as a whole. Datim play an ever larger role in the army, with their proportion among combat units' officers steadily increasing. Datim are also involved in all aspects of society, including academia, science, and high technology.

Non-Orthodox Judaism

The Jewish Reform and Conservative movements were relatively late in establishing themselves in Israel, remain very small there—less than 1 percent of the Jewish population are adherents—and are still generally seen as non-Israeli approaches to religion that have merely accompanied some Western immigrants from their native countries. Shlomo Avineri made a famous statement on this issue when he said, "The synagogue I don't go to is Orthodox." In other words, nonreligious Israelis perceive religious Judaism of either the Haredi or Dati variety as normative.

In Israel, the Conservative movement runs a number of TALI schools (TALI is the Hebrew acronym for "Enriched Jewish Studies"). They are somewhat equivalent to a North American Jewish day school, and their curriculum is somewhere between that of the national religious schools and the secular state schools. In Israel, the movement has more than fifty congregations.

The Reform movement in Israel began with the founding of the Leo Baeck school in Haifa in 1939. The first modern Reform synagogue in Israel, the Harel synagogue in Jerusalem, was founded in 1958, and the Israel Movement for Progressive Judaism, a grouping of non-Orthodox synagogues, was incorporated as a movement in 1971. Today the movement comprises twenty-eight congregations, two kibbutzim, and a communal settlement.

Both the Reform and the Conservative movements provide alternatives to Orthodox services. They each have their own *beit din*s (religious courts) for conversions, although the state does not accept the conversions they supervise within Israel for immigration or personal status purposes. Advocates from these two groups argue that their version of Judaism is well suited to non-Orthodox Israelis looking for a level of observance outside a total commitment to Orthodoxy. They have also tried to appeal to Russian-speaking immigrants. But few native-born Israelis show enthusiasm, since they already live in a Jewish environment, speak Hebrew, and receive basic Jewish education in school.

WOMEN IN SOCIETY

In Israel, the formal acceptance of women's status as equal to men's dates back to the pre-state years, when socialist ideals of equality and a challenging new environment provided ample opportunity for women to play important roles in working and fighting. Women are and always have been equal in Israeli doctrine. The pioneering woman and the woman warrior are staple historical images.

Israel has offered paid maternity leave and affordable child care services since the 1950s. But Israel also lagged behind many Western countries in ensuring women's equal status during the latter decades of the twentieth century. Once the myth that gender equality had already been achieved was successfully challenged in the 1970s and 1980s, legislation was passed that has helped women take advantage of the same opportunities as men.

Still, equality between the sexes varies depending on the population sector, with Arab women playing much more traditional roles, according to their community's norms, than Jewish women and being almost completely absent from the political scene. Among the Mizrahim and later the Ethiopian immigrants, women also filled more traditional roles, with concomitant lower education rates and lower workforce participation. Gaps between men and women, and between native-born women and immigrant women, have declined over time.

Elements of sexism are still present in Israeli society, especially in the workplace. In addition, while women's overall participation in the workforce is high, more women than men work part-time and in lower-paying jobs. Domestic abuse is a problem on a par with that in other Western societies, and several shelters exist to help victims. There is also illicit sex trafficking, although Israeli authorities are becoming stricter about punishing those involved, including clients.

Some challenges to full equality between the sexes in the society stem from the patriarchal nature of both traditional Judaism and Islam given the lack of separation between religion and state. Religious courts have jurisdiction over personal status matters for each religious community. This means that women often find themselves at a disadvantage in cases of divorce and inheritance, although women have won the right to be members of regional religious councils. Furthermore, despite the proclamation of equality in the Declaration of Independence, religious parties were able to block the explicit mention of gender equality in the Basic Law on Human Dignity and Liberty—a part of Israel's constitutional legal framework—because they feared that it would interfere with matters under religious jurisdiction.

Numerous women's organizations provide services and advocate for a variety of issues of concern to women and society at large. Successful lobbying has brought laws that assure women's representation on the boards of public institutions; stipulate equal pay for equal work; prohibit sexual harassment in the workplace; and improve conditions for rape victims at trials. Women are represented in politics, the military, the workforce, and the cultural world.

In 1897, at the First Zionist Congress, 17 women were present among the 200 participants; most were accompanying their husbands. One exception was Rosa Sonneschein, a Hungarian-born U.S. citizen who came as a representative for *The American Jewess*, a journal she founded and published. Women were given the right to vote in the Zionist movement in 1900, at the Third Zionist Congress.

In the Second Aliya, 1904–1913, women accounted for 17 percent of the mainly Russian immigrants. Many of them were committed to challenging traditional female roles by doing hard physical labor. By the standards of the day, they were well educated, and their socialist doctrine emphasized equality between the sexes. A dynamic example was Manya Shohat, who came from a wealthy, educated family and had been a Socialist Revolutionary Party member in Russia dedicated to overthrowing the tsarist regime.

Shohat's brother wrote her from the Land of Israel claiming to be ill and asking that she come to help him. Actually, he was trying to save her life, since he was sure that her revolutionary activities would lead to her execution. After she came to Israel, Shohat, who had studied the Talmud and was fluent in Hebrew, helped found the first Jewish agricultural workers' collective at Sejera in the Galilee. There, women undertook many of the same jobs as men, including plowing and doing guard duty. Later, Shohat smuggled in arms, was arrested by the Ottoman authorities, and was sent into exile. After World War I, she returned and continued her pioneering activities.

Other women, however, had different experiences. The kibbutz system promised to liberate women from the yoke of domestic responsibilities. Children were to be raised communally in special children's houses. All meals were to be prepared communally with the work shared by everyone so that women did not have to do it all. Even laundry was done communally.

Despite socialist ideas of equality, women were passed over for the most important, high-status jobs, such as being guards, and were often shunted to the communal kitchens and laundries. As one pioneer woman, Zippora Bar-Droma, put it, while men "were 'building the country,'" women "would take care of everyday matters of the 'builders of the country.'" In a 1975 book, *Women in the Kibbutz*, anthropologists Lionel Tiger and Joseph Shepher concluded that the majority of women were cooking, cleaning, and child-rearing while men were harvesting, planting, guarding, and building. Women composed only 14 percent of those at the highest level of kibbutz management.

In 1911, Hannah Meisel, an agronomist from Russia, established the first women's training farm for agricultural workers. Other training farms followed, where women learned about livestock, dairy, and vegetable farming until the British authorities closed them after World War I. Although many men ridiculed these communes, and they never attracted large numbers of students, their graduates used their new skills.

The women of the Third Aliya, 1919 to 1923, from Eastern Europe, made up almost 20 percent of the total. Included among them were some who had trained on model farms in Europe where they had successfully insisted that men help in the kitchen. These new immigrants demanded road-building work and became 300 of the 3,000 workers in those jobs, although some did cooking, cleaning, and nursing.

In 1920, women gained the right to vote in elections for the Yishuv's decision-making body. The next year, forty-three women established the Working Women's Movement, which provided vocational courses for women. By 1937, some of them held jobs as construction workers, painters, farmworkers, and day laborers.

Women were also involved in self-defense activities in the Haganah, the Yishuv's paramilitary organization while Palestine was a British mandate. From 1936 to 1939, hundreds of women guarded roads during the Arab rioting. In 1941, the Haganah created the Palmach, a full-time elite military unit. Although women were not supposed to be in it, one commander assembled a small group of women in Jerusalem and taught them how to use weapons. During World War II, about 9,000 women joined the British army, serving as radio and radar operators, parachute inspectors, and truck or ambulance drivers. A few, most famously Hannah Senesh, parachuted behind enemy lines in Europe.

Women worked in the illegal immigration movement and fought during the War of Independence. They composed about 20 percent of the membership of military organizations—mainly in supply, communications, and medical aid. Five women commanded combat units, and thirty-three were killed in battle during the war.

Israel's Declaration of Independence assured all female citizens that they could vote and run for office. In fact, Israel was the first country in the Middle East that gave Arab women the right to vote. In the first Knesset, elected in 1949, there were eleven women lawmakers, about 10 percent of the total.

Women also participated in the army after Israel became a state. Upon reaching age eighteen, all Jewish women were drafted for twenty-four months. Religious and married women, as well as all those with children, were exempt. Prime Minister Ben-Gurion stated, "The army is the supreme symbol of duty, and as long as women are not equal to men in performing this duty, they have not yet obtained true equality [and] . . . the character of the community will be distorted."

Still, women did not achieve any semblance of equality with men in the military. For many years the army had a policy of avoiding endangerment to women's lives; their death or capture, especially given the serious likelihood of rape, would be demoralizing, it was believed. As a result, more than half of all military job specialties were long closed to women, a higher percentage even than in the U.S. Army. Most women served in administrative and clerical jobs. Since a successful army career was often the basis for obtaining important jobs later in civilian life, the disparity in military jobs denied women this advantage.

In 1951, Rachel Kagan, a member of the first Knesset and one of the two women to sign the Declaration of Independence—along with Golda Meir—sponsored the Equal Rights for Women Act. It called for gender equality before the law, including the right to sign contracts, own property, and bring lawsuits. In her initial draft of the legislation, Kagan included a provision for civil marriage and divorce. David Ben-Gurion told Kagan that he could not support that provision because of his promise to give the Rabbinate control over those personal status issues. The bill passed without that provision, but Kagan voted against it in protest.

Under Jewish religious law, women cannot be rabbis or witnesses at weddings, but a woman is most vulnerable when divorce occurs. The man must give a *get* (the divorce document) to the woman, who needs this paper in order to remarry. Sometimes men withhold this document to make the wife forgo financial support or even child custody. If the husband cannot be found or he is mentally incapacitated, a get cannot be provided. The only way for a woman to obtain a divorce in such cases is to have the marriage dissolved by the rabbinical courts. But all the judges are men, and women are not allowed to give evidence. On the other hand, a man whose wife does not accept the get—because she is unwilling, missing, or mentally ill—can obtain a divorce and remarry with permission from 100 rabbis, a difficult but not impossible process.

To address the double standard, at least in part, legislation was passed in the late 1990s enabling rabbinical courts to punish men who refused to give their wives gets by canceling their drivers' licenses, passports, and credit cards or even sending them to jail. But women in such situations wait an average of three and a half years to get a divorce and sometimes as long as ten years. One source estimated the number of such cases at 10,000 in 2003, although according to a rabbinical court statement in 2007, the annual number of such cases is less than seventy.

The second woman to sign the Declaration of Independence was Golda Meir, who, in 1969, became the third woman in the twentieth century to be an elected national leader and the first to do so without ties to a famous father or husband. Among her earlier posts were ambassador to Russia, minister of labor, and foreign minister.

Israel's modern feminist movement began with two Israelis who had emigrated from the United States and were then teaching at the University of Haifa, Marcia Freedman and Marilyn Safir. They started courses on women's issues and opened the first day-care center on campus. A series of other firsts followed—a women's bookstore, a feminist conference in Israel, a shelter for battered women, and women's magazines.

In 1973, feminist activists joined forces with Shulamit Aloni, who had fought and been captured in the War of Independence and who was later a Labor Party Knesset and cabinet member. She was a founder of the Citizens' Rights Movement, a political party that sought civil marriage and divorce in Israel, among other things. When Freedman and Aloni were elected to the Knesset, they pushed issues of importance to women's activists, including legal abortion and awareness of domestic violence.

In 1985, Alice Shalvi, a Dati professor of English at Hebrew University, became chair of the Women's Lobby, an umbrella organization for feminist activity in the country. In 1997, the group became the Israel Women's Network (IWN), the central nongovernmental group lobbying for women's rights.

Some of the greatest gains for Israeli women have been made through the Supreme Court. In 1988, the court agreed that women could participate in choosing the chief rabbis of cities and could run as candidates for religious councils. The court also ruled in 1995 in favor of Alice Miller, a licensed pilot who wanted to serve as such in the air force. Although Miller failed the course, she laid the foundation for Roni Zuckerman to become the first woman fighter pilot in 2001. The air force also has women navigators, transport pilots, and helicopter pilots. In 2007, a woman became the air force's first woman deputy squadron commander.

By 2005, women were permitted to serve in 85 percent of all positions in the military, compared to 73 percent a decade earlier, and 56 percent twenty years earlier. By 2005 there were 450 women in combat units. The following year, Keren Tendler, who died when a helicopter was shot down over Lebanon, became the first woman killed in combat service since the War of Independence. Only 2.5 percent of women soldiers are in combat units, however. By 2007, there were three female brigadier generals and twenty colonels.

With the rise in opportunities, Israeli women have also advanced politically. In 1992, a group of women Knesset members started the Committee on the Status of Women with both male and female members to promote women's issues and increase the number of women in the Knesset. In 2005, the committee successfully supported legislation that gave additional government funding to political parties whose Knesset delegations were more than 30 percent female.

Nevertheless, only 17 members of the 120-member Knesset elected in 2003 were women. That number fell by one in the 2006 elections, although that year Dahlia Yitzhak became the first woman speaker of the Knesset. She also served as acting president when Moshe Katsav was forced to resign following a sexual harassment scandal. In the 2009 election, with a woman, Foreign Minister Tzipi Livni, leading the Kadima Party ticket as its candidate for prime minister, 21 women were elected to the Knesset.

Women are also underrepresented in business leadership positions. A 2006 survey by Dun and Bradstreet found that while 46 percent of the working population consisted of women, they were only 2.5 percent of those serving on boards of Israeli companies. The same report found that women were only 6.6 percent of all heads of companies, 11.8 percent of senior vice presidents, and 14 percent in all senior management positions. Nevertheless, Israel's wealthiest citizen is a woman. Shari Arison, controlling stockholder of Bank Hapoalim, Israel's largest bank, and of the nation's largest construction company is the richest woman in the Middle East and, in 2007, was the only woman among the Middle East's top twenty richest people.

Israeli women have been protected in the workplace by the Equal Employment Opportunities Law, passed in 1988, which made illegal all forms of discrimination in the workplace on the basis of gender, marital status, and parenthood. The Israeli Prevention of Sexual Harassment Law was passed in 1998 protecting victims of this crime. Since then, Israel has had several sexual harassment scandals reaching into the highest levels of government. Minister of Justice Haim Ramon was forced to resign in 2006 after kissing a woman soldier against her will. Not long afterward, Israel's president, Moshe Katsav, was forced to resign after being charged with rape and sexual harassment of several women, crimes for which he was convicted.

By 2009, several women were in top positions in Israeli society: six of the twelve Supreme Court justices in Israel were women, including the Supreme Court president, Dorit Beinisch; Livni was head of a major political party; and Yitzhak was Knesset speaker. Still, Jewish women in Israel will continue to struggle against discrimination in those areas controlled by religious authorities, especially in matters of divorce.

GAY AND LESBIAN ISSUES

Despite the presence and influence of conservative religious and ethnic minorities, Israel is a very tolerant society with regard to sexual minorities. There was never a taboo against gays serving in the military, and the few restrictions that did exist were erased by legislation in the 1990s. Tacit acceptance notwithstanding, for many years homosexuality was not really discussed, and many gays and lesbians found it difficult to come out because of the macho culture and the emphasis on family. Gay rights began to be part of the national discourse in the 1980s. The first legal victory came in 1988 with the repeal of a sodomy law. Although religious parties oppose homosexuality, the Knesset vote was arranged for a time when they would not be present, and the repeal passed with little opposition or attention.

Legal and judicial victories for gay rights continued in the early 1990s, with an amendment to the Equal Workplace Opportunities Law outlawing discrimination on the basis of sexual orientation and a Supreme Court ruling that the Israeli airline El Al must offer gay partners of its employees the same benefits it offers spouses. More recently, gay couples who marry abroad have been permitted to register as married with the Interior Ministry to receive benefits. Gay couples are also permitted to adopt children.

Gay Pride participants mingle with IDF soldiers in Jerusalem's Gay Pride Parade, June 2009. (Getty Images / Image Bank.)

Part of the reason for these legal successes is that the issue is not associated with any particular political stance, aside from religion. The fact that religious parties are opposed actually helps gay rights activists win support, since many secular Israelis who might not otherwise care about the issue view gay rights as another battlefield against the religious.

In 1998 an Israeli transsexual, Dana International, whose family originally came from Yemen, became a national hero after winning the Eurovision song contest and hosted the 1999 contest held in Jerusalem. The mixing of influences in Israel is manifest in her choosing as the theme song in Jerusalem one based on the writings of a famous Yemenite Jewish religious poet.

The same year, the first openly lesbian politician, Michal Eden, was elected to the Tel Aviv City Council. Tel Aviv annually holds a gay pride parade and film festival. Gays and lesbians in the Arab and Haredi sectors have a harder time, as these groups are not tolerant of homosexuality, but there are organizations that seek to help people in these communities.

Haredi protesters demonstrate against gay parades in Jerusalem; at the 2005 parade, a Haredi man stabbed and wounded three marchers. Other protesters argue that the preferences of the majority and the holy nature of the city make gay parades there distasteful, even if they are acceptable in other cities. Activists, however, point out that the parade does not go through Haredi neighborhoods, and the annual celebration continues.

THE MILITARY

Israel's army, the Israel Defense Forces, has three defining characteristics. First, it was designed as a people's army modeled after that of Switzerland. This means a relatively small standing army, a mandatory draft, and a large reserve force—whose members can be called back to active duty when necessary. This model was also chosen in the belief that near-universal service would weld the country's people together, develop the virtues of service to society, and help build the nation.

Compulsory military service for most segments of Israeli society is thus understood not only as a security requirement but also as fulfillment of the duty of citizens to share in national defense. This dynamic means that participation in the army creates solidarity, contributes to a shared education, and produces a melting pot effect that spreads to the country's diverse groups. Yet the demands of modern warfare increasingly push toward the creation of a smaller, more highly trained professional army, a situation that somewhat conflicts with the people's army concept.

A second defining element of the Israeli military is a focus on quality over quantity. Priority is placed on the cultivation of highly educated, well-trained forces; good relations between officers and enlisted soldiers; officers trained to take the initiative; research and development; and the use of technological force multipliers. The IDF also tries, not always successfully, to avoid the old problem of fighting the last war by a frank evaluation of past mistakes and a strong consciousness of what is necessary for the next one. Precisely because soldiers are so vocal, have widely different political views, and can mobilize popular support, and also because so many former officers are in the Knesset and hold other political leadership positions, problems cannot be swept under the rug.

For example, even as the Lebanon War was still raging in 2006, IDF committees reevaluated tactics and equipment to recommend changes. Often what is involved is the need to make life and death choices about what to procure on the basis of available resources. Before the war, expensive upgrades of tank armor that let it repel rockets were not made, as funding went instead to planes designed to strike at Iranian missile sites if necessary.

But given Hizballah's possession of world-class antitank weapons supplied by Russia, this decision resulted in higher casualties for Israel. Afterward, the tanks were improved, and helicopter-fired projectiles were purchased so that tanks did not have to undertake risky missions against reinforced enemy positions.

The third factor characterizing the IDF is Israel's strategic doctrine. Given the state's small territory, the emphasis has been on successful deterrence, on persuading enemies that any attack would bring high costs and ultimate defeat for them. But if attack cannot be avoided, Israel's armed forces must be ready to go on the offensive and take the battle into the enemy's territory. In recent years, pursuing this strategy has involved the use of airpower, smart bombs, and unpiloted airplanes.

The Lebanon War showed the limits of this strategy, especially overdependence on the air force. Thus, the need to adjust to enemy tactics, to keep ahead in technological terms, to decide what weapons to build or acquire, and to determine what tactics and training are needed is a continuous process. Israel can simply not afford waste or incompetence in this area.

Israeli society is constantly evaluating how it stands regarding these three defining factors, which are always in flux. Clearly, the relationship of the military to society has changed in several respects since the 1973 Yom Kippur War. The media is more critical, the courts are more ready to investigate and order changes in tactics and rules of engagement, and soldiers' parents intervene far more to protect their children's interests.

Every Jewish, Druze, and Circassian Israeli citizen is drafted after his or her eighteenth birthday. Exemptions are granted to Haredi men and to both Haredi and Dati women. Some male Bedouins volunteer, as do some Jews from abroad. Entering a university or the workforce is put on hold until after army service, except the case of a few temporary deferments to study high technology, medicine, or other specialties. Psychological or medical problems are also sometimes a basis for exemption. Police, diplomats, and intelligence service personnel are permanently exempt from duty in the regular forces.

Despite a growing sense that not everyone does military service any more, it is still viewed as an honorable and important component of Israeli life. Though less so than in the past, a non-Haredi man still finds it embarrassing to admit that he did not serve, even though changing norms in Israeli society have somewhat eroded what was once seen as a sacred duty, with dishonor the price of failing to serve. Evading a reserve call-up is somewhat easier but involves letting down comrades-in-arms. Studies of armies have shown that the obligation one feels to fellow soldiers is one of the most powerful incentives to serve and show courage on the battlefield.

Historically, men did three years of mandatory service, although this has been lowered to twenty-eight months in recent years. Women's time in the army was traditionally two years but has been lowered to eighteen months. A four-year commitment is required of those who want to become officers and an even longer one for pilots. Any soldier has the opportunity to excel and become an officer.

Enlistees take physical and intelligence tests that result in two profiles, which help determine what kind of job they get. As long as an enlistee's profiles match the requirements of a requested position, there is a real chance of obtaining it. Nonetheless, entry into the top combat units is competitive. In 2009, seven recruits vied for each spot in the most popular unit, the Golani Brigade. At the end of 2010, the IDF reported that over 74 percent of those with adequate health profiles wanted to serve in combat units (compared to about 64 percent in previous years), the highest percentage in that decade.

Enlistees can specify the navy, air force, or ground forces, although they are not guaranteed their choice. It is a point of honor to serve in elite combat units. Conversely, people who work in offices are known as *jobniks*—the term is not complimentary. Despite many articles bemoaning declining volunteerism, the proportion of young people who sign up voluntarily remains quite high. In 2009, for example, 73 percent of eligible men enlisted; of those who did not, over 11 percent did not do so because of religious exemptions (Haredim mainly); 7 percent had medical or psychological exemptions; and 4 percent were abroad, temporarily or permanently. Only 4.5 percent of eligible men shirked the draft (and this number includes those with criminal records).

Religious women and Arabs have the option of signing up for national service instead of military service. This option is popular among religious women but not among Arabs. National service covers a broad range of opportunities, from working with the disabled or engaging in other social welfare activities, including helping new immigrants adjust. Immigrant men, but not women, who arrive when they are in their mid-twenties or older, may be required to perform a truncated military service, the main purpose of which is to familiarize them with the country and train them for reserve duty.

Most men leave the army at around age twenty-one, and women at age twenty, unless they opt to stay on for a military career. It has become customary for those who have finished their service to go on a long trip—generally to Asia or Latin America—to relax and see more of the world. Israelis generally enter college after either finishing their military service or completing such travels, or they may begin their careers. Since students are older and more mature as a result of their experiences, Israeli college students are generally more serious and dedicated to their studies than their younger counterparts in other countries.

After finishing their mandatory service, all men must go on reserve duty for a number of days per year (which varies based on their job in the military and the army's current needs) until the age of forty, officers until age forty-five, and a few until age forty-nine. Single women generally serve in the reserves until age twenty-four. In the past, around thirty days of reserve duty a year was roughly average, with thirty-nine days as the maximum, although the time spent could be extended in times of emergency.

Reserve duty places a heavy burden on civilians, even though, over the long term, the number of reserve days has tended to decline—for example, from 9.8 million days in 1988 to less than 6 million in 1995. It rises again during times of crisis, as it did in the 2000–2005 intifada.

In 1995, only one-third of reservists were called up, with about half serving less than ten days and only 2.3 percent serving longer than thirty-three days.

Increasingly, though, the burden is unequal. Those in combat and technological units spend more time doing service. In 2008, a law was passed limiting reserve duty during a three-year period to a maximum of fifty-four days for enlisted men, seventy days for noncommissioned officers, and eighty-four days for officers. Call-ups can be for a single day—to refresh soldiers' knowledge of equipment—or a short period for maneuvers, or for a longer period in case of war or the need to provide security in the territories captured in 1967.

The regular career army is small. The reserve system is designed to enable a quick call-up of a large portion of the population for emergencies while minimizing disruption of the economy and the lives of civilians during quieter times. Generally, reservists stay with the same unit for their whole career. This practice brings them together with friends and builds the personal bonds of trust and comradeship necessary for army units to work smoothly together. Reservists on active duty do not lose vacation days from work, and their employers must hold their jobs open for them. While on call-ups, however, reservists do not receive their normal salaries. According to a 2008 law, they are paid about $1,000 a month, a bit less than half of an average salary, plus they receive tax breaks.

Service branches and specialized units often have their own spirit and style. These include the artillery and the armored corps; the Galei Tzahal military radio station (which in peace-time provides regular news and music); the media office; the paratrooper units; the elite head-quarters' reconnaissance unit, which carries out covert missions and is considered the most select group of all; the elite navy frogmen; and many others.

The Nahal units bring together soldiers interested in forming an agricultural community that would continue after they leave the military. There is also a Nahal Haredi unit, a Nahal paratrooper unit, and the Hesder units for Datim, which combine combat training and religious study. The Tracking Unit is largely Bedouin; its members use skills developed to track stray animals from their herds to find infiltrators and terrorists.

Because Israel is a small country, much of its defense is carried out close to home, and many reservists or regular-duty soldiers have jobs that permit them to go home every night. Soldiers are supposed to carry their weapons even when off duty in case of terrorist attacks, although noncombat soldiers no longer take guns home with them. Soldiers do not normally patrol towns and cities, but seeing soldiers on leave, doing their jobs, or traveling is common, and they blend into daily life.

Despite the large social role played by Israel's citizen army, Israeli society is not militaristic. Indeed, it is more accurate to speak of a civilianized military in which soldiers feel free to speak their minds and discipline is rather informal. Soldiers may argue with their officers or with each other about specific orders.

Aside from the IDF, Israel's other security organizations include law enforcement and intelligence agencies. The main law enforcement agencies are the police and the Border Police. The police force fights crime and upholds public safety, as in other democratic countries. Israel is unique, however, in that the 30,000 civilian police officers are under national control. There are no municipal police.

Crime in Israel consists most commonly of burglary and car theft but also includes drug-selling, money-laundering, demands for protection money from small businesses, murder (most often a result of family conflicts), and human trafficking—largely from former Soviet areas—for prostitution. Crime rates remain lower than those in most Western countries. Hashish, and to a lesser extent marijuana and heroin, are smuggled mainly from Lebanon and Egypt. There has also been considerable concern over excessive drinking among young people and increased low-level violence in schools, two developments that contrast with past Israeli social patterns. Organized crime is small-scale and organized around a half-dozen families, notably the Alperons and the Abergils. The former family's leader, Ya'akov Alperon, was assassinated in a gang conflict in 2008 that led to retaliation against rival groups.

The Border Police (known as the Magav, for the Hebrew acronym) is the military branch of the police force. It operates in the West Bank, rural areas, and along the borders to deal with such difficult problems as counterterrorism and riot control. It has about 6,000 members, many of whom are Druze. People can opt to serve in the Border Police instead of the IDF for their mandatory service.

Israel's intelligence agencies include the Israel Security Agency (Shin Bet, or Shabak) and the Mossad. The Shabak is roughly comparable to the FBI in that it is responsible for Israel's internal security. It reports directly to the prime minister, and its duties include intelligence gathering, interrogation, and other counterterrorist activities; guarding against foreign spies; and protecting state officials, buildings, and embassies. It also works in the territories captured in 1967.

The Mossad, which also reports to the prime minister, is, like the CIA, responsible for foreign intelligence gathering. Its many successes have given it something of a legendary reputation. It has become internationally famous for daring operations that have played a major role in the country's strategic successes, although at times failed or controversial projects have created problems for Israel.

THE EDUCATION SYSTEM

The education system is another important institution that has shaped Israeli society. Like the army, it has traditionally been a place where values are passed on to the next generation. Education is mandatory from kindergarten through tenth grade and free through high school. The compulsory education law is strictly and widely enforced. An estimated 50 percent of three-year-olds and 75 percent of four-year-olds also attend preschools, which are often funded by local municipal councils.

Overall, expenditures on education account for about 8.5 percent of Israel's gross domestic product (GDP). Israel has five separate educational systems, all of which are funded through the Ministry of Education. One is the Arabic-language school system, although Arabic-speaking students can attend Hebrew-language schools if they wish. The four other systems are primarily for Jews:

- State: Though referred to as secular, state schools provide instruction on religious history and the Bible, taught with an emphasis on its historical aspects.

- State-religious: These schools, intended for Datim, have a full curriculum on both secular and religious subjects.
- Haredi: These schools emphasize religious subjects.
- Shas: The newest in Israel, these schools are a Mizrahi alternative in between the Haredi and the state-religious models with an emphasis on Sephardic Orthodox teachings.

Aside from all of these systems, small, extreme Haredi groups in Jerusalem seek to avoid even minimal contact with the state authorities by having their own schools that accept no state funding. There are also TALI schools run by the Masorti (Conservative) religious movement and state boarding schools for problem students and children from troubled homes, but there are virtually no private schools.

Most students attend state schools, which offer a general academic curriculum with some historically oriented religious study. The quality of these schools varies depending on the region and the socioeconomic status of the students. In Hebrew-language schools, students study English and Arabic as foreign languages. State-religious schools, which cater to the Datim, supplement academic studies with a more intense Jewish education focusing on the Bible, the Talmud, and Jewish law. Some private Dati yeshiva high schools offer more religious study and stricter observance than the state-religious schools do.

The Arab schools teach in Arabic and offer a curriculum that focuses on Islam, history, and culture. Haredi and Shas schools cater to the Haredi population and focus mainly on Jewish religious subjects. Unlike the other systems, Haredi and Shas schools are run independently of the Ministry of Education, but in order to receive government funding they must teach a basic core curriculum.

Although the Ministry of Education oversees the entire country's school systems, every municipality has its own education department overseen by the mayor and the local council, which are responsible for such local matters as selecting principals and approving specific educational programs—for example, spoken Arabic is taught at the elementary school level in Haifa's state schools although instruction in that language starts later elsewhere. This arrangement gives schools some autonomy from the ministry.

Specialty schools have increased in number, accompanying a rise in parent-funded and nongovernmental-organization-funded education. These schools receive some state funding, but parents have decided to supplement it. Some types of specialty schools include democratic schools (where students choose the curriculum) and Russian-language schools. In Tel Aviv, there are nature-oriented and performing arts schools, among others. While each school has a specific district, at the secondary level it is possible for students to apply to any nearby or specialized school.

Israeli education works on a matriculation system, and students in high school must pass examinations (*Bagrut*) in various subjects in order to matriculate at a university. Today, 85 percent of Israelis graduate from high school (although graduation is different from receiving a matriculation certificate, which is required to pursue higher education). More than 42 percent go on for further schooling.

Primary and secondary school education have been in somewhat of a crisis because of the low wages that teachers earn and their difficult working conditions. In 2007, the teachers' union held a long strike to protest their working conditions. Teachers are underpaid, but their union has also at times blocked educational reforms intended to improve the educational system. The problems include a classroom shortage, particularly but not exclusively in Arab schools, and an insufficient number of teachers, which leads to large and potentially unruly classes.

The general informality and aggressiveness of Israeli society extends to the classroom, where teachers sometimes have trouble controlling students. Low-level violence among students has also become an important concern in some schools. At the same time, though, there is a special emphasis on teaching students to get along well in social terms. An aspect of this effort is that elementary school classes are kept together over several years.

Many parents are concerned that standards have declined in recent years and that Israel has not done as well as it should compared to other countries in providing education. Test results have shown Israeli schools to be lagging behind in academic instruction.

Israel's universities maintain high standards and include several semipublic institutions: the Hebrew University of Jerusalem, Tel Aviv University, the Technion (a science and engineering institute), Ben Gurion University, Bar-Ilan University (a Dati institution), the University of Haifa, and the Open University (which engages in much adult education). The Weizmann Institute in Rehovot, a world-class research center for science, also grants graduate degrees.

Many colleges providing bachelor's degrees have sprung up around the country, usually as branches of universities. College tuition is kept low compared to the rate in other countries.

The Interdisciplinary Center (IDC) in Herzliya is the country's first private institution of higher education. Founded by faculty dissatisfied with other institutions who wanted to follow more innovative methods, it specializes in law, communications, high technology, international affairs, and business.

A large number of specialized research centers have developed, often affiliated with universities, focusing on wide-ranging topics from agriculture to religious studies to international affairs. Israel has become a leading country in Middle East studies and counterterrorism studies. The quality of the faculty is generally high.

Still, the university system has faced problems. Hebrew and Tel Aviv Universities have had major budgetary deficits due to overexpansion and the general international economic downturn, since donations from foreign Jews are important elements in university budgets. Students strike periodically to protest rising tuition, and professors strike to protest low wages. Compromises end immediate conflicts, but the issues remain unresolved.

THE HEALTH-CARE SYSTEM AND NATIONAL INSURANCE

Israel has a universal health-care system, which means that by law every citizen is entitled to medical treatment. The Ministry of Health oversees health services and owns and operates many of the country's larger hospitals. Health care represents nearly 10 percent of Israel's GDP.

Health care is administered through four "sick funds," which are health maintenance organizations (HMOs). The largest historically, Kupat Holim Clalit, is run by the Histadrut, the trade union federation. Two others, Maccabee and Meuhedet, are commercially run. The last, Leumit, is a small fund associated with the Likud Party. The sick funds operate clinics throughout the country, where members can go to receive basic care. Local Ministry of Health branches, municipalities, and the sick funds also run mother-and-childcare centers to monitor child development, provide immunizations, and help new mothers.

Every citizen is entitled to a minimum level of tax-financed coverage through one of the funds and can also purchase supplementary insurance. Basic health insurance covers doctor visits; hospitalization; surgery; dental care for children; medical services at the workplace; treatment for drug abuse and alcoholism; obstetrics and fertility treatment; and many medications, among other things. Members with supplemental insurance, which costs an additional small monthly fee, are entitled to more goods and services, such as a longer list of subsidized medications, alternative medicine treatments, and smoking cessation seminars.

The "health basket" of medications and services available to basic and supplemental insurance holders is updated annually to include the newest medicines. Medications are far less expensive than in other countries. But not every treatment makes it onto the list, and there is greater investment in more glamorous areas like new technology than in long-term basic services like home care for the elderly.

All care begins with a visit to a general practitioner. Medical records are completely computerized on a national level. The original doctor may provide a letter allowing visits to specialists. For some operations and other treatments, there might be a waiting list. Doctors can also choose to offer private treatment for pay if their obligations to the sick fund are fulfilled.

Israel has many state-of-the-art hospitals, and the country is a global leader in medical procedures, innovations, and research, including genetic research. Israel has the professional and technological capacity to provide the highest levels of care currently possible to all types of patients. A typical scene in a Jerusalem emergency room includes religious, secular, Arab, Russian, and Ethiopian patients waiting to be treated by a medical staff just as diverse.

Israel invests in the development of biotechnology, and the public is well informed of medical advances. There is strong public support for investments in life-saving technologies and therapies. The Jewish principle of taking extraordinary measures to save a life guarantees backing for practices considered controversial in some other countries such as embryo research and reproductive cloning.

One problem in the Israeli health-care system is the lack of doctors, especially in certain fields. In the 1990s, Russian immigrants who had been doctors before coming to Israel were able to fill needed positions; but as the population continues to grow and immigration slows, Israel is again experiencing a shortage. Doctors make far less money than in other countries, which adds to the problem.

In addition to universal health care, Israel also has a National Insurance Institute (Bituach Leumi) that provides monetary assistance to unemployed and underprivileged members of society. Employer contributions, along with a portion of everyone's salary, go to the National Insurance Institute through taxation to ensure that unemployment benefits can be allocated when necessary. The National Insurance Institute is also responsible for allocating child subsidies and payments to single mothers.

WAR'S EFFECT ON SOCIETY

The premise of the terrorist campaigns against Israel is that constant threats and warfare will eventually break down the confidence of Israeli society and even its ability to function. These predictions have proven wrong. As PLO leader Yasir Arafat explained in 1968, violence should be focused on Israeli citizens and facilities "to create and maintain an atmosphere of strain and anxiety that will force the Zionists to realize that it is impossible for them to live in Israel." Two years later he added, "The Israelis have one great fear, the fear of casualties."

Arafat also predicted that attacks on civilians would "prevent immigration and encourage emigration, destroy tourism, prevent immigrants from becoming attached to the land, weaken the Israeli economy and divert the greater part of it to security requirements." By achieving these objectives, the PLO would "inevitably" lead to Israel's disintegration. "A quick blow by the regular [Arab] armies at the right moment," Arafat said, would then finish Israel off.

Yet Israeli society worked despite threats and tensions, although there was certainly trauma. Israel's wars and the widespread participation of Israelis in the military mean that there are many military casualties, and these losses have affected everyone in society. It is said that every Israeli knows someone who has fallen in military service. Such losses take a toll in a country whose citizens are used to facing security threats and death.

In general, Israelis deal with events by moving on, although the need for psychological help and counseling has become increasingly recognized in recent years. The fallen are commemorated, and dead soldiers are elevated to mythical status in the Israeli narrative. The poet Natan Alterman immortalized those who died in the War of Independence as the "silver platter" upon which the state was served.

On the annual Remembrance Day (Yom Ha-Zikron), held the day before Independence

A memorial outside the Frank Sinatra International Student Center at the Hebrew University in Jerusalem, August 7, 2002, following a terrorist attack there in which seven people were killed. (Getty Images/Image Bank.)

Day, a siren is sounded in the evening and in the morning, during which time virtually the entire nation stands at silent attention. Only Arabs, for political reasons, and most Haredim, who say that reading religious texts is a more Jewish way of honoring the dead, do not participate. A national commemoration ceremony is held at the Western Wall in Jerusalem, and each community holds its own memorial service for members who have given their lives. People often attend communal sing-alongs, where they sing sad nationalist songs attesting to the struggle for existence and commemorating sacrifices and loss.

During the day, it has become traditional to visit the graves of fallen soldiers at the national military cemetery, where there is another national memorial service. At the end of this day, after the sun sets, another national ceremony is held, and then celebrations erupt as people move from mourning the dead to honoring Independence Day.

SOCIAL TRENDS AND INFLUENCES: DECLINING COLLECTIVISM

Israeli society is open to change and more readily imports foreign ideas and trends than other countries do. On the whole, Israelis welcome exposure to new cultural influences, for they are not afraid of jeopardizing their own identity, especially since cultural elements are adapted to the Israeli vision. Over time, the socialist and collectivist approach, so hegemonic during the country's early years, has declined significantly, however, to be replaced with a more market-based, individualistic approach to the organization of society.

The degree of change should not be exaggerated. Israeli society has strongly established patterns and features that rest on the country's experiences and unique aspects. Predictions of dramatic alterations have been repeatedly proven wrong or overstated. Many of these trends are normal ones for countries that have gone from the flux of being established to a more routine stability.

Israeli society is characterized by a general decline in the primacy of the collective. Previously strong institutions in Israeli life such as political party affiliation, the Histadrut trade union federation, and even the army have all been affected by this trend. Ideological Zionism is also of less interest, in large part because its main goals have been fulfilled. Socialism is seen, without bitterness or controversy, as a system that was simply necessary at an earlier stage but not today.

Many of the changes affecting Israel are typical of those happening elsewhere in the Western world. Supermarket chains and malls with national and international retailers are replacing neighborhood grocery stores (*mekollet*) and outdoor markets (*shuk*). The availability of affordable plane travel, the Internet, and the communications revolution in general have also had a huge effect—augmented in Israel by Israelis' facility with languages and technology. For many years, Israel's society was shaped by geographical constraints due to neighbors' hostility. Now, Israel has gone from a large degree of isolation to easy or instantaneous interaction with the world.

These developments do not mean that localisms have vanished. Many cities still boast thriving shuks, with stalls operated by the same families that have run them for generations. Still, even these traditional Middle Eastern shopping places are being gentrified. In Jerusalem, for example, expensive designer shops are squeezed in between the vegetable stands and spice booths of Jerusalem's traditional open air market. The change can be attributed to globalization—specifically Americanization, some would say.

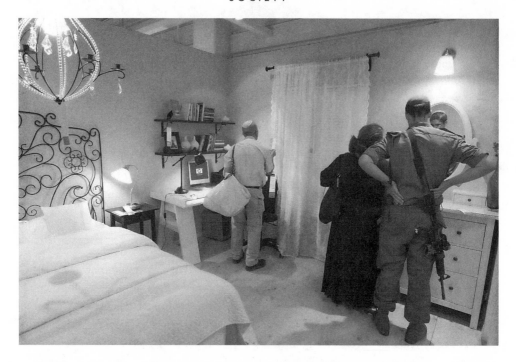

Israelis shop at the local outlet of the Swedish furniture store IKEA in Netanya, north of Tel Aviv, August 2009. (Getty Images / Image Bank.)

The Americanization trend was already evident in Israel in the 1960s, when jeans became a popular clothing item. In the 1970s the Coca-Cola company began manufacturing profitably in Israel. In the 1990s malls sprouted up across the country. In 1993 the first commercial Israeli television channel, Channel 2, was launched, changing the face of advertising and television programming. Political parties began holding primaries to choose candidates—a practice inspired by the U.S. model. Aside from the global power of American influences, Israelis felt a special bond between the two countries. Jews have contributed significantly to American cultural, business, and intellectual life, so many of its features are congruent with Jewish attitudes and history.

During the 1980s and 1990s in particular, the Americanization of Israel was a prime subject of debate, although the country had historically looked more toward Europe. One set of examples offered was political: the portrayal of Prime Minister Benjamin Netanyahu as an American-style politician, the decline of ideology and party allegiance, and the use of American political consultants and methods in campaigning.

But the changes were limited: the number of floating voters increased somewhat and party loyalty declined. Israeli elections may not revolve around ideology any more, but they focus on issues rather than personalities or campaign gimmicks. Indeed, shifts were far more often on superficial levels than on fundamental ones.

For example, English words and phrases are making their way into Hebrew, just as Russian and Arabic words have. Many of these English words have to do with banking, computers, and technology. Given the need to modernize an ancient language, however, this borrowing does not disturb cultural or national sensitivities.

The same point applies to consumer choices. American businesses have proliferated, including McDonald's, Home Depot, and other such stores. The first Gap franchise opened in summer 2009 and sold much of its merchandise within the first few days. American television shows, music, and fashion have also entered the country and won audiences and customers.

Yet all of these influences go through an Israeli filter. Commonly, the imported ideas, products, and services that initially attract customers quickly fade away once the Israeli taste for novelty is sated. Starbuck's cafés failed because Israelis have very decided tastes in coffee that do not include weaker or flavored varieties. Even more commonly, the new import is interpreted in an Israeli way. Many McDonald's franchises in Israel are kosher, for example, and Jerusalem's upscale mall is built out of Jerusalem stone and connects the modern downtown area with the historical Old City.

Much of the copying is also superficial. Israeli chain stores give themselves American-style names, for example. Israel now has its own version of Best Buy. Restaurants like to name themselves after popular American trends, so Jerusalem now boasts a pizza place called American Pie Pizza and another called Pizza Obama. American reality shows are very popular in Israel, but by the time *Survivor*, *The Amazing Race*, or *American Idol* is made in a local version with Israeli contestants, it is transmuted into something remarkably different and quintessentially Israeli.

Another key reason why Israeli social identity does not erode under the American influences is that there are so many diverse foreign influences, and most are adapted to Israeli preferences. Just as there are American influences, there are also considerable European, Russian, and Mediterranean influences. The easing of trade regulations with the European Union, for example, has brought an influx of products from those countries.

The scope and implications of influences coming from the Russian immigrants is not yet clear. There is definitely a push toward secularism in social terms and conservatism in political terms. Immigrants hailing from the big cities in the former Soviet Union consider themselves highly cultured, like the German-speaking immigrants who arrived in the 1930s and 1940s. To what extent their sophistication will revitalize and alter the country's intellectual life remains a question. On the contrary, the immigrants may themselves adapt to Israeli norms. In the short term, however, there is some upsurge in the quality of cultural life.

Another influence on Israeli life, especially in the cultural center of Tel Aviv, is Mediterranean. Israel does have a great deal in common with southern Europe—a warm climate and an informal, passionate social atmosphere. Mediterranean food and music meet with a positive reception.

Israel both does and does not suffer from an inferiority complex, which partly explains the debate over foreign influences and the mixed and unpredictable response to them. On one hand, the country is young, small in size and population, and committed to using a language that has little international importance, which supports a self-image as a vibrant, creative, courageous country.

Yet a portion of the elite—especially artists and many intellectuals—see Israel as provincial, idealize the United States or Europe, wish to escape the country's semi-pariah political status, and resent religious, right-wing, or "too Middle Eastern" compatriots, whom they blame for ruining the country or throwing away chances for peace. This accounts for the strong leftist tinge in many areas of culture, although this situation also characterizes many other Western countries.

If many changes come from abroad, some are also internal—specifically, changes in the role of and attitudes toward the kibbutz, whose decline can been seen as significant. The kibbutz, which is both a community and a collective economic cooperative stressing egalitarianism, symbolizes the socialist Zionist ideals that directed the early years of the country. Today only a small minority of Israelis live on a kibbutz, a situation with more of a symbolic than a material effect on the country.

As Israeli society has changed, the kibbutz has lost its privileged position in the Israeli social consciousness for several reasons. Mizrahim, who formed many of the later waves of immigrants, had little interest in this way of life. Over time, too, the economy shifted away from agriculture. Building up a kibbutz and maintaining it proved to be very different kinds of activities, and the first or second generations born on kibbutzim often wanted to leave to determine their own lifestyle. The experiment of communally rearing children also met with many criticisms after years of experience, especially from those who grew up on kibbutzim.

Kibbutzim are spread throughout the country, with the majority located in away from the major urban centers. The kibbutz prototype is secular, but there are also a few religious kibbutzim. Typically, a kibbutz has several hundred members, each admitted by a vote of the membership. The grounds include a residential area with very modest homes, a post office, a dining hall, an industrial zone, a cowshed, and agricultural fields. Traditional kibbutzim also have children's homes, schools, and a small service center for technicians such as electricians. All automobiles are owned by the kibbutz and available for use by members who need them. This collectivist framework is far less common now.

Kibbutz residents traditionally saw themselves as the embodiment of society's values of equality and working the land: they were pioneers settling the new land. Other Israelis admired them, sometimes envied them as privileged—although those privileges were based on very hard work—and made fun of them as naive. For the most part, they no longer feel that they are at the forefront of an important movement but rather that they have chosen a way of living with low stress and high quality of life.

The decline of the kibbutz was accelerated in the 1980s by the economic crisis that hit the entire country. Having borrowed funds in previous years, many kibbutzim were forced to sell off assets and adjust to changed circumstances. The more successful kibbutzim turned to making income from tourism and went into high technology and a wide variety of specialized enterprises. The most successful were those in good locations for engaging in innovative enterprises. One kibbutz, formerly a poor place relying on fishing, parlayed its location on the Tel Aviv–Haifa road into prosperity by establishing and running a huge shopping center—where stores can stay open on the Sabbath since it is private property—a water park, and a zoo. Other kibbutzim on the periphery remain in financial trouble.

The other type of agricultural community, the moshav, has adjusted to changes over time more easily. On a moshav, property is privately owned but machinery may be owned and marketing may be done cooperatively. Many moshavim have become suburban housing areas at least in part. Homes have been sold, and agricultural activities are carried out by individuals or companies.

LOOKING TO THE FUTURE

Israel has had to contend with many internal challenges since its establishment in 1948, among them determining the proper balance between religion and other institutions in a Western, democratic, Jewish state; integrating diverse groups of immigrants while providing space for them to maintain elements of their own cultures; overcoming the prejudices of the early years of statehood and the institutionalized discrimination that resulted; figuring out how to accord a large, distinct ethnic and cultural minority maximum rights; and dealing with the decline of the collectivist ethos.

In many ways, societal gaps are closing, and there is now little difference between native Israelis of Western and Eastern extraction. Immigrants from Ethiopia and the former Soviet Union are becoming part of Israeli society despite challenges. Women have equal rights in law and increasingly in practice, with some personal status exceptions, and sexual minorities enjoy legal rights and growing social acceptance. Religion remains a contentious arena, with Haredim becoming more comfortable in Israeli society while resisting change. Diversity of religious expression and practice in Israeli society is on the rise, although institutionalized forms developed in the Diaspora may be adapted instead of strictly maintained.

The historic dividing lines between secular and religious and between Ashkenazic and Mizrahi are declining in importance. Among most Israeli Jews a secular lifestyle is coupled with a sentimental, not always rigorous attachment to symbols of Judaism. The blend is recognizably Israeli. Jewish traditions are taken for granted.

This blurring of dividing lines has been linked to the growing pluralism of society. In the early days of statehood, secular Jews of European origin dominated most areas of society. This is no longer the case. Religiously observant Israelis, immigrants from Russia, and Israelis of non-European origin all help shape the country today. These groups, whatever their continuing distinctions, appear to be linked by a loosely defined but deeply felt perception of shared Jewish-Israeli identity. The emergence of this link is one of the most important aspects of modern Israeli society and marks Israel's maturity—although, as any Israeli would quickly point out, the country is far from perfect.

Many of the traditional assumptions in Israeli society have been overturned, which has led to considerable debate and some anxiety, though neither instability nor crisis. The old values of socialism and austerity are being replaced by capitalism and materialism, a process that has also produced a more pluralist society. The military and the education system remain instrumental in shaping Israelis, and they are tasked with integrating new immigrants and with instilling the nation's youth with a respect for pluralism, democratic values, a sense of civic responsibility, and pride in their country.

In some specific ways, Israel is different from other Western countries. Indeed, these differences are often the cause of antagonism toward Israel, which possesses characteristics that some Europeans and Americans now reject in their own societies. Salient among these are respect for the military and a readiness to fight in defense of one's country; an important role for religion, its practices, and values; and a strong sense of nationalism, the affirmation of Jews' and Israelis' identity as a distinct people, and belief in the importance of country and patriotism. In any case, the real Israel does not correspond with the frequently voiced impressions of it by foreign observers, whether negative or sympathetic.

Within Israel, the Jewish-Arab gap shows signs of narrowing socially and economically, though not politically. Still, the Israeli Arabs do not see—nor have they rallied around—any particular alternative, especially when they compare their situation with that of Arabs in the West Bank, the Gaza Strip, and elsewhere in the region. Israeli Arabs are dissatisfied with many aspects of the status quo, even deeply resentful, but the majority doubt that things are going to change and are quite divided over what they want, not to mention very aware of the unpleasant alternatives. The gap between themselves and the Palestinians of the West Bank and Gaza Strip is growing wider as well. And Islamist ideology, the very factor that makes some increasingly radical, makes others wary of supporting a movement that would put them under a dictatorship or an Islamist state.

As for the Jewish majority, two points inhibit their understanding of the Israeli Arabs' situation. One is their attempt to draw parallels between Israeli Arabs' experience and others' experiences elsewhere, Jewish or not. The second is a tendency of all Israelis to reflect the views of Israel's traditional elite, who see the country's first years as a heroic time and any change since then as unwelcome and who also see any decline in their own power as inherently negative.

Jonathan Spyer has summed up the overall trends and changes in his book *The Transforming Fire*:

> The Israeli-Jewish society that has emerged . . . is a real, breathing, living country that gets up in the morning and works and argues and reconciles and makes its loyalties in its own language and in its own interests. . . . The Zionist project has been achieved and transcended. The European nationalist outlook that formed modern Zionism is fading. But beneath and around it is growing something else that is being formed through the fusion of Jewish sovereignty, Jewish tradition, and Middle Eastern reality.

In other words, a new synthesis of "Israeliness" is emerging. The old secular Ashkenazic, socialist-oriented elite that has built so much is itself being rebuilt. The infusion of ideas, attitudes, and customs from Mizrahi Jews, Datim, and immigrants from the former Soviet Union is having a revitalizing effect, adding in different proportions the strengthening influences of energy, faith, confidence, strength, and thirst for knowledge. However multicultural these factors, they are not divisive precisely because they are feeding into a collective consciousness. The emerging Israeli identity is more inclusive than the old one. It is still a Jewish consciousness, but it is quite different from what existed in the past or now prevails in Diaspora Jewish communities.

BIBLIOGRAPHY

Aridi, Naim. "The Druze in Israel," December 23, 2002. Israel Ministry of Foreign Affairs, http://www.mfa.gov.il/MFA/MFAArchive/2000_2009/2002/12/Focus%20on%20Israel-%20The%20Druze%20in%20Israel.

Avni, Idan. "Nobody's Citizens." *Ynet News*, October 16, 2006. http://www.ynetnews.com/articles/0,7340,L-3315769,00.html.

Azaryahu, Maoz. "The Golden Arches of McDonald's: On the 'Americanization' of Israel." *Israel Studies* 5, no. 1 (Spring 2001): 41–64.

Bassok, Moti. "Don't Worry, Be Israeli: 82 Percent of Adults Satisfied with Life." *Ha'aretz*, November 7, 2005. http://www.haaretz.com/print-edition/news/don-t-worry-be-israeli-82-percent-of-adults-satisfied-with-life-1.173462.

Ben-Dor, Gabriel, and Ami Pedahzur. "Civil-Military Relations in Israel at the Outset of the Twenty-First Century." In Uzi Rebhun and Chaim I. Waxman, eds., *Jews in Israel: Contemporary Social and Cultural Patterns*, 331–344. Waltham, MA: University Press of New England, 2004.

Ben-Rafael, Eliezer. "The Faces of Religiosity in Israel: Cleavages or Continuum." *Israel Studies* 13, no. 3 (2008): 90–113.

Ben-Rafael, Eliezer. "Mizrahi and Russian Challenges to Israel's Dominant Culture: Divergences and Convergences." *Israel Studies* 12, no. 3 (2007): 68–91.

Ben-Rafael, Eliezer, and Menachem Topel. "The Kibbutz's Transformation: Who Leads It and Where?" In Uzi Rebhun and Chaim I. Waxman, eds., *Jews in Israel: Contemporary Social and Cultural Patterns*, 151–171. Waltham, MA: University Press of New England, 2004.

Bilu, Yoram, and Eliezer Witztum. "War-Related Loss and Suffering in Israeli Society: An Historical Perspective." *Israel Studies* 5, no. 2 (2000).

Cashman, Greer Fay. "Poll: Israel's Biggest Patriots in the West." *Jerusalem Post*, January 18, 2006.

Central Bureau of Statistics, State of Israel. *The Arab Population in Israel*. Statistilite series. November 2002. http://www.cbs.gov.il/statistical/arabju.pdf.

Central Bureau of Statistics, State of Israel. *The Arab Population in Israel: 2008*. Statistilite series. March 2010. http://www.cbs.gov.il/www/statistical/arab_pop08e.pdf.

Central Bureau of Statistics, State of Israel. *Statistical Abstract of Israel, 2009*. http://www.cbs.gov.il/reader/shnatonhnew_site.htm.

Central Bureau of Statistics, State of Israel. *Statistical Abstract of Israel, 2010*. http://www.cbs.gov.il/reader/shnatonenew.htm.

Chafets, Ze'ev. *Heroes and Hustlers, Hard Hats and Holy Men: Inside the New Israel*. New York: William Morrow, 1986.

"Characteristics and Influences of the Immigration from the Former Soviet Union." *People Israel—Your Guide to Israeli Society*, http://www.peopleil.org/details.aspx?itemID=7571&nosearch=true&searchMode=1. [In Hebrew.]

Cohen, Asher, and Bernard Susser. "Jews and Others: Non-Jewish Jews in Israel." *Israel Affairs* 15, no. 1 (2009): 52–65.

Cohen, Stuart A. "Tensions between Military Service and Jewish Orthodoxy in Israel: Implications Imagined and Real." *Israel Studies* 12, no. 1 (2007): 103–126.

DellaPergola, Sergio. "Demography in Israel at the Dawn of the Twenty-First Century." In Uzi Rebhun and Chaim I. Waxman, eds., *Jews in Israel: Contemporary Social and Cultural Patterns*, 20–43. Waltham, MA: University Press of New England, 2004.

Dloomy, Ariel. "The Israeli Refuseniks: 1982–2003." *Israel Affairs* 11, no. 4 (2005): 695–716.

Elazar, Daniel J. "Education in a Society at a Crossroads: An Historical Perspective on Israeli Schooling." *Israel Studies* 2, no. 2 (1997): 40–65.

Elon, Amos. *The Israelis: Founders and Sons*. New York: Holt, Rinehart, and Winston, 1971.

Friedman, Ron. "Buffett: 'Israel Has a Disproportionate Amount of Brains.'" *Jerusalem Post*, October 13, 2010. http://www.jpost.com/Business/BusinessNews/Article.aspx?id=191215.

Frisch, Hillel. "Israel and Its Arab Citizens." *Israel Affairs* 11, no. 1 (2005): 207–222.

Gavison, Ruth. *The Law of Return at Sixty Years: History, Ideology, Justification*. Jerusalem: Metzilah Center for Zionist, Jewish, Liberal and Humanist Thought, 2010. http://metzilah.org.il/webfiles/fck/File/ShvutENG.pdf.

Gorny, Yosef. "The 'Melting Pot' in Zionist Thought." *Israel Studies* 6, no. 3 (2001): 54–70.

Habib, Jack. *The Arab Population in Israel: Selected Educational, Economic, Health and Social Indicators*, November 2008. Myers-JDC-Brookdale Institute, http://brookdale.jdc.org.il/_Uploads/dbs AttachedFiles/ArabIsraelisBackgroundDocumentENG-Nov2008.pdf.

Herzog, Hanna. "Women in Israeli Society." In Uzi Rebhun and Chaim I. Waxman, eds., *Jews in Israel: Contemporary Social and Cultural Patterns*, 195–217. Waltham, MA: University Press of New England, 2004.

Horowitz, Tamar. "The Integration of Immigrants from the Former Soviet Union." *Israel Affairs* 11, no. 1 (2005): 117–136.

Kaplan, Steven, and Hagar Salamon. "Ethiopian Jews in Israel: A Part of the People or Apart from the People?" In Uzi Rebhun and Chaim I. Waxman, eds., *Jews in Israel: Contemporary Social and Cultural Patterns*, 118–147. Waltham, MA: University Press of New England, 2004.

Kemp, Adriana, and Rebecca Raijman. "'Ovdim Zarim' B'Yisrael" ["Foreign Workers" in Israel]. *Meda Al Shivyon* 13 (June 2003). [In Hebrew.]

Leshem, Elazar, and Moshe Sicron. "The Soviet Immigrant Community in Israel." In Uzi Rebhun and Chaim I. Waxman, eds., *Jews in Israel: Contemporary Social and Cultural Patterns*, 81–116. Waltham, MA: University Press of New England, 2004.

Levy, Shlomit, Hanna Levinsohn, and Elihu Katz. "The Many Faces of Jewishness in Israel." In Uzi Rebhun and Chaim I. Waxman, eds., *Jews in Israel: Contemporary Social and Cultural Patterns*, 265–284. Waltham, MA: University Press of New England, 2004.

Levy, Yigal. "Is There a Motivation Crisis in Military Recruitment in Israel?" *Israel Affairs* 15, no. 2 (2009): 135–158.

Liebman, Charles S. "Reconceptualizing the Culture Conflict among Israeli Jews." *Israel Studies* 2, no. 2 (1997): 172–189.

Ministry of Foreign Affairs, State of Israel. "Culture," November 28, 2010. Israel's 60th Anniversary Edition. http://www.mfa.gov.il/MFA/Facts%20About%20Israel/Culture/Culture.

Newman, David. "From Hitnachalut to Hitnatkut: The Impact of Gush Emunim and the Settlement Movement on Israeli Politics and Society." *Israel Studies* 10, no. 3 (2005): 192–224.

"The Official Summation of the Or Commission Report." *Ha'aretz*, September 1, 2003.

Raday, Frances. "Women's Human Rights: Dichotomy between Religion and Secularism in Israel." *Israel Affairs* 11, no. 1 (2005): 78–94.

Rebhun, Uzi. "Major Trends in the Development of Israeli Jews: A Synthesis of the Last Century." In Uzi Rebhun and Chaim I. Waxman, eds., *Jews in Israel: Contemporary Social and Cultural Patterns*, 3–17. Waltham, MA: University Press of New England, 2004.

Rebhun, Uzi, and Chaim I. Waxman. "The 'Americanization' of Israel: A Demographic, Cultural and Political Evaluation." *Israel Studies* 5, no. 1 (2000): 65–91.

Regev, Motti. "Present Absentee: Arab Music in Israeli Culture." *Public Culture* 7, no. 2 (1995). http://publicculture.dukejournals.org/cgi/pdf_extract/7/2/433.

Regev, Motti, and Edwin Seroussi. *Popular Music and National Culture in Israel*. Berkeley: University of California Press, 2004.

Rekhess, Elie. "The Arabs of Israel after Oslo: Localization of the National Struggle." *Israel Studies* 7, no. 3 (2002): 1–44.

Rekhess, Elie. "The Evolvement of an Arab-Palestinian National Minority in Israel." *Israel Studies* 12, no. 3 (2007): 1–28.

Roffe-Ofir, Sharon. "Rift between Druze, Israel Growing." *Ynet News*, January 18, 2008. http://www.ynet.co.il/english/articles/0,7340,L-3495934,00.html.

Rudge, David. "Most Israeli Arabs Support 67 Borders." *Jerusalem Post*, May 16, 2004.

Schafferman, Karin Tamar. "Arab Identity in a Jewish and Democratic State." *Parliament*, May 5, 2008. Israel Democracy Institute, http://www.iataskforce.org/sites/www.iataskforce.org/files/identity 14.pdf.

Shalev, Carmel. "Health Rights." *Israel Affairs* 11, no. 1 (January 2005): 65–77.

Shavit, Zohar. "Back to the Cultural Core." *Panim* 20 (Spring 2002): 113–122. [In Hebrew.]

Sheffer, Gabriel. "Individualism vs. National Coherence: The Current Discourse on Sovereignty, Citizenship and Loyalty." *Israel Studies* 2, no. 2 (1997): 118–145.

Smooha, Sammy. "Ethnic Democracy: Israel as an Archetype." *Israel Studies* 2, no. 2 (1997): 198–241.

Smooha, Sammy. "The Jewish-Arab Relations Index 2007." University of Haifa web page, http://soc.haifa.ac.il/~s.smooha/download/Index_2007_Highlights_Eng.pdf.

Smooha, Sammy. "Jewish Ethnicity in Israel: Symbolic or Real?" In Uzi Rebhun and Chaim I. Waxman, eds., *Jews in Israel: Contemporary Social and Cultural Patterns*, 47–75. Waltham, MA: University Press of New England, 2004.

Spyer, Jonathan. *The Transforming Fire: The Rise of the Israel-Islamist Conflict.* New York: Continuum, 2010.

Stadler, Nurit, and Eyal Ben-Ari. "Other-Wordly Soldiers? Ultra-Orthodox Views of Military Service in Contemporary Israel." *Israel Affairs* 9, no. 4 (2003): 17–48.

Stern, Yoav. "Druze Women Protest in J'lem, Calling for Opening of Golan Border Crossing." *Ha'aretz*, September 10, 2007.

Tabory, Ephraim. "The Israel Reform and Conservative Movements and the Market for Liberal Judaism." In Uzi Rebhun and Chaim I. Waxman, eds., *Jews in Israel: Contemporary Social and Cultural Patterns*, 285–311. Waltham, MA: University Press of New England, 2004.

Waxman, Chaim I. "Religion in the Israeli Public Square." In Uzi Rebhun and Chaim I. Waxman, eds., *Jews in Israel: Contemporary Social and Cultural Patterns*, 221–237. Waltham, MA: University Press of New England, 2004.

Ya'ar, Ephraim. "Continuity and Change in Israeli Society: The Test of the Melting Pot." *Israel Studies* 10, no. 2 (2005): 91–128.

Yonah, Yossi. "Israel as a Multicultural Democracy." *Israel Affairs* 11, no. 1 (2005): 95–116.

Yuchtman-Yaar, Ephraim, and Ze'ev Shavit. "The Cleavage between Jewish and Arab Israeli Citizens." In Uzi Rebhun and Chaim I. Waxman, eds., *Jews in Israel: Contemporary Social and Cultural Patterns*, 345–367. Waltham, MA: University Press of New England, 2004.

Chapter Five

GOVERNMENT AND POLITICS

Israel is defined in its laws as a Jewish and democratic state. It has a parliamentary system in which the executive is subject to the legislature and the judiciary is independent. The parliamentary, judicial, and electoral systems are adapted from the British model in place before the state was established. As in other democracies, members of the legislature are freely elected, and citizens live under the rule of law and enjoy many freedoms. As in the United Kingdom, Israel has no written constitution. Instead, the political structure and fundamental rights are set out in a series of Basic Laws that are interpreted by the judiciary. Unlike the United States, Israel has no clear separation of religion and state.

The head of state is the president, elected by the Knesset, but the president's role is mainly symbolic and ceremonial. The national legislative body, the Knesset, is composed of 120 members elected on party lists, rather than individually, and all chosen on a national level, not as representatives of local districts. The prime minister heads the government. Given the large number of political parties in Israel, the government has always been a coalition, and the prime minister is the head of the party with the most seats in the Knesset or the leader of a party who, in the president's judgment, has the best chance to form a majority coalition. The prime minister forms a cabinet composed of ministers who come from the coalition parties and who are almost always also Knesset members.

Every government in Israel has been based on multiparty coalitions because both the number of political parties and the highly proportional election regulations favor coalition building. The system was deliberately designed to allow for maximum pluralism among communities. No party has come close to gaining a majority in its own right.

LEGISLATIVE BRANCH: THE KNESSET

The Knesset, Israel's legislative body, is similar to European parliaments. Its name—taken from the Knesset Hagedola (Great Assembly), the representative body of ancient Israel—harks back to Israel's Jewish and democratic roots. Like its predecessor, the Knesset has 120 members.

The modern Knesset was established in 1949, replacing the temporary Representative Council created at the time of Israel's independence. There was an attempt to prepare a consti-

The Knesset, Israel's parliament building in Jerusalem. (Getty Images/Image Bank.)

tution, but the religious and secular parties failed to agree on how to define the state-religion relationship.

The members of the Knesset, or MKs, are elected for a period of four years. But each Knesset may dissolve itself during its term by passing a no-confidence motion, although this rarely happens, or the prime minister may dissolve it. Once it is dissolved, an election is held to form a new Knesset, after which the prime minister is once again selected. More than 40 percent of governments in Israel's history have gone to elections before reaching the four-year mark.

Elections are nationwide; MKs represent the whole country, not just a region or district. On election day, voters cast a ballot for a political party's list of candidates, drawn up in the party's order of priority. To win a seat in the Knesset, a party must gain at least 2 percent of the popular vote. Every party gaining more than that percent minimum receives seats in proportion to the number of votes obtained. Candidates become elected MKs depending on their order on the ballot. The first person on the list is the party's candidate for prime minister. In recent years, the larger parties have held primaries to choose some candidates, with the rest being picked by party committees.

Basic Laws (*Hokei Yesod*)

The Knesset has passed a number of Basic Laws. These have precedence over other laws—and will, in theory, some day add up to a comprehensive constitution. Despite the many attempts to write a full constitution, however, most Israelis consider the completion of such a document to be unnecessary.

The first Basic Law passed was the Knesset Law of 1958, which confirmed existing arrangements: Jerusalem was declared the country's capital and the place where the legislature would meet. And the Knesset was asserted to consist of 120 elected members. Over the next thirty years, eight more Basic Laws were passed. They dealt with various governmental institutions and, again, mostly enshrined existing procedures. The Israel Lands Law (1960) ensures that state lands remain national property. The Law on the President (1964) defines the president's duties. The State Economy Law (1975) outlines a framework for the budget law and regulations for other economic matters. The Military Law (1976) subordinates the military to the government and provides for compulsory military service for citizens over age eighteen. The Capital Law (1980) declares Jerusalem's status as the capital and deals with holy places. The Judiciary Law (1984) provides regulations for courts. The State Comptroller Law (1988) addresses the comptroller's fiscal and auditing duties. The Government Law (1978; amended in 1992 and 2001) concerns voting and the executive branch. This last law was amended to allow for the prime minister's direct election then changed again to repeal that amendment.

In 1992 two additional Basic Laws were passed to protect human rights. The Basic Law on Freedom of Occupation gives every resident of Israel the "right to engage in any occupation, profession or trade" and has been used for the purposes of gender equality. The Basic Law on Human Dignity, which says its purpose is "to defend Human Dignity and Liberty," was passed "in order to establish in a Basic Law the values of the State of Israel as a Jewish and democratic state." It does so by delineating several freedoms: the freedom from violations of life, liberty, and property; the freedom to leave and enter the country; the freedom of privacy and the freedom from a search of private property; and the freedom from violations of confidentiality in speech and writing. The law does not explicitly mention equality or free speech, but it—together with the Basic Law on Freedom of Occupation—has been interpreted by the Supreme Court as upholding these rights as derivations of "freedom of dignity."

Functions and Powers of the Knesset

The Knesset is the supreme legislative authority in Israel, a unicameral parliament that drafts and passes laws, levies taxes, investigates issues of public interest, and sets the budget. The Knesset also has the responsibility for overseeing the government's work and the implementation of laws. Its committees and subcommittees focus on investigating specific issues and preparing legislation.

One of the Knesset's main tasks is to supervise the government, and it does so in a number of ways—by passing or not passing laws, defining the powers of the executive branch, determining whether the prime minister and the cabinet stay or fall, and controlling finances. The Knesset also possesses the right to request information and status reports from the government.

In monitoring the government, the Knesset uses two highly respected institutions, the offices of the state comptroller and the ombudsman, which report on problems, including corruption, and evaluate the performance of agencies. Elected by the Knesset for a seven-year term, the state comptroller and the ombudsman audit all ministries, government institutions, the defense establishment, political parties, and local municipalities for accountability, efficiency, and corruption.

The state comptroller's office publishes an annual report that makes very specific criticisms of institutions and individuals. The ombudsman's office responds directly to specific complaints made by citizens.

The Plenum and Committees

The Knesset's work is carried out largely in the plenum and in committees. The plenum, when all members meet together, has two sessions each year that last for a total of eight months. It elects a speaker, who is responsible for arranging the Knesset's schedule. The plenum sessions enable all members, including MKs who are also cabinet ministers, to debate issues, introduce and vote on bills and the government budget, and ask questions of the executive branch—which must be answered within two days.

Individual MKs can propose private bills not supported by their whole parties or the government. Sometimes a bill's sponsors may come from several different parties. After its first reading, a member-backed or party-backed bill is assigned to a committee, which may discuss its provisions, add amendments, hold hearings, or kill the proposal. If the committee passes the bill, the bill returns to the plenum for a second reading. After discussion, MKs vote on whether to make any amendments, after which there is a third reading to decide whether the bill should be passed into law.

A simple majority of the MKs in the Knesset chamber at voting time is sufficient for passage, no matter how few MKs are present. Basic Laws, however, require an absolute majority of at least sixty-one votes. If passed, the bill is signed by the Knesset speaker and published in the *Gazette*, the Knesset's official publication.

There are twelve permanent Knesset committees, the most important being those on foreign affairs and defense, economy, education, and the environment. Their membership, which includes both government and opposition MKs, is determined at the start of every new Knesset term. The composition roughly resembles the ratio of each party in Knesset. The ruling party determines the makeup of committees, often using the assignment of leadership or membership positions in more important committees as bargaining chips in coalition negotiations.

Opposition parties sometimes lead less important committees. At times, the Knesset establishes special committees to deal with new issues that arise or to conduct major investigations, including complaints against specific MKs. Chairing a committee or being on a key committee greatly enhances an MK's power and ability to push his or her party's agenda.

Members of the Knesset (MKs)

The individual Knesset members do not have a great deal of autonomy vis-à-vis their party since they are in office as party members rather than as individuals. MKs' power rests on an ability to build coalitions within the party and across party lines to back their proposals. Ultimately, though, it is the party that determines an individual's place in the political hierarchy—by choosing who is to be on the party list of candidates, setting positions on the list, giving out cabinet posts and committee assignments. Knesset members who decide to leave their party can still remain in the Knesset either by serving as an independent, joining another party, or establishing a new party with others.

EXECUTIVE BRANCH

Israel's prime minister is head of the executive branch and the country's leader. According to Israel's Basic Law on Government, the prime minister need only be an Israeli citizen and a permanent resident of the country. A prime minister supposedly serves a four-year term, but most prime ministers do not remain in office four straight years, being removed by resignation, death, illness, the loss of a Knesset majority, a personal decision to dissolve the Knesset and go to elections, or a no-confidence motion passed in the Knesset.

The prime minister is also head of his or her party, which is usually (but not always) the party with the most votes and hence the most Knesset seats. During Israel's history the prime minister has become increasingly more powerful. Nevertheless, given party factions and the need to maintain a multiparty coalition, since no single party is able to win a Knesset majority, the prime minister is probably somewhat less powerful than the leaders of the United States, France, or the United Kingdom .

The prime minister's staff and the staffs of regular MKs are quite small. The prime minister's most important advisors are the director-general of the prime minister's office, the cabinet secretary, and the media and military advisors. The prime minister also supervises the country's two intelligence services: the Mossad (corresponding to the CIA) provides the prime minister with reports on international intelligence, and the Shin Bet (known as the Shabak and corresponding to the FBI) provides reports on intelligence on Israel and the territories captured in 1967.

Ministries and Coalition Building

The prime minister chooses the cabinet, although the needs of powerful individuals within the prime minister's own party and the distribution of seats based on agreements with the government coalition partners restricts the prime minister's choices. Since the cabinet includes the coalition party leaders, it is more powerful than in other Western democracies, and the prime minister must win a majority in it, not just give it orders.

Following each election, the president, elected by the Knesset for a seven-year term, nominates a prime minister after consulting with all the political parties. The main criterion is being the party leader who has the best chance of forming a coalition with a majority in the Knesset of at least sixty-one MKs. After the 2009 elections, for example, Livni's Kadima Party had won one seat more than Benjamin Netanyahu's Likud Party, but President Shimon Peres, previously a member of Kadima himself, chose Netanyahu as the next prime minister. Discussion with all the parties showed that Netanyahu, but not Livni, had support from more than sixty-one MKs.

Once selected, the president's choice for prime minister must be approved by the Knesset in a symbolic vote of confidence. The prime minister-elect then has twenty-eight days to assemble a formal coalition of political parties that agree on the government's platform—both its stances on issues and the legislation it will work to pass. The prime minister–elect and those designated for the purpose meet with all other parties that might join the coalition. The negotiations focus on what the leading party will offer and the smaller parties take in terms of appointments for ministers, deputy ministers, and committee chairs. Offering the prestigious—but not intrinsically powerful—title of deputy prime minister to the leader of the second-biggest party can be an attractive sweetener of a coalition deal, as can promises of budgetary support for a party's constituents.

Usually the distribution of power in the coalition is based on the relative size of the parties. The most sought-after posts are those of foreign, defense, and finance ministers. Haredi parties do not want to take ministerial positions and so prefer to be deputy ministers or chairs of Knesset committees as their price for joining a coalition.

Sometimes certain parties—usually religious parties and advocates of secularism—refuse to belong in the same coalition. Equally, religious parties compete for specific offices, notably control of the ministries of religion and the interior, which can provide funds for their constituents. Ethnic parties whose voters are from the former Soviet Union want to control the Ministry of Absorption, which deals with immigrants.

The prime minister must juggle different possible numerical combinations to achieve the greatest possible majority with the fewest likely problems. It has often been shown, however—in making and in maintaining coalitions—that a clever, persistent politician can overcome even the shrillest demands and the strongest insistence that no compromise is possible. After all, the chance of participating in the government, gaining the prestige of high office, having power over budgets and decision making, and providing benefits for one's supporters are high incentives for politicians. Still, leaders can reject such incentives in matters of principle and cases of high-priority policies.

Thus, while parties join a coalition to exercise power and patronage by getting legislation passed and by controlling ministries, they will not join a coalition—and are more likely to leave one—if they have substantive disagreements on important issues. During an entire term, the prime minister must thus take care to retain a majority. Creating and maintaining coalitions is a game of leverage, compromise, and, at times, threats; the prime minister may express a readiness to let the government fall—and sometimes implement those warnings—or may throw out dissenters. Parties may threaten to walk out of the coalition to force an election, and they sometimes do so. But if the coalition partners believe on the basis of polls that they will lose seats in an election, they usually want to avoid being responsible for a dissolution of the Knesset and an early election that damages their party.

Sometimes a coalition can survive with only a minority of MKs but can stay in power with a majority on the basis of votes from non-coalition parties. On at least two important occasions—the peace treaty with Egypt and the disengagement from the Gaza Strip—a Likud-led government could not depend on all its members to support the proposal and required outside support from Labor and Meretz MKs for its majority on those votes.

All ministers must be Israeli citizens and residents. However, they are not necessarily experts on the issues their ministries cover. As in the British system, they usually depend on career civil servants, and especially the permanent secretaries, to run the ministry. A minister may or may not take a strong interest in the ministry's business. There are also often ministers without portfolio who sit in the cabinet without a specific assignment. This is often a way for the prime minister to give an additional benefit to coalition partners or to include valued individuals in high-level discussions.

In assembling the cabinet, the prime minister has a fairly free hand in breaking up or combining existing ministries to create additional cabinet positions or create new ones. Cabinets have tended to grow larger over time for coalition purposes, even to the point that money is wasted and efficiency impaired. Those whose careers are upward bound will move to increasingly more important ministries. Here as elsewhere, a central theme of Israeli politics is to favor long careers and the accumulation of experience.

A common pattern is for the ruling party to retain the job of either foreign or defense minister, or, more rarely, finance minister, and give the other two jobs to leaders or top figures in the largest coalition parties. A prime minister may also keep one or even two ministries to avoid squabbles among coalition parties competing for that job or trying to entice another party that wants that position to join.

The cabinet meets at least once a week, more often if necessary. Its decisions address the most important issues facing the country. There is often lively debate in the cabinet, and there are often leaks to the media. The prime minister may call for a vote to put members on the record or simply announce a consensus. An official communiqué is released to cover each meeting's outcome, although many decisions—or at least their details—are kept secret. Most legislation begins in the cabinet. MKs who are cabinet members or whom the party assigns to the task then present the legislation to the Knesset for consideration.

Many prime ministers have smaller informal groups of perhaps a half-dozen ministers who may be called on to plan strategy or formulate proposals. The prime minister can use such a group to test the level of support for alternative policies. Golda Meir had her "kitchen cabinet," although the term "inner cabinet" is in more frequent use. Ministers of the ruling party may also meet as a forum for discussion with a more partisan edge. In the Labor Party era the forum was called the *sareinu* (our ministers') group.

Israeli Prime Minister Benjamin Netanyahu with German Chancellor Angela Merkel (left) and Israeli Foreign Minister Avigdor Lieberman (right) during a visit to Berlin, January 2010. (Getty Images / Image Bank.)

Generally, each government minister is responsible for deciding and formulating the policies of just one ministry. But when a decision needs to be made about an issue of extreme importance, all government ministers discuss and decide on it, and the ministry in charge of the matter oversees and ratifies implementation.

The defense minister is almost always an experienced former general or someone with expertise in military affairs. On one of the rare occasions that this was not the case, when former Histadrut chair Amir Peretz held the job during the 2006 conflict with Hizballah, Peretz's poor performance undermined the war effort. Being finance minister is usually not a stepping stone to the top job, but Netanyahu's good performance in that post, from 2003 to 2005, did help pave the way for his return to be prime minister.

Prime Ministers and Political Parties

During Israel's first fifteen years, politics was dominated by Prime Minister David Ben-Gurion. He was the only real contender for the post, except when he temporarily withdrew from politics. It should be noted, however, that even with his tremendous power, he often was in conflict with his own Labor Party (then called Mapai) and did not always win battles. During these periods of conflict he enjoyed the loyalty of two second-generation Israelis, Shimon Peres and Moshe Dayan. When Ben-Gurion formed his own small party, Rafi, for several years, Peres and Dayan joined him.

When Ben-Gurion stepped aside for a time, he was replaced by his sometime foreign minister Moshe Sharett. When Ben-Gurion retired in 1963, his colleagues Levi Eshkol and, after Eshkol's death, Golda Meir became prime minister. To some extent, it can be said that all four of these leaders governed in partnership with the Labor Party. In later years, prime ministers became more independent of such constraints. Israeli-born Yitzhak Rabin, who became prime minister in 1974, was the first to do so from the second generation of leaders and was the first former career military man to hold the post. His protégé, Ehud Barak, was the only other former general ever to be prime minister.

Each of these early leaders was brought down by a mainly non-electoral event. Sharett was removed by Ben-Gurion, who felt his own strong hand was needed to manage the growing friction with Egypt; Eshkol died in office but had been regarded as weak; Meir was discredited by failures immediately prior to the Yom Kippur War of 1973; Rabin left office when his wife, in a technical violation of a then-existing law, left a foreign bank account open after Rabin left his post as ambassador to the United States.

While these early prime ministers all had vulnerabilities, the Labor Party's dominance combined with the first generation's solidarity—not excluding Ben-Gurion's various disputes with Labor—ensured electoral victory. The party's leader became prime minister.

The 1977 election brought the first great transition. The victory of the sixty-four-year-old Menahem Begin marked a break from Labor Party, socialist, and Ashkenazic control. Although Begin was from Poland, a large portion of his voter base was Mizrahi. His election also attested, however, to the continued authority of the founding generation. Like most of his predecessors, a perceived partial failure—in Begin's case, the Lebanon War of 1982—along

ISRAEL'S PRIME MINISTERS

Name	Years in Office	Political Party
David Ben-Gurion	May 1948–January 1954	Mapai
Moshe Sharett	January 1954–November 1955	Mapai
David Ben-Gurion	November 1955–June 1963	Mapai
Levi Eshkol	June 1963–February 1969	Mapai
Yigal Allon (interim)	February–March 1969	Labor (Alignment)
Golda Meir	March 1969–June 1974	Labor (Alignment)
Yitzhak Rabin	June 1974–June 1977	Labor (Alignment)
Menahem Begin	June 1977–October 1983	Likud
Yitzhak Shamir	October 1983–September 1984	Likud
Shimon Peres	September 1984–October 1986	Alignment
Yitzhak Shamir	October 1986–July 1992	Likud
Yitzhak Rabin	July 1992–November 1995	Labor
Shimon Peres (interim)	November 1995–June 1996	Labor
Benjamin Netanyahu*	June 1996–July 1999	Likud
Ehud Barak*	July 1999–March 2001	Israel Ehad / Labor
Ariel Sharon*	March 2001–April 2006	Likud / Kadima
Ehud Olmert (interim)	April–May 2006	Kadima
Ehud Olmert	May 2006–March 2009	Kadima
Benjamin Netanyahu	March 2009–Present	Likud

* Elected as prime minister in direct elections.

with failing health led to his departure from office. He was replaced by Yitzhak Shamir, only two years younger, who was also a founding father of the country.

Following the long single-party dominance of Labor, Israel seemed to turn into a two-big-party system, with Labor and Likud dominating. This system remained in place until 2003, when Sharon split Likud, his new centrist Kadima Party drew leaders from both Labor and Likud, and Kadima replaced Labor as the alternative leading party. That did not mean other parties lost their importance and bargaining leverage, but no one party has been able to establish a long-term hegemony as Labor did during Israel's first three decades.

After the 1984 election, this new bipolarity was underlined by the power-sharing arrangement between Labor, led by Shimon Peres—who, like Rabin, was a member of the second generation to become prime minister—and Yitzhak Shamir. Each man held the office for two years before the Likud Party regained power in 1988. Two features of this period were the struggle for leadership within the Labor Party between Rabin and Peres, and Peres's persistent and failed attempts to bring down the Shamir government.

Israel's prime minister and co-winner of the Nobel Peace Prize in 1978, Menahem Begin (1913–1992), on the CBS current affairs program *Face the Nation,* June 1982. (Getty Images / Image Bank.)

The alternation between Labor and Likud prevailed between 1977 and 2003. Thus, Rabin won the 1992 elections; Peres took over when Rabin was assassinated in 1995; Peres lost the 1996 elections and was replaced by the first third-generation Likud leader, Benjamin Netanyahu. Netanyahu served as prime minister from 1996 to 1999. Deep conflicts in the Likud Party helped lead to the victory of Netanyahu's contemporary and Rabin's protégé, Ehud Barak, in 1999. The failure of the Oslo peace process then brought into office the Likud's Ariel Sharon in 2001.

This complex history reflects the simple duality of a struggle between two parties for power. Each party had a set of more and of less reliable potential coalition partners. The parties to the left of center favored Labor, those to the right of center were more willing to join with Likud, and the religious parties basically held the balance. Still, even added together, the two main parties did not have more than about 60 percent of the total Knesset seats in the 1981, 1984, 1988, and 1992 elections. Their share has fallen even more since then with the rise of several medium-sized parties.

The 1990s saw an attempt to institutionalize the two-main-party system by the direct election of prime minister, and it was under those rules that the 1996 and 1999 elections were held. This experiment was ultimately deemed unsatisfactory, however, because a division of control over the prime minister's office and the Knesset made Israelis worry about the government's ability to act decisively. On the first occasion, Labor won the most seats in the Knesset, and Likud's Netanyahu became prime minister. On the second occasion, Labor's Barak won the most Knesset seats, but Labor still held only a little more than 20 percent of them, the lowest total ever for a ruling party. Afterward, the country's return to a single vote for a party list to elect the Knesset, with the prime minister thus being chosen indirectly, enjoyed overwhelming support.

Ehud Barak (front left) and Benjamin Netanyahu (front right) at the handover-of-office ceremonies in the Prime Minister's Office following Barak's 1999 election victory. (Getty Images / Image Bank.)

While there has been some debate from time to time over whether the prime minister's office is becoming too strong or too weak, this has never developed into a major concern. The principal critique of the system is the need to make so many coalition partnerships, which is perceived as producing corruption, waste, and an excessive influence for special interest groups.

This last point is usually made by secular forces complaining about the leverage of religious parties, although the latter's rivalries and the ease with which a Labor or Likud prime minister can play them off against one another somewhat reduces their power. The concerns have lessened as immigration from the former Soviet Union proportionately reduced the religious parties' power.

The third era of Israeli politics was ushered in by Ariel Sharon. Elected prime minister in 2001, he wanted to build a centrist base for his strategy of unilateral withdrawal from the Gaza Strip and concessions on some Palestinian-related issues that went beyond what his Likud Party was willing to give. Consequently, he split from the party, which he had played a central role in forming, while also taking defectors—including Peres—from Labor. The new party was called Kadima (Forward).

It seemed that Israel would now have a three-main-party system. Kadima remained in power after Sharon suffered a disabling stroke. His designated heir Ehud Olmert replaced him but resigned in a corruption scandal, necessitating elections in 2009. Following a very close election between Benjamin Netanyahu and Tzipi Livni, Netanyahu won because he was able to form a coalition. Far more parties felt closer to his views than to Livni's.

Former Israeli prime minister Ariel Sharon, January 2006. (Getty Images / Image Bank.)

His most important coalition partner was Barak, who became minister of defense. Remaining in the coalition not only accorded with Barak's policy views generally and his powerful role as defense minister but also ensured his continued leadership of Labor despite growing criticism. In 2011, the majority of Labor MKs split with Barak, took the party out of the coalition, and moved toward the left. Barak, with a minority of Labor MKs, stayed in the government and formed his own party. It seemed as if the long role of Labor as a leading party was at an end.

An apparent theme of contemporary Israeli politics is a competition to be seen as centrist enough to pull in a variety of voters. This means that parties with a stronger ideological bent, a specific constituency, and more extreme stands may become middle-sized parties or coalition partners but cannot hope to play the leading role.

The most likely possibility for the future is a Likud-Kadima competition for leadership, with Labor sinking to the status of a permanent middle-sized party. Other middle-sized parties include Shas, with its Sephardic-Mizrahi, religious-ethnic base, and Avigdor Lieberman's Yisrael Beiteinu, with its base mainly of immigrants from the former Soviet Union. The more left-wing, right-wing, and religious parties generally remain quite fragmented.

JUDICIAL BRANCH

Israel's judicial system is independent from the other two branches of government by law, although the Ministry of Justice manages the system. Prior to the establishment of the State of Israel in 1948, the British Mandate established a judicial structure based entirely on the British judicial system. It included peace courts, whose responsibilities coincided with those of justices of the peace in the United States, along with district courts and a high court.

Today the court system in the State of Israel contains elements of British, Ottoman, and Jewish law. Since 1948, a body of Israeli case law has been built up, and this has become an important component of the legal system. In 1948, after Israel declared its independence, the British judicial system previously in effect was retained. But the British system had never completely displaced its predecessor, and the current use of religious courts governing matters of personal status is a continuation of the pre-1918 Ottoman system.

In 1953 the law regarding the appointment of judges transferred authority from the prime minister to the president, who would be guided by input from a committee made up of Supreme Court judges, members of the bar, and public figures, to ensure the courts' independence from the executive branch.

An even more important, and still controversial, change came in 1995, when the Supreme Court established its right to review laws to make sure they did not violate the Basic Laws. This ability to rule laws as unconstitutional solidified the superiority of the Basic Laws and greatly added to the power of the court. While generally accepted, the right to review sometimes makes religious and conservative groups angry, for they see the court as acting more like a court of the political and secular left than like the court of the state as a whole. The court system is nevertheless one of the institutions in which the Israeli public consistently reports high levels of trust.

The judiciary in Israel is divided into two sections: the general law courts, also known as the civil courts, and the tribunals. The general law courts have authority over criminal, civil, and administrative issues; the tribunals have more specific and personal jurisdiction. The religious Jewish courts, which are considered tribunals, rule mainly in matters of personal status—for example, in such family matters such as marriage and divorce. No courts in Israel operate using a jury system.

Supreme Court

At the top of Israel's judicial hierarchy is the Supreme Court, which also has the tricky job of finding the correct balance between individual rights and the needs of the state. The Supreme Court comprises ten justices appointed by a special commission made up of the justice minister, another cabinet minister, two serving Supreme Court justices, the president, two Knesset members, and two members of the Israeli Bar Association. Justices serve until death, resignation, or mandatory retirement at age seventy. A justice can be dismissed if the president or another justice recommends it and if seven of the nine commission members agree.

The Supreme Court is situated in the capital city of Jerusalem and has jurisdiction over the entire country as both the high court of appeals and as the High Court of Justice for special or severe cases that do not fall under the jurisdiction of other courts or tribunals. All rulings by the Supreme Court have precedence over other courts or previous rulings.

In recent years, the Supreme Court has usually included at least one Dati and one Arab judge. Three to five justices rule on regular cases. Under certain circumstances, the Supreme Court has the authority to order a retrial. Cases also reach the Supreme Court when a petition is brought against a government body, in which case the Court functions as the High Court of Justice. Palestinians in the West Bank often take this route to pursue grievances, such as objections to the route of the security fence.

The six mid-level district courts have regional jurisdictions. The judges preside over criminal and civil cases for which the potential punishment is a jail term above seven years or a fine of over one million shekels. These courts also rule in prisoner appeals, company and partnership cases, and tax matters. Usually one judge is appointed to handle a case.

Israel's twenty-nine magistrate or peace (*shalom*) courts deal mainly with criminal and civil offenses in which the penalty is under seven years' imprisonment or a fine of under a million shekels. They also function as municipal, family, small claims, traffic, and tenancy courts. One judge generally presides in each case unless the president of the court decides otherwise.

Defendants who are minors generally stand trial in juvenile courts, to which special judges are appointed by the Supreme Court's president with the justice minister's approval. In some cases in which the minor committed a first offense, the judge may give a lenient penalty, such as house arrest instead of imprisonment.

The Israeli legal system also includes tribunals that focus on religious, military, or labor issues. Each type of tribunal answers to a different higher agency: religious to the relevant religious authorities, military to the Defense Ministry, and labor to the Justice Ministry.

Religious tribunals always existed in Jewish communities but were granted official status in 1922, under British rule. They deal with such matters as marriage, divorce, and family disputes. Jews go to a rabbinical court, and Muslims attend a court operating under shari'a law, which is based on the Quran. Druze and Christians have their own religious courts. The Ministry of Justice is responsible for appointing judges (*dayanim*) to the rabbinical courts. The Knesset is responsible for electing the Muslim and Druze judges (*qadis*).

Military tribunals are held to try soldiers accused of military offenses or civilian offenses committed while they are serving as soldiers. These courts were established in 1955 under the Military Justice Law. Generally, a military tribunal panel comprises two officer judges and one judge appointed by the minister of defense. Under rare circumstances, serious cases may be moved to the Supreme Court for a ruling.

In 1969 the Knesset established the labor court system under the Ministry of Justice to handle the rising number of labor-related cases. Regional labor courts hold the trials and national labor courts deal with the many submitted appeals. The cases concern disputes involving workers, employers, workers' unions, and employer organizations regarding such issues as pension fund agreements, salaries, and unlawful dismissal claims.

Under ordinary circumstances, a panel of three sits on the regional courts—one judge and two public representatives who act for the employees and employers in the cases. The national courts, which are higher than the regional courts, usually seat between three and five judges at appeal hearings, depending on the severity of the issue.

Administrative tribunals are ad hoc courts designed to deal with specific legal issues that require a specialist's assessment to determine an outcome. These tribunals deal with social benefits, contracts, trade practices (such as antitrust suits), tax liability, injury compensation, and other such matters. A single judge usually sits at the head of these tribunals, which come under the direct jurisdiction of the Ministry of Justice.

The government has the authority to set up other one-time tribunals known as commissions of inquiry to investigate government actions. These are usually related to the conduct of wars or high-profile scandals. Members of these commissions are appointed by the head of the Supreme Court. Important commissions of inquiry include the Agranat Commission (1974) that investigated the management of the Yom Kippur War of 1973; the Kahan Commission (1984) that investigated the Sabra and Shatila massacre during the First Lebanon War; and the Winograd Commission (2006) that investigated the handling of the Second Lebanon War.

In addition to the courts, the political system attempts to uphold the rule of law through the attorney general. The attorney general is appointed by the government but acts independently in representing the state for all civil, criminal, and administrative matters. Further, the attorney general tells the government what actions he or she finds illegal, and has jurisdiction over questions of parliamentary immunity. The attorney general can transfer cases between civilian and military courts. Not infrequently an attorney general investigates and even indicts politicians in the government that appointed him or her.

Judicial Activism

Since the 1990s the Supreme Court has used its power in a broader way than in the past, using "judicial activism" to influence policy. Chief Justice Aharon Barak stated judicial activism was intended to increase freedoms in line with the values of the enlightened part of Israeli society. Barak said he preferred the Knesset to act, but in cases where it did not, he maintained that the court could do so. Any Israeli can bring a case to the court to challenge a government action.

Religious groups viewed judicial activism by the Supreme Court as a way to reduce their own power, for example, by breaking the Orthodox monopoly on religious conversions in Israel. The argument was that this decision bypassed the Knesset and the agreement to maintain the status quo—that is, the balance between religious and secular power in personal status matters. Antagonized by the court's activities, a leading rabbi, David Yosef, asked the crowd at a 1997 Shas rally, "What do you think of the rule of law?" and was answered with thousands of jeering whistles.

Some secular Israelis see such comments as posing a theocratic threat to their way of life and to democracy. As with many such passionate conflicts in Israel, however, this verbal debate has little or no actual effect. The Supreme Court's unilateral expansion of its powers, a major shift in the national political structure, has been accepted with surprising equanimity.

The Supreme Court has ruled mainly against laws having to do with extremist incitement, violations of rights, and antidiscrimination issues, as well as with laws and policies having to do with the administration of the West Bank and the Gaza Strip. In 1999, for example, the Supreme Court ruled that security agencies could not use torture in investigations of terrorists. It also has issued important rulings on the precise location of the security fence built to protect Israel from terrorist attacks.

PRESIDENCY

According to the Basic Law on the President of 1964, the president is the head of the State of Israel, but the position must be apolitical and is separate from the three branches of the government. While the president's position is mainly symbolic, it is also important because the president represents national unity, consensus views, and the people as a whole. The president is elected for seven years and may only serve one term. Members of the Knesset nominate candidates and elect the president in a secret ballot. Any citizen is eligible by law to be elected president.

Traditionally, the position of president was given to an older person as a final post after a long record of service in politics, science, or academia. In earlier years, the president was often elected with only token opposition. Since 1983, however, the position has been more competitive, with some of the largest parties nominating their own candidates.

The Law on the President specifies that the role of the president includes signing every bill before it becomes law; accepting a prime minister's and a government's resignation; overseeing the government's general actions; approving the appointment of Israel's diplomats and receiving foreign diplomats; approving international treaties and agreements that have been approved by the Knesset; and participating in the appointment of court judges, rabbinical dayanim, and other high-profile state officials, such as the governor of the Bank of Israel and members of the Council of Higher Education.

The president must carry out these tasks regardless of personal preferences. At other times, the president makes decisions. After elections, the president must select the candidate thought capable of forming a stable government. The president also has to decide whether to give a government permission to dissolve itself. The most controversial duty is pardoning criminals or prisoners deemed to be rehabilitated. The president can erase convictions and reduce sentences or penalties.

Israel's first presidents were men selected because of their high levels of service to the state, but not necessarily because they were active in politics. Israel's first president was Chaim Weizmann, a chemist who had been international leader of the Zionist movement for thirty years. Indeed, that appointment was thought by many to be Ben-Gurion's method of getting Weizmann out of his way by neutralizing a man who had led the movement abroad but had no actual experience in the Yishuv.

Following Weizmann's death in 1952, the presidency was offered to another scientist, Albert Einstein, but he declined, and Yitzhak Ben-Zvi became Israel's second president. He was a leading figure in the Labor Party and Israel's struggle for independence, although he was seen as a historian rather than a politician. Other presidents followed the pattern of being a scientist or politician.

ISRAEL'S PRESIDENTS

Name	Years in Office
Chaim Weizmann	1948–1952
Yitzhak Ben-Zvi	1952–1963
Shneur Zalman Shazar	1963–1973
Efraim Katzir	1973–1978
Yitzhak Navon	1978–1983
Haim Herzog	1983–1993
Ezer Weizman	1993–2000
Moshe Katzav	2000–2007
Shimon Peres	2007–Present

Former Israeli prime minister and Labor Party chair Shimon Peres speaking at an assembly of the Jewish Agency for Israel, June 2004. (Getty Images / Image Bank.)

In 1978, Yitzhak Navon became the first Mizrahi Jew to become president, and in 2000, Moshe Katzav became the first president born in a Middle Eastern country besides Israel (Iran). His presidency ended in disgrace owing to allegations of sexual harassment. Shimon Peres's election to the presidency in 2007 was seen as a way both to honor the country's elder statesman and to restore honor, after Katzav's scandalous conduct, to the country's most prominent position.

CIVIL SERVICE

The ministries and departments that make up the public sector of the government are run by the civil service bureaucracy. In the 1950s the post of civil service commissioner was created to keep the bureaucracy from being politicized. Among the twenty permanent ministerial-level agencies are the Prime Minister's Office and the Ministries of Defense, Foreign Affairs, the Treasury, Justice, Education and Culture, the Interior, Agriculture, Industry and Trade, Transportation, Health, Labor and Social Welfare, Immigrant Absorption, Tourism, and Environment Quality.

The Prime Minister's Office formulates the government's main policies and strategies. Given the growing complexity of policymaking and the problems faced by Israel, this office has grown rapidly in size. Its subsidiaries include the National Security Council, whose formation Netanyahu pushed in the 1990s to copy the American model; other prime ministers have mostly ignored it. The National Economic Council advises the prime minister on economic matters. The Government's Press Office deals with media attention and foreign correspondents, a much bigger job than in comparable small countries.

The Foreign Ministry is a highly professional organization but understaffed and insufficiently financed given the many issues and pressures faced by Israel. It is also responsible for Israel's informational struggle, called *hasbara*; for running embassies abroad; and for dealing with foreign diplomats in Israel. Career diplomats periodically complain that prime ministers often give top ambassadorships to political appointees.

The prime minister can also take over key issues—especially relations with the United States—or circumvent a foreign minister who doesn't enjoy the leader's confidence for policy or personal reasons. It is important to remember that the foreign minister is usually not someone freely chosen by the prime minister but is instead likely to be either the prime minister's rival within his or her own party or the leader of the number-two coalition party.

Israel's security situation and the threats of war and conflict make the Ministry of Defense especially important, and prime ministers, as well as Knesset members, usually heed advice from that quarter. Not only does the ministry run the armed forces and handle all weapon purchases, but it also runs several defense industries. For the sake of its own security, the Defense Ministry is the only government institution headquartered in Tel Aviv rather than Jerusalem.

The prime minister usually has more freedom in choosing the defense minister, since it is widely recognized that the country cannot afford the risk of picking someone who is not fully qualified. The problems with Peretz during the 2006 war underlined that point. Another important factor is that the prime minister relies primarily on information supplied by military intelligence, not, as in most other democratic states, on information supplied by civilian intelligence agencies.

LOCAL GOVERNMENT

As a geographically small nation with a small population, a focus on security and foreign policy, and a political system that treats the whole population as a single constituency, local government may seem less important than in other countries. Indeed, the local institutions do not have much power, although they are responsible for elements of education, health, social welfare, infrastructure, sanitation, and culture. A local authority might implement certain policies, but it is by and large the national government that makes the decisions. Utilities, construction, education, and the police force are all directed from national ministries through their own local agents.

The Ministry of the Interior oversees the network of local authorities and provides them with funds. Additional income comes from local taxes, but the Ministry of the Interior controls the level of tax each municipality is permitted to collect, making local governments even more dependent on the national government.

Local governments' main powers are in education and religion. Educational policy is set by the national Ministry of Education, but municipalities can raise money for schools. Then the local boards of education can decide which policies to implement and how to do so. Local councils can also decide the level of public religious observance that will occur in the area under their jurisdiction, such as whether or not public transportation is permitted on the Sabbath.

There are three kinds of local governments. Municipal governments serve large urban areas. Local councils serve towns of 2,000 to 20,000 residents. Regional councils manage associations of small, nearby villages. Residents of each local government elect a mayor or chair and a local council. As with Knesset elections, those who serve on the local council are determined by the votes each party receives. The Ministry of Interior sets the number of seats on each council depending on population. Elections occur every five years.

Voting rates among Israeli Jews in municipal elections are typically low, although some races become more heated if hot-button topics like public religious observance are up for debate. On the other hand, voting rates among Israeli Arabs in municipal elections are generally very high, both out of loyalty to their candidates and out of a sense of empowerment, since local government is one area of Israeli politics in which Israeli Arabs, often the majority in towns and villages, have the most direct control in government.

ELECTORAL SYSTEM

Israel's national electoral system is based on proportional representation. The number of votes each party receives translates directly into the number of seats the party receives in the Knesset. The only exception is that a party needs to pass a minimum threshold by receiving at least 2 percent of the vote to gain a seat in the Knesset. The purpose of that rule was to reduce the number of small parties, although its effect has been limited.

Although the large number of parties is often decried, there is no serious movement to change the system. Having many parties and government by coalition makes government less efficient and forces the making of many deals that many people do not like. Yet the situation also makes representation more directly possible for diverse groups. In the 2009 election, for example, thirty-three parties were on the ballot, and twelve obtained seats. Of these, three had the minimum of three seats (left-wing Jewish, right-wing, and Arab); another three had four seats (a right-wing and two Arab parties); and one had five seats (Haredim religious). The result was that twenty-six seats, more than 20 percent of the total, were tied to small parties. The two biggest parties (Likud at twenty-seven seats and Kadima at twenty-eight seats) together had somewhat fewer than half the seats.

The system, then, ensures that electoral power is dispersed. The larger parties argue that since what is most important is which leader and party rule the country, voting for a small party is a wasted ballot. Small parties respond that a vote for them ensures the existence of a force to push the government to the left or the right—depending on the party—and makes it more responsive to religious, secular, immigrant, or Mizrahi interests.

Since voters support a party as a whole rather than a specific person, they do not influence the careers of individual candidates, except the prime minister's, and even that indirectly. Voting by party puts more of a focus on issues than does the common Western model in which voters may vote for individual politicians merely because they are charismatic, good-looking, or articulate on television. Voting by party also encourages parties to take stances that are clearly different from their rivals'. In much Western politics, the tendency is for each party to try to appeal to all voters.

By holding primaries, as some parties do, voters who are party members can participate in selecting the candidates on party ballots. Primaries also provide an incentive for citizens to join a party formally, counteracting the general trend in Western democracies toward reduced party loyalty. But the party leaders still determine the precise lineup in the party list.

The order of the candidates on the list is extremely important. After an election, the total number of votes is divided by 120, the number of seats in the Knesset. The number resulting from the division is used to calculate how many seats each party will have. Parties that win at least 2 percent of the vote gain one seat for each multiple of the index number.

In 2009, for example, there were roughly 3.3 million valid votes. About 100,000 of them went to parties that did not make the minimum of 2 percent. Thus, a party received one seat for approximately every 27,000 votes received. The 100,000 "wasted" votes were then redistributed to those parties closest to gaining another seat. Two parties often make vote-sharing agreements to pool their "extra" votes. The partner that gets the most votes above what is needed to earn its last seat gets the "extra" votes of both, thus gaining one more representative.

The Basic Law on elections (the Knesset Law) calls for Knesset elections to be secret, direct, nationwide, and based on proportional representation. Every Israeli citizen over the age of eighteen has the right to vote. Elections are managed by the Central Elections Committee (CEC), which comprises one Supreme Court justice and members of the parties represented in the outgoing Knesset. The CEC has the right to decide whether a candidate or a party violates the laws governing who can run, a decision that can be reviewed and overturned by the Supreme Court.

It is not difficult to form a party or list to run for the Knesset. Before the elections, each party must present a platform and its candidates listed in order of preference. A candidate who drops out or resigns is replaced by the next name on the list. Anyone over the age of twenty-one—aside from the incumbent president, judges, state comptroller, senior public officials, and chief of staff—is eligible to be a candidate. Parties sitting in the outgoing Knesset are automatically qualified to run; new parties must put down a monetary deposit and collect 2,500 signatures to present to the Central Elections Committee.

The thirty-three parties that ran in 2009 exceeded the previous record of thirty-one in 1981. Parties have the option of running a joint list, which increases their chance of passing the threshold and obtaining more seats. At times, these alliances seem natural, as when Ashkenazic and Mizrahi Haredi parties run under one banner or when a group of left-wing parties merged to run together as Meretz. Sometimes partnerships are more unlikely, as when the religious, left-wing Meimad teamed up with the Green Movement in 2009 or when the Holocaust Survivors Party ran on a ticket with the pro-marijuana Green Leaf Party in the same election. In neither case did the alliance pass the threshold percentage of votes.

Some campaigning begins as soon as an election is announced, but campaigning cannot legally begin until three weeks prior to election day. On the opening date, posters and advertisements sponsored by the parties plaster the country and fill the airwaves. Each party is given a set amount of free television time based on how many votes it received in the previous election.

Election corruption in Israel is limited to disputes in each election about whether false ballots were cast in one or two precincts. The main problem is campaign contributions that break regulations strictly limiting fund-raising. High-ranking officials of different parties have been prosecuted, sometimes successfully, over violations, which sometimes involve illegal foreign contributions.

It should be stressed, though, that the level of spending does not make a big difference, nor does clever advertising sway many votes, since there are clear reasons for voters to choose the party they support. A key calculation is whether to back a smaller party that more closely corresponds to one's views or a larger party that could form the government and thus have greater power to implement change that voters want. Roughly half the voters choose according to one or the other of these options.

In 1988 an unusual scandal erupted when Shas "bought" votes by promising to give religious benefits. After that, it became illegal for parties to "buy" votes with blessings or amulets (or to withhold them or to curse those who voted for a different party), just as it is illegal to buy votes with money or political favors. Nonetheless, a certain amount of buying continues on a small scale among religious constituencies.

On election day, the voter steps into a curtained booth and chooses from a tray of small slips of paper on a shelf, each carrying the name of a party and its symbol. The Labor Party, for example, is represented by the letters that spell out the Hebrew word for "truth"; Kadima, by the letters that spell out "yes." New parties can choose their letters, but traditionally the fifth letter of the Hebrew alphabet is not used, because it is also the symbol for God's name.

MAJOR POLITICAL ISSUES

Politics in Israel tend to revolve around a few major questions. Since 1967 the main focus has been on a cluster of security issues: the fate of the West Bank, the Gaza Strip, and the Golan Heights; the potential for peace with the country's Arab neighbors and the Palestinians; and the degree of civilians' safety from terrorist and military attacks. Political parties, as well as members of the electorate, generally identify as right, left, or center based on their views. The left end of the spectrum places a higher premium on negotiations and concessions in the belief that these could achieve peace; and the right end, on skepticism, security, and—though more so before 2000 than afterward—retention of territories captured in 1967.

In addition to matters of peace and security, religion is a major political (as well as social and cultural) factor in Israel. Of the religiously identified sectors, however, the Dati Party (National Religious Party) has focused increasingly on security issues, while the Sephardic and Mizrahi Haredi party (Shas) emphasize constituency services.

The National Religious Party's failure to make its voters' needs its priority was a cause of its downfall. Since Shas has put the emphasis on obtaining and spending funds, its critics have complained about the amount of money it has received and about corruption. With United Torah Judaism and the Ashkenazic Haredi party, the controversies revolve around whether secular voters perceive them as trying to expand religious observance in society at large.

The (Ashkenazic) Haredim advocate enforcing certain religious practices in public, such as stopping public transport on the Sabbath and confirming rabbinic control over personal status issues. They also want to maximize budget allocations for their school systems, maintain military exemption for Haredi men, and retain high child allowances for families with more than five children. Those on the most secular end advocate separation of religion and state, including the establishment of civil marriage. Small secular parties highlighting the issue have come and gone without retaining enough leverage to change much. Most Israelis are content to maintain the status quo. The main parties—Likud, Labor, and Kadima—would not sacrifice the ability to form a coalition to push through such changes. Thus, the secular-religious balance remains very stable over time despite much controversy and debate.

The Arab parties, though considered to be on the left, are actually interest-group parties. But they are divided because of strong ideological differences between Islamist, Communist, and Arab nationalist standpoints. The Islamists back Hamas; the Communists supported the Soviet Union until its disintegration and Fatah afterward; and the nationalists support Fatah. None of these parties has challenged the Muslim clerical domination of most Arabs' personal status issues.

Yet many Arabs, almost half, also vote for ostensibly Jewish parties to take advantage of the parties' links to the Histadrut, patronage networks, and other institutions. At times, for example, a surprising number of Arabs have voted for Shas in exchange for financial support to their towns from ministries that it controlled. Arab ties to the Labor Party have traditionally been through trade unions.

The third, though less important, focal point of Israeli politics is economic. In Israel's earlier political history, there was an ideological divide between socialists and economic liberals. Since the 1980s, modernization, privatization, and globalization have made these differences largely disappear. Israel retains aspects of a welfare state, yet a consensus across the political spectrum accepts these features. Although Amir Peretz tried to revive Labor's socialist rhetoric in the 2004 elections during his brief time as party leader, his reversion did not stem the party's decline. Consequently, the main parties in contemporary Israel do not differ greatly in economic ideology.

Entitlements have been kept at a low enough level to be sustainable, unlike in many other Western countries, where such government payments have swamped the national budget and contributed to massive debt. To some extent, the need for high levels of defense spending has made excessive entitlements impossible, and because the public understands the necessity of the defense priority, it has accepted that orientation.

Aside from these issues, the major impetus for creating parties is to champion a single issue or constituency. Small parties have been created around the interests of immigrants from the former Soviet Union, the environment (there have been several green parties), pensioners' rights, and even the legalization of marijuana.

Historically, one other motive for creating parties has been the idea that a centrist group, located between Labor and Likud, could muster wide support. The electorate might well vote for a party that could presumably provide good government and consensus policies. Parties

An Israeli Arab woman casts her ballot at a polling station in the Israeli Arab town of Kfar Qara, February 2009. (Getty Images / Image Bank.)

formed to fill the gap have generally been short-lived. Although Kadima was not founded on this basis—but rather on the basis of Ariel Sharon's personal choices and security issues—it has used such arguments in seeking voter support during elections with a large degree of success.

POLITICAL PARTIES

Israel is often defined as a party state, meaning that political parties rather than personalities drive politics. Elections and trends in public opinion since the 1990s show a slight shift. The perceived character of the candidate for prime minister is important, especially whether that person can be trusted with the nation's security and survival. For Israel, character is no abstract issue.

Most voters know where they fit most comfortably. Often the main decision they must make is whether to vote for a big party that they feel will implement their general ideas or a smaller party that reflects their views more closely. Historically the main choices would be between Labor and a small left-wing party (for those left of center); Likud or a small right-wing party (for those right of center); or—for Datim—their community's religious party, a small right-wing party, or Likud.

Israel's party system evolved from the world Zionist movement of the pre-state era. Many contemporary parties—holding almost half the Knesset seats after the 2009 election—are in fact descendants of Eastern European Zionist organizations that were part of the movement and had their own newspapers, sports clubs, health insurance, youth movements, and labor unions. The party system based on Zionism existed in full force until the 1970s, and remnants of it still exist with party youth movements and some other institutions.

Jerusalem's main soccer team still bears the name Beitar, identifying it with the Likud, which probably remains the political choice for most of its fans. The Tel Aviv teams in the Premier League have parallel names: Hapoel (Labor), Maccabi (descended from centrist-liberal parties that no longer exist), and Bnai Yehuda (Datim). Haifa's main team is also named Maccabi.

The Labor Party's predecessors in particular developed strong organizations that touched the lives of most citizens. The main organizations include the Histadrut labor union, which also controlled the biggest health-care fund, and most of the kibbutzim and cooperative villages (moshavim). By the 1990s a combination of influences—consumerism, globalization, a substantial immigrant influx, the growth of grassroots' volunteer groups, and rising individualism—led to a decline in the strength of permanent party loyalties in general and the prominence of party-controlled organizations in particular.

Still, political parties remain by far the main framework through which politics is conducted in Israel, and loyalties are strong by the standards of comparable societies. The main change in Israel has been that a floating vote actually exists; also, some historic Labor and Likud voters switched to Kadima.

Left-of-Center Parties

The left side of the political spectrum among Jewish voters in Israel derives from the heritage of the Labor Zionists, who coupled socialist ideology with Jewish nationalism. Two streams—Mapai (ancestor of the Labor Party) and the further left Mapam (ancestor of Meretz)—defined themselves against the anti-Zionist Communist and Bundist left of that era. It should be noted that both Labor and Mapam and descendent parties have often elected Arab and Druze members as candidates on their lists.

Labor

The Labor Party was formed as such in 1968, although it is basically the same party as the one that ruled Israel during the previous two decades under the name Mapai. Its formation was facilitated by a sense of national unity following the Six-Day War in 1967. Although the left-wing Mapam Party did not join Labor, it formed a joint electoral list with Labor for some years, mostly between 1969 and 1991, known as the Labor Alignment. The early years of the Labor Party were marked by tension between the old guard—exemplified by Prime Minister Golda Meir's reliance on her "kitchen cabinet"—and younger leaders.

The Labor Party began to change after the Yom Kippur War in 1973 and the subsequent inquiry (Agranat Commission) that judged the government's preparedness for the war harshly. Meir and her associates stepped down. Yitzhak Rabin, a younger, native-born leader associated with the 1967 victory in the Six-Day War but not the 1973 war (since he was ambassador to the

United States at the time) became the new party leader. Rabin was not closely associated with any of the three factions that made up Labor, and the other top slots in the party—defense minister and foreign minister—went to Shimon Peres and Yigal Allon, respectively.

Despite internal reorganization, several factors—the 1973 war, allegations of corruption, and tension with the religious parties—forced early elections in 1977. The results of those elections, which brought Likud to power, signaled the end of the left's three-decade-long reign and marked a turning point in Israeli politics and history.

In the three decades following that watershed event, Labor's fortunes have been mixed. It has won only a few elections but has served in the coalition government for about half of those years. In 1984, Labor once again became the largest party in the Knesset, but it was unable to form a coalition by itself, the same fate that befell Likud in 1988.

In 1992, to reverse Labor's fortunes and restore it to the power it once held, the party tried to redefine itself by deemphasizing its connection with socialism, the kibbutz movement, and the Histadrut labor union. With the more centrist and popular Rabin beating Shimon Peres in the party primary, the party rebranded itself as "Labor Headed by Rabin" to attract voters.

The changes were effective, as was Labor's ability to appeal to new immigrants, and it won the most seats in 1992. After Rabin's assassination, Peres again took over. While the earlier reforms were kept, Peres lost the 1996 elections, for a variety of reasons, but his low personal popularity was clearly a factor, especially since the prime minister was elected directly that year.

Since then, Labor's number of Knesset seats has steadily declined. In 1996 it gained thirty-four seats, but the number fell to twenty-six in 1999, to an average of twenty in the 2003 and 2006 elections, to thirteen in 2009, and then down to eight after party leader Ehud Barak's decision to quit the party with three other MKs in January 2011. Barak's decision left Labor at a historic nadir, facing an uncertain future as a minor, second-tier presence on the Israeli political stage.

What caused this decline? The main external factor was the failure of the peace process in 2000. Labor had staked its reputation on the success of the peace process. The attempt to achieve a full peace treaty with the Palestinians in exchange for major concessions was the culmination of arguments the party had been making for the previous three decades.

Many of the causes of the decline can be traced to mistakes by the party's leadership. Sharon's decision to create the Kadima Party came at the precise moment when the Labor Party was in turmoil following Amir Peretz's purge of many from leadership positions (including Peres) when he took power in 2005. Consequently, Kadima received several high-level Labor defectors as well as the support of many of the party's voters.

A second internal problem was the party's lack of identity. Promoting socialism and what used to be called Labor values was no longer viable in a much-changed Israeli society. Dovish stances were not politically profitable after 2000. The party was not able to come up with a new approach, and when it moved to the left, the decline became steeper.

Third, the party had weak leadership, especially compared with the giants of the past. Amram Mitzna (2002–2003) and Amir Peretz (2005–2007) were poor party leaders; voters saw the former as naive and condemned Peretz for his poor performance in the 2006 war with Hizballah. Ehud Barak (1996–2001; since 2007) had to deal with the failed peace process. No one denied his high intelligence, but nobody claimed that he had any charisma either. Equally, his arrogance and lack of political skills created much conflict within the party.

Finally, the party drifted too far to the left in 2002–2007, which was especially damaging since voters were headed in the opposite direction. Barak brought it back toward the center, but it remains unclear whether he or anyone else can rebuild Labor into a ruling party.

Meretz

Meretz, a left-wing secular party, was formed from the small Ratz, Mapam, and Shinui parties prior to the 1992 election. Its name is an acronym standing for Mapam and Ratz and means "energy." The party's platform called for ending the Israeli presence in the West Bank; equality for Israeli Arabs, women, and homosexuals; and separation of religion and state.

In the 1992 election, at the peak of hopes for a breakthrough to peace, Meretz won twelve seats, an all-time high for a left-wing party. It became the third-largest party in the Knesset and joined the center-left coalition. Its number of seats fell somewhat in 1996 and 1999 but, after the failure of the peace process, declined sharply to only six seats in 2003, when the widely respected Yossi Sarid resigned as party leader. Meretz disbanded and reformed as Yahad (Together).

Yahad sought to resuscitate the Israeli left-wing peace camp, which had been decimated by events, with very limited results. In 2005 the party added Meretz back into its name to attract voters, eventually dropping "Yahad" altogether. The reformulation and name changes did not bring electoral triumph, and the party won just five seats in 2006. In 2009 the party tried merging with the New Movement (HaTnua HaHadasha), but even together, under the leadership of Peace Now founder Haim Oron, the two parties won only three seats. The party's response to the electorate's shift toward the center has been to move further left, which has not proven a successful strategy.

Meimad

Meimad is a left-of-center religious party of Datim that takes positions similar to those of the Labor Party. It is the only religious party that does not support the religious status quo but argues that coercion alienates mainstream Israelis from the Jewish religious tradition. Thus, for example, it argues that places of entertainment should be legally open on Shabbat even though this is contrary to religious law. Meimad has a complex history of allying with Labor and other parties. With a limited constituency and a position contrasting with the views of most Datim, it has never won a seat on its own.

Arab Parties

In classifications of Arab politics, Israel's Arab parties are often said to be left-wing. This designation is misleading. They are first and foremost interest-group parties that are also opposed to Israel's existence as a Jewish state. Their emphasis on the latter issue minimizes their ability to gain state services for its constituents, which is why a large portion of Arabs vote for Zionist parties. Their basic rejection of the status quo prevents them from joining government coalitions or bargaining to provide their votes in the Knesset in exchange for benefits.

A second critical reason for these parties' failure to win more votes is the deep and bitter rivalry among the Arab parties, which reflects clear ideological differences between Communists, Islamists, and Arab nationalists. In addition, party loyalties are linked to family and clan allegiances which makes it difficult for constituents to shop among the parties in order to get the greatest advantage for themselves. In 2009, for instance, the three Arab parties received eleven seats with about 9 percent of the total ballots, only half the Arab portion of the population. One of the parties, Balad, barely exceeded the minimum vote for getting any representation at all. They thus remain small and ineffective.

At one time, several Arab lists existed in affiliation with Mapai, allowing Arab candidates to be simultaneously independent and linked to Mapai. This system ended when Labor lost control of the government in 1977. By the 1980s, Israel's security situation had relaxed, and a new opportunity arose for Arab parties to participate in politics on the national level.

The Supreme Court has upheld the right of Arab parties to run in elections and the right of their members to serve in the Knesset despite a law stating that parties running for the Knesset must uphold the principle of Israel as a Jewish and democratic state. The Arab parties, at least those other than the Communists, do not meet that standard.

Hadash (Communists)

The Palestinian Communist Party was founded in 1924. Most members of this party were Jews sympathetic with the Soviet Union who viewed Zionism as a bourgeois movement. When it tried to become a Jewish Arab party, differences between the two constituent groups often divided them. In 1948 the Palestinian and Jewish factions reunited. They maintained their opposition to Zionism but pledged loyalty to the state.

The party followed Soviet policy—which supported Arab nationalism and opposed Israel but never criticized the treatment of Jews in the Soviet Union—and gradually lost almost all of its Jewish members, becoming in effect an Arab nationalist party. As a result, the party split in 1965. The Jewish party, Maki, disintegrated in 1973; the new Rakah Party went further in the Arab nationalist direction.

In 1977 the party changed its name to Hadash (Democratic Front for Peace and Equality) when it tried to join with other left-wing, non-Communist groups in a failed attempt to attract more Jewish voters. The Soviet Union's fall eliminated its sponsor and reduced the party's assets. For example, one of its traditional points of appeal was the ability to provide scholarships for Israeli Arabs to study in Soviet bloc countries.

Hadash's platform calls for establishing a Palestinian state and demands recognition of Israeli Arabs as a national minority with special rights. The party has held between three and five seats in the Knesset and sometimes runs Jewish members as candidates. In an unusual development in 2008, Dov Khanin, a Jewish member of the party, made a serious run to be mayor of Tel Aviv on the City for Everyone ticket. Although he eventually lost with 34 percent, his list gained 15 percent of the city council seats.

United Arab List (Ra'am)

The United Arab List, an Islamist party, has its roots in a nationalist predecessor that was taken over. In 1988 the Arab Democratic Party (ADP) became the first solely Israeli Arab party in the Knesset when Abd al-Wahab Darawshe, a Labor MK, left his party to protest its stance on the First Intifada. The party went through a series of alliances, from which it gained from a high of four to a low of one seat in the Knesset.

In 1996 the southern faction of the Islamic Movement in Israel, a group that promotes Islam among Israeli Arabs, gained control of the United Arab List upon merging with it. Formally, to meet the legal requirements for a party to run in an Israeli election, the United Arab List advocates the existence of two states, Israel and Palestine, but Islamists in fact desire to turn Israel into an Islamist Palestine under shari'a law. Since the merger, the party has won between two and four seats in the Knesset.

The Islamist Movement's northern faction split away from the Islamic Movement because it opposed the 1996 merger with the United Arab List. It boycotts electoral politics in Israel altogether, regarding participation as a recognition of the State of Israel. The Islamists all view Israel as an illegitimate country but claim to use only democratic means as they work to replace it by an Islamist state.

The leader of the northern faction, Ra'id Salah, is the son of a retired Israeli police officer, has two brothers still on the force, and draws a government pension as a former mayor of Umm al-Fahm. Northern faction members have occasionally been involved in terrorist attacks. Both the northern and the southern factions maintain social welfare and educational groups to mobilize support and promote Islamic piety and traditional social behavior.

Balad (National Democratic Alliance)

Balad is based on an old Arab nationalist group but did not become a party until 1996, under Azmi Bishara's leadership. Formally, the party platform calls for making Israel into "a state of all its citizens" and recognizing Israeli Arabs as a national minority. It calls for two states (Israel and Palestine) and the right of return for Palestinian refugees. Although the party leaders' preference is for Israel to be transformed into a Palestinian Arab state and despite the fact that its close ties with Syria were clearly expressed, the Supreme Court overturned a CEC ruling in 2003 and 2009 that the party should be not be allowed to run in Israeli elections.

Accused of having close ties with Hizballah and other anti-Israel terrorist forces, Bishara fled Israel and openly came out as a backer of these groups in 2007. The party has won between two and three seats in the Knesset since 1999.

Center Parties

Center parties have never done well in Israel for two reasons, at least before the establishment of Kadima. First, voters had strong party loyalties to Labor and Likud, while supporters of interest-group parties proved loyal to their single-issue approach (religious or secular, left- or right-wing, or immigrants' issue) and were even more hostile to the political center. Second, center parties thought that if they focused on issues other than the Israel-Palestinian question, voters would flock to their support. Voters generally disagreed with that assessment.

Indeed, the success of Kadima as a centrist party was in contrast to both points. It drew from Labor and Likud because popular leaders in both parties left to join it. In addition, Kadima succeeded precisely because of its emphasis on a specific strategy toward the conflict.

Several parties have occupied the political center historically, including the General Zionists (later the Liberals); the Progressive Party (later the Independent Liberals); Rafi (Ben-Gurion's split from Labor); the Democratic Movement for Change (an ambitious 1977 project that ended by ensuring a Likud victory); the Center Party; Shinui; the Pensioners Party; and Kadima. The fact that all of these are defunct except Kadima, which followed a different course, indicates the problem with the centrist orientation.

The story of the Pensioners Party (Gil) provides a good example of single-election success followed by collapse. The Pensioners Party burst onto the scene in the 2006 elections on a platform of improving the status of retired people. In a major surprise, it won seven seats in the Knesset, entering the government as an important coalition partner. In 2009, however, it received few votes and lost all of its seats. Disappointed at the failure to win the promised reforms or tired of the party now that it was no longer a novelty, voters returned to their traditional loyalties.

Kadima

Prime Minister Ariel Sharon formed Kadima in 2005 by splitting from his own Likud Party in the face of extensive opposition to his plan for a unilateral disengagement from the Gaza Strip. The new party put forth the argument that maintaining Israel as a Jewish and democratic state was more important than trying to hold onto the Gaza Strip and the West Bank. It put religious and Arab candidates on its list, as well as ex-Labor and ex-Likud leaders. The party took more leaders and seats from Likud than from Labor, since many from the former party followed Sharon into Kadima. Because of Sharon's subsequent coma, Likud's Ehud Olmert took over the mantle of Kadima leadership and led the party to victory in 2006. For the first time in Israeli history neither Labor nor Likud had won an election, and for the first time a splinter party was victorious over the party that it had left.

Kadima's first term was plagued with problems, however. There was a great deal of criticism over its conduct of the Lebanon War of 2006, and there were numerous scandals. Olmert eventually resigned, and Tzipi Livni was chosen as Kadima Party leader. Livni, however, who had barely won the party primary and who had not rebelled against Olmert even when he was in serious trouble owing to credible bribe-taking accusations, failed to save her coalition.

In the February 2009 elections, Kadima won one seat more than Likud did, but because Livni appeared to be unable to form a new majority coalition, President Shimon Peres asked Likud leader Netanyahu to do so. Kadima opted to sit in the opposition, but Livni was unable to parlay her position as leader of Kadima into a strong role as opposition leader. And since Likud and Labor had both moved toward the center, it was not clear that Kadima had popular alternative solutions to offer for key political concerns.

One of the central questions in Israeli politics is whether Kadima will survive as one of the two big governing parties or, like previous centrist parties, prove to be short-lived. If the

Israeli Foreign Minister Tzipi Livni, Kadima Party candidate for prime minister, casts her ballot in a Tel Aviv polling station in February 2009. (Getty Images / Image Bank.)

latter, historians will probably see Kadima as an extension of Sharon's power and particular circumstances that could not long survive his demise. Otherwise, Kadima could be the long-term replacement for Labor in a two-party-dominated system.

Right-of-Center (Nationalist) Parties

The mainstream right in Israel is derived from Revisionist Zionism (the nationalist faction in the Zionist Movement) and the Herut Party, although some small parties also drew members from the Labor and National Religious Parties. Conservative nationalist ideology in Israel is nationalism that places a premium on meeting the security threat to the country and doubts that the Palestinians and Arabs will make and maintain peace with Israel.

From 1967 to the mid-1990s, nationalist parties generally favored holding onto all the territories captured in the 1967 war. It was the conservative Prime Minister Menahem Begin, however, who gave up the Sinai Peninsula in exchange for peace with Egypt. Today the centrist Likud Party has accepted the withdrawal from the Gaza Strip and favors holding onto the West Bank on pragmatic grounds given the absence of peace. But it has also offered to give up almost all of that territory if there is a prospect of a real and lasting peace.

Historically, parties of the right favored a more capitalist economy based on free enterprise, but with the general abandonment of socialism, this, too, has become a consensus issue. Much the same can be said about the Likud's championing of Mizrahi interests in the 1970s and 1980s, which has led to social change.

The key to understanding the Israeli right is the issue of Likud versus smaller parties. The smaller parties argue either that the Likud has become too moderate and thus must be opposed or that Likud must accept being influenced by themselves as rightist coalition partners.

The Likud's counterargument is that by voting for small parties, rightists are merely putting the left into power. In the 2009 elections, for example, the Likud obtained twenty-seven seats, compared with seven seats for the smaller parties. Support from the smaller parties was one factor in Netanyahu's being able to obtain a parliamentary majority and take office. Once in power, Likud prime ministers have tried to propitiate small rightist partners but have also been willing to dare them to leave the rightist coalition and bring it down, which happened in 1992.

Yisrael Beiteinu can be considered a right-of-center party, but its main identity is as a party of immigrants from the former Soviet Union. Still, in considering the size of the Israeli right, its large base of support should be taken into account.

Likud

The roots of Likud are in Herut, a party founded in 1948 and based on the ideology of Revisionist Zionism, established in the 1920s by Vladimir Jabotinsky. The main tenets of Revisionist Zionism in those days were a militant belief that all of the Palestine Mandate and Jordan should become a Jewish state; that a tough line should be used against the British authorities; and that large-scale Jewish immigration should begin immediately. The Revisionists, as they were called, left the World Zionist Congress in 1935 and set up their own institutions, including a labor federation, military forces (Irgun, or the IZL), and a health fund.

Once the State of Israel was established, the Revisionists formed the Herut Party and softened their positions. Still, for many years the Labor Party–dominated establishment treated Herut like a pariah. Outcaste status only intensified the inner-group loyalty of its supporters, and Herut quickly became the second-largest party in the Knesset, leading the opposition. It is part of Israeli political lore that the animosity between Ben-Gurion and Menahem Begin, the Herut Party leader, was so great that Ben-Gurion refused to call Begin by his name, instead referring to him only as the "man seated next to Dr. Menahem Bader," another Herut MK.

A major step out of isolation was the formation of the Gahal bloc with the Liberals, who formed a moderate, respectable, and middle-class group. Begin was able to increase Herut's support further by appealing to Mizrahi immigrants who felt ignored by the establishment. This strategy won the Gahal bloc twenty-six seats in the Knesset in 1965. Then Begin entered the government during the 1967 war and remained there for two years. In 1973, Gahal merged with three small groups—the State List, Free Center, and the Land of Israel Movement—to form the Likud Party.

What mainly brought the groups together was a nationalist ideology that opposed the return of territory captured in the 1967 war. A centrist party, the Democratic Movement for Change, took votes from Labor in 1977. That, added to support from the Mizrahim, gave Likud its first electoral victory, signaling the first regime change in nearly thirty years of independence.

In its first term, Likud signed a peace agreement with Egypt, destroyed Iraq's nuclear reactor, and implemented Project Renewal, a program aimed at developing poor neighborhoods. On the other hand, inflation increased dramatically, and the country's economic performance was poor. Although Begin's flexibility in making peace with Egypt enhanced the party's standing with Israelis, it also led rightists who opposed the deal to split off from the party. Despite the poor economic policy and the split-offs, Likud won reelection in 1981, but the Lebanon War in 1982 undermined its position, much the way perceived failures in the 1973 war had brought down Labor.

Netanyahu revitalized the party and marked its generational transition: he was the first second-generation leader. From 1996 on, he was the party's head except from 2001 to 2006, during Sharon's leadership. Netanyahu's term as prime minister from 1996 to 1999 was especially significant in the party's history, because he accepted the Oslo Accords and the principle of trading territory for peace, the party's first move toward becoming more centrist.

In 2001, Sharon brought Likud back to power in the aftermath of the collapse of the peace process. Sharon had long been a controversial figure; he was seen as too extreme to lead the country. Yet because Israel had changed and Sharon had moved toward the center, he was quite popular during his term in office. Netanyahu, as finance minister, also gained in popularity; even some of his most determined enemies approved of his handling of delicate privatization issues.

When Sharon announced his plan to withdraw unilaterally from the West Bank and the Gaza Strip—an idea rooted in previous Labor Party thinking—he gained approval from many left-of-center Israelis. His new popularity did not benefit the Likud, however, since Sharon left the party to join Kadima. Netanyahu, who opposed disengagement, returned to the party leadership, but it was hard hit by the defections. In the 2006 election, its voting base reached an all-time low.

Left with the party's more conservative forces, Netanyahu began moving them toward the center, which he succeeded in doing without additional defections and despite inner-party grumbling. In the 2009 election, when many voters returned from their infatuation with Kadima, Likud's vote rose by 250 percent and the party returned to the government. Netanyahu had succeeded in making Likud into a more centrist party, but with constant pressure from the right, the party could again split in the future.

National Union and HaBayit HaYehudi

Israel's farthest right-wing parties emerged mostly from two groups: those who defected from Likud and those remaining after the disintegration of the National Religious Party (NRP). The National Union and Jewish Home parties both strongly support the Jewish settlements in the West Bank and oppose withdrawal from any more territory. The main difference between them is that the former—which absorbed the old Dati NRP in 1999—has a more religious complexion. The two parties have worked together at times, but all attempts to unify the right have failed. In 2009 the National Union won four seats. HaBayit HaYehudi gained three and joined Netanyahu's coalition.

Religious Parties

Historically, the three main Jewish religious communities in Israel each had its own political party: the Mizrahi Haredim had Shas; the Datim had the National Religious Party (NRP); and the Ashkenazic Haredim had the United Torah Judaism (UTJ) Party. The NRP no longer exists as such. First it became a right-wing party, focusing on the single issue of Jewish settlements, and then it disintegrated completely, with the remnants joining the National Union. A fourth religious party, Meimad, represents the left-of-center Datim disenchanted by the NRP's rightward turn.

Other than Meimad, religious parties have been socially and politically conservative, although their primary focus is religion and the welfare of their religious constituents. They will form coalitions with left-of-center parties if it benefits their goals. Shas, many of whose supporters are traditional in religious terms, has at times taken mildly dovish positions.

The religious parties do more than just run candidates. They also provide social services to their voters, including education and cultural services, and they sponsor youth groups, newspapers, and religious institutions. When in the government, they use their power to obtain jobs and funding for their constituents. They are not seeking state power, the transformation of society, or the conversion of the majority to their way of life.

National Religious Party (NRP, Mafdal)

The NRP—or, to use its Hebrew acronym, the Mafdal—grew out of the pre-state Dati Zionist-religious organization. The NRP wanted the state to maintain the religious status quo, support the state-religious school system, adhere to kashrut (Jewish dietary laws) in public institutions, and preserve rabbinic control over such personal status issues as marriage, divorce, and adoption. Its youth movement was Bnei Akiva.

During the period of Labor Party dominance, the NRP was a reliable coalition partner. The party's character took on a more nationalist bent after 1973, following Rabbi Zvi Yehuda Kook, the leader of religious Zionism who believed that Jewish settlement in the West Bank was a portent of redemption. The NRP became closely associated with Gush Emunim (Bloc of the Faithful), the main settlement movement, most of whose members were Datim. Gush Emunim eventually drifted away from the NRP and toward the smaller right-wing parties before itself disintegrating.

Until 1981, the NRP held between ten and twelve Knesset seats, making it an important party for coalition building. In 1981 the voters gave the NRP only six seats, many of them apparently having decided that if the main priority was settlement rather than Dati communal interests, they might as well support one of the smaller right-wing parties completely focused on settlement. In 1984, because of competition from Shas, the NRP's place in the Knesset shrank further, to only four seats, and Shas replaced it as Labor's perennial religious coalition partner. The defection of the NRP left to Meimad in 1988 was a further blow.

Beginning in the 1990s, the NRP asserted its nationalism more strongly. In 1992, for the first time in twenty years, it did not participate in Labor's coalition. After Rabin's assassination in 1995 it lost a great deal of support because the public blamed it for helping to incite feelings against Rabin. Although the party revived to some extent between 1999 and 2005, internal disputes finally blew the party apart in 2005. When Sharon announced his intention to withdraw from the Gaza Strip, one faction wanted to leave the government to oppose the pullout, and the other wanted to stay in the government to pursue its own ambitions for office, to continue to serve the Dati constituency, and to keep the NRP alive. The members feared that becoming a one-issue party would destroy the NRP. The party split, and after a complex series of partnerships with other small right-wing parties, it disappeared completely in 2009.

Agudat Israel (United Torah Judaism)

Agudat Israel represents the Haredim, themselves a very diverse group. Large segments of the community have moved from a historically anti-Zionist stance to a non-Zionist one. They participate in the Israeli political system and run as candidates in every election. In deference to their position that divine law supersedes state law, MKs will take posts only as deputy ministers and not as full ministers to avoid participating in cabinet meetings.

Agudat Israel represents a merger of two distinctive Haredi groups: the Hasidim and the Mitnagdim (often in Israel called Lithuanians, after the place of the movement's origin). The party is controlled by the Council of Sages, a committee of senior rabbis, who choose the candidates and decide on the party's positions. The party is not interested in gathering support outside its own sector. It is mostly concerned with practical issues that affect its constituents—namely, government subsidies to large families, funding for its own school system and other institutions, opposition to mandatory military service for Haredi men, and preserving (or slightly altering in its favor) the status quo.

Agudat Israel ran in its current form for the first time in 1992 and stayed in government for most of that decade. When Barak went to Camp David to negotiate with Yasir Arafat in 2000, Agudat Israel left the government out of fear that Barak might agree to divide Jerusalem—despite the fact that the party itself does not take a position on Zionist issues such as land concessions. When the Agudat Israel has not been in government, as in 2003, child subsidies and education allocations—two of their top-priority issues, given the large size of Haredi families—have been greatly reduced.

Since its support is often valuable for maintaining a coalition majority, the party has sometimes wielded more leverage than its small number of seats (between four and six) suggests. The party likes to control the Housing Ministry and the Knesset Finance Committee, which allocate funds to Haredi educational institutions. At the same time, Agudat Israel has a great deal to lose by walking out of governments, and demographic shifts have made it less powerful in Israel though more powerful in Jerusalem's municipal government.

Shas

Shas (an acronym for the Hebrew name, Sephardic Guardians of the Torah) emerged as a party in 1984 when Agudat Israel refused to place more Mizrahi candidates on its list. The Sephardic chief rabbi, Ovadia Yosef, formed his own political party in protest, serving as its spiritual leader and selecting its candidates. Shas works to uphold the religious status quo and to obtain financing and jobs for its supporters.

Most Shas voters are from the poorest Mizrahi sector; they often identify with traditional Judaism but are not necessarily religious by Orthodox standards. This practical consideration has two effects on Shas. One is pragmatism. Shas realized that flexibility on national security issues would give it an advantage over the staunchly nationalist NRP, even if its constituents

Eli Yishai, leader of the Shas, a Sephardic and Haredi political party, arrives for consultations with President Shimon Peres about forming a new coalition government after the 2009 elections. The president meets with party heads after the votes are counted to get their views on who best can form a government. (Getty Images / Image Bank.)

wanted a harder line. The other is that the constant pressure to provide more funds for constituents has led party leaders into corruption.

Shas served in the governments of the 1980s, replacing the NRP as the sole religious party in the Likud and Labor coalitions. In 1993, Shas abstained from voting on the Oslo Accords, making it possible to move the agreement through the Knesset. Shas finally left the government coalition, not because it objected to the peace process, but because Aryeh Deri, the party's leader, was caught up in a corruption scandal.

In 1996, Shas became the largest religious party in the Knesset, with ten seats. Shas's electoral success was even greater in 1999, when it won seventeen seats. Although it has been unable to repeat that feat, it has won eleven or twelve seats in each election since, making it a powerful voice in Israeli politics, and eclipsing its religious rivals.

Former Soviet Union (FSU) Immigrant Parties

When the massive wave of immigration from the former Soviet Union began in the early 1990s, the major political parties courted their votes. Likud was heading the government, and immigrants associated it with bureaucracy and the difficult conditions they faced upon arrival. As a group, they therefore voted for Labor, making exactly the opposite choice of the earlier, Mizrahi immigrants.

This unwillingness to support Likud did not last, and the FSU voters helped elect Netanyahu (Likud) in 1996, returned to help elect Labor in 1999, supported Likud again in 2001 and 2003, and then helped elect Kadima in 2006. It should be stressed that this was not a bloc vote

Israeli politician and former Soviet dissident Natan Sharansky on the Mount of Olives, Jerusalem, October 2007. (Oren Fixler / Flash90.)

and that evaluation is made on the main choice of the immigrant voters, not any exclusive loyalty. Since 1996, the Soviet immigrant vote, though generally conservative, has been split between mainstream and FSU immigrant communal parties.

Despite a history in Israel going back to 1977, no FSU immigrant communal party was able to win any Knesset seats until 1996, when the Yisrael B'Aliya Party passed the 2 percent threshold. The best-known political leader of this community at the time was Natan Sharansky, although he eventually retired from politics.

Yisrael Beiteinu (Israel Our Home)

Yisrael Beiteinu (Israel Our Home) was formed in 1999 when Avigdor Lieberman and other FSU immigrant Likud supporters broke with Netanyahu in opposing territorial concessions made in negotiations with the Palestinians. They were joined by a number of MKs of the Yisrael B'Aliya Party, who also opposed the concessions.

Though often portrayed as an extreme right-wing party, Yisrael Beiteinu is more complex than that description indicates. Lieberman's land-exchange proposal is at the heart of the party platform: to trade some largely Arab areas of Israel to a Palestinian state in exchange for Jewish-populated areas in the West Bank. Although this approach appears to be hawkish, it provides an opening for trading land for peace and is similar to land-swap proposals made by the Labor Party.

Yisrael Beiteinu is widely known for another of Lieberman's controversial proposals—to require Israeli Arabs take a loyalty oath—although he has never pushed this idea when in the government. More immediately, Yisrael Beiteinu favors the separation of religion and state as well as the institution of civil marriage, issues important to many FSU-origin Israelis who are not religious or, in some cases, not considered Jewish according to Jewish law as interpreted by the Rabbinate.

Despite the party's role as a communal vehicle for FSU immigrants, it never describes itself as such. Many FSU immigrant voters prefer it this way, since to support an immigrant party would make them feel less integrated into Israeli life. In the party's big breakthrough election in

2006, it won eleven seats, nine of which came from FSU immigrant-sector votes. The number of seats grew, in 2009, to fifteen, making it the third-largest party after Kadima and Likud, and it joined the government coalition.

The party has attracted many votes from beyond the FSU immigrant sector, and some believe that it should no longer be considered an ethnic party because of its broader appeal. It is also, in effect, the largest personal party in Israel's history, given Lieberman's unchallenged leadership.

Banning Political Parties

There are few limits on who can run for Knesset. According to the 1985 Basic Law on the Knesset, it is illegal for any party denying the existence of Israel as a Jewish and democratic state to run. Thus any party seeking to turn Israel into a binational, Islamist, or Arab state or to create a Jewish theocracy can be banned. This regulation has not been enforced against Arab parties by the courts despite accusations that they do have as their goal a binational, Islamist, or Arab nationalist state.

It is also illegal for parties to espouse a racist message. The Supreme Court subsequently ruled that this law, too, was applicable only in extreme cases. Further, for a party to be banned, the offensive message must be central to the party's platform, and it must be proven that the party is actually trying to implement the racist position. The Basic Law was amended in 2002 to include party support for terrorist activity as grounds for disqualification.

The law was originally passed as a reaction to the extreme right-wing Kach Party, based on the Jewish Defense League, which advocated the deportation of Israel's Arabs as part of its 1984 platform. The Central Elections Committee banned the party, claiming that it stood against the state's democratic values. The Supreme Court overturned the ban, and Kach won one seat in 1984. An amendment to the Basic Law was subsequently passed, and, in 1988, the Central Elections Committee again disqualified Kach. This time, the Supreme Court upheld the decision, ruling that Kach was a racist party that violated the law.

The issue came up again regarding the Progressive List for Peace (PLP), the first independent Arab party, in 1992. In that case, the Supreme Court found that the PLP did not violate the law, and the party was permitted to run. Then, in 2003, the Central Elections Committee invoked the later amendment to ban Balad because of statements made by MK Azmi Bishara supporting Hizballah and rejecting Israel's existence as a Jewish and democratic state. Nevertheless, the Supreme Court again overturned the ban, arguing that while Bishara's statements did qualify as support for a terrorist organization, it was not proven that he supported "armed struggle," so the demands of democracy and free speech permitted him to run. In 2009, Balad, together with the United Arab List–Ta'al, was again banned by the Central Elections Committee; the Supreme Court permitted both to run.

VOTING TRENDS AND POLITICAL ACTIVITIES

Voting in Israel is taken very seriously. The minimum voting age is eighteen, and every citizen over this age has the right to vote. Election Day is a national holiday, and voters are reimbursed for transportation to get to their polling places. Israeli citizens residing or traveling abroad cannot vote by absentee ballot, but voting provisions are made for all IDF personnel as well as for merchant seamen on ships on that day, members of the diplomatic corps stationed abroad, hospital patients, and prisoners. Voting turnout among both Jews and Arabs has traditionally been very high, with 65 percent of all voters casting ballots in 2009, up 2.5 percent from the percentage three years earlier.

Party loyalty has decreased, however, with the exception of supporters of the Haredi parties, and voting on issues has increased. Voting analysis shows that gender has never played a role in political preference and that the correlation between income and political preference is weak. Degree of religiosity is also still a strong factor in voting preference.

Of the twelve parties winning seats in the 2009 elections, seven of them appeal to specific constituencies: there were three Arab parties, three Jewish religious parties (including the National Union), and an FSU immigrant-oriented party.

The politicans themselves are mostly male. For many decades, Israel's political elite were men of Eastern European origin, members of the Mapai (later Labor) Party, and residents of a big city or a kibbutz. The composition of the elite has steadily changed as more and more Jews of Mizrahi background and a few women have come to hold powerful positions. Breaking into politics from places other than through party or army hierarchies has also become easier.

Israelis express their political views through a very large number of nongovernmental organizations, not just through political parties. These include groups lobbying on everything from environmental issues to child welfare, human rights, and government reform. Their public interests are wide-ranging. Voluntary membership groups use all sorts of methods to try to persuade people to support them, including demonstrations, interviews with the media, and educational activities.

While voluntary groups addressing social issues tend to be durable, their size and influence rises or falls depending on public views and the importance of issues at any particular time. For example, Peace Now on the left and Gush Emunim on the right were major organizations during the 1980s, but both faded into insignificance within a few years. Other temporary but influential protest movements include the Four Mothers group, urging a withdrawal from southern Lebanon, and the "orange" movement, opposing withdrawal from the Gaza Strip.

In 2011, a large social protest movement began in Israel, creating tent cities and holding demonstrations that drew many tens of thousands of people who opposed high consumer and housing prices. The movement's leaders included those focused on these specific issues and others seeking to use the protest to rebuild the political left.

POLITICAL CORRUPTION AND SCANDAL

In the 2009 Transparency International Corruption Perceptions Index, Israel tied with Spain for number 32 of 180 countries (1 being the least corrupt), ranking ahead of all Middle Eastern countries except for Qatar (22) and the United Arab Emirates (30) and such European countries as Portugal (35), Poland (49), and Italy (63). The United States is number 17, the United Kingdom 15, and Canada 8.

Polls show that Israelis, whose resentment of corruption is very high, tend to overrate its level in their country. The most notorious scandals in Israel have involved politicians from all parties, including both financial and sexual misdeeds. The scandal surrounding Aryeh Deri implicated many politicians. Deri, the founder of Shas, was convicted in 1999 while serving as an MK. The charges were bribe taking, fraud, and breach of trust. While director-general of the Interior Ministry and later interior minister in the late 1980s, he accepted bribes from three associates in return for funneling public funds to a yeshiva. Released from jail on parole in 2002 after serving two years of his three-year sentence, Deri was prohibited from participating in politics until September 2003, the end of his original jail term. He was subsequently barred, under Israeli law, from serving as a cabinet minister for a period of ten years.

Haim Ramon, then minister of justice and an MK for the Kadima Party, was convicted in 2006, one day after the start of the Second Lebanon War, on the charge of forcibly kissing a female soldier. Ramon admitted to the kiss in court but claimed that it was consensual. The three-judge panel agreed unanimously to convict Ramon, who was sentenced to community service. He resigned from the Knesset after his conviction, to return in July 2007 and join Prime Minister Ehud Olmert's government. In June 2009 he resigned once again, this time to become chair of the Kadima Council, the party's most important body.

MKs are not the only members of the political elite who get caught up in scandals. Dan Halutz, for one—the chief of staff who oversaw the disengagement from the Gaza Strip and the Second Lebanon War—was strongly criticized following revelations that after Hizballah kidnapped two Israeli soldiers, an act that triggered the Second Lebanon War, he quickly liquidated his entire investment portfolio. Many across the political spectrum demanded his resignation because he had not given priority to his duties and took advantage of inside information. Halutz finally resigned in January 2007 amid criticism over the IDF's performance in the war.

Outgoing prime minister Ehud Olmert speaks at the Interdisciplinary Center, Herzliya, March 2009. (Getty Images / Image Bank.)

Historically, the president has been seen as being above reproach, so it was devastating to the Israeli public when Moshe Katzav was charged with rape, sexual harassment, fraud, and obstruction of justice during his presidency. Katzav resigned in 2007, although he continued to insist on his innocence.

Nor have prime ministers been immune to scandal. Ehud Olmert of Kadima was involved in several major corruption scandals during his tenure as prime minister. In the first, Olmert faced a criminal investigation on suspicion that in 2006, as finance minister, he had interfered with a privatization tender for selling Bank Leumi in order to benefit a businessman bidding on the company. Later an American businessman, Morris Talansky, testified that he gave Olmert $150,000 over the years, much of it in cash-stuffed envelopes. Evidence was also disclosed that Olmert had double-billed charities and government agencies for his various travel expenses. In July 2008, Olmert, facing myriad charges, resigned under pressure.

Although these and other scandals did not involve the overall direction of the country or huge amounts of money, they had a demoralizing effect on the Israeli people. Many felt that the scandals of greed and debauchery were a sign of how far the country had fallen since its founding, a time of idealism and utopianism when leaders prided themselves on Spartan living conditions and citizens put the nation's welfare first.

POLITICAL REFORMS

Since 1948, the political system in Israel, like the economic system, has become more open and democratic. When the state was first founded, a small group of veteran politicians controlled the parties, chose the leaders, and set the agendas. Today most of the major parties have mechanisms in place to allow the public a greater role in party decisions and to disseminate more information.

One of the main reforms took place in the 1990s with the introduction of party primaries and the passage of two Basic Laws that established the concept of judicial review and opened the way for the Supreme Court to play an activist role in determining the legality of new laws. In 2003, however, a third reform, direct elections for prime minister, was repealed.

Labor was the first party to institute primaries, in 1992. Instead of party leaders choosing the list of candidates for elections, as was the case until the 1970s, and instead of party institutions selecting the leaders, as was the case for the next two decades, party members were now able to vote for their preferred candidates. By the mid-1990s the major political parties (with the exception of religious parties) were holding primaries. By 1999, however, Likud had abandoned this practice, concerned that candidates were signing up people as party members just to win the primaries—candidates needed a certain number of signatures in favor of their candidacy in order to run—and struggling with the difficulties of creating a balanced candidate list. Instead, the party instituted a system in which only veteran party members could vote for candidates in the primaries.

Direct election of the prime minister failed because it did not achieve the intended goal of making governing coalitions more stable by reducing the power of small parties. Instead, the opposite happened because people felt free to cast a vote for the prime minister candidate of a big party and then give their Knesset ballot to a smaller one. The law was repealed before the 2003 elections.

Israelis often speak about the weaknesses that they perceive in the party system. The inability of any party to achieve a majority in its own right and the need to recruit and satisfy multiple coalition partners dilutes the government's effectiveness and favors patronage politics. Some believe that electing MKs from local districts rather than at the national level might make the government more responsive to citizens' needs and gain more resources for neglected regions. But there is little impetus to make changes. People have become used to the system, have seen the problems that reforms can bring, and are more concerned with more immediate problems.

FOREIGN POLICY

Israel has several distinct disadvantages in international dealings. Most notably, it is a country small in territory and population, lacking considerable natural resources and facing enemies who are big, strong, and naturally endowed. Making its situation more difficult is the hostility of almost all Muslim-majority, Communist, and radical Third World countries and the frequently less-than-full support of Western countries. Among Israel's opponents have been countries with massive financial surpluses based on oil and natural gas exports. This wealth enables them to be attractive trading partners. They can also buy a certain amount of influence in other countries.

Israel tries to counter its disadvantages by developing good relations with countries that have the same enemies or face similar threats. In addition, it carries out an energetic, though small-scale, aid program, especially in Africa, and is active in humanitarian projects and relief efforts.

Other Israeli assets include the backing of Jewish communities around the world, the respect that other countries' armed forces and intelligence services have for their Israeli counterparts, and a strong economy. Many countries find Israel to be a useful trading partner for their imports and exports, as well as a source of innovative technology.

Also ameliorating its handicaps is the sympathy that Israel received after World War II in the reaction against the Holocaust. The European left also identified with Israel's socialist agenda during the country's earlier years. In the 1950s and most of the 1960s, France was also Israel's patron, for it saw Arab nationalism as subverting its empire in North Africa. This patronage ended in 1967, when President Charles de Gaulle jettisoned the alliance with Israel to build relations with Arab states.

The overarching international framework during Israel's first four decades was the Cold War. As early as 1950, Israel cast its lot with the West by supporting the Korean War against the Soviet Union and its allies. With the turn of several Arab regimes toward Moscow during the 1950s and 1960s, the Cold War context of Israel's own conflict intensified.

The United States took its first steps toward supplying Israel with arms covertly in the mid-1960s. Israel's victory in the 1967 war, when it inflicted a humiliating defeat on Soviet-supplied Soviet allies, and its secret successful intervention with Syria in 1970, warning it not to invade

Jordan, convinced U.S. leaders that Israel was a real asset in the Cold War. Thus began the special U.S.-Israel relationship.

After the Cold War ended in the early 1990s, a new phase in Israel's foreign policy began. The Israel-Palestinian peace process was under way and many of Israel's former enemies had fallen from power when the Soviet Union and its Communist government collapsed. This combination of factors led to some major Israeli gains. Its relations normalized, improved greatly, and even became friendly with many previously aloof countries—including Russia and all the former Soviet satellite states in Europe, as well as China and India.

In contrast, a strong leftist sector among the Western intellectual and cultural elite became increasingly critical of or hostile toward Israel after the collapse of the peace process in 2000. By negotiating with the PLO and the Palestine Authority in the 1990s on the basis of a projected two-state solution, Israel inadvertently created the impression that the Palestinians merely sought a two-state solution rather than Israel's extinction, or so many in the West came to believe. Ironically, by 2000, few Israelis still shared that view.

Fear of terrorism, especially after the September 2001 attacks in the United States, and the rise of Islamist radicalism made some Western attitudes more favorable to Israel—especially in previously largely unfriendly conservative circles—and some less so, depending on whether Israel was seen as an ally and bulwark against the threats or as a cause of the violence and enmity expressed toward the West. The rise of political correctness and multiculturalism often made Israel's role as a Western country allied with the United States, formerly an asset, into a reason for criticism when Palestinians were viewed as the oppressed underdog. Moreover, there was a strong resurgence of antisemitism throughout the world. Still another issue was whether people blamed Israel for the failure of the 1990s peace process or saw it as a victim of that outcome.

An unusual feature of Israel's foreign policy is hasbara: the war of image and interpretation waged by Israel and its opponents to gain the support of foreign public opinion, opinion makers, and policymakers. Although Israelis regard hasbara as an important front, Jewish communities abroad feel that it is even more important. Shimon Peres expressed the Israeli attitude when he remarked that if Israel had a good policy, it did not require good hasbara. Israelis are also aware of the irony of being criticized for withdrawing from territories that it captured, for taking great risks (which resulted in many Israeli casualties), for making many concessions, and for announcing its willingness to accept an independent Palestinian state. It was criticized much less before it proceeded with a mostly unilateral peace process.

While Israel's foreign policy has changed somewhat—the government now takes campaigns to delegitimize Israel seriously, for example—Israel's government still puts a higher priority on the actual situation than on public relations. Foreign criticism, media stories, and unpopularity are evaluated both in terms of policy options—whether an alternative that could change adverse opinions exists—and factors outside Israel's control, including personal hostilities or domestic political factors in other countries that will not be altered by factual arguments.

Israel is given disproportionately large attention in the Western media, and often the attention involves criticism and the misrepresentation of Israel and its actions. In certain foreign nongovernmental organizations and international bodies, Arab countries, Muslim-majority states, and other countries push hard to condemn Israel. The treatment of Israel as a pariah state, or at least an attempt to put it into such a category, has become a major feature of contemporary international relations.

Attitudes in foreign countries toward Israel vary in three distinct groups: policymakers, opinion makers (journalists, academics, intellectuals, and cultural figures), and the general public. It is with the second group—often the most visible though not the most important in policy terms—that Israel faces the greatest problems.

None of these developments, however, have made Israelis feel insecure, nor have they affected the pursuit of policies deemed necessary for the nation's security and interests.

THE FUTURE OF ISRAELI GOVERNMENT AND POLITICS

The political questions that Israel has struggled with for many years will not go away. Two specific issues—those relating to its security situation and the role of religion—go to the heart of Israeli democracy. What does it mean to be a Jewish and a democratic state? What will happen with Israel's Arab minority? What is the role of religion in a democracy? And what does it mean for a democracy when the security situation is so dire?

On the domestic front there is also debate over whether the country's idealism and its citizens' willingness to put the community before the individual have eroded beyond some point of no return. There is also disillusion with existing leaders and parties due to corruption.

These problems are countered by a high level of national consensus on key issues, the near resolution or decline of many past issues, lowered expectations, and a sense of national self-confidence that coexists with intense self-criticism.

Despite internal scandals, popular disillusionment with politics, and especially the challenges arising from the conflict with the Palestinians and Israel's neighbors, Israeli democracy remains vibrant and resilient.

BIBLIOGRAPHY

Amara, Muhammad H. "Israeli Palestinians and the Palestinian Authority." *MERIA Journal: The Middle East Review of International Affairs* 4, no. 1 (March 2000). http://www.gloria-center.org/meria/2000/03/amara.html.

Arian, Asher. *The Second Republic.* Chatham, NJ: Chatham House, 1998.

Arian, Asher, and Michal Shinar. "A Decade Later, the World Had Changed, the Cleavage Structure Remained: Israel, 1996–2006." *Party Politics* 14, no. 6 (2008): 685–705.

Bick, Etta. "A Party in Decline: Shas in Israel's 2003 Elections." *Israel Affairs* 10, no. 4 (Summer 2004): 98–129.

Brown, Cameron S. "Israel's 2003 Elections: A Victory for the Moderate Right and Secular Center." *MERIA Journal: The Middle East Review of International Affairs* 7, no. 1 (March 2003). http://www.gloria-center.org/meria/2003/03/brown.html.

Diskin, Abraham. *Elections and Voters in Israel.* Santa Barbara, CA: Praeger, 1991.

Diskin, Abraham, and Reuven Y. Hazan. "The Knesset Election in Israel, March 2006." *Electoral Studies* 26 (2007): 699–724.

Diskin, Abraham, and Reuven Y. Hazan. "The 2001 Prime Ministerial Election in Israel." *Electoral Studies* 21 (2002): 649–680.

Dowty, Alan. "Israeli Foreign Policy and the Jewish Question." *MERIA Journal: The Middle East Review of International Affairs* 3, no. 1 (March 1999). http://www.gloria-center.org/meria/1999/03/dowty.html.

Facts about Israel. Jerusalem: Israel Information Center, 2003.

Frisch, Hillel. "Israel's Arab Parties." In Robert O. Freedman, ed., *Contemporary Israel: Domestic Politics, Foreign Policy, and Security Challenges*, 115–134. Boulder, CO: Westview Press, 2009.

Garfinkle, Adam. *Politics and Society in Modern Israel.* Armonk, NY: M. E. Sharpe, 1997.

Gerstenfeld, Manfred. "The Run-up to the Election." *Israel Affairs* 13, no. 2 (April 2007): 251–265.

Goldberg, Giora. "The Electoral Collapse of the Israeli Doves." *Israel Affairs* 10, no. 4 (Summer 2004): 36–55.

Hazan, Reuven Y. "Kadima and the Centre: Convergence in the Israeli Party System." *Israel Affairs* 13, no. 2 (April 2007): 266–288.

Hazan, Reuven Y., and Abraham Diskin. "The 1999 Knesset and Prime Ministerial Elections in Israel." *Electoral Studies* 19 (2000): 615–646.

Hazan, Reuven Y., and Abraham Diskin. "The Parliamentary Elections in Israel, January 2003." *Electoral Studies* 23 (2004): 329–360.

Khanin, Vladimir (Ze'ev). "Israel's 'Russian' Parties." In Robert O. Freedman, ed., *Contemporary Israel: Domestic Politics, Foreign Policy, and Security Challenges*, 97–114. Boulder, CO: Westview Press, 2009.

Knoller, Ephrat. "Change (Shinui) in the Centre." *Israel Affairs* 10, no. 4 (Summer 2004): 73–97.

Lahav, Pnina. "Israel's Supreme Court." In Robert O. Freedman, ed., *Contemporary Israel: Domestic Politics, Foreign Policy, and Security Challenges*, 135–152. Boulder, CO: Westview Press, 2009.

Lim, Kevjn. "Neither Left nor Right but Backwards: The Failure of Centrist Parties in Israel and Their Relationship to the Multiparty System." *Israel Affairs* 15, no. 1 (January 2009): 28–51.

Mahler, Gregory. "Israel's New Electoral System: Effects on Policy and Politics." *MERIA Journal: The Middle East Review of International Affairs* 1, no. 2 (June 1997). http://www.gloria-center.org/meria/1997/07/mahler.html.

Mann, Kenneth. "Judicial Review of Israeli Administrative Actions against Terrorism: Temporary Deportation of Palestinians from the West Bank to Gaza." *MERIA Journal: The Middle East Review of International Affairs* 8, no. 1 (March 2004). http://www.gloria-center.org/meria/2004/03/mann.html.

Navot, Suzie. "Fighting Terrorism in the Political Arena: The Banning of Political Parties." *Party Politics* 14, no. 6 (2008): 745–762.

Peleg, Ilan. "The Israeli Right." In Robert O. Freedman, ed., *Contemporary Israel: Domestic Politics, Foreign Policy, and Security Challenges*, 21–44. Boulder, CO: Westview Press, 2009.

Peretz, Don, and Gideon Doron. *The Government and Politics of Israel.* Boulder, CO: Westview Press, 1997.

Rahat, Gideon. "Trial and Error: Electoral Reform through Bypass and Its Repeal." *Israel Affairs* 14, no. 1 (January 2008): 103–117.

Rodman, David. "Israel's National Security Doctrine: An Introductory Overview." *MERIA Journal: The Middle East Review of International Affairs* 5, no. 3 (September 2001). http://www.gloria-center.org/meria/2001/09/rodman.html.

Rosenblum, Mark. "After Rabin: The Malaise of the Israeli Zionist Left." In Robert O. Freedman, ed., *Contemporary Israel: Domestic Politics, Foreign Policy, and Security Challenges*, 45–75. Boulder, CO: Westview Press, 2009.

Rubin, Barry. "External Factors in Israel's 1999 Elections." *MERIA Journal: The Middle East Review of International Affairs* 3, no. 4 (December 1999). http://www.gloria-center.org/meria/1999/12/rubin .html.

Rubin, Barry, and Judith Colp Rubin. *Yasir Arafat: A Political Biography.* Oxford: Oxford University Press, 2003.

Rynhold, Jonathan. "The View from Jerusalem: Israeli-American Relations and the Peace Process since Camp David." *MERIA Journal: The Middle East Review of International Affairs* 4, no. 2 (June 2000). http://www.gloria-center.org/meria/2000/06/rynhold.html.

Sandler, Shmuel, and Aaron Kampinsky. "Israel's Religious Parties." In Robert O. Freedman, ed., *Contemporary Israel: Domestic Politics, Foreign Policy, and Security Challenges*, 77–93. Boulder, CO: Westview Press, 2009.

Sandler, Shmuel, and M. Ben Mollov. "Israel at the Polls 2003: A New Turning Point in the Political History of the Jewish State?" *Israel Affairs* 10, no. 4 (Summer 2004): 1–19.

Sandler, Shmuel, and Jonathan Rynhold. "Introduction: From Centrism to Neo-Centrism." *Israel Affairs* 13, no. 2 (April 2007): 229–250.

Spyer, Jonathan. "Downfall of a Dominant Party: The Likud and the 2006 Election." *Israel Affairs* 13, no. 2 (April 2007): 289–304.

Spyer, Jonathan. "Forward to the Past: The Fall and Rise of the 'One' State Solution." *MERIA Journal: The Middle East Review of International Affairs* 12, no. 3 (September 2008). http://www.gloria-center.org/meria/2008/09/spyer.html.

Spyer, Jonathan. "The Netanyahu Government at Its Halfway Point: Keeping Things Quiet?" *MERIA Journal: The Middle East Review of International Affairs* 14, no. 3 (September 2010). http://www .gloria-center.org/meria/2010/09/spyer.html.

Susser, Bernard. "The Retirees' (Gimla'im) Party: An 'Escapist' Phenomenon?" *Israel Affairs* 13, no. 2 (April 2007): 187–192.

Torgovnik, Efraim. "Shinui's Attempt to Capture the Centre of Israeli Politics." *Israel Affairs* 10, no. 4 (Summer 2004): 56–72.

Chapter Six

ECONOMICS

Israel's economy ranks high among the world's wealthiest and most technologically advanced. Its industry specializes in cutting-edge communications, electronics, and medical technology and shows an increasing capacity for developing consumer products and services. Its business sector is entrepreneurial and dynamic.

A full-fledged participant in the global economy, Israel exports about one-third of its gross domestic product (GDP) and attracts billions of dollars in foreign investment every year. Its financial markets are sophisticated. Business and financial regulations are efficient if heavy-handed by the standards of the United States and much of Europe. Its GDP per capita, a measure of a country's relative wealth, was about $28,500 in 2009, about the same as the GDP of Italy, Spain, Greece, and South Korea.

In the World Economic Forum's annual survey of national competitiveness, Israel placed 27th among 134 countries in 2009 and rose to 24th in 2010. Measured against social indicators such as access to health care and life expectancy—to which economists are giving increasing weight—Israel also stands among the world's most developed economies. The United Nations Human Development Index—which gauges health, knowledge, and standard of living—ranked Israel at 15th out of 169 surveyed countries in 2010.

None of these achievements was inevitable. When the first Jewish immigrants motivated by Zionism arrived in the last quarter of the nineteenth century, the economy was poor by the standards of the time. The land had few of the natural resources that traditionally underpin modern agriculture and industry. In the years that followed, the conflict with the Arabs hampered economic development and forced the young State of Israel to devote disproportionate financial and human resources to security.

Growth was repeatedly interrupted by wars and the struggle to cope with successive waves of immigration. The ideological imperatives of creating a new society and state often came into conflict with economic efficiency. Indeed, Israel went through more than a decade of economic stagnation in the 1970s and 1980s before it made the transition to a full-fledged market economy.

That Israel finally overcame these obstacles is a testament to its people's dynamism, entrepreneurial drive, and intellectual resources. Yet the economy continues to face critical challenges. The country remains isolated from its immediate neighbors in the Middle East,

Relative Wealth GDP per capita among developed economies 2008 (U.S. dollars*)

Country	GDP per capita
Norway	
U.S.	
Switzerland	
Netherlands	
Canada	
Australia	
Denmark	
Sweden	
Finland	
Britain	
Germany	
Belgium	
Japan	
France	
Spain	
Italy	
Greece	
Israel	
Korea	
New Zealand	
Czech Rep.	
Portugal	
Slovakia	
Hungary	
Poland	

10,000   20,000   30,000   40,000   50,000   60,000

*At purchasing power parity.

While Israel ranks among the world's wealthiest economies as measured in per capita GDP, it remains poor relative to Western Europe and North America. (Data: OECD; Chart: David Rosenberg. Drawing: Bill Nelson.)

which prevents the free flow of trade, labor, and capital. Although defense costs are smaller as a percentage of GDP than in the past, they continue to be heavy. In addition, Israel has higher rates of poverty and income inequality than its peers in the developed world.

The primary and secondary educational system—a critical foundation for the technology industry—performs poorly by international standards. Universities are underfunded even though more Israelis than ever are getting a higher education. Compared to the world's wealthiest economies, Israel still has catching up to do. Its GDP per capita is equal to about 60 percent of the U.S. GDP and 81 percent of the average for countries belonging to the Organization for Economic Cooperation and Development (OECD), which assesses the world's industrialized economies and to which Israel was admitted as a member in 2010.

The Israeli economy and the ideological assumptions behind it evolved over the past century in parallel with the global debate over the relative merits of the socialist and capitalist models of economic development. In the Yishuv, socialism emerged early on as the prevalent ideology and held sway in Israel for the first three decades of the country's history. The global tide turned in the face of economic malaise in the United States and Western Europe during the 1970s, which pointed up the inefficiencies of state intervention, and finally with the collapse of Communism in 1989. Israeli policymakers, starting with the 1985 Economic Stabilization Plan, took their cue not only from local conditions but from events around the world and began to implement policies that rolled back the state's role in economic life, a process still going on today.

Poor Israelis wait to receive food aid from the private Pithon Lev charity just before Rosh Hashana, the Jewish New Year, in Rishon LeZion, September 2005. (Getty Images / Image Bank.)

THE ECONOMY OF THE YISHUV

The mainstay of economic life for the mostly Arab population of Ottoman-ruled Palestine in the last quarter of the nineteenth century was subsistence agriculture. Much of the land had been abandoned over the centuries to swamps and desert. The few Jews already living there depended on financial assistance from abroad (*haluka*).

Jewish immigrants from central and Eastern Europe, who constituted the great majority of immigrants before Israel was created in 1948, were ill suited for the tasks of developing the country. Most had been legally barred from engaging in agriculture in their home countries and had no knowledge of the climate and the other conditions they were facing. They possessed little or no capital.

Nevertheless, they had good reasons for emigrating. Apart from growing antisemitism in the Russian Empire, the Pale of Settlement, where the majority of Russian Jews were confined, was under immense economic pressure. Industrialization and urbanization had reached Eastern Europe in the last quarter of the century, pushing small-time Jewish craftsmen and service providers out of business even as the Jewish population grew rapidly. In the 100 years before the outbreak of World War II, some four million Jews emigrated from Eastern Europe. Given the poor prospects in Palestine, only about 4 percent chose to go there.

The agricultural communities of this First Aliya (wave of Jewish immigration) faced financial collapse not long after the first of them was established in Israel in 1882. Baron Edmond de Rothschild, a scion of the great European banking family, agreed to supply financial and managerial aid. He saved the settlements, but at a price. By the time the next wave of immigrants began to arrive in 1904, in the Second Aliya, the settlements had all but abandoned the goal of creating self-sustaining Jewish agricultural cooperatives; they relied instead on Rothschild and Arab labor. In Zichron Ya'akov, where Rothschild sponsored the opening of a branch of the Carmel wineries, some 200 Jewish farmers employed 1,200 Arabs.

In pre-state Palestine, the socialist ethos was developed into a concrete reality with the establishment of the Histadrut (trade union federation), the kibbutzim and moshavim, and an array of other economic institutions. With the Ottomans and later the British ruling Palestine, the Zionist establishment could not impose a socialist economic structure, but it created one for the Jewish population through quasi-official institutions, building a system from scratch in an economy that had virtually no modern infrastructure. Many in the Zionist leadership shared the philosophy of the most ideological socialists, believing that the economy was not simply a tool for providing goods and jobs but could serve as a platform for remaking people and society. For them, Zionism meant remaking the Jew and creating an ideal society in the Jewish homeland.

Inspired by the socialist ideas prevalent in Eastern Europe at the time, the Second Aliya immigrants were very different from their predecessors. They saw Jewish life in Europe, dominated as it was by petty traders and craftsman, as economically and socially distorted. They believed that Jews should use the new homeland they were building to develop a working class engaged in manual and agricultural labor and in class struggle. Without any local industry, however, the new arrivals had no choice but to seek work with the veteran Jewish farmers and form independent labor brigades.

Oddly, at a time when the most advanced economies were industrializing, these Labor Zionists saw the foundation of their social revolution in agriculture, hence the pride of place given to the kibbutz, which married the two goals into a single institution. "We saw in Zionism a revolution in the life of the Jewish people and its economic structure, a transition from a nation of intermediaries to a nation of real workers," Eliezer Kaplan, then treasurer of the Jewish Agency, wrote in 1935. "Agriculture and the conquest of labor are therefore a necessary condition for the fulfillment of our desires."

The ranks of the agricultural workers and their ideological proclivities were reinforced by another wave of newcomers arriving in the Third Aliya after World War I, by which time the country had passed to British control. The first two decades of the twentieth century saw the establishment of many of the Israeli economy's founding institutions—the kibbutz, the Histadrut, and an array of social and educational networks—that reflected the view of those in the Second and Third Aliyas that economic life was inseparable from political, social, and cultural life.

TWO COMPETING STRATEGIES: CAPITALISM AND SOCIALISM

The debate over the two competing strategies for building up the Jewish homeland—capitalism and socialism—came to a head at the Zionist Congress of 1920. On the one side were American Zionists led by Louis Brandeis, a Supreme Court justice who wanted private investors to spearhead economic development. They argued that the Zionist movement's economic organizations, such as the Jewish National Fund, should act as a quasi-government, building infrastructure and ensuring social welfare. Opposing them was Chaim Weizmann, champion of the European Zionists, who wanted the movement to buy land and sponsor agricultural settlements. The Europeans took the view that Zionism was not a business enterprise but a social revolution, which would be driven by the collective farmers of the kibbutzim and moshavim. Conditions were too primitive for capitalism to work, they argued.

Weizmann and his allies prevailed, but private enterprise nevertheless remained a powerful force in the years that followed. The next two waves of immigration mainly consisted of small entrepreneurs and professionals. The first were Polish Jews, many of them owners of small businesses escaping the growing antisemitism of the early 1920s. They were followed in the next decade by German Jews fleeing the Nazis. These immigrants came with capital and skills, which they used to set up small factories in the cities.

The Zionist institutions set up to realize the movement's socialist goals were inefficient and underfunded. From 1932 to 1937 private capital accounted for 87 percent of all investment in Jewish Palestine. Finally, World War II provided a boost to private industry: British forces in the Middle East, isolated from their regular suppliers back at home, came to rely on local factories and workshops for uniforms and other provisions. The stress on agriculture by the Yishuv's official institutions meant that the development of industry was left largely to the private sector.

On the eve of the War of Independence, the Jewish population had overcome considerable obstacles to create a small but quite modern economy. Fueled by immigration and the capital that immigrants and Zionist institutions brought to the country, as well as by British investment in infrastructure and the war effort, the economy of the country's Jewish population expanded an average of about 14 percent annually between 1920 and 1947.

A WAR-SHATTERED ECONOMY

The nascent Jewish state inherited the Yishuv's ideology. Even if its leadership never actively pursued a sweeping program of creating the "New Jew," its government took over nearly all the economic institutions previously controlled by the Yishuv. Many of the biggest private enterprises came under government control, though more because of the absence of private investors than for ideological reasons. The Histadrut retained its business empire as well as a key role in the economy and stood in the unusual situation of being both a union and an employer.

In the first years of the state, given the dominant ideology, the private sector and the profit motive were looked at suspiciously by the government, but officials were by no means determined to do away with the private economy altogether. Instead, economic policy could be termed "national" in the sense that decisions were driven by what the government deemed best for building the country.

In contrast to the conventional view today, capitalism was seen as wasteful and unproductive; capitalists invested resources where profits could be most easily made rather than where they were needed by the nation. Small business was tolerated, though dismissed as filling a socially useless role as "middleman" rather than making a useful contribution.

Whether the economy could have been developed with private enterprise—or, at the very least, whether it could have been developed more efficiently—remains a matter of debate. To be sure, the rapid growth of the early years was a function of massive inputs—specifically, immigration, which expanded the labor force and imported capital that paid for the development of industry and infrastructure. There was egregious waste and mismanagement that almost certainly would have occurred on a far smaller scale if private enterprise had been given more leeway. But given the immense pressures facing Israel in the early years—isolation from its neighbors, its perpetual war footing, and mass immigration—it seems unlikely that private enterprise could and would have met the challenge.

The economy of the nascent Israeli state emerged shattered from the 1948 war. Many industrial enterprises were destroyed or damaged, much farmland was now outside Israel's borders or laid to waste, and the country was cut off from its closest trade partners. The new nation faced massive defense and rebuilding costs, but at the same time it opened its doors to hundreds of thousands of immigrants, the great majority of whom were poor and unskilled. Between May 1948 and the end of 1952, some 690,000 Jews arrived in Israel, nearly all of them refugees from war-shattered Europe or from the underdeveloped economies of the Middle East and North Africa. There were so many that the number almost equaled Israel's 1948 population. The newcomers all required housing, basic necessities, and jobs.

In response, the government imposed rationing in 1949 on everything from food and clothing for consumers to raw materials for industry. Known as the *Tsena*, the program was mostly dismantled in 1953 (although some rationing continued as late as 1959) because it was having the perverse effect of creating shortages and, consequently, a black market and inflation. But the bigger problem for Israel's leaders was how to undertake badly needed economic development.

GROWTH YEARS

Israel did not have the financial resources to pay for investment and development, particularly when a population that more than doubled in a very short period needed housing. For housing, it turned first to the Jewish communities of the United States and Europe, which provided some $750 million in aid between 1949 and 1965. The U.S. government also helped by donating agricultural surpluses and providing loans, but the biggest single contributor was West Germany, which agreed in 1952 to compensate Israel for Jewish property plundered by the Nazis. Over the next twelve years, German reparations provided Israel with $833 million, which was used for everything from buying manufacturing equipment to underwriting a fleet for the national shipping company, Zim. Driven by investment and immigration, Israel's gross domestic product grew 10 percent annually from 1954 to 1965.

Although the State of Israel never formally adopted a socialist model, much less the expansive social goals set out by Labor Zionist thinkers, the 1950s saw the gradual development of an economy dominated by the state and allied Histadrut and kibbutzim institutions. Key industries, such as Dead Sea Works and the Haifa oil refineries, passed from private to state control. Other industries, such as the defense industries, were created by the government from scratch. The state and the labor union–affiliated companies built homes—indeed, whole towns; operated the phone and transportation networks; and controlled access to credit and finance. The state took over farmland and property left by the British Mandate authorities and Palestinian

SHARE OF CAPITAL IMPORTS IN TOTAL RESOURCES AND
GROSS INVESTMENTS IN ISRAEL, 1950–1967 (ANNUAL AVERAGE)

	Total Loans, Investments, and Grants ($ millions)	Total Resources ($ millions)	Gross Domestic Investment ($ millions)	Ratio of Capital Imports to Resources (%)	Ratio of Capital Imports to Investments (%)
1950–1954	274	1,157	394	17.6	69.5
1955–1959	398	2,071	497	19.2	80.1
1960–1964	697	3,165	667	22.0	104.4
1965–1967	805	4,399	834	18.3	96.5
Full period	515	2,620	572	19.7	90.0

Source: Michael N. Barnett, *Confronting the Costs of War: Military Power, State, and Society in Egypt and Israel* (Princeton, NJ: Princeton University Press, 1992)
Note: Capital imports financed nearly all of Israel's investment needs during the first two decades of the country's history.

Arabs in the 1948 war, leaving it in control of 95 percent of the country's land. A private sector existed alongside the government-Histadrut economy, unmolested and even encouraged, but constricted by regulations.

At times, these national imperatives came into conflict with the government's official so-cialist ethos. In the late 1950s, Pinhas Sapir (who—together with Levi Eshkol—dominated economic policymaking during Israel's first three decades, serving first as industry minister and later as finance minister) blocked a plan by the Histadrut's industrial arm, Solel Boneh, to greatly expand its empire by building a steelworks in Acre. Sapir saw the growing power of the Histadrut as a threat to private enterprise. At about the same time, Sapir began recruiting local businesspeople and foreign investors to develop the textiles industry. Indeed, Sapir was instrumental in bringing private foreign investment by Diaspora Jews to Israel. But the state decided where and what kind of factories would be built.

The years of rapid growth were briefly interrupted by a recession from 1966 to 1967 that was in part engineered by the government. Concerned that rising incomes were creating unacceptably big trade deficits and inflation, the Finance Ministry tightened credit and re-duced the state development budget. The timing was poor: a host of big infrastructure proj-ects, such as the development of the Ashdod port and the construction of the National Wa-ter Carrier (which pipes water from the Sea of Galilee to the highly populated center of the country and to the northern Negev), were being completed, causing construction activity to

ISRAEL'S ECONOMIC GROWTH IN SELECTED PERIODS, 1950–2009

Years	Average Annual Change (%)
1950–1965	10.6
1966–1967	1.7
1968–1972	11.8
1973–1977	3.6
1978–1984	3.3
1985–1989	3.8
1990–1996	6.1
1997–1999	3.3
2000	8.9
2001–2003	0.4
2004–2006	5.2
2007	5.2
2008	4.0
2009	0.7

Source: Israel Central Bureau of Statistics.
Note: Israel experienced recessions in 1966–1967,
1997–1999, 2001–2003, and 2008–2009, as well as a
prolonged period of slow growth in 1978–1984.

decline. GDP growth slowed to 1.7 percent in the two years of the recession, which in per capita terms was equal to a decline of 1.2 percent, and the unemployment rate jumped to 10 percent. Unaccustomed to recession, the slowdown had an unusually deleterious effect on national morale. Some Israelis chose to emigrate in search of opportunities elsewhere.

The slowdown evaporated in the aftermath of the June 1967 Six-Day War. Construction resumed as the army built installations in the newly captured Sinai, West Bank, and Golan Heights. The arms embargo imposed by France forced Israel to accelerate development of its own defense industry, giving a boost to the electronic and metal sectors. The victory also ushered in a new era of optimism, encouraging investors and immigration just as the doors of the Soviet Union briefly opened to Jews wanting to leave.

THE YOM KIPPUR WAR AND HYPERINFLATION

The 1973 Yom Kippur War brought the era of expansion to a halt. For more than a decade, the economy was mired in slow growth and accelerating inflation. The GDP expanded at an average rate of more than 3 percent annually, a pace insufficient to keep up with population growth, while inflation reached a rate of 450 percent in 1984. The immediate causes of the problem were the war's huge human and financial costs and the jump in world energy prices. Defense spending reached 30 percent of GDP in the mid-1970s—more than three times the U.S. level during the Cold War.

The government exacerbated the crisis by allowing its budget to grow so quickly that rising taxes could not offset a widening deficit and growing debt. The Bank of Israel was beholden to the government to create money as needed to cover the state's overspending. The widespread use of inflation indexing—automatically raising wages to keep pace with prices—designed to protect savers and wage earners from price rises was also exacerbating the problem while reducing the political pressure to take steps to stop it.

But there were deeper problems. The state-directed economic model was no longer working. The era of big infrastructure projects that had generated so much growth was over, making it increasingly obvious that the government and the Histadrut-owned companies dominating economic life were bloated and inefficient.

Unlike the United States (but much like Europe), Israel was reluctant to embrace capitalism in the 1970s and 1980s, even as the quasi-socialist economic model that had previously served it so well was obviously failing. The rise of Menahem Begin and the Likud Party to power in the 1977 elections, ending twenty-nine years of Labor Party rule, should have ushered in a new era of freer enterprise. The party was hostile to the Histadrut, the kibbutzim, and the other components of the Labor establishment, but the Likud's primary ideological concern was cementing Israeli rule over the West Bank and the Gaza Strip by constructing settlements.

To the extent that the Likud Party had an economic policy, it was populist, not capitalist. Its few efforts at liberalization were overwhelmed by the depth of the economic crisis that it was contending with and by a lack of commitment. In fact, welfare spending and the size of government grew during the first years of Likud rule. When the Economic Stabilization Plan was adopted eight years later, it was adopted by a Labor-Likud coalition government.

In July 1985, the government responded to economic failure with an Economic Stabilization Plan. The budget deficit was slashed, the shekel, Israel's unit of currency, was devalued by 20 percent, cost-of-living allowances were suspended, and price controls were imposed. The U.S. government pitched in with $1.5 billion in aid. By 1986 inflation was down to about 20 percent. The government also undertook a long-term program to sell off state-owned companies (privatization), deregulate markets and foreign trade, and reduce state spending. The Economic Stabilization Plan was more than a policy change: it marked the end of the socialist era of Israel's economy. While the state's role remained substantial, the principle that private enterprise and free markets were the key to economic growth and development now came to the fore.

REFORM AND REBOUND

With GDP growing at an average annual rate of 3.8 percent from 1986 to 1990, renewed economic growth took longer to achieve than economic stabilization. The immediate impact of the Economic Stabilization Plan was to choke off easy credit and reduce the stimulus of government spending, forcing businesses to cut back or even close. But eventually the plan set the stage for the two decades of rapid expansion that followed. Immigrants began pouring in from the Soviet Union in 1990, fortifying the economy over the next decade with about one million people who were disproportionately young, skilled, and educated.

Meanwhile, the Madrid peace conference and the Oslo peace process weakened the Arab economic boycott of Israel that had deprived Israel of imported products and services, foreign investment, and export markets. Many companies saw the signing of the Oslo Accords as a signal that they could do business with Israel and not suffer Arab retaliation. Finally, the new, liberalized economic environment helped let loose a high-technology sector, driven by entrepreneurialism and innovation. By the end of the 1990s, technology had emerged as Israel's flagship industry.

The first decade of the twenty-first century tested the new economic regime repeatedly. The year 2000 saw the outbreak of the Second Intifada, followed in short order by the collapse of the global high-tech industry. In 2006, the economy suffered another security-related blow with the Second Lebanon War, which lasted little over a month but paralyzed one-third of the country under a rain of rockets. A year later, a new threat emerged when the collapse of the U.S. subprime mortgage market set off a global financial crisis.

In fact, Israel experienced three full-fledged recessions over the decade—in 1997–1998, in 2001–2002, and in 2008–2009—but they were manageable and were not caused by fundamental flaws in the economy. Israel was among the last developed economies to be pushed into recession by the subprime crisis and was among the first to emerge from it, after only two quarters (six months) of negative GDP growth. As much of the developed world struggled with the aftereffects of the global recession in 2010, Israel's GDP expanded 4.5 percent, compared with 2.7 percent for industrialized economies. Just as significant, the economy rebounded very rapidly after the Second Lebanon War, a testament to its ability to cope with war, at least a brief one.

The private sector proved able to absorb repeated external shocks, moving quickly to cut costs, keep production lines running even in wartime, and to seek out new markets and opportunities. The government's policies of fiscal restraint also helped shield the economy from shockwaves set off the by subprime crisis. Yet recent experience also shows the limitations of unfettered free-market policies. Israel did not go to the lengths the United States did to deregulate its financial markets, a hesitancy that subsequently spared it the banking and financial crisis that the United States suffered.

With the electorate and the political establishment both preoccupied by the political and security challenges facing Israel, economic issues have never been at the forefront of policy debate. This differentiates Israel from most Western societies and may explain why the government has often been slow to address economic issues. Nevertheless, today there is a very broad ideological consensus among Israeli policymakers in favor of smaller government and a free market. Although the Likud has led seven governments since 1985, Labor four, and Kadima one, all the governments have pursued the broad outlines of economic management—privatization, deregulation, and careful fiscal policy.

LEADING INDUSTRIES

Because of the very small domestic market, most of Israel's biggest industrial companies are focused on selling overseas, in many cases generating just a few percentage points of their total sales at home. Companies have to operate in multiple foreign markets with differing regulations, business practices, and currencies while they contend with the disadvantages of high costs and the unfavorable economies of scale at home. Given the challenges faced, Israeli managers must act nimbly, adapting quickly to changing market conditions and swiftly developing innovative products. Israel's leading manufacturing industries are machinery and electronics, defense, chemicals and pharmaceuticals, food, plastics, and transportation equipment.

Industry made its first appearance in the 1920s when entrepreneurial immigrants arriving from Poland set up small textile factories. The Poles were later joined by German business-people who founded bigger enterprises, including the Ata Textile combine, the biggest industrial employer in the 1940s. However, attempts in the early years of the state to build heavy industries like steel and automobiles failed in the absence of sufficient economies of scale and raw materials. Instead, textiles became the focus of a government-led program of subsidies and other incentives for private business starting in 1957.

Protected from import competition and boosted by financial aid, the industry employed about 15 percent of the country's industrial workforce by 1985. But by the late 1980s, the government began removing protection for local industries. Textiles and Israel's other traditional industries could no longer compete with lower-cost producers abroad, leading to painful factory closures and rising unemployment. Technology, pharmaceutical, and other industries where innovation was more important than cost gradually took the place of the traditional industries.

High Technology

Technology emerged as Israel's leading industry in the 1990s. In 2008, it accounted for about 20 percent of Israel's industrial output and about one-quarter of its exports of goods and services, employing about 168,000 people, 7 percent of the country's private-sector labor force. The foundation of Israel's technology sector was made possible by the country's institutions of higher education and science, which even in the early years of the state were of an unusually high caliber thanks to the immigration of scientists from Europe. Israel's workforce also had a large proportion of scientists and engineers. Today, it counts 140 scientists and technicians and 135 engineers for every 10,000 people, the highest ratio in the world.

But technology is not only a function of raw scientific ability. Creating the start-up companies that turn new ideas into commercial products requires a cadre of entrepreneurs and a specialized financing system—namely, venture capital. Israel has succeeded in bringing all these ingredients into the mix. Even the army has played a critical role as the source of many of the industry's innovations and as a training ground for future managers.

The country's technological know-how was initially devoted to defense, especially after France, then the country's chief arms supplier, imposed an embargo on Israel in 1967. The

Innovation

Research and Development - Civilian spending % GDP 2007

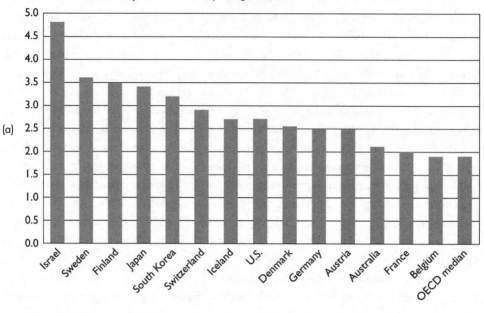

(a)

Utility Patents - Number/million population 2008

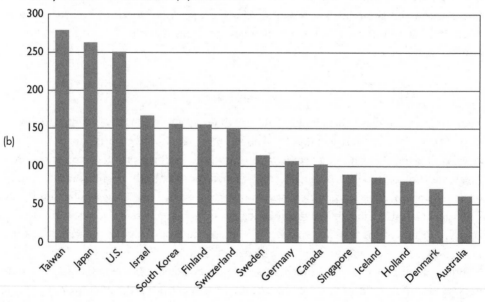

(b)

(a) Israel spends more per capita on research and development than any developed economy and (b) is among the world leaders in patents granted per capita. (Data: OECD; Chart: David Rosenberg. Drawing by Bill Nelson.)

transition to civilian markets began after a major defense project, the Lavi fighter jet, was canceled in 1987. This put thousands of engineers out of work, at just about the time that new opportunities were being created from the deregulation of the global telecommunications industry and the development of new technologies, principally the Internet.

The government played a critical role in helping to lay the foundation for a venture capital industry, sponsoring technology incubators where entrepreneurs could develop new products, and subsidizing corporate research and development. Among Israeli innovations were the first generation of Internet chat software and the first solid-state flash drive. Israel-based engineers were also responsible for the design of some of Intel's most important computer chips.

Two decades after the industry got under way, Israel's technology sector remains focused on innovation. At the core are start-up companies developing cutting-edge communications and computer products and medical devices. In 2008, Israel spent 4.8 percent and, in 2009, 4.3 percent of its GDP on research and development, in each case the highest percentage in the world. Where the industry has been less successful is in marketing and building large and sustainable enterprises.

Israeli start-ups frequently pioneer a technology only to sell to a foreign rival, leaving them the choice of turning to another market niche or selling themselves to a larger, overseas competitor. The founders typically form a new company with a new core technology and target market, repeating the cycle. That strategy has been criticized for its short-term outlook and for depriving Israel's economy of the income, skills, and jobs that large and growing multinational companies generate.

Chemicals and Pharmaceuticals

One of Israel's few natural resources with industrial value is the combination of phosphate, potash, and other mineral deposits from the Dead Sea and adjacent areas, used mainly in making fertilizers. As opposed to everywhere else in the world where these minerals are mined, at the Dead Sea they are collected at much lower cost in huge salt evaporation pans that occupy the entire southern end of the lake. These minerals were first exploited by the Palestine Potash Company, founded in 1930 by Moshe Novomeysky and his British partners after they obtained an exclusive license from the British authorities.

The Israeli government took over the company in 1952, changing its name to Dead Sea Works. Over the years, other chemical businesses were added to form what is now Israel Chemicals, which was privatized in 1995. Besides fertilizers, the company makes flame retardants and chemicals for the oil industry and has bought companies in the United States and Europe to expand beyond its Dead Sea base.

Israel has also developed a large pharmaceuticals sector thanks to one company, Teva Pharmaceutical Industries, the world's largest producer of generic drugs. More recently, Israel's biotechnology industry has sought to replicate the model used to develop electronics and communications start-ups, which relied on government backing and venture capital for finance. In place of the army, which often served as the source for innovations in communications and computers, the country's academic institutions serve as biotech companies' source for basic innovations. Today, Israel has about 300 biotechnology companies, most of them start-ups. About two-thirds of them are dedicated to developing new therapeutic drugs, the remainder to developing diagnostic kits and research tools.

Defense

Faced with high defense costs even in times of relative peace, as well as the threat of embargos by foreign suppliers, Israel came inevitably to develop and produce its own arms and defense materials. Although the Israel Defense Forces relies on the United States for its principal weapons platforms, Israeli companies develop and manufacture technologies to enhance them. They also produce missiles, drones, communications equipment, and a host of other military-electronics equipment and even make the IDF's main battle tank, the Merkava. Unlike Israel's other industrial sectors, most of the defense industry is under government control. Among the largest state-owned companies are Israel Aerospace Industries (drones, missiles, and defense electronics, as well as civilian business jets and satellites), Rafael (defense electronics), and Israel Military Industries (ammunition, missiles, defense electronics). Elbit Systems, a maker of defense electronics, is the biggest private-sector company.

Though large by international standards, Israel's defense procurements are insufficient to cover the costs of developing new military technologies. The industry therefore has emerged as a major exporter to the United States, Europe, Asia, and Latin America. In many cases, Israeli companies have to set up local subsidiaries or joint ventures with local partners to meet domestic production requirements. Although reliable dollar figures are difficult to obtain, Israel is probably among the world's five largest arms exporters.

Fashion and Textiles

Israel's textile industry has declined since the days of government backing. The companies that survived did so by adopting strategies to reduce costs and upgrade their product lines. Many have moved part of their production out of Israel, most often to Jordan or Egypt, where labor is cheaper than at home. Typically, companies have garments designed and cut in Israel and send the most labor-intensive sewing operations to neighboring countries. The other strategy is to employ proprietary technology, like that developed by Tefron to make seamless undergarments, to ensure a competitive advantage of lower-cost rivals. Other companies have concentrated on the highest end of the apparel market, where costs are less of an issue than design and quality, or niches, as Gottex did with swimsuits.

Like Israel's other leading industries, the textile industry is geared toward exports. Free-trade-area agreements with its two biggest markets, the United States and Europe, entitle Israeli-made products to tariff- and quota-free access, helping to offset higher costs of production. Israeli plants in Jordan and Egypt are located in qualified industrial zones (QIZs) that give them duty-free access to the U.S. markets so long as a minimum percentage of the garment's value is produced in Israel.

Energy

Israel's natural resources only recently came to include natural gas. Israel imports most of its energy, which is both very costly and carries major security risks. The Arab boycott prevents it from importing oil from its immediate neighbors, so Israel depends on Russia and the former Soviet republics for most of its petroleum.

Beginning in the 1950s, the government encouraged exploration for oil and gas, but the effort did not yield any significant finds. Israelis joked that Moses took the Israelites in the wrong direction after he led them out of Egypt, turning left into Canaan rather than right into what is now petroleum-rich Saudi Arabia. In fact, however, there are large reserves of natural gas off Israel's Mediterranean coast, created over the millennia by organic matter carried by Egypt's Nile River into the sea and up the coast.

The first major find occurred in 1999, when the Yam Thetis group found reserves of natural gas amounting to 1.236 trillion cubic feet (35 billion cubic meters) in the Mediterranean near Ashkelon at the Mari B and Noa fields. A decade later, considerably larger discoveries were made in Israeli waters 56 miles (90 kilometers) offshore from Haifa. The Tamar field is estimated to contain about 211.88 trillion cubic feet (6 trillion cubic meters) of gas, enough to supply Israel's needs for the next two decades. Mari B, where production began in 2004, will probably run dry by 2012 or so, at which point planners are counting on the Tamar field to take its place. In 2010, by far the largest field in Israel was discovered. Called Leviathan, it is estimated to hold 16 trillion cubic feet (453 billion cubic meters) of gas and could supply Israel's domestic needs for the next six decades. The find is so extensive that Israel could, if it chooses, become a major gas exporter.

Starting in 1995, before the first domestic reserves were identified, Israel embarked on a long-term program to boost its gas consumption by 2014 to 40 percent of the total energy used, replacing much of its imported coal. The reason for the program is that building gas-fired power stations is relatively cheap, and the plants themselves take up little space. Unlike coal-burning plants, which must be built close the shore to receive the imported coal from ships, gas plants can be sited anywhere. Gas, however, is transported most cheaply and efficiently by pipeline, so a critical part of Israel's gas program includes a network of pipelines carrying gas from the wells to power plants and big industrial users.

Big new natural gas discoveries off the Mediterranean coast may make Israel a major exporter, as well as replacing imports from Egypt, jeopardized by sabotage attacks on the pipeline and political hostility after that country's 2011 revolution.

AGRICULTURE AND KIBBUTZIM

In the state's early days, oranges were the economy's flagship product and the sturdy *kibbutznik* (kibbutz resident) was the archetypal Israeli. Even if the kibbutzim did not as a rule grow citrus, Jaffa oranges were Israel's biggest export, and collective agriculture was the focus of economic development. The immigrants in the first wave arriving in Israel after 1948 were settled as much as possible in kibbutzim or in other collective settlements, called moshavim; in these the land is held privately for the most part but the purchase of supplies and the sale of produce are done by the community.

Farming accounted for about 17 percent of employment in 1950. Only later in the 1950s, when it became evident that the agricultural sector could not generate enough jobs and housing for all the arrivals, did the government's focus turn to industry. The decision was a wise one, for agriculture has grown more efficient, reducing the number of jobs in the sector even as output has grown. In 1955, one Israeli farmer could feed 15 people; by 2007 one farmer could feed 100. Agriculture today directly employs less than 3 percent of the labor force and accounts for about the same proportion of GDP.

Farm products have fallen as a percentage of Israel's total exports, but even today about one-quarter of Israel's harvest is sold abroad. Like industry, agriculture faces problems of high costs and small scale in competing in overseas markets. To overcome them, growers use research and development to identify new products and niche markets. They also employ advanced growing technology, such as drip irrigation, to use water efficiently, and greenhouse technologies to control heat, light, and humidity.

Citrus accounted for only 5 percent of Israel's $5.5 billion in agricultural output in 2007, but in its place Israel now exports exotic fruits and flowers and has been at the forefront in innovations allowing it to sell off-season fruit and vegetables abroad, an effort now emulated by Chile and other developing countries. Vegetables accounted for 24 percent; other fruit and cattle made up another 17 percent each.

In spite of the progress made in increasing output and exploiting limited resources, Israel suffers serious constraints in expanding its agriculture. A small country with an arid and semi-arid climate, only about 20 percent of its land is arable. Much of the best land, most notably the orange groves that once surrounded Tel Aviv, has been given over for homes, factories, and offices as the country's population has grown.

Israel's Mediterranean climate means that rainfall occurs only between October and April. To ensure sufficient water for crops year-round, about 40 percent of the country's arable land is irrigated, about six times the rate in 1948. About one-half the country's potable water goes to

Fresh-picked grapefruit are loaded into bins before being trucked to a juice factory near the town of Hod Hasharon in central Israel, March 2008. (Getty Images / Image Bank.)

farming, even though the sector accounts for only a tiny proportion of GDP. Although Israel is developing a network of desalination plants and recycles sewage, it runs a water deficit—that is, it uses more water every year than is renewed by rainfall. Hence it must draw on underground aquifers.

Israel is addressing its water shortage in part by building a network of desalination plants that will provide about 26.486 billion cubic feet (750 million cubic meters) of water. The largest of them, a 4.48-billion-cubic-foot (127-million-cubic-meter) facility in Hadera, is capable of providing 20 percent of the country's household water consumption needs and is the largest in the world using reverse-osmosis technology. Israel is planning an even bigger facility in the coastal city of Ashkelon; it will have a minimum capacity of 5.297 billion cubic feet (150 million cubic meters).

Kibbutzim: A Struggling Experiment

Not only has the role of farming diminished in Israeli society, so has the place of the kibbutz. The combined population of the kibbutzim never exceeded a few percentage points of Israel's population, but kibbutzim supplied Israel with many of its political and military leaders and even today account for a disproportionate share of Israel's farm and industrial output. No less important, in their heyday, kibbutzim embodied something close to the socialist ideology in its purest form, to which many in the Yishuv aspired.

Kibbutz members held all their property in common. Resources—clothing, travel, or spending money—were divided according to need, not according to the value of a particular member's contribution or job. Indeed, in the classical kibbutz model, members were compensated for their work in kind, receiving housing, food, clothing, and the like in exchange for their labor. Major decisions were made collectively by the entire membership at regular general assemblies, which were much like New England town meetings. The kibbutz came close to the ideal of a single, all-encompassing community, erected on the foundation of a collective economic structure that provided for all its members' needs—child rearing, education, culture, health, and retirement.

The first kibbutz, Degania, was founded in 1910 close to where the Jordan River flows out of the Sea of Galilee by a group of eleven young men and women. Although conditions were difficult, the idea caught on quickly, and within a decade there were twelve kibbutzim numbering 805 members. Kibbutzim formed alliances among themselves along ideological lines and gained further impetus from the backing of the Yishuv leadership.

European Jewish youth movements encouraged and trained a new generation of young people for agricultural life over the next two decades. By 1940, 27,000 people lived in 82 kibbutzim. In the first years of the state, the government made a great effort to settle new immigrants in the kibbutzim, which boosted the number of settlements to 229 and their combined population to almost 78,000.

In the earliest years, life on a kibbutz resembled life in other experimental communes, with characteristically strong ideology, high expectations, and intense personal and political relationships. Unlike most experiments of this sort, however, the kibbutz endured as an institution. But the collectivist values that once formed its foundation began to dissipate in the 1960s and 1970s as Israeli society grew wealthier and more individualistic. Kibbutzim supplemented their traditional farming economy with industry and tourism and established other enterprises that brought in increased revenue and profits. Indeed, even as the kibbutzim's population continued to grow, the number of members engaged in agriculture was dropping. By 1990, more were working in industry than in farming. Some members also left, attracted by the material and other advantages of city life.

The real blow to the movement came in the 1980s as the hyperinflation that struck the Israeli economy caused the kibbutzim's debts to balloon and exposed their economic inefficiencies. In 1989, they reached the first debt bailout agreement with the government and its bank creditors. Kibbutzim were forced to sell land and industrial enterprises, including the giant dairy cooperative Tnuva in 2008, and to begin running their operations on a business basis. By 2009, the great majority of the kibbutzim had solved their debt problems.

In the wake of the debt crisis, the kibbutzim also did away with much of their collectivist structure, a process informally called "privatization" even though each community remains under collective ownership. In most kibbutzim today, members can work outside the settlement at salaried jobs, outsiders rent homes in the settlement, and professional managers run kibbutz-owned enterprises. Rather than being allocated goods and services in kind, members are paid stipends for their work, which they can spend on meals in the dining hall, clothing, and entertainment. Indeed, in 2007, three years short of its centennial, Degania (now called Degania Aleph to differentiate itself from a sister kibbutz, Degania Bet, formed in 1920) privatized itself.

Even if privatization has meant jettisoning many of the movement's original values, it has helped the kibbutzim to recover from the crisis of the 1980s. After declining in the following decade, their combined population has slowly begun to grow again, and since 2005 the kibbutzim have attracted more new members than they have lost. Their combined membership stood near 130,000 in 2011, close to its record high seven years earlier.

INVESTMENT, SAVINGS, AND MONETARY POLICY

In the early years of the state, Israel was faced with the enormous task of building an economy, as well as industry, homes, and infrastructure, with few domestic resources to meet the challenge. Although Israel's private savings rate was high, it was not high enough to meet the economy's needs, in part because the government has almost always had a net negative savings rate through nearly all of its history.

The solution to the shortfall was twofold. First, Israel became an importer of foreign capital in the form of loans, such as Israel Bonds, which were first issued in 1950, and grants and gifts, which amounted to $2.2 billion between 1952 and 1960. Second, the government gradually established an almost complete monopoly on the allocation of capital to various sectors of the economy. The government gave itself the authority to decide where banks would lend money (a practice known as directed credit), when and how companies could turn to the capital markets to raise funds, and where institutional investors, such as pension and provident funds, could invest their assets. By assuming control over access to capital, the government effectively assumed control over the entire economy.

Why did the state come to supplant the banks and financial markets? Certainly one critical factor was the private sector's inability to raise capital on its own. There was little cross-border investment in the 1950s, and Israel was an unlikely candidate to capture what little there was. It had just emerged from the War of Independence, and its long-term survival was still in doubt. Thus, Palestine Potash was taken over by the Israeli government after its private-sector shareholders failed to secure financing to rehabilitate its facilities.

In any case, most of the unilateral transfers of the 1950s were intergovernmental, which left little alternative but for the state to become the conduit to invest in the economy. But there was also an ideological imperative. The socialist ethos of the Labor Zionists held that economic development should be steered by the government rather than by market forces, which they regarded as fickle and unreliable.

The system worked well enough in the 1950s and early 1960s, but as the economy grew more sophisticated, its inefficiencies became more apparent. Moreover, in the aftermath of the Yom Kippur War of 1973, the government was having an increasingly difficult time controlling its current expenditures—the money spent on budget items such as defense, education, and social welfare. By 1985, 96 percent of all the capital raised in Israel (state loans, bonds, and equity issues) went to the government, and increasingly not to develop finances but to cover current expenditures on defense and education, among other things.

The bank shares' collapse of 1983 illustrated the problem created by the state's excessive involvement in finance. The banks had so much of their capital tied up in directed credit that they turned to the stock market as an alternative, unhindered source of capital. To convince investors to buy their stock, the banks ensured attractive returns by buying it themselves. By the early 1980s, the strategy was no longer sustainable: the price of the shares had risen far beyond their underlying value.

When the banks could no longer afford to prop up their stock, investors sold their holdings and prices collapsed. To prevent the losses from reverberating through the economy, the government was forced to step in. It bought the banks' shares from investors at close to their pre-crash value and assumed ownership of the banks, a cost that was covered by printing money, thereby exacerbating the country's inflation problem.

In the wake of the Economic Stabilization Plan, the government gradually reduced its involvement in finance. Quotas imposed on institutional investors to hold non-tradable government bonds were lowered, enabling the investors to choose what kinds of assets to invest in. The government itself began issuing increasing amounts of tradable bonds, and companies no longer had to get official approval to issue bonds. Directed credit, which in 1985 accounted for two-thirds of all bank lending, was gradually eliminated.

The shekel was gradually made fully convertible, so that by 2003 Israelis could buy and sell foreign currencies for business, travel, or investment without any restrictions. As budget deficits fell over the years, the government no longer needed to monopolize capital for itself.

Government debt as a percentage of GDP fell from a high of 284 percent in 1984 to about 80 percent in 2008 and 70 percent in 2010. Though high by the standard of 60 percent set by the European Union, it nevertheless represents a significant achievement. Israeli government debt accounted for about 19 percent of all financial assets held by the public in 2009, but the corporate debt market has been able to grow as well, and it accounted for about 11.5 percent.

Although the government continues to have a negative savings rate, the figure has dropped to the low single digits, while the private savings rate has been about 10–12 percent since 1990.

Foreign Investment

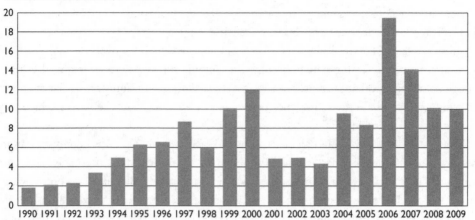

Overseas investment in Israel, U.S. dollars billions

Foreign investment, which has grown since implementation of the Oslo Accords in 1994, was given further impetus by the growth of the high-tech sector starting in the late 1990s. (Data: Israel Finance Ministry; Chart: David Rosenberg. Drawing by Bill Nelson.)

Indexation (linking the value of assets to the rate of inflation) no longer has the stranglehold on the economy it once had as inflation slowed: in 2008, about 40 percent of the government debt traded on the Tel Aviv Stock Exchange was linked to the consumer price index (CPI).

Since 2002, Israel has been a net creditor to the rest of the world, and since 2003, it has had consistent surpluses in the current account of its balance of payments. Liberalization has also spurred overseas investment in Israel, with foreign direct investment (money used to buy real assets, such as control of companies and real estate) totaling around $10 billion in 2009. Likewise, it has enabled Israelis to invest more freely and efficiently, whether they manage a company buying an overseas rival or are household savers looking for the best return on their portfolios.

Inflation

Although inflation has been brought under control since the middle 1980s, high inflation was a major element of Israeli economic life for much of the state's history. The first serious inflation occurred in the early 1950s, when rationing led to a black market at the same time that the government was printing money to cover widening budget deficits. Prices rose 66 percent in 1952 alone. Although the pace of inflation subsequently fell, the government introduced indexation in 1956, pegging the price of its bonds to either the consumer price index or the exchange rate.

The banks followed suit in 1962 with partially indexed savings plans. The labor market also adopted the practice, with cost-of-living allowances (COLAs) becoming a permanent feature of collective labor agreements starting in 1957. Indexation was understandably welcomed by the public as a way of protecting the value of their financial assets and wages. But businesses

seeking financing to invest and expand were in no position to match the government's gener-
ous terms.

After fifteen years of single-digit price rises, Israel's CPI climbed by a rate of 13 to 14 percent
annually in 1971–1972. It reached 80 percent a year at the end of the decade and moved into
the triple digits during the early 1980s. Although inflation has many causes that economists did
not fully understand, undoubtedly excessive budget deficits financed by the Bank of Israel's
printing money contributed to inflation. Indexation exacerbated the problem by automatically
passing along price rises as a kind of inflationary aftershock.

Inflation undermined economic growth because it made planning for business more difficult, thereby discouraging investment. Indeed, even as prices rose, Israel's economic growth
slowed in a phenomenon known as stagflation. While much of the world suffered stagflation
in the 1970s, Israel felt its effects longer and more deeply than most others. Moreover, once inflation reached a rate of 10 to 20 percent per month, indexation could no longer shield people
from the effects of price hikes.

Inflation in the 1970s and 1980s eroded so much of the Israeli currency's value, as well as the
public's confidence in it, that it had to be replaced twice in the space of five years. In 1980, the
lira (plural, lirot), the Israeli pound, in use since 1948, was succeeded by the shekel at a rate of
ten lirot for every shekel. In 1985, the government replaced the inflation-battered old shekel
with a new shekel, this time at a rate of 1,000 old shekels for each new one. The new shekel remains in use today. The 1985 Economic Stabilization Plan finally returned the inflation rate in
the second half of the 1980s to the lower double digits. Since 1999, the CPI has remained under
5 percent each year, in line with the CPI in other developed economies; the low CPI has been
a factor in the economic growth since the 1990s.

Inflation

Consumer price index, annual % change (Dec. to Dec.)

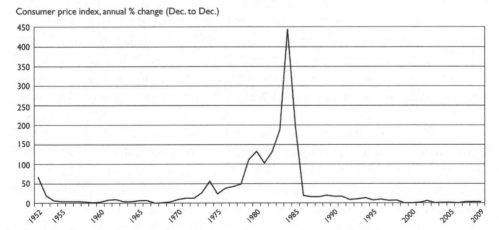

Inflation began to accelerate in the 1970s and was not brought down until after the 1985 Economic Stabilization Plan. It took another fifteen years to achieve consistent single-digit CPIs. (Data: Israel Central Bureau
of Statistics; Chart: David Rosenberg. Drawing by Bill Nelson.)

Monetary Policy

The responsibility for maintaining price stability falls on the Bank of Israel, the country's central bank, the equivalent to the U.S. Federal Reserve. Like its peers, the Bank of Israel seeks to stabilize prices by controlling the amount of money circulating in the economy (money supply) and the short-term interest rates. Interest rates that are too low encourage the economy to expand too quickly and contribute to inflation. Conversely, rates that are too high can choke off economic growth. The bank was set up in 1954, but for the first thirty years of is existence, its ability to ensure price stability was severely constricted. It operated principally by raising and lowering the amount of money it required the banks to put on deposit (the reserve requirement).

Since 1985, however, the Bank of Israel has gradually adopted the same set of tools for controlling money supply used by other central banks in the developed world. The foremost of these are monetary auctions, in which the country's commercial banks bid for deposits or loans from the central bank, thereby setting a baseline for the lowest rate of interest in the economy. Another tool is *Makams* (short-term loans, called by their Hebrew acronym), which are bonds issued by the central bank for terms of up to one year. By issuing Makams, the Bank of Israel ties up the cash used to purchase them for a year; buying them back or letting them mature has the reverse effect. Since 1992 the government has set an inflation target, which defines the boundaries of "acceptable" inflation. In recent years, the target has been set at 1 to 3 percent annually.

The Shekel and the Exchange-Rate Policy

The legal tender of pre-state Palestine and Israel has gone through several changes over the past century. Under Ottoman rule, Turkish currency was the official medium of exchange, and it remained so after the British conquered Palestine (although the Mandate authorities also let the Egyptian pound circulate, as Egypt was then under British rule as well). In 1927, Palestine got its own currency, the Palestinian pound, which was linked to the British pound.

In a move that would have long-term implications for the Israeli economy, Britain imposed exchange controls on the Palestinian pound during World War II. These remained in effect after the war and were adopted by Israel when it was declared a state in 1948. Even as Israel moved to its own currency, the lira, and later to the shekel and the new shekel, exchange controls remained in force to one degree or another—with two brief interruptions—until 2005.

Exchange or currency controls set rules about who can buy and sell foreign currency at what price and for what purposes. The idea behind them is that in an economy that has limited foreign currency assets, the government should allocate them where they are most critically needed (for instance, to support food imports instead of vacations abroad). Indeed, it might even use the exchange rate to foster other economic policies, such as making exports more price competitive by reducing the currency's international value (a devaluation).

Many governments, including Israel's, have imposed multiple exchange rates, setting their currency's value at different rates depending on the purpose for which it is being bought or sold. Of course, the value of a currency hinges on a host of factors, such as inflation and a country's balance of payments (its total international transactions for a period of time), which cannot all be successfully managed all the time by policymakers. A black market exchange rate, based on what ordinary people and businesses think the currency is really worth, inevitably develops alongside the official exchange rate. For a small country like Israel that is heavily reliant on foreign trade, the exchange rate and the policies adopted to manage it play a major role in the economy.

Although Israel periodically devalued the lira in the 1950s and 1960s, the exchange rate remained relatively stable until inflation began to gather steam and the country's balance of payments deteriorated after the Yom Kippur War. In response, the government adopted a crawling peg in 1975 under which the lira depreciated in value at a steady, predictable rate of about 2 percent a month. When the Likud Party took power in 1977, one of the few concrete steps it took to liberalize the economy was ending most currency controls and allowing the lira exchange rate to be set by the market (to float). But without other measures to correct the economy's serious imbalances, the policy was a failure.

During 1983 and 1984, Israel resumed fixing its currency (by now called the shekel) and reimposed exchange controls. However, neither the lira nor the shekel exchange rates were stable during the years that the exchange rate was fixed. The government frequently stepped in to readjust its value lower, sometimes by as much as 20 percent at a time; but it was the government that set the rate, not the markets.

The modern era for currency began, like much else in Israel's economy, with the 1985 Economic Stabilization Plan and the end of hyperinflation. Together they created a foundation for a more stable shekel and enabled the government to embark on a slow evolution toward a free-floating currency—this time with all the elements in place to make it work. In 1989, the fixed rate was made more flexible and responsive to the market, allowed to trade up to 3 percent above or below a midpoint set by the government. Over time, this band was widened to such an extent that, for all intents and purposes, the shekel was free floating. The Bank of Israel, which was responsible for the exchange rate, would intervene only if it reached either end of the band.

As the band grew wider, Israel acted to remove controls over buying and selling foreign currency. In 1989, for instance, it began to lift restrictions on capital inflows, enabling Israelis to borrow abroad; and in 2004, it abolished taxes on investments. By 1997, the Bank of Israel no longer needed to intervene in the foreign currency market to ensure the shekel exchange rate. Finally, in June 2005, the band was eliminated, and the shekel exchange rate officially became completely free floating.

Thanks to the performance of the economy, the shekel has demonstrated consistent strength since 2003. Israel's current account has been in surplus, and foreigners have invested record amounts in Israel—all of which creates demand for shekels. Ironically, the Bank of Israel was finally forced in 2008 to begin intervening in the currency market to prevent the shekel from appreciating too much and making it hard for exporters to price their products competitively. But the central bank was not setting the exchange rate as in the past. Rather, it was trying to influence the market temporarily by buying dollars with shekels.

Banking and Financial Markets

Israel has about twenty-five banks, including mortgage lenders, foreign institutions operating in Israel, and other financial service companies. But the industry is dominated by five major groups that account for more than 90 percent of all assets. That is a high degree of concentration even for a small economy like Israel's, and in recent years the trend has grown more pronounced as larger institutions have bought up smaller ones. Israeli banks are universal banks in the sense that they provide a host of functions besides offering loans and deposits. They underwrite the sale of new securities, provide brokerage services to stock market investors, manage investment portfolios for clients, sell insurance, and issue credit cards.

Israel's larger banks have traditionally had a large presence abroad, mainly in the United States and Europe, where they attract foreign-currency deposits from Diaspora Jews. In more recent years, as the opportunities for growth at home have been constrained by industry concentration and regulators, the largest banks have sought to expand abroad, mainly into Eastern Europe and the countries of the former Soviet Union.

Regulators have sought over the past decade to pare back the role of the banks to increase competition in the financial services industry and prevent the conflicts of interest that arise when a single institution offers an array of financial products. In 2005, the banks were ordered to divest their management of mutual and provident funds and have been forced to limit their holdings in nonbank companies. As a result, insurance companies and institutional investors have become a major source of corporate finance: they buy company bonds and make direct investments in infrastructure and real estate projects.

The Tel Aviv Stock Exchange (TASE) is Israel's only market for trading stocks and bonds. About 630 companies are listed on it, and its aggregate worth (market value) stood at $134 billion at the end of 2008, accounting for about 67 percent of GDP, compared with a ratio of 83 percent for the United States (both percentages represent relatively low levels after the collapse of share prices in 2008, but Israel's percentage is consistently lower than that of the United States). The twenty-five largest companies by market value form the exchange's benchmark index, the TA-25, or Maof. The TASE also trades government and corporate bonds, whose market value stood at $189 billion at the end of 2008. In addition, the exchange serves as a marketplace for trading options on the TA-25, individual stocks, foreign currency, and about 350 financial products that track various global indices. Foreign investors held 21.5 percent of shares traded on the TASE in 2008.

Many Israeli companies choose to list on overseas stock exchanges instead of, or in addition to, the TASE. About 150 Israeli companies are traded in the United States, primarily on the Nasdaq Stock Market, where Israel has the second-largest contingent of non-U.S. companies. More are listed on European exchanges, mainly the one in London. Listing abroad gives companies easier access to foreign investors and raises their profile among foreign customers. This is especially the case for Israel's high-tech companies, which do almost all their business outside Israel and account for the bulk of the Israeli companies traded in foreign markets.

Venture capital is another critical component of the Israeli financial system—indeed, more so than in nearly any other country—because it is the chief source of finance for technology

People watch a board showing stock fluctuations at the Tel Aviv Stock Exchange, November 22, 2007. (Moshe Shai / Flash90.)

start-ups. The industry plays a critical role in providing not only finance but the management skills that young companies need to evolve from pure research and development to manufacturing and marketing. The venture industry has about eighty funds, including about thirty-five foreign funds, with total capital of about $10.6 billion at the end of 2008. Israeli venture funds invested just over $2 billion in approximately 480 technology companies in 2008, making it the largest venture industry in the world after that of the United States.

Regulation of Israel's markets and financial services industry is divided among three principal authorities. The Bank of Israel supervises banks. The Finance Ministry's capital markets division supervises foreign insurance companies and pension and provident funds. The Israel Securities Authority, an independent agency, regulates the stock market and securities industry. With the deregulation of financial markets and the blurring of distinctions among the players, there have been calls to merge most or all of these bodies into a single unit.

THE PUBLIC SECTOR

Israel's government has traditionally played a large role in the economy—at times an exceedingly large role—in terms of taxes and spending, regulation, finance, and outright ownership of businesses. In part, this has been because of the country's heavy defense burden; both the cost of maintaining a large army and national security considerations require the state to intervene in areas normally left to the private sector. Until the 1980s, ideology was also a factor. Policymakers believed that the state was the best mechanism for managing the economy. Even if it was not the most efficient mechanism, it was still the one best suited to ensure the needs of national development.

Although the government was deeply involved in almost every aspect of economic life in the 1950s, the portion of GDP paid to taxes (the tax burden) was a relatively low 15 percent, because the state financed a large portion of its activities through loans and grants from abroad. The burden gradually increased to 28 percent in the mid-1960s, then accelerated in the 1970s and 1980s to more than 40 percent. Defense costs had climbed in the wake of the Six-Day (1967) and Yom Kippur (1973) Wars, and the government had expanded its welfare programs. Before 1967, government expenditure claimed on average 35 percent of GDP.

Between the Yom Kippur War and 1985, government expenditure more than doubled, reaching 77 percent of GDP, the highest rate among Western economies, an increase made possible by significant U.S. aid. Even as taxes rose, spending grew faster, leaving the government with widening fiscal deficits. On average, they amounted to 14 percent of GDP in the years 1974 to 1985; government debt was equal to 145 percent of GDP at the end of that period.

The government's impact on the economy during those years went beyond taxes and spending. Although Israel always had a large private sector, the government and the labor union establishment gained control of an increasingly large segment of manufacturing and services. The state acquired control of companies such as Palestine Potash and the Haifa Oil Refineries and set up most of the defense industry. Government ministries or companies ran the telephone system, provided water and electric power, operated a fleet of ships (Zim) and an airline (El Al), and controlled monopolies on radio and television broadcasting and on agricultural product sales. In 1983, in the wake of the bank shares crisis, it took control of four of the five biggest banks. As noted earlier, the state was actively involved in industrial development and gradually monopolized finance. Regulations cut deep into economic life.

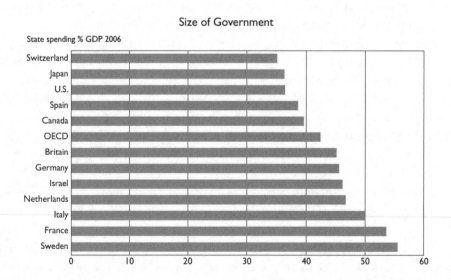

Although Israeli government spending has fallen since 1985, when the Economic Stabilization Plan was put in place, it continues to account for a large proportion of the economy compared to government spending in other developed economies. (Data: OECD; Chart: David Rosenberg. Drawing by Bill Nelson.)

The trend toward growing state intervention came to an abrupt halt in 1985 with the Economic Stabilization Plan. Among its key planks was a sharp cut in government spending, which led to declining budget deficits and an end to nearly all subsidies on consumer goods. The tax burden drifted lower to an average rate of 37.6 percent by 2004–2006. The government undertook measures to deregulate the economy and sold off many of its biggest businesses, including Israel Chemicals (1995), telephone operator Bezeq (2005), and Oil Refineries (2007).

Between 2003 and 2008, Israel kept its deficit under 4 percent of GDP, which let it pay down debt and reduce its borrowing. In fact, the government's financial picture improved to the point where it had earned enough confidence from foreign investors that it could borrow money abroad without U.S. guarantees. The deficit widened to 5.8 percent in 2009 in an effort to counterbalance the effects of the world recession, but that was a small increase by the standards of developed economies, and by 2010 the figure was below 4 percent again.

Nevertheless, by U.S. standards, Israel's government continues to occupy a very large place in the nation's economic life. At 44.2 percent of GDP in 2007, government spending was higher than the OECD average. Israel's debt burden fell to 79.8 percent of GDP in 2007, but that was still twenty points higher than the OECD average. State-owned enterprises still control electricity, water supply, and ports and make up the lion's share of the defense industry.

U.S. AID

Israel is the biggest single recipient of U.S. foreign assistance since World War II. Today it receives more money annually than any country other than Iraq (an average of about $3 billion annually since 1985), even though by every measure Israel has a wealthy, developed economy. Moreover, Israel gets its aid money under far less restrictive terms than other countries do. The United States has also helped Israel by guaranteeing bonds issued by its government abroad.

The first large-scale U.S. assistance program began after the Yom Kippur War, and in subsequent years the aid made a substantial contribution to the economy. In the 1980s, for instance, U.S. aid equaled about 14.5 percent of GDP, and now, even with Israel's much larger GDP, it equals about 1.5 percent. However, as Israel's economy has grown, the relative importance of U.S. aid has shrunk. The aid now goes almost entirely to military spending, and three-quarters of that is spent by law in the United States. While that eases Israel's defense burden, the main beneficiaries of the sales and jobs created by the aid are U.S. companies and workers.

HUMAN RESOURCES

By global standards, Israel's labor force is small and high cost, two characteristics that long handicapped it in developing large and competitive industries. Where its comparative advantage lies is in skills and education. Both have proven to be invaluable resources as the world economy moves toward more knowledge-intensive industries and services.

The proportion of people in the labor force with sixteen or more years of schooling was 30 percent in 2006, the same level as in the United States and the second-highest level in the world. Two decades earlier, the figure was 16 percent; but in the interim Israel's higher-education system expanded immensely. The number of university graduates grew almost fourfold in the two decades before 2008; now about 55,000 graduate annually. In addition, immigrants arriving from the former Soviet Union in the 1990s had an exceptionally high level of schooling, bolstering the ranks of Israel's skilled and educated workforce.

Israel, however, has failed to utilize its human resources fully. At 57.3 percent in 2010, the percentage of the working-age population holding or actively seeking a job (the labor force participation rate) is low by the standards of developed countries (in the United States, for example, it is 66 percent).

Part of the reason is that young people enter the job market later than in most countries because of army service; but even adjusting for this, the rate remains low. The main reason is that two large segments of the population have much lower rates of participation. The rate for Israeli Arabs lags behind the national average owing to social and cultural norms that discourage women from seeking employment. And the rate for Haredi Jews has even fallen over the past thirty years. It was about 30 percent below the average rate in 1980 and today

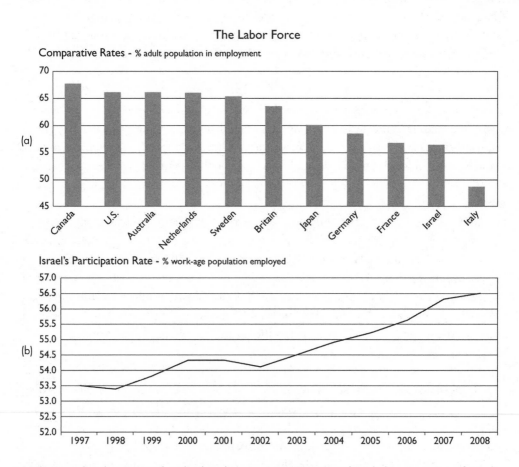

The Labor Force

Comparative Rates - % adult population in employment

(a)

Israel's Participation Rate - % work-age population employed

(b)

(a) Compared to the rate in other developed economies in 2008, a relatively low proportion of Israel's working-age population is employed or seeking employment, (b) but Israel's labor force participation rate has risen in recent years. (Data: Monthly Labor Review, U.S. Department of Labor; Israel Central Bureau of Statistics. Chart: David Rosenberg. Drawing by Bill Nelson.)

is about 60 percent below. In the Haredi world, it is men who do not take jobs; they wish to devote their time to religious study. In both cases, Israel is losing the productive power of a large segment of its population at a cost to the overall economy in the form of lower GDP and higher taxes on the relatively small working population.

As is often the case in wealthy economies, the least desirable jobs are performed by outsiders. In Israel, these were Palestinians from the West Bank and the Gaza Strip through the 1990s, increasingly foreign guest workers thereafter. Guest laborers work for lower wages than Israelis will accept, often without social benefits and frequently in violation of the law.

The influx of outside laborers began after the Six-Day War of 1967, when the border between Israel and the newly conquered West Bank and Gaza Strip opened up. Working principally as day laborers in construction, agriculture, and domestic services, the Palestinians accounted for as much as 10 percent of Israel's labor force.

After the outbreak of the First Intifada in 1987, the flow of Palestinian labor was gradually curtailed. Palestinians were replaced by foreign guest workers from Eastern Europe, Asia, and Africa. In 2008, 61,000 Palestinians and 203,000 non-Palestinian guest workers worked in Israel, accounting for close to 12 percent of Israel's labor force. About half of these guest workers resided in Israel without a permit.

Organized Labor

During the Mandate era and the first thirty years of statehood, the Histadrut labor federation had a major role in the economy, acting not only as a labor union but as an employer, banker, provider of health, education, and culture, and pension manager. Together with the Jewish Agency, it served as a quasi-government for Palestine's Jewish population before the State of Israel came into being and only reluctantly surrendered many of its powers to the new government. In its heyday, the scope of the labor federation's activities was without parallel in the Western world. In the 1950s, about 70 percent of the country's workforce was organized in Histadrut-affiliated unions, and its business, controlled through its Hevrat Ha'Ovdim holding company, accounted for as much as 20 percent of the country's economic output.

As early as the 1950s, the government sought to curtail the Histadrut's expansion. But the real collapse of the labor-union empire began after the 1977 elections, when the Labor Party, which was closely allied with the Histadrut, lost power for the first time in Israel's history. The hyperinflation had saddled its business empire with enormous debts while slow economic growth exposed its inefficiencies. The economic problems also led to the demise of the most heavily unionized industries in the private sector.

Under the weight of debts, the Histadrut was forced to divest its business holdings. It lost control of Bank Hapoalim in the 1983 bank shares crisis, and in 1995 it was forced to give up control of the Kupat Holim Clalit health maintenance organization, which deprived Histadrut of a major source of members and dues. The government took control of its pension funds in 2003. Today, the Histadrut is an ordinary labor-union umbrella group. Most of its members are employed in the civil service and the remaining state-owned monopoly companies, such as Israel Electric Corporation and those in the defense industry. The new economy that arose in the 1990s, led by high technology, has almost no union presence.

Poverty and Inequality

The rapid economic growth and liberalization that Israel has experienced since the 1990s has not solved the problems of poverty and income inequality. In fact, the situation has worsened. The country enjoyed some of the highest levels of income equality in the world in the 1950s and 1960s. But in the early part of the twenty-first century, 20 percent of all Israelis had incomes under 50 percent of the national median (the poverty line). Middle-class consumers have been squeezed by high prices for homes and consumer goods plus stagnating incomes. These problems became so acute that in the summer of 2011, Israelis erected tent cities across the country and staged mass demonstrations demanding that the government address them.

Several factors have contributed to raising the poverty rate. One is the low labor force participation rate, especially among Israeli Arabs and Haredi Jews. Those families are less likely to have two breadwinners and often lack even one. For cultural reasons, both groups have larger-than-average families, thereby exacerbating the problem of child poverty, which in 2007–2008 was 34.3 percent, almost nine percentage points above the total rate.

A second factor is immigration. While most of the last wave of newcomers—those arriving from the former Soviet Union in the 1990s—were successfully absorbed into the economy, a large number remain unemployed or underemployed. Third, the transition of the economy to technology-intensive industries and the concomitant loss of jobs in traditional sectors have left a great many Israelis permanently unemployed for lack of appropriate skills or education. Nor has Israel been exempt from the global increase in income inequality, as those with the greatest skills and education have captured a growing portion of earnings and wealth.

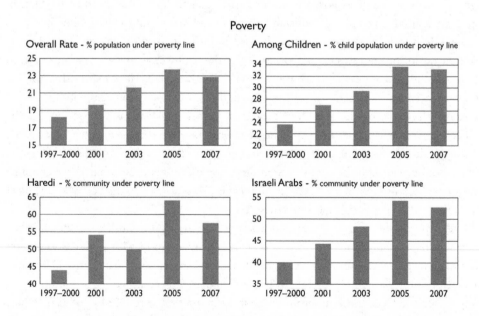

Poverty is highest among Haredi Jews and Israeli Arabs, both of whom have low rates of labor force participation and larger-than-average families. (Data: Bank of Israel; Israel National Insurance Institute. Chart: David Rosenberg. Drawing by Bill Nelson.)

Finally, the Israeli government has pared back social welfare spending since 2004, and that has added to the ranks of the poor by reducing or eliminating state aid. Before the cutbacks, benefits to the poor had been growing since the 1970s, surpassing the size of the defense budget. But policymakers came to the conclusion that the benefits were serving as a deterrent to employment as evidenced by Israel's low labor force participation rate.

FOREIGN TRADE

Given a small economy with few natural resources, Israel is highly reliant on imports for basic necessities. Its imports range from energy and transportation equipment to farm products and defense materials, and even its exports contain a high proportion of imported raw materials or components and are manufactured with imported machinery. Polished diamonds, for example, are Israel's single biggest export item in dollar terms, with sales overseas amounting to $9.6 billion in 2007. But cutters and polishers had to import all their rough stones at a cost of $8.8 billion.

To cover the country's import bill, Israel must export, thereby making trade an especially large component of the economy. Exports account for about 30 percent of Israel's output, and imports make up about the same proportion of resources available to the economy. But for nearly all of Israel's history, its trade balance has been in deficit. In 1950, imports were seven times the level of exports, and although this gradually narrowed over the next three decades to a ratio of 2:1 in 1960 and 1.3:1 to 1.4:1 in the 1970s and 1980s, they remained high by global standards.

Not until 2004 did Israel post its first-ever trade surplus, counting both goods and services. There are two reasons for the improved trade picture. The first is the high-technology sector, whose products now account for about one-third of Israel's industrial exports. Not only did technology exports jump fourfold between 1995 and 2008, but their profit level is also considerable.

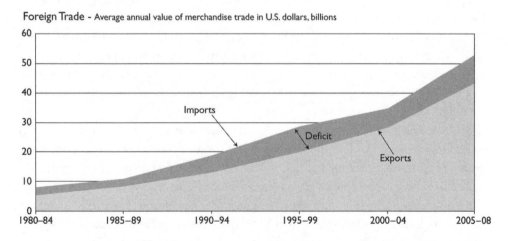

Foreign Trade - Average annual value of merchandise trade in U.S. dollars, billions

Although Israel has persistent merchandise trade deficits, they have generally grown narrower over the past three decades. The deficits temporarily widened in the early 1990s as a surge in immigration increased demand for imports. (Data: Israel Central Bureau of Statistics. Chart: David Rosenberg. Drawing by Bill Nelson.)

Composition of Merchandise Exports

1995   2007

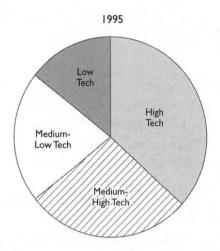
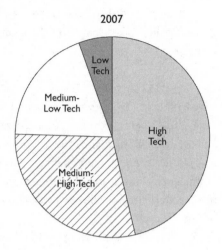

High technology has led export growth as the total value of Israeli exports (not counting diamonds) climbed to $34.3 billion in 2007, about three times the level in 1995.

High tech: computers, electronics, aircraft, and pharmaceuticals
Medium-high tech: chemicals, machinery, electrical gear
Medium-low tech: rubber/plastic, metals, jewelry
Low tech: food, textiles, paper

(Data: Israel Central Bureau of Statistics. Chart: David Rosenberg. Drawing by Bill Nelson.)

The second factor is the growth of service exports, which include items ranging from consulting services to tourism (a hotel providing a room or a restaurant serving a meal to a foreigner is considered a service export). Service exports grew about threefold in the same period, and since 2002, Israel's current account has consistently been in surplus. The same increase can be looked at from another perspective: Israelis have in recent years begun to invest far greater amounts abroad (to export capital) than foreigners have invested in Israel, leading to a deficit in the country's financial account. This, many economists believe, has been the driving force behind the economy's shift into current account surpluses.

After 1948, Israeli policymakers saw the solution to the country's trade challenges in a highly regulated trade regime aimed at discouraging imports and aiding exporters. In the late 1980s, however, Israel jettisoned the old policies, and it has gradually put into practice the principles of a liberalized system. The centerpiece is a series of bilateral free-trade area (FTA) agreements, which bar tariffs, quotas, and other restrictions on trade. The most important FTAs are with the European Union (1975) and the United States (1985), but Israel also has accords with five other countries and the European Free Trade Association. It is pursuing others.

Along with the rest of the world, Israel has liberalized its trade regime as well. Starting in 1990, it removed nontariff barriers, such as compulsory licensing for importers, on manufactured goods and, later, on farm products. While high tariffs were initially substituted for the nontariff barriers, tariffs began coming down after 1992. To even the playing field for both imports and exports, Israel eliminated exchange rate insurance and preferential interest rates for exporters during the 1990s.

Israel's two biggest overseas markets are the European Union (33 percent of total exports in 2008) and the United States (28 percent), a function of cultural ties and the nature of most of Israel's exports, which are for wealthy, industrialized markets. As the balance of world economic power shifts to East Asia, Israel has sought to increase trade with China and the other industrial powers of the region. Asia took 16 percent of exports in 2008.

Israel's trade with the Arab world, except for energy imports from Egypt, is minimal. The Arab boycott of foreign companies doing business with Israel withered away in the early 1990s as the peace process with the Palestinians got under way. A host of imported consumer products never previously available came into Israel, and new overseas markets opened up for Israeli companies. Israeli companies, however, remain subject to the boycott in most of the Arab world. Even if businesses in Egypt and Jordan, the two Arab states with which Israel has diplomatic relations, do not formally subscribe to it, they shun business relationships with their Israeli counterparts.

ISRAEL IN THE DEVELOPED WORLD

In 2010, acceptance into the Organization for Economic Cooperation and Development was a sort of matriculation ceremony, admitting Israel to the exclusive club of developed nations. Membership requires Israel to meet the world's highest standards on matters like protecting the environment and fighting corruption. Its ability to thrive does not hinge on developing the basic skill sets of a twenty-first century economy—its citizens already have those—only in taking the right steps to ensure they are not lost or squandered.

BIBLIOGRAPHY

Unfortunately, very few books have been published on the Israeli economy in English for nonspecialists. Moreover, so much of the economic environment has changed since the 1990s that books published before 2000 are often out of date in addressing contemporary issues.

Aharoni, Yair. *The Israeli Economy: Dreams and Realities*. London: Routledge, 1991.

Ben-Bassat, Avi, ed. *The Israeli Economy, 1985–1998: From Government Intervention to Market Economics*. Cambridge, MA: MIT Press, 2002.

"Beyond the Start-Up Nation," *The Economist*, December 29, 2010. http://www.economist.com/node/17796932.

Breznitz, Dan. *Innovation and State: Political Choice and Strategies for Growth in Israel, Taiwan and Ireland*. New Haven: Yale University Press, 2007.

Klein, Michael. *A Gemara of the Israel Economy*. Cambridge, MA: National Bureau of Economic Research, 2005.

Knowledge@Wharton. "Israel and the Innovative Impulse." Wharton, University of Pennsylvania. http://knowledge.wharton.upenn.edu/special_section.cfm?specialID=105.

Morag, Nadav. "The Economic and Social Effects of Intensive Terrorism: Israel, 2000–2004," *MERIA Journal: The Middle East Review of International Affairs* 10, no. 3 (September 2006). http://www.gloria-center.org/meria/2006/09/morag.html.

Organization for Economic Cooperation and Development (OECD). "Accession: Estonia, Israel and Slovenia Invited to Join OECD," May 10, 2010. http://www.oecd.org/document/57/0,3343,en_2157 1361_44315115_45159737_1_1_1_1,00.html.

Plessner, Yakir. *The Political Economy of Israel: From Ideology to Stagnation.* Albany: State University of New York Press, 1993.

Rabinovitch, Ari. "Israel Opens Largest Desalination Plant of Its Kind," May 16, 2010. Reuters, http://www.reuters.com/article/idUSTRE64F1O820100516.

Razin, Assaf, and Efraim Sadka. *The Economy of Modern Israel: Malaise and Promise.* Chicago: University of Chicago Press, 1993.

Rivlin, Paul. *The Israeli Economy from the Foundation of the State through the 21st Century.* New York: Cambridge University Press, 2010.

Rosenberg, David. *Cloning Silicon Valley.* London: Pearson, 2001. See the chapter on Israeli high technology.

Rosenberg, David. "The Israeli Economy: After the Financial Crisis, New Challenges." *MERIA Journal: The Middle East Review of International Affairs* 14, no. 1 (March 2010). http://www.gloria-center.org/meria/2010/03/rosenberg.html.

Senor, Dan, and Saul Singer. *Start-up Nation: The Story of Israel's Economic Miracle.* New York: Twelve, 2009.

Shachar, Arie. *Israel: An Emerging Node in the Global Economy.* Bronfman Lectures. Jerusalem: Urban and Regionals Studies, Hebrew University of Jerusalem, 2006.

Sharaby, Linda. "Israel's Economic Growth: Success without Security." *MERIA Journal: The Middle East Review of International Affairs* 6, no. 3 (September 2002). http://www.gloria-center.org/meria/2002/09/sharaby.html.

Websites

Bank Hapoalim. http://www.bankhapoalim.com/wps/portal/!ut/p/_.cmd/cs/ce/7_0_A/s./7_0_DJ/_s.7 _0_A/7_0_DJ. This is one of two Israeli banks that publish information and analysis in English on a regular basis.

Bank Leumi. http://english.leumi.co.il/LEBusinessBanking/Economic_Reports/5731/. This is one of two Israeli banks that publish information and analysis in English on a regular basis.

Bank of Israel. http://www.bankisrael.gov.il/firsteng.htm. The Bank of Israel publishes quarterly and other reports in English on economic developments.

Central Bureau of Statistics (CBS), State of Israel. English: http://www.cbs.gov.il/reader/?MIval=cw_ usr_view_Folder&ID=141. All of the CBS's English-language material appears on this separate home page.

Central Bureau of Statistics (CBS), State of Israel. Tables: http://www.cbs.gov.il/reader. The CBS publishes current and historical economic data. Although with a few exceptions, the text appears only in Hebrew, the tables are in English.

Globes. http://www.globes.co.il/serveen/globes/nodeview.asp?fid=942. Although the *Jerusalem Post* and *Ha'aretz* report English-language economic and business news in print and online, the most comprehensive coverage appears on the website of the *Globes* financial daily.

Ministry of Finance, State of Israel. http://147.237.72.111/mainpage_eng.asp. Israel's Finance Ministry also publishes information in English, although the material does not come out on a timely basis.

Chapter Seven

CULTURE

During Israel's pre-state period and early years of statehood, culture was used to promote the creation of a coherent people, identity, and nation. In later decades, Israeli artists often took a very critical stance, using art forms to examine their society's values and actions. Israeli culture can only be described as widely varying. As in other facets of Israeli life, the variety of themes, forms, and cultural output is remarkable for such a small country. Today, Israel boasts a vibrant art, theater, music, and dance scene and produces nearly 7,000 new books per year, mostly in Hebrew.

Key expressions of culture evolved in Israeli society over the years. These include literature, poetry, film, music, theater, and dance, as well as food and sports. Integral to the expression and evolution of culture are the media—including newspapers, radio, and television. The proliferation of Internet access, together with the growth of the Internet itself, now gives Israelis increased access to the global community and has further influences on the evolution of Israeli culture.

LITERATURE

For many centuries, the Hebrew language existed almost exclusively in connection with Jewish religious literature. But since Hebrew was the language of the ancient Jewish nation, the Zionist movement was determined to revive it. For Hebrew to be used as a modern language it had to be adapted to secular needs and acquire a vocabulary for everyday life and all other aspects of contemporary culture. A key role in this process was played by Eliezer Ben Yehuda, who compiled the first modern Hebrew dictionary.

The new literature drew on tradition, took in foreign influences, and developed distinctive characteristics to encompass the experiences of a reborn country. But the development of modern Jewish literature actually began in the 1880s, with works in both Hebrew and Yiddish, written mainly by Jews living in Russia.

Jewish authors had to decide which language to write in, although some used both at different points in their career. Hebrew was associated not only with Zionism but also with sophistication, while Yiddish was often perceived as a dialect, lacking the exalted association with religion and ancient Israel. Yiddish remained generally more popular, though, precisely because it was the daily means of communication for most Jews. But around the time of World

War I, Hebrew took on symbolic value for those who wanted to break with the poverty and oppressed state of existing Jewish communities in Eastern Europe. It was also important as a bridge among all Jews, including non-Yiddish speakers whose first language was German, English, or French but who also knew Hebrew.

For the Israeli writer, the Hebrew language is both confining and a source of richness. Hebrew does not have a large vocabulary, but precisely for this reason, a single word can contain diverse meanings, which the poet can use to add connotations and allusions.

Founders of Israeli Literature

During the first decades of the twentieth century, many prominent Hebrew-language authors and poets from Russia and Poland immigrated to the Land of Israel. These included Yosef Haim Brenner (1881–1921), Shmuel Yosef Agnon (1888–1970), and Haim Hazaz (1898–1973). As a result, the center of activities of the big Hebrew publishing houses located in Odessa and Warsaw soon moved too. This also led to the creation of new local literary magazines. The Land of Israel became the main Hebrew literary center. During this period, Hebrew consolidated its role as the language of the new nation, despite the sentimental attachment of many— including the celebrated poet Hayim Nahman Bialik—to Yiddish.

Agnon, the most renowned figure in modern Hebrew literature, is the only Hebrew writer to have received the Nobel Prize in Literature, which he did in 1966. His writing career spanned six decades. While most Israeli Hebrew writing focused on the new secular society developing in the Land of Israel—deliberately breaking with the exiled past—Agnon, who was also Dati, remained loyal to classical Jewish culture and traditional Jewish life. His rich depictions of small-town Jewish life in Europe often focused on the clashes and transitions between traditional and modern Jewish life. Agnon developed his own Hebrew style, which often played on and extended the Biblical and religious Hebrew meanings of words into modern situations.

Yet Agnon also set works in the Land of Israel. In *Only Yesterday* (1945), he follows an earnest but naive young Zionist who immigrates before World War I and experiences both the good and bad sides of the Yishuv, in the countryside and in Tel Aviv. *Shira* (1971) does the same thing for Jerusalem during World War II, but here Agnon views the clash between the highest level of rationalism and the wildest shores of romanticism in the experiences of a dry, scholarly German immigrant professor at the Hebrew University in Jerusalem.

Not just authors of novels and short stories but poets were at the forefront of the renewal of Hebrew as a spoken, modern language, and until the middle of the twentieth century, their poetry was considered a national achievement of the greatest importance. Hayim Nahman Bialik (1873–1934) and Saul Tchernichovsky (1875–1943) were two major poets who became national heroes. Their poetry echoed themes of Israeli pioneering and national self-assertion. Like Agnon, they felt comfortable in referring to both Jewish traditional and Jewish modern life. Bialik became such a national institution and was so showered with praise that he found his celebrity status burdensome.

Bialik and Agnon are considered the founders of modern Hebrew literature: Bialik for poetry and Agnon for prose. Their main contribution was the way they used words or concepts

Israeli writer Shmuel Yosef Agnon at home in Jerusalem after the announcement that he had won the Nobel Prize in Literature, October 1966. (Getty Images / Image Bank.)

from religious imagery and practice in creating a new literary language. Their generation of readers, having been schooled in religious yeshivas before breaking with tradition, understood their multilayered references.

The Palmach Literary Group

During the 1930s, a second generation — born in the Land of Israel or at least locally raised — that had neither come from Europe nor been raised religiously developed a literature more in tune with its experiences and needs. These authors, with their emphasis on the Zionist-national idea and labor movement values, were called the Palmach generation, named for the Haganah's elite military arm that fought in the War of Independence. Their work was published by publishing houses founded by Labor Party institutions, including Am Oved (Working People), HaKibbutz HaMeuhad (United Kibbutz), and Sifriyat HaPoalim (Workers' Library).

This second generation's most prominent prose writers included Moshe Shamir, Aharon Meged, Hanoch Bartov, Yigal Mosinzon, Nathan Shaham, Benjamin Tamuz, Amalia Kahana-Carmon, and Yoram Kanyuk. They wrote about settling the land, serving in the army, and engaging in the other activities involved in creating a new country. Their writings developed the idea of the "New Jew," or Sabra, each a healthy, handsome, secular, and socialist person engaged in building a new society. Their characters devoted themselves to the welfare of nation and community.

Unlike the previous generation's works, the writings of the Palmach generation had ever-present elements of death, war, and self-sacrifice as a heroic act. The writers of this "1948 generation" were linked in their shared belief that it was their duty to advance the Zionist movement and Israel's creation as a national homeland. The characters had personal difficulties to overcome too, but their dedication to the collective was also central in their lives.

Moshe Shamir's popular wartime hero characters in *He Walked Through the Fields* (1947), which became the first play performed in the country after independence, and *With His Own Hands* (1951) reflected the "religion of labor" and collectivist ideology of the youth movements and the kibbutzim. The latter work is a tribute to the life of Shamir's brother, a young Haganah fighter killed in the 1948 war while defending an aid convoy on the road to besieged Jerusalem.

The Holocaust in Israeli Literature

Israeli writers who had been in Europe during World War II, and thus had not shared the early experiences of the Palmach generation, also tried to deal with the Holocaust, the most traumatic event in the Jewish people's modern history. Two Holocaust survivors and authors, Uri Orlev and Aharon Appelfeld, were the main pioneers in the effort; Appelfeld is considered the most prominent writer on the Holocaust. While Orlev wrote of the memories of a child wandering in the death camps, Appelfeld focused on the period following the Holocaust, during which many surviving Jews were refugees in Europe. His characters live in the past and cannot awaken from the horrors they have seen and suffered.

The Holocaust remained proportionately less important for Israeli writers than for Jews outside Israel. During the 1980s, a new wave of Holocaust literature appeared whose writers, notably David Grossman, sometimes violated the earlier taboo that the Holocaust could be addressed in fiction only with the utmost seriousness. In *See Under: Love* (1986), the main character, Momik, is a child of Holocaust survivors. Momik is deeply affected by his parents' experience and weaves surrealistic fantasies that he is channeling writers who were killed in it.

Creating Modern Hebrew Poetry

The attitudes and experiences of succeeding generations shaped poets as well as fiction writers. Nathan Alterman (1910–1970) and Avraham Shlonsky (1900–1973), best known in the second generation of poets, moved beyond exhortations to aid in the national revival to verse about the Land of Israel. They used a modernist style quite different from the style of their predecessors, who were still using the forms of traditional Hebrew poetry.

Alterman was so fiery and influential that the British Mandate authorities banned many of his poems, which heightened their popularity in the Yishuv. After Israel's independence, Alterman attained the type of status that had been accorded to Bialik. His work *The Seventh Column* was so renowned that a cultural journal was named after it, and his poem "The Silver Platter" virtually became the country's anthem. It tells those who come later to remember they received

A portrait of the Israeli national poet Leah Goldberg, April 4, 1946. (The Government Press Office, Israel / Eldan David.)

Israel on a silver platter, as a gift from those who gave their lives to achieve independence. In addition to writing original poetry, plays, and essays, Alterman also translated into Hebrew the writings of Shakespeare, Molière, and other great European writers.

Shlonsky got his start as an editor and translator of great works of Western literature, such as *Hamlet* and *King Lear* and Russian classics. Much of his influence came through his Ktuvim (Biblical Writings) center, which attracted young, talented poets who themselves would become household names, including Alexander Penn and Leah Goldberg.

Leah Goldberg (1911–1970) was a renowned poet, in addition to being a successful children's author, theater critic, translator, and editor. In 1952, she established the Department of Comparative Literature at the Hebrew University of Jerusalem and remained its head until her death. During her career, Goldberg published nine books of poetry, two novels, three plays, six books of nonfiction, and twenty children's books. She won many prizes, including the Israel Prize in Literature in 1970.

Although many or most of them were on the political left, two significant poets joined the nationalist right. Uri Tzvi Greenberg was born in Ukraine in 1896 and immigrated to Israel in 1924. Writing in both Yiddish and Hebrew, he won the Bialik Prize for Literature three times. He became a member of the Irgun underground militia during the time of the British Mandate. Like others of his generation, he mixed Jewish religious sources and depictions of Jewish life in Europe with the Yishuv experience.

Uriel Shelah, best known by his pen name Yonatan Ratosh, was born in Poland in 1908 and immigrated with his family in 1921. He edited the Irgun's magazine. In 1939, however, he helped start the Canaanite movement, which—while never attracting more than a tiny group of people—created great controversy by declaring that it wanted to return to pre-Judaic, ancient Israelite cultural roots.

Literary life in Israel during the 1950s and 1960s centered on a prominent group called Likrat (Towards). In contrast to their predecessors, this group was more influenced by German and English than by Russian or French culture, used an existentialist and ironic rather than socialist realist style, and focused more on individual than on public issues. In retrospect, these differences were a sign that Israel was moving toward the post-heroic stage of its history. The remarkable variety of talented writers included Yehuda Amichai, Nathan Zach, Moshe Dor, Pinhas Sadeh, David Avidan, Dahlia Ravikovitch, and Israel Pinkas.

Yehuda Amichai (1924–2000) was Israel's most renowned poet throughout the second half of the twentieth century. Unlike most of his contemporaries, he came from an Orthodox family and was born in Germany, and he coined many new words combining classical Hebrew and modern Hebrew slang and fusing prose phrases and poetic rhythm. Quite prolific, he wrote novels, short stories, plays, and children's books, and his work was widely translated and studied abroad. While he dealt with many subjects, Amichai was particularly loved for presenting a personal perspective that readers felt also captured their own feelings.

No particular poet can be said to be the leader of contemporary Israeli poetry since the 1980s. The number of people writing poetry has increased while the number reading it has declined. The revolutionary poetic passion prevalent in the 1960s and 1970s ended when postmodern ideas emphasizing individual experience, complex language, and style became dominant. In retrospect, these works of political or cultural radicalism represented a natural rebellion against the homogeneity of earlier patriotic and nationalist writing.

The Israeli Novel

Since the 1960s, the two most prominent Israeli novelists have been Amos Oz and A. B. Yehoshua. The kibbutz-raised Oz wrote books and stories providing allegories for Israel's complicated history, often from a highly critical perspective, including *Where the Jackals Howl* (1963), in which he gives his negative assessment of the kibbutz: the jackals symbolize the enemies beyond the gates. In some of his later works, he questioned every aspect of Israel, including its very creation. Yehoshua, in contrast, focused increasingly on Mizrahi life, both historically and within Israel.

The 1970s saw the rise of writing about women's issues by such authors as Amalia Kahana-Carmon and Ruth Almog. There were also stylistic innovations, including writing in a more colloquial style and bringing in elements of popular culture. A very popular imported idea was the magical realism style that originated in Latin America.

In *Past Continuous* (1977), Yaakov Shabtai does for Tel Aviv what James Joyce did for Dublin. A 2007 survey of publishers and editors judged it the best book written since independence. Shabtai, who died at the age of forty-seven, was a successful playwright, and this was his only novel. Still, the style of writing resembles that of a play.

By the end of the 1970s, two powerful themes emerged that some earlier writing had prepared the way for, but the new works stood in sharp contrast to most of the previous literary output. One theme was a highly critical approach to Israeli politics and society. Instead of considering themselves a supportive part of the national project, those in the cultural sphere took on the role of opposition. Literary work was influenced both by international cultural trends and by dramatic events in Israel, notably the 1967 and 1973 wars and the end of Labor's long political control in 1977. *The Voyage of Daniel* (1969) by Yitzhak Orpaz, for example, about an exhausted war veteran who finds redemption through a mystical experience, was a direct reaction to the state of shock Israeli society was in after its unexpected victory in the Six-Day War in 1967.

A few years later, the Yom Kippur War cracked the image of the glorified hero, a constant portrayal in Israeli fiction up through the Six-Day War. The new writers exposed existential national fears behind the mask of confidence. Following the Yom Kippur War, the editors of *Achshav* (Now) magazine wrote an "I told you so" editorial, as if Israel's losses in the war were a kind of moral victory for avant-garde literature.

The left wing's struggle for peace became a central issue in Israeli fiction. The optimistic view of peace being attainable if Israel only wanted it badly enough was coupled with a pessimistic perception that peace was not being achieved. Most of the post-realistic literature fell on the left side of the political spectrum, and only a few authors, mostly the older ones, disputed its themes.

In part, the leftist orientation of literature was a reaction to the perceived political defeat of the Israel that the literary elite had championed: the Israel of Labor Party hegemony. But the 1977 triumph of Likud, with its large Mizrahi constituency, and the opening up of "ethnic" issues also produced an upsurge in works that described the culture and experiences of Mizrahi Jews. Yehoshua's first novel, *The Death of an Old Man* (1962), tells a story of neighborhood people getting rid of a troublesome senior citizen. Many interpreted the book to be about Israel's new generation overthrowing the country's founders. One prominent new voice on the poetry scene was Erez Biton, who was born in Algeria and arrived with his family in Israel in 1948 as a six-year-old. Biton began publishing poetry in the late 1970s at the same time that he was a leading figure in the Mizrahi consciousness movement.

Older writers like Yehoshua also wrote more about their roots. Yehoshua's book *Mr. Mani* (1990) is a story about five generations of a Mizrahi family. Sami Michael, born in Iraq, also brought to life the Mizrahi experience in the "old countries" and in Israel. In the novel *Victoria* (1995) he describes his mother, the spirit of the women from Middle Eastern countries, and the hardships encountered in the new state.

The development of a mass market for books—as Israelis had more leisure time, education, and income as well as improved technology for producing, selling, and distributing them— brought a dramatic increase in the number of books published in Israel during the 1980s and 1990s. Several Israeli writers achieved international recognition, including Oz, Yehoshua, Yoram Kaniuk, Appelfeld, David Shahar, Grossman, and Meir Shalev. At the same time, a favorite Israeli outlet for publishing fiction—literary magazines—declined, as did the publication of short stories in newspapers.

Yet precisely because of the development of the market, a literary split formed between elite works aimed at a small, high-brow public and popular novels that sold a high number of copies in a very short time. Many of the latter are translations of foreign books, especially best-sellers, but such potboilers also appear from Israeli authors.

Still, new authors continued to appear who used innovative methods to describe Israeli life and society. David Grossman is considered the main heir of the 1960s generation. In *See Under: Love*, he demonstrated his talent at using varied international styles. Another writer who built on the innovations of the 1960s generation is Meir Shalev, who produced sociohistorical pieces that mixed nostalgia, realism, and magical realism in original ways. In *The Blue Mountain* (1988), Shalev satirized the kibbutz through his main character, who becomes the kibbutz undertaker, a reflection on the institution's moribund aspects. Shalev's novel *Esau* (1991) includes two popular themes in Israeli fiction: a reworking of Biblical material and a leading character who leaves the country. *As a Few Days* (1994), set in the 1930s, is about three very different men competing over who will get a woman and who will raise her son.

Among internationally successful works is Ron Leshem's first novel, *If There is a Garden of Eden* (2005; better known by its English title, *Beaufort*). This story of an Israel Defense Forces unit at the strategic Beaufort Castle in southern Lebanon just before the Israeli withdrawal in 2000 was made into a film that was nominated for an Academy Award in 2007. Dorit Rabinyan's first novel, *Persian Brides* (1995), is a magical realist tale about a Jewish family—and especially the young women in it—in a small Iranian town at the start of the twentieth century. The novel was featured on the cover of the *New Yorker* in 2007. Gail Hareven's *The Confessions of Noa Weber* won Rochester's Best Translated Book Award in 2010. The book describes a middle-aged writer's love for a man she made a marriage of convenience with.

Israeli fiction thus encompasses the whole gamut of styles and themes, from mysteries to best-sellers to ambitious novels seeking to sum up Jewish existence in Israel or thousands of years of Jewish life in the Diaspora.

Women Writers

Women authors of Hebrew works have proliferated only recently. The best-known woman author in Israel's early years was Naomi Frankel (1918–2009), who wrote the notable trilogy *Saul and Johanna* (1956–1967) about an assimilated German Jewish family in pre-Nazi Germany whose daughter becomes a Zionist. The book was somewhat autobiographical, since Frankel was born in Berlin, immigrated to Israel at age sixteen, and lived on a kibbutz for several decades.

The author most prominent in creating a feminist consciousness in Israel, beginning in the 1960s, was Amalia Kahana-Carmon. She dealt with relations between men and women and with family experiences in various periods, regions, and classes in Israel.

During the 1970s and 1980s, when new influences affected Israeli fiction, the feminine voice almost disappeared. The stereotype of women's fiction as dealing with family issues seemed to contradict the tide of writing about political and societal subjects. In fact, the only field in which women were dominant during the 1970s and 1980s was in children's and juvenile literature, Devorah Omer and Galila Ron-Feder being the best known.

In the late 1980s, many important women writers appeared on the literary scene both because of Israeli readers' changing interests and because of the wave of women's fiction abroad.

These included Savyon Liebrecht (*Apples from the Desert*; 1986), Leah Aini, Yehudit Katzir, Hannah Bat-Shahar, Dorit Peleg, Nava Semel, and Orly Castel-Bloom, who all gave a new feminine perspective to old subjects. Castel-Bloom wrote about the condition of contemporary women in *Dolly City* (1997), a novel set in a futuristic city; in it a woman doctor finds a baby, gives up her laboratory, and becomes an obsessive, destructively overbearing mother in a society riddled with war and bizarre behavior.

Israeli Arab Writing

The works of most Israeli Arab writers are written in Arabic. The best known among them is Emile Habibi, a veteran Communist who was a member of the Knesset in the 1950s and 1960s and who won the Israel Prize (the country's highest honor) for Arabic literature in 1992. He quit politics in 1974 to focus on writing, and his most famous novel, *The Secret Life of Said the Pessoptimist*, was published that year. It tells the story of an Israeli Arab hero through satire. There are also a few major Israeli Arab poets, such as Mahmoud Darwish (1941–2008) and Samih al-Qasim (b. 1939), whose works have been translated into Hebrew. The themes dominant in the poetry of Israeli Arabs are longing for Palestine, the experience of being uprooted, and resistance to the current state of affairs.

The most famous Arab poet, originally a citizen of Israel, is Mahmoud Darwish, who began his career as a journalist and political activist and later turned to poetry. He published his first collection, *Wingless Birds*, in 1960, but it was his 1964 volume, *Olive Trees*, that established his reputation as the "poet of the Palestinian resistance." Two of Darwish's famous poems are "Identity Card" (1964) and "State of Siege" (2002). He left Israel in 1970 to study in the Soviet Union, joined the PLO, and called for Israel's elimination. In 1995 he moved to Ramallah in the West Bank, where he died in 2008. In 2000, a debate occurred when the education minister, Yossi Sarid, added Darwish's poetry to the Israeli public school curriculum, a decision that was eventually revoked.

The most prominent Israeli Arab fiction writer today is Sayed Kashua, who explores what it means to be both an Arab and an Israeli; that was a theme particularly in his first novel,

Israeli Arab journalist and writer Sayed Kashua speaks at the International Writers' Festival held in Jerusalem on May 4, 2010. (Miriam Alster/ Flash90.)

Dancing Arabs (2002). Both of his novels were written in Hebrew. A popular newspaper columnist for the Hebrew-language daily *Ha'aretz,* Kashua often uses humor and a sense of the absurd to explain to mainstream Israeli audiences the trials of being Arab in Israeli society.

Authors who emerged in the 1950s and 1960s—Amos Oz, A. B. Yehoshua, Meir Shalev, and David Grossman, among others—still dominate the Israeli literary world. Yet a remarkably varied literary scene has emerged around them. Since many Israelis can read works in more than one language, Hebrew-language Israeli authors are free to focus on the particular experience of life in Israel and the characters, groups, and feelings found there. Their specialization leaves the field wide open to exploration and has perhaps advanced the quality of original Hebrew literature, since "low-brow" tastes in prose (thrillers, mysteries, and romances) are already largely met by translated material from abroad.

FILM

The history of Israeli film has parallels with the history of Israeli literature. Both film and literature had a state-building role in the 1930s and 1940s, featured heroic nationalist epics in the 1950s and 1960s, and became hypercritical of Israeli politics and society in the 1970s and 1980s. Afterward, the tendency was to take an intermediate position and to deal with more personal issues.

One critical difference between the two media is that while Israeli literature has a strong audience because of its use of Hebrew and Israeli situations, feature films are extraordinarily expensive to make and the dialogue of foreign films is easily put into Hebrew subtitles. Some great Israeli films have been made, but imported competition is far more pressing than in the field of literature. Israeli film thus exists largely because of government subsidies. Many productions offer the kinds of stories shown in other countries. Yet independence from audience tastes and the predominance of left-wing filmmakers have also made it possible to produce films with a strongly critical bent.

Origins of Israeli Cinema

Israeli cinema goes back to documentaries depicting the Zionist movement's achievements. Mostly financed by Jewish and Zionist institutions, they depicted the movement's early history, showing proud Jewish pioneers working the land, often in the propagandistic spirit of socialist realist films produced at that time in the Soviet Union. The first early filmmaker was Ya'akov Ben Dov, who immigrated from Russia and photographed scenes from the pioneers' daily lives as well as historical events, such as the British army's conquest of Jerusalem in 1917. Around that time, Baruch Agadati, a painter, dancer, and choreographer, founded Aga Films with his brother Yitzhak. Aga Films and Moledet-Carmel Films competed in making newsreels. These two companies formed the basis of Israel's cinematic industry.

The first feature-length Hebrew film was *Oded the Wanderer,* made by Axelrod and Haim Halahmi in 1932. This silent film tells the story of a dreamy child who loses his way during a class trip. His attempts to find his way back to his classmates provide a panoramic view of Zionist settlement in Palestine. Another landmark film of the period was *This Is the Land,* Baruch Agadati's film part documentary and part fiction, made in 1935. It tells the story of the first fifty years of Zionist settlement in Palestine. It was the first Zionist talkie produced entirely in Israel.

Another key figure of the early period was Helmar Lerski, a German-born theater actor and later a famous still photographer who became known for his award-winning portraits. He worked as a cinematographer in the German film industry and in 1935 was hired to direct a film on Zionist achievements in Palestine. *Avoda* was a documentary that followed a Zionist pioneer as he took part in building the Tel Aviv port, paved roads, drained swamps, and dug for water. The film is known for expressive cinematography that emphasizes the muscular bodies and suntanned faces of the New Jews. It competed in the Venice Film Festival.

The Holocaust became a prominent theme in post–World War II films, albeit with an emphasis on rehabilitating its victims. Among these films were *The Illegals* (directed by Meir Levine, 1947), *The Great Promise* (Joseph Lejtes, 1947), and *The Faithful City* (Joseph Lejtes, 1952). Holocaust survivors are depicted undergoing a conscious change and being reborn as New Jews. The quick and successful repression of a traumatic past and "old identity" symbolizes the survivors' rehabilitation and their identification with the Zionist vision as they turn away from both the Jewish past and the more recent catastrophe.

War Films

The majority of films made in the fifteen years after Israel's independence in 1948 depicts its struggle against the surrounding Arab states and portray an idealized Israeli warrior. This heroic-national genre, as it was called, centered on mythic Israeli heroes—Sabras, kibbutzniks, and soldiers—mainly in the context of the Israeli-Arab conflict.

Most noted among these films is *Hill 24 Doesn't Answer* (1955), directed by Assi Dayan, about four fighters during the War of Independence who are assigned to hold a strategic hill. Their life stories unfold in flashback, as does the story of their desperate battle against overwhelming odds. This was the Israeli film industry's first major production, made with a considerable budget of $400,000. It achieved critical and commercial success both in Israel and abroad.

A key episode depicts the Sabra as a humanistic soldier who, in the course of a hard battle, notices a wounded Egyptian soldier. Risking his own life, the Israeli soldier hurries to aid his enemy, but while carrying him on his back to a safe place, the latter tries to kill him first with a pistol and then with a hand grenade. Finally, while finding cover in a nearby cave, the Israeli soldier is surprised to find out that the wounded "Egyptian" is actually a German Nazi fighting on the Arab side. A quick circular camera movement shows the Jewish soldier again, this time dressed as a Jew from the ghetto, wearing the yellow patch on his clothes that the Nazi government required Jews to wear. The same camera movement turns him back into the Sabra soldier. Yet he does not kill the man, who is already mortally wounded.

In no area of Israeli culture did Americanization have as much effect as in films made after 1967 that borrowed from the epic style and "larger than life" protagonists of Hollywood war films. Such was the first Israeli film that dealt with the war, *Is Tel-Aviv Burning?* (Kobi Jaeger, 1967). Others following this pattern include *He Walked Through the Fields* (Yosef Millo, 1967), based on Moshe Shamir's novel and play about Uri, a kibbutznik who is torn between his love for a new immigrant from Europe and his commitment to his country and the Palmach; *The Eagles Attack at Dawn* (Menahem Golan, 1970), in which an Israeli commando group is sent to Syria to rescue captive Israeli soldiers; and *Azit, the Paratrooper Dog* (Boaz Davidson, 1972), in which the canine protagonist carries out heroic missions beyond enemy lines.

Modernist Cinema

In the mid-1960s a new type of film, influenced by European modernist cinema, was introduced to the Israeli public. This "new sensibility" style was a reaction against the "death ethos" and "martyrology" of films that focused so heavily on death, battle, and self-sacrifice for people and country.

One leader of this Israeli "new wave" was David Perlov, who in 1963 made *In Jerusalem*, a forty-minute documentary directed with a unique and lyrical style; it was composed of shots of stonemasons, beggars, children playing with his camera, peddlers, and people from different groups. Unintentionally, the film caused a scandal, since Perlov "dared" to film beggars. Because the film gave what was considered an "unsuitable" portrait of the holy city, Israeli officials opposed its release. Only after Prime Minister Levy Eshkol became involved could the film be screened.

The second leader of Israeli modernist cinema was Uri Zohar, actor, director, and comedian. His *A Hole in the Moon* (1965) is one of the most experimental Israeli films ever made. The film starts with Zohar himself as Zelnik, a Zionist pioneer who arrives in Israel on a raft, dressed in a suit, drinking whiskey, and smoking a cigar. He then goes to the desert and opens a kiosk in the middle of nowhere and yells, "Lemonade!" The scene refers to the well-known story of David Ben-Gurion, Israel's first prime minister, who while touring the southern Negev stopped in the middle of nowhere, looked around, pointed at the sand, and announced, "Here a city will rise."

Zelnik wakes up in the morning only to find another kiosk, just opposite his, whose owner is Mizrahi. The two decide to make a Western movie. Their movie includes a documentary episode, cinema verité style, in which Zohar auditions young women aspiring to be actresses, parodies passionate Zionist speeches, and presents three Arabs who beg to be portrayed as the "good guys" and sing a Zionist song. In another scene women wait in line to enter a tent and then exit pregnant in order to increase the national birthrate. The film ends with its two film-within-a-film makers being executed by the angry women, who have been pregnant for eleven months and have yet to give birth.

Later, Zelnik's and Mizrahi's ghosts stand opposite their graves. A lone horseman (potentially either an Arab or a Zionist pioneer) rides toward them and shoots the ghosts. Then a Jesus-like shepherd walks on water and sinks. An end title reads, "This is the end (of the Zionist vision?)." Ironically, in a uniquely Israeli twist, Zohar himself later gave up performing and became a Haredi Jew.

A Hole in the Moon was the first Israeli film to criticize the Zionist vision, which it compared to a chaotic studio. In the spirit of the French New Wave, the actors improvised; the camera was hand-held; the references were cinematic; the editing was swift and associative; and the overall atmosphere was free-spirited and joyful. *A Hole in the Moon* was the pioneer "auteur" film in Israel—that is, it was a personal film with a wildly idiosyncratic style.

Like many of their contemporary counterparts in literature, poetry, and theater, the Israeli modernist filmmakers avoided national ideologies (themes of war and building the land) in favor of more universal and intellectual themes, as well as demythologization of the Sabra.

Bourekas Films

The second type of film to emerge in the mid-1960s was a popular comedy genre. *Bourekas* films, as they were called, dealt with ethnic tensions between Mizrahi and Ashkenazic Jews. Their heroes were poor but sly Mizrahim who usually fell in love with a rich Ashkenazic counterpart. Although the woman and man come from different social strata, love overcomes all obstacles (mainly the Ashkenazic parents' prejudices). Conflict is usually resolved by marriage between the sons and daughters of rival families, thus establishing the idea of Israeli society as a melting pot for Jews migrating from different parts of the world.

The pioneer in this genre of satirical comedies was Ephraim Kishon, Israel's greatest comic writer, whose *Sallah* (1964) is about a Mizrahi immigrant, played by the Israeli star Haim Topol, and his clashes with the Ashkenazic establishment. *Sallah* was the first Israeli film to be nominated for an Oscar, and it is one of the most popular and successful ever made.

When Sallah and his large family arrive in Israel in the 1950s, they are sent to a transit camp (ma'abara). Sallah is not pleased to live in a ramshackle shack and is determined to move his family to a nearby housing complex. Meanwhile, he passes his time playing backgammon with his idle neighbor and tries his luck at occasional jobs. *Sallah* satirizes the Israeli establishment by depicting the arrogance of members of a nearby kibbutz (who are not enthusiastic in their support of the new immigrants) and governmental authorities indifferent to the immigrants' distress.

The film's ridicule of such icons as the kibbutz and the Sabra was a daring act. Golda Meir, former foreign minister and prime minister, objected to the film because of a scene portraying a Jewish National Fund official changing signs with the names of donors each time a different donor arrived to see the forest planted with his money.

Bourekas films were made by Ashkenazic producers, directors, and screenwriters—among them Boaz Davidson, Menahem Golan, and Eli Tavor—and some of the Mizrahi protagonists were played by Ashkenazic stars as well. Yehuda Barkan, for one, played the leading role in Davidson's *Charlie and a Half* (1974), as Topol did in *Sallah*.

Sallah is noted for being the first film to present a Mizrahi protagonist and deal with issues of ethnic discrimination as well as for being the prototype for the bourekas films that flourished during the 1970s. The films were seen as vulgar and "low" cinema by critics and by modernist filmmakers, who pointed to their stereotypical characters, predictable plots, superficiality, and popularity.

Politically Critical Cinema

The turbulent events of the 1970s and early 1980s led to a wave of politically critical films. Uri Barbash's *Beyond the Walls* (1984), for example, takes place in an Israeli prison where Jewish and Palestinian convicts are locked up together. The story revolves around Mizrahi and Palestinian prisoners who join forces in a struggle against the oppressive Ashkenazic management in what can be seen as an allegory of the Israel-Palestinian conflict and of the

Mizrahi-Ashkenazic political divide within Israel. The film gained critical and commercial success and was nominated for an Oscar.

Another three films together symbolize the ideological change in Israeli cinema in the late 1970s: Ram Levy's *Hirbet Hiz'ah* (The Ruined Village; 1978) was the first Israeli film to deal with the Palestinian Arab narrative of the 1948 War of Independence. The film was based on a story by the distinguished writer Yizhar Smilansky and aroused a public and political debate when it was broadcast on Israeli television. The second film was Judd Ne'eman's *Paratroopers* (1977), which subverted the image of the Sabra warrior by telling the story of the abuse and eventual suicide of a young recruit. The third film, *Wooden Gun* (Ilan Moshenson, 1978), dealt with the trauma of Holocaust survivors for the first time.

Prominent among the films examining the Israel-Arab conflict was *Avanti Popolo* (1986), directed by Rafi Bukai and considered to be one of the best Israeli films ever made. This surrealist tragicomedy tells the story of two Egyptian soldiers in the Sinai desert, right after the declaration of the ceasefire ending the Six-Day War, who are trying to find their way home. In the course of their wanderings, the lost soldiers encounter a reconnaissance squad of the victorious Israeli army, which opens fire on them. In the hope of obtaining some water from them, the Egyptians run toward the Israelis. When the Israelis prevent them from approaching the water container in their possession, one of the Egyptians, a stage actor by profession, begins reciting Shylock's famous monologue from Shakespeare's *The Merchant of Venice*, "I am a Jew. Hath not a Jew eyes? Hath not a Jew hands, organs, dimensions, senses, affections, passions? . . . If you prick us, do we not bleed? If you tickle us, do we not laugh? If you poison us, do we not die?" In response, one of the startled Israeli soldiers mumbles: "He's got his part mixed up."

Instead of the fearless, morally superior fighting Sabra (as represented in the national-heroic films of the 1950s and 1960s), these films present a faded, shattered image. The Israeli warrior is damaged both physically and mentally, confined to a wheelchair or shell-shocked. *The Vulture* (Yaki Yosha, 1981), based on a book by Yoram Kanyuk, deals with the moral corruption of an Israeli officer and the cynical use of the commemoration of war heroes. *Don't Give a Damn* (Shmuel Imberman, 1987), based on a book by Dan Ben Amotz, is about a young soldier, paralyzed from the waist down, who abuses his family and close friends. *Buba* (Doll; Ze'ev Revah, 1987) features as protagonist a secluded man who came out of the Yom Kippur War with shell shock; and *The Night Soldier* (Dan Wollman, 1984) focuses on a young man whose exemption from military service leads him to murder soldiers. All these films are manifestations of a critical perspective characterizing Israeli cinema after the Yom Kippur and Lebanon Wars.

Parallel to this demystification of the Israeli soldier was a shift in the representation of the Palestinian. Among the films made were *Hamsin* (Daniel Wachsmann, 1982), about the expropriation of Palestinian land in the northern Galilee; *Fellow Travelers* (Judd Ne'eman, 1983), whose protagonist is an Israeli political activist who finds himself chased by both Israeli security agents and Palestinian extremists; and *A Very Narrow Bridge* (Nissim Dayan, 1985), which tells a Romeo and Juliet–like story about an Israeli military reservist and a young Palestinian widow. *Smile of the Lamb* (Shimon Dotan, 1986), based on David Grossman's best-selling novel, tells the story of friendship between an Israeli military doctor in the West Bank and an elderly Palestinian man; and Haim Bouzaglo's *Fictive Marriage* (1988), in which a Jerusalem teacher impersonates a deaf-and-dumb Palestinian construction worker and forms a friendship with a group of Palestinian workers, depict attempts at close relationships between Israelis and Palestinians. These narratives usually lead to tragic endings that express Israelis' disbelief in the likelihood of real and lasting peace. These films include Palestinian actors and actresses playing the Palestinian parts.

In another trend, the Holocaust survivor becomes a more complex character, not just a total contrast to the New Jew, the Sabra. In early Israeli films, the emphasis was on erasing traumatic memories in order to adapt to the Zionist experience. Now the painful past is brought into the open. *Wooden Gun* (1978), for example, tells the story of a Sabra boy in the 1950s who is a member of a youth gang. One day he shoots the leader of a rival gang with a slingshot (the wooden gun of the title). The leader falls down, bleeding from his forehead, and the protagonist, fearing he has killed, runs away. In the course of running away, he hurts his knee and is taken care of by a disturbed woman who lost her family in the Holocaust and lives alone by the sea. Her shack is a shrine to her dead family. The boy feels tremendous empathy toward this woman, whom he and his friends used to taunt, and he walks out a different, more sensitive Sabra.

Nihilistic Cinema

The outbreak of the First Intifada in December 1987 stilled the wave of politically critical cinema. Instead, in a time of Palestinian violence toward Israel, films that avoided any direct political message, often taking a nihilistic stance, became prominent. One major work from the decade after the uprising began is Assi Dayan's apocalyptic *Life According to Agfa* (1992). The film—a critical and commercial hit—stirred a huge debate over its depiction of current Israeli society as violent, oppressive, and nihilistic. Set in a forlorn Tel Aviv pub, used as a metaphor for Israel, the story, shot in a stark black and white, centers on a group of customers and staff, each representing a part of Israeli society: a few soldiers, a policeman (representing a distorted image of the heroic Sabra), a Mizrahi, a Palestinian—all men—and some women. The characters are all perceived as victims of their own violent, militaristic Israeli psyches. The film ends with a massacre carried out by some drunken soldiers who kill everyone in the pub.

Agfa was the first in a trilogy of films written and directed by Assi Dayan, the son of Moshe Dayan, Israel's minister of defense during the 1967 war. Dayan had been the star of *He Walked Through the Fields*, in which he played the ultimate embodiment of the heroic Sabra. The two other films constituting Dayan's "nihilist trilogy" are *An Electric Blanket Named Moshe* (1995), a surreal fantasy that follows a homeless person, a Romanian prostitute, and her philosopher pimp (a character that first appeared in *Agfa*) on a Dantean journey; and *Mr. Baum* (1997), which unfolds in real time—the last ninety-two minutes in the life of Micky Baum (played by Dayan himself), a successful businessman who suffers from an incurable disease, which symbolizes the tension between personal and national that exists in all of Dayan's works.

Mr. Baum includes a scene in which a surrealist exhibition publicly displays a magnified, detailed recreation of ordinary objects—a half-eaten apple, a parking ticket, a set of keys— that are related to Baum's last moments. In that way, Baum's life and death become a satirical comment on a society that lives on the myths and rituals of heroic-national death. In yet another powerful scene of full frontal nudity toward the end of the film, Mr. Baum takes his clothes off in order to have one last shower. Dayan's personal physical degeneration from the handsome young man he was when he appeared in *He Walked Through the Fields* to his run-down image due to drug and alcohol abuse could be taken as symbolizing the decay of the Sabra image.

Death, self-annihilation, aimless existence, and the search for a national identity in a time of historical crisis are prominent features of Dayan's nihilistic cinema. Dayan's trilogy and other films of this era are a result of what the filmmakers see as confusing shifts. They broke away from the politically critical cinema of the 1980s, where the protagonist and apparent victim of the political complexity was the conscientious and usually leftist Sabra. This brought about the rise of escapist films that avoided taking a direct political stance by blurring the Israeli-Zionist identity (of locales, characters, and story), as well as allegorical films that depicted an apocalypse awaiting Israeli society and the Zionist vision.

Pluralism and Beyond

Israeli films after 2000 often tend to depict the lives and culture of sectors of Israeli society that rarely—if ever—appeared in local films before. *Late Marriage*, for example, directed in 2001 by newcomer Dover Kosashvili, portrays life within a family of Georgian immigrants who mostly speak Georgian (it was screened with Hebrew subtitles). Surprisingly, this little film brought over 300,000 viewers to the cinemas, received rave reviews, and was considered the beginning of a new phase in Israeli filmmaking.

Though not the first, *Late Marriage* was a key film in the current wave of ethnic or multi-cultural Israeli cinema. Films in this genre are made mainly by young and promising directors from diverse backgrounds and depict life in different sectors: the Orthodox right wing (*Time of Favor*, Josef Cedar, 2000); new immigrants from Russia (*Yana's Friends*, Arik Kaplun, 1999); veteran Iraqi Jews (*The Barbecue People*, David Ofek, 2003); Moroccan women oppressed by their patriarchal and religious families (*To Take a Wife*, Ronit and Shlomi Elkabetz, 2004); gays (*The Bubble*, Eytan Fox, 2006); foreign illegal workers mostly from Third World countries; and even Haredim, in *The Holy Guests* (Gidi Dar, 2004), a tale about a poor childless Jewish couple in a Haredi Jerusalem neighborhood during the Sukkot (Feast of Tabernacles) holiday. This unique film was produced under the supervision of the Rabbinate and starts with a title card reading "With divine providence," a traditional phrase that religious Jews place on anything they write.

The film *Sh'hur* (Shmuel Hasfari, 1994), an autobiographical film based on the memoirs of its screenwriter-actor, Hana Azoulay-Hasfari, tells the story of a Jewish family, originally from Morocco, living in a southern Israeli town in the 1970s. The story is told through the eyes of the youngest and only Sabra (that is, Israeli-born) member of the family, the adolescent girl, Heli. It raises doubts about the identity of second-generation immigrants.

Thus, the "westernized" Heli is not exactly a model for success: the settings—a television studio, her home—are shown in cold and alienating bluish colors, while the past is shown in warm reddish colors reminiscent of the warm, hearty Mizrahi environments depicted in the bourekas comedies of the 1970s. The "unauthentic" Heli also has no emotional connection with her autistic daughter, who bursts into frantic screams when she tries to approach her. Her husband is far away (his voice is heard only on the telephone), and she hardly ever smiles.

This approach is a direct product of cultural and political upheavals in Israeli society since the early 1990s: the massive immigration of Jews from the former Soviet Union and the rise of Shas, a Mizrahi Orthodox political party whose voters are mainly Jews of North African origin. These films acknowledge Israel as a diverse society.

Contemporary Israeli cinema has enjoyed both domestic and international success. Etgar Keret, a popular and startlingly original comic writer, and Shira Geffen co-directed *Jellyfish*, which won the Camera d'Or award at Cannes in 2007; Sasson Gabai won the European Film Award for Best Actor in 2007 for his portrayal of the chief of the Egyptian Ceremonial Police Orchestra in *The Band's Visit* (Eran Kolirin, 2007); and Joseph Cedar's *Beaufort* won the Silver Bear for Best Direction at Berlin in 2007. *Beaufort*, about Israeli soldiers during the last days before the Israeli withdrawal from Lebanon in 2000, was also nominated in 2008 for an Academy Award for Best Foreign Language Film.

Poster for the Israeli animation documentary *Waltz with Bashir* (2008), directed by Ari Folman. The film was winner of the Golden Globe Award for Best Foreign Language Film and an Academy Award nominee. (Getty Images / Image Bank.)

What *Beaufort*, along with *Waltz with Bashir* (Ari Folman, 2008), a groundbreaking animation documentary; *Forgiveness* (Udi Aloni, 2006); and *Walk on Water* (Eytan Fox and Gal Uchovsky, 2004) have in common is that they deal with national traumas by exploration of private ones. *Waltz with Bashir* deals with repressions of traumatic memory—that of an IDF soldier (Folman himself), who was in Lebanon at the time of the Sabra and Shatila massacre and is haunted by guilt. Through a mix of two seemingly contradictory art forms—documentary and animation—*Bashir* creatively re-creates and explicates memories. The film won the Golden Globe Award for Best Foreign Language Film in 2009 and was nominated for an Academy Award in the same category.

Israel continues to develop its rich cinematic tradition, producing both critical and popular films that reflect and critique societal trends. In the pre-state and early state years, Israeli films served to solidify and strengthen Zionist ideology, Jewish connection to the land, and the rebirth of the New Jew. Since then, Israeli cinematography has gone through many stages as it has developed, portraying and including marginalized voices in society, examining and challenging certain central ideas of society, and ultimately coming to use the art form as a means for examining and dealing with troubling, traumatic events in the nation's past and the daily lives of its people in the present.

MUSIC

Music is central in shaping and understanding what it means to be Israeli. Each musical style has struggled for recognition, legitimacy, and dominance as the true Israeli national music, or at least for a significant part of that title. At the same time, musical developments express and emphasize important Israeli social and political developments. The result is the creation of a unique national musical culture.

Early Folk Music

In the early years of statehood, the lyrics of folk songs, known as songs of the Land of Israel (*Shirei Eretz Yisrael*), revived the Hebrew language and expressed a sense of what it was like to be an Israeli. The songs were often sung by large choirs or performers together with the audience. Such sing-alongs, a main form of entertainment during a period of austerity and in a pre-television era, were a chance for the population to experience a feeling of membership in the new nation. From 1948 to 1973, from independence to the Yom Kippur War, folk songs were also a major component of music lessons in the education system and of broadcasts on the radio.

Religious songs, often focusing on a future return to the Land of Israel, had been a staple of Jewish religious services for a thousand years. Songs expressing similar longings in a modern Zionist—that is, secular and political—mode already existed in Europe by the end of the nineteenth century. Songs that reflected a sense of the Hebrew nation, however, were not produced until around 1930. In the following years, a group of composers and lyricists (among them David Zehavi, Mordehai Zeira, and Alexander Argov) wrote the songs that became symbols of Israeli rootedness and the use of Hebrew language.

Prominent poets, including Ya'akov Orland, Alexander Penn, and Nathan Alterman, wrote lyrics that were adaptations of Biblical texts and Jewish prayers translated into a Zionist context, thus lending cultural value to the corpus of Israeli song. These folk songs were meant to unify people through communal songs by praising the Zionist pioneers and celebrating the revival of the land. The music itself was a blend of Middle Eastern musical elements with Eastern European melodies. Israeli folk songs, then, ranged in style from Russian ballad to Balkan folk dance (such as the hora) to Arab melody (such as the *debka*).

Naomi Shemer, one of the most famous composers and lyricists of Israeli folk music, created songs that quickly became classics. Her songs dealt with Israeli landscapes, society, and events. Shemer's "Yerushalaim Shel Zahav" (Jerusalem of Gold), written in the anxious days just before the Six-Day War in 1967, became almost a second national anthem.

The fact that Israeli folk songs were not usually recorded when they were composed led to the production of *shironim* (songbooks), small booklets containing their lyrics and sometimes musical notes. These shironim were distributed widely among music teachers, youth movements, and others who taught the new songs in all types of group gatherings. Another form of music consumption was *shira betzibur* (communal singing), where people sang the lyrics from the booklets accompanied by an accordionist who also acted as the conductor. Shira betzibur were important social events that brought people together, strengthening the new nation's communal and emotional unity.

Army Ensembles

Military entertainment units called *lehakot tzvaiot* (army ensembles) were created to entertain soldiers and raise morale during war. They were also supposed to embody the esprit de corps and prestige of the particular unit or command to which they belonged. The first army ensembles were established in 1948 during the War of Independence. The most famous was the Hizbatron, which furnished a model for those to come later: a group of young male and female soldiers performed sketches and sang folk songs that reflected a spectrum of feelings from joy to heroism to melancholy. Many leading musicians learned their craft and began their rise in these units.

The first period of the lehakot tzvaiot, from the mid-1950s until 1967, featured simple musical and stage productions. Low budgets made simplicity a necessity, but simplicity was also seen as a core national virtue. The typical instruments were limited to an accordion and a *darabuka* (goblet drum). The second period, from 1967 to 1975, was characterized by more elaborate productions with more instruments: drums, electric guitars, organ, and bass. For two decades, between the mid-1950s and the mid-1970s, the repertory of the lehakot tzvaiot dominated Israeli popular music.

The Rise of Israeli Rock

The musical works today considered the first masterpieces of Israeli rock had three characteristics: they were typical rock songs with electric instruments and personal lyrics; they used melodies and lyrics similar to traditional Israeli music; and most of the musicians were graduates of the army entertainment ensembles, which meant that their version of rock was part of mainstream Israeli culture. The early days of Israeli rock, the 1970s, featured collaborations by a prominent group of talented musicians, many of whom are stars to this day.

Arik Einstein has been the most prominent popular music performer in Israel since 1965. With over twenty-five albums, Einstein has largely defined Israeli music. Outstanding examples of his work include "Poozy" (1969) and "Shablul" (1970). Einstein fronted what was considered the first typical rock band with an international style. His other style, which dominated his records in the late 1970s, was more home grown: his music consisted of versions of Israeli folk songs with lyrics adapted from well-known poems. In a series of seven albums entitled *Good Old Land of Israel*, Einstein adapted these traditional works into a pop/rock style.

Shalom Hanoch was Arik Einstein's right-hand man for many years and played and sang as part of Einstein's group. Hanoch's gentle, serious, and poetic lyrics set his music apart from that of other rock musicians. In the mid-1970s, after working on "Shablul," Hanoch left Einstein's group to become the lead singer of the band Tamuz, whose only record is considered a masterpiece. After leaving Tamuz, Hanoch continued as a solo musician. His solo breakthrough came during the 1980s with one of his most popular songs ever, "Mehakim Le-Mashiah" (Waiting for the Messiah). His music ranges from soft acoustic ballads and Beatles-like pop/rock to hard rock and even "stadium rock."

Arik Einstein (left) performs with Shalom Hanoch, November 4, 1979. (The Government Press Office / Sa'ar Ya'acov.)

Shmulik Kraus was one of the first musicians to work with Arik Einstein. He was the main creative force behind the High Windows trio, of which Einstein was also a member. In 1970, Kraus formed another group, Cape of Good Hope, whose song "Ballad to a Kibbutz Leaver"— a mockery of kibbutz life, previously the symbol of Israeli-ness, and an appraisal of city life— symbolized the rebellion of Israeli rock.

Kaveret (Beehive) was an original, creative group unlike any that had previously existed in Israel. The seven members wrote their own songs and even produced their own records. The sales figures of their three records from 1973 to 1975 were unprecedented in Israel. Their original creations consisted of catchy tunes, Beatles-like harmonies, and sophisticated sketches with clever nonsensical humor. They occasionally used Eastern melodies and instruments to accompany sarcastic lyrics that exposed prominent taboos in Israeli society. Lines from their songs are still often quoted.

Despite these early stars, Israeli rock remained far from dominant in Israeli music as late as 1980, with traditional folk songs still generally considered more Israeli than anything else.

Popular Song Festivals

Beginning in 1960 and continuing for four decades, Kol Israel (later the Israeli Broadcasting Authority) sponsored a song contest to encourage new Hebrew songs. By the early 1970s, this event, generally called the Song Festival, had become the model for many other song contests in the country. These festivals had a huge impact on music, especially in the 1970s and 1980s, giving new performers and writers a venue for introducing new songs and a way to build their careers.

Since the original festival became mainstream by the 1970s, the music world pressed for additional festivals, one focusing on music more popular among Israelis of Middle Eastern origin and another on religious music. These festivals became two additional dimensions of authentic Israeli music. Private entrepreneurs also began children's song festivals, which were very successful. All these festivals became national events, often broadcast live on radio and television. Many of the new songs, especially the contest winners, became hits, and the albums became commercial successes.

Israeli Pop/Rock

By the mid-1980s, local pop/rock had become the dominant Israeli music. The sociologist Motti Regev argues that during this time, while folk and Middle East–oriented music were still popular, it was rock that spoke to the younger generation and reflected its desire to see Israel as an integral part of contemporary Western society. American and British innovations as well as Mediterranean music were all significant influences shaping this Israeli music. Russian, religious, and Arab influences were less prominent influences. Two of the biggest music companies—CBS-Israel and Hed Arzi—concluded that there was a strong market for locally produced rock.

As companies offered more and more contracts to local rock musicians and promoted their work, the industry became more and more successful. A notable example of success is Yehuda Poliker, whose roots were in Greek music. His career with his band Benzeen earned him recognition as one of the best rock musicians in Israel. After leaving Benzeen, he made two "back to the roots" records. The first was a rock-oriented interpretation of contemporary Greek songs translated into Hebrew. Then, in 1988, together with his regular lyricist and co-producer Ya'akov Gilad, he made what most critics regard as his masterpiece—*Ashes and Dust*. In this record, he merged a variety of musical influences—rock, punk, Eastern European, Greek, and Arabic—as an expression of his and Gilad's experiences growing up in Israel as sons of Auschwitz survivors. The blend was not only remarkably appealing emotionally and musically but also distinctively Israeli in its hybrid mixture of style and theme.

As in Western music, the classic rock era was followed by a period of soft rock. Sentimental ballads were produced by singer-songwriters such as Rami Kleinstein, inspired by Elton John. Glamorous female singers also became popular, of whom the single-named Rita was perhaps most famous. Yehudit Ravitz, whose unglamorous persona was the perfect reflection of the Israeli self-image, brought a wave of original songs that included a South American influence.

Especially popular on the contemporary rock scene in the early twenty-first century is a gentle music with ballad overtones, including songs by musicians like Yoni Bloch and the bands HaYehudim (The Jews) and Beit Habubot (House of Dolls). Groups like the Mercedes band also have complex and sophisticated lyrics, which to some extent take on the role once occupied by poetry.

Musika Mizrahit (Middle Eastern Music)

In the country's earlier years, *musika mizrahit* (Middle Eastern music) had an almost underground quality, but it emerged in the early 1970s to become quite successful (though never dominant). It can be defined as a blend of Middle Eastern musical styles and Greek-Turkish-Mediterranean influences, infused with some Western-style pop spirit. Such music used both rock (electric guitar, bass, synthesizer, and drums) and traditional instruments (the qanoun, oud, and bouzouki). Sometimes artists nearly copied foreign works, substituting Hebrew lyrics by Israeli composers to make the songs Israeli. Beginning in the 1980s, this type of music become mainstream national music not connected to a particular ethnic group.

Since musika mizrahit has less commercial backing and radio play and fewer sales than its rock rivals, performers rely more on live performances. In the early 1980s, after a decade of work by bands like Tzliley HaOud and Tzliley HaKerem, musika mizrahit crystallized in the music of the singers Zohar Argov and Haim Moshe. In 1983 they crossed over to the mainstream market with two classic albums, Argov's *Nahon LeHayom* and Moshe's *Ahavat Hayai*. Their success led to recognition of this type of music as mainstream, and its supporters demanded more radio time at the expense of Anglo-American and Israeli rock music.

Since all Israeli radio stations were public until 1995, this demand became a political issue intertwined with the campaign by Israeli Jews with Middle Eastern roots to achieve more recognition for their culture and traditions in Israeli society. On one hand, this music was seen as asserting this group's particular identity; on the other hand, it was seen as representing authentic Israeli music.

Different strategies have been used to popularize the music. One approach has been to incorporate elements of folk songs into musika mizrahit. Another has been to insist on the music's distinctiveness and importance to Israeli culture. Zohar Argov employed the latter strategy in a career that has been compared to that of Elvis Presley in American music. Argov too was called "the king." His tragic death in 1987 turned him into a cultural hero of the Mizrahi underclass. Yet by the 1990s, musika mizrahit was still relatively—though far from completely—absent from radio and television. Its supporters continued to demand recognition and legitimacy.

A major turnaround in the status of musika mizrahit occurred in the 1990s, when radio and television stations began to adapt to increasing pressure from those demanding greater air time for this musical style. Today the status of the performers is stronger than ever. They are heard and seen everywhere, much more than their peers of pop/rock music, and are repeatedly elected "singers of the year." This change in status demonstrates the diminished power of cultural elites (in this case, music editors and producers).

Today, the popular musika mizrahit is widely considered Israel's most successful musical genre. Among its contemporary stars are Dudu Aharon, who has revitalized the genre by bringing in new influences from other styles of music, and Sarit Hadad, who represented Israel in the Eurovision Song Contest in 2002 and was crowned best Israeli female singer of the 2000s in October 2009.

Classical Music

The center of classical music is the Israel Philharmonic Orchestra, founded in 1936 by the violinist Bronislaw Huberman. It played "HaTikva," Israel's national anthem, during the ceremony at the state's founding. In December 1950 the orchestra, with the famous American conductor Leonard Bernstein, went on its first tour in the United States. In the following years, the orchestra toured Europe as well, and after the end of the Cold War and the opening of diplomatic relations with countries around the world, it went on to perform in the countries of the former Soviet Union, China, and India.

Many talented young musicians were discovered in the first decades of the orchestra's existence. These include the violinist Yitzhak Perlman and the pianist Daniel Barenboim. In 1968 the world-renowned conductor Zubin Mehta was made musical consultant to the orchestra. This appointment was considered a tremendous achievement for the Israeli orchestra. In 1981, Mehta was appointed the orchestra's musical director for life.

Over the years, the Israeli orchestra has gained a worldwide reputation. A radio orchestra, known today as the Jerusalem Symphony Orchestra, was also established, and its concerts are broadcast to tens of thousands of listeners, bringing classical music to the public's awareness and to the education system. One of the state-run radio stations plays classical music exclusively. Immigration from the former Soviet Union also brought many professional musicians, including instrumentalists, singers, and music teachers, to Israel and led to the formation of new symphony and chamber orchestras as well as smaller classical ensembles. The new immigrants also brought tremendous additional talent and musical expertise to schools, conservatories, and community centers.

Since the 1990s, awareness of classical music has grown. Leading groups include the Israel Camerata and the chamber orchestra of the IDF Education Corps. Many cities and towns sponsor their own choirs, and several festivals are devoted to choral music—such as the vocal music in the churches of Abu Ghosh. Musical performances, from recitals to full symphony concerts, are held in a variety of venues, from the restored Roman amphitheaters in Caesarea and Beit She'an to concert halls and art centers around the country.

Israel also hosts many world-class classical music events, such as the International Harp Contest and the Arthur Rubinstein International Master Piano Competition. It also has local festivals, such as the Music Festival at Kibbutz Ein Gev and the Chamber Music Festival at Kibbutz Kfar Blum. The Israel Festival in Jerusalem is considered the most prestigious cultural event in Israel. Though initially a classical music festival, today it includes jazz, Israeli music, and other musical genres, as well as dance and theater performances by groups from all over the world. The final hallmark of the importance that classical music has gained in Israeli culture is the opening of various musicology departments and the establishment of research in musicology at institutions of higher learning.

Jazz

Jazz has a major presence on Israel's music scene. There has been an explosion of talent, and names like Iris and Ofer Portugali are prominent. The International Red-Sea Jazz Festival in Eilat held every August has increased its popularity. Israeli performers have also done well on the American jazz scene. The bassist and jazz composer Avishai Cohen was discovered

A performance by New Orleans's Los Hombres Calientes and the Olympia Brass Band at the annual International Red-Sea Jazz Festival in Eilat, August 2000. (Getty Images/Image Bank.)

by the legendary Chick Corea, for example. That Israel produces strong, original jazz, a musical genre seemingly so far from its own roots, demonstrates the musical versatility of its culture.

Trends in Israeli Music

Today's Israeli music scene is influenced by two key trends: greater variety and popular interest and a growing exposure to international music. These trends mean that every global style, from hip-hop to techno-pop to rap, has found distinctive Israeli expression.

The Israeli version of hip-hop music, for example, began in the 1990s with the band Shabak Sameh and became popular nationwide by 2003. Politics also makes its way into hip-hop music. Two of the most popular bands are the left-leaning HaDag Nahash (literally, "Snakefish" but also a pun on the Nahag Hadash, or "New Driver," auto decal used by those who have just received their driver's licenses) and Subliminal, which is rightist-oriented. HaDag Nahash members call themselves "the hip-hop Zionists," while Subliminal has a Star of David on its album and wrote a song called "HaTikva" (Hope, which is also the name of Israel's national anthem). A breakthrough for HaDag Nahash was the use of its music in the American film *Don't Mess with the Zohan.*

Perhaps Israel's wittiest band is Teapacks, led by Kobi Oz. Teapacks performed "Push the Button," a song about Iran's acquiring nuclear weapons, at the 2007 Eurovision Song Contest; it was the object of an ultimately unsuccessful attempt at censorship.

Another ensemble that shows the ability to borrow from different cultures and integrate them into the local Israeli culture is the Idan Raichel Project. The group, which started with Ethiopian music, borrows musical elements from all over the world and combines them with Middle Eastern, soul, and religious music to create some very original masterpieces.

Many of the newcomers to the Israeli music pop scene were discovered on the *Kochav Nolad* (A Star Is Born) television program, Israel's version of *American Idol,* the U.S. hit television show. In a small country where a fad can appeal to a large proportion of the population very quickly, *A Star Is Born* has produced many success stories. Ninet Tayeb is one of Israel's biggest stars. Shiri Maimon and Shai Gabso, the other two finalists in the first year's show, have also done very well.

With the appearance of so many new and talented singers, the Israeli music industry, focused more narrowly in the 1990s and early twenty-first century, has now moved toward more popular music and undergone a renaissance. The popularity of public communal singing has also returned and can be seen in television shows and nightclubs. In Israel, the success of commercialized pop music has encouraged the popularity of all types of music in general, notably traditional Israeli songs.

A crucial element in the international success of Israeli music has been the ability of singers to perform in English, something they would not have dared to try in earlier years. The first big international breakthrough in the 1990s was that of the singer Ofra Haza, who won acclaim because of her extraordinary voice and innovative use of her Yemenite roots. The first decade of the new century brought even wider international recognition for all genres of Israeli music. Surprisingly, however, the most successful was a previously marginal style, electronic trance music; the bands Astral Projection and Infected Mushroom have become globally recognized in this genre.

Music has also come to play a new role in Israel as a sort of secular equivalent of prayer. Israeli music is given a special place in Memorial Day commemorations, on holidays, and in various types of ceremonies. Prime Minister Yitzhak Rabin's peace rally in Tel Aviv in 1995 is a prominent example. His last action before leaving the stage was to sing a song; and after he was assassinated, young people began to mourn by singing songs.

THEATER

Theater was virtually unknown among Jews until the late nineteenth century. Yet in its Israeli incarnation, various genres are blended to create a distinctive national theatrical style. The HaBima Theater, founded in Moscow in 1917, marked the beginnings of Israeli theater. This Hebrew-speaking company was under the leadership of the Russian director Constantin Stanislavski, perhaps the single most influential theorist on acting in the modern Western world. Its famous actress Hanna Robina (1892–1980) went on to became the "first lady" of Hebrew theater. The theater was established to further the national revival of the Jewish people while simultaneously setting a high artistic standard in the performance of ideological plays. In 1931 the entire company immigrated to the Land of Israel, settled in Tel Aviv, and became the national theater of Israel.

Plays written during the first years of statehood mirrored contemporary events and portrayed a composite of stories of heroic victory. Because they tended to align with the core values of the state and the establishment, they rarely included Arab characters or open criticism. In fact, they criticized deviations from this standard. The most prominent playwrights were Moshe Shamir (*He Walked Through the Fields*, 1947), Yigal Mosinzon (*On the Negev*, 1949), Nathan Shaham (*They'll Arrive Tomorrow*, 1949), Nissim Aloni (*Most Cruel the King*, 1954), Aharon Megged (*Hedva and I*, 1954), and Ephraim Kishon (*His Name Precedes Him*, 1953).

Most of these pioneers were in the same age group, shared the same background, and employed similar writing styles. Many eventually shifted to prose and left theater altogether. Only Nissim Aloni remained in the of theater. His most extraordinary play was his first, *Most Cruel the King*, in which he makes use of perspectives and historical analogies to relate to the present.

Experimental Theater

Theater in the 1960s was characterized by experimentation and adaption of influences from Europe and the United States. Among the strongest of these influences was the work of the German poet and playwright Bertolt Brecht; other influential writers were Pirandello, Samuel Beckett, Eugene Ionesco, and Jean Genet. Their work had a tremendous influence on the writings of four prominent playwrights who effectively created the new Israeli drama and theater: Nissim Aloni, Nathan Alterman, Yosef Bar-Yosef, and Hanoch Levin, with Aloni and Levin the most prominent among them.

Aloni's most important work, *The King's New Clothes* (first produced at HaBima in 1961), opened a new chapter in the evolution of Israeli drama. Aloni's plays were mostly anchored in the worlds of myth, the grotesque, and fantasy. They were characterized by brilliant dialogue, extensive vocabulary, and allusions to different cultures and exotic locations. Aloni directed many of his own plays, the most prominent of which were *The American Princes* (Season Theater, 1963), *The Bride and the Butterfly Hunter* (HaBima, 1967), and *Aunt Lisa* (Bimot, 1969).

The main revolutionary of Israeli theater was Hanoch Levin, who rose to prominence following the Six-Day War. In 1969, when the feelings of excitement surrounding the military triumph were still reverberating, Levin tried to undermine the general sense of euphoria. He and a group of students produced a satirical evening at the Bar-Barim club in which they attacked the political and military establishment and mocked the pathos and sentimentalism that characterized the literature and most of the journalism of the time.

One of Levin's famous plays, *You and Me and the Next War*, is an antiwar satire in the traditional style of political cabaret. Levin presents this war, and all the wars of Israel, from a pacifist and an antimilitaristic point of view. Levin disconnected the theme of war from the historical Israeli context. This satire evoked a very emotional public debate, which followed Levin's works for many years. *You and Me and the Next War* and *The Queen of the Bathtub* portended the satiric, antiheroic attitude of the 1970s and the 1980s.

During the 1960s and 1970s, Israeli theater also gradually moved away from the original tradition of the HaBima and Cameri theaters, both in Tel Aviv, with many small theaters considered avant-garde and daring starting to develop. Gradually, the small theaters' innovations were reflected in the big theaters. Besides small theaters established in the 1950s, such as Do Re Mi, Zutta, and Zavit (Angle), new theaters became very active. Among them were the Onot (Seasons) Theater, with Nissim Aloni as a central player; Bimat HaSahkanim (Actors' Stage), with Oded Kotler and a group of actors; and Bimot (Stages), with Ya'akov Agmon. In addition, Israeli poets and playwrights began to translate the classic plays of Shakespeare, Molière, and Chekhov into Hebrew, which created a new reservoir of drama, both classic and modern.

Realist Theater

The drama of the 1960s, especially before 1967, was escapist. The drama of the 1970s, on the other hand, crashed into harsh reality following the Yom Kippur War and tended to be naturalistic and satirical. A bitter doubt about the national purpose was emerging in intellectual and artistic circles, and the theater was a leading forum in which to express this doubt. Criticizing the life of the individual in favor of the collective—communal life was an absolute value in the early years, as expressed in such plays as *He Walked Through the Fields*—was beginning to become outdated, and criticism of the collective was losing its social taboo.

The Haifa Theater, under the management of Oded Kotler and Nola Chelton, contributed to this shift during the mid-1970s. This theater became a platform for the expression of what was known as "the second Israel." Productions featured Middle Eastern and North African Jews, Arabs, and other such characters for the first time. Chelton also recruited Tel Aviv University theater students to embark on special projects—for example, living in deprived communities and producing docudramas. Chelton's work at the Haifa Theater produced a whole school of new writers and actors, including Yehoshua Sobol, Itzik Weingarten, and Hillel Mittelpunkt.

Theater and War

A crack in Israel's national consensus caused by the Lebanon War of 1982 was immediately expressed through theater, both in original dramas and in interpretations of translated classics. The collegiality of the earlier period was replaced by antagonisms so great that some theater groups and intellectuals supported attempts to censor Hanoch Levin's bitter antiwar satire *The Patriot*, in sharp contrast to their opposition to any similar action toward *The Queen of the Bathtub* in 1970. The post–Lebanon War years led to the creation of a protest theater. The new trend in theater was sober, with warring sentiments; plays simultaneously praised the Zionist dream and spoke of its demise.

During this time, the unique Acco (Acre) Festival of Alternative Theater was initiated by Oded Kotler, becoming a showcase for experimental theater. Yet the Haifa Theater remained the leader where delicate topics were concerned. For example, plays produced there discussed the Israeli-Arab conflict to a much greater extent and used more Arab actors. It managed to express their identity conflict in plays like *The Island* by Faugard, of which two versions were produced—one in Hebrew and one in Arabic (1983); *Waiting for Godot* in a Hebrew-Arabic version (1984); and *The Palestinian Girl* by Yehoshua Sobol (1985).

However, by the end of the decade, the sounds of protest and criticism were silenced as the public grew less interested in heavy topics. The dramatic change in the theatrical scene, after which theater in Israel was never again the same, occurred in the summer of 1987 with the staging of the play *Les Misérables*, performed in the Cameri Theatre. The play was Israel's first theater spectacular, produced with sophisticated light and sound equipment never before used in Israel. For the first time in an Israeli theater the audience and the critics cheered the technical achievement itself. Michael Handelzlats, theater critic for the *Ha'aretz* newspaper, called the applause a "production value"; technical efficiency was valued over substance, unlike in traditional theater in the state's early days.

This change indicated, on the one hand, the technical maturation of Israeli theater and the public's demand for high standards. Yet it also signaled that important ideological messages were no longer considered sufficient by the theatergoing public. The repertory theaters started to produce more plays with a commercial orientation. Among them were musicals, which until then had been seen as too professionally challenging and demanding for the actors. Even the daring Acco Festival began to follow this trend; the artists who participated used it mostly as a springboard to join the establishment and not as a laboratory for daring artistic experiments. Young acting-school graduates, who were recruited to the institutionalized theaters straight from school, were primarily interested in acting as a career path. Though these standards are normative in Western countries, in Israel they reflected a change.

Contemporary Theatrical Trends

At the eleventh Acco (Acre) Festival in 1990, the first-place prize was awarded to the play *Reulim* (Veiled), the first play by the young playwright Ilan Hazor. It was the first Israeli play that dealt with the intifada. Yet apart from a few notable exceptions like this, the theater of the 1990s became less political. Plays that dealt with the individual, the personal quality of life, and self-fulfillment replaced political works. The general tendency was toward entertainment, though not necessarily through comedies and musicals. This tendency made stand-up performances, a new genre of theater, very popular. Stand-up became an acceptable form of entertainment for young people and took the place of the satire, which nearly disappeared. Young stand-up artists usually avoided direct political statements about the situation in Israel and preferred to deal with personal situations, taken from their daily lives.

In recent years, Israeli theater has notably combined the old with the new and local identities with imports from abroad. By the 2000s, about half the plays produced were original Hebrew works. Each year, more theater classes are offered in Israeli high schools, more theater teachers are trained, and acting schools reject growing numbers of theater aspirants.

There are six government-subsidized public theaters, HaBima, the Cameri, and Beit Lessin in Tel Aviv, the Municipal Theaters in Haifa and Beersheva, and Jerusalem's Hahn Theater. HaBima and the Cameri have a wide repertoire of original Israeli and translated foreign plays. Beit Lessin and the Haifa theater, though historically they sought controversy, have now turned to musicals and more commercial plays. The well-known Gesher Theatre in Tel Aviv–Jaffa was founded by Russian immigrants.

Since the 1970s, there have been several attempts to establish a professional theater to serve Arabic speakers, but among them only the Beit HaGeffen Theater, located in the Arab-Jewish cultural center in Haifa, has survived. Its repertoire consists of pieces written in Arab states and contemporary pieces translated into Arabic. Arab actors acquire diplomas in act-

Israeli Arab actress/singer Mira Awad (right) and Israeli Jewish singer Ahinoam Nini representing Israel at the first semifinal of the Eurovision Song Contest on May 11, 2009, in Moscow, Russia. (Getty Images/Image Bank.)

ing schools and have been active in Hebrew theater since the beginning of the 1980s. Some well-known actors are Salim Dau, Muhammad Bakri, Salma Nakara, Makram Khouri, and Mira Awad.

Since the beginning of theater in the new state, Israel has sustained a proportionately high number of theatergoers compared to other Western countries.

DANCE

Dance in Israel has developed along two parallel paths—folk and professional. Dance performances used to be a central element in holiday ceremonies, especially in the kibbutzim and moshavim. However, in the pre-state years, the most popular folk dances were foreign imports, mostly from Jews in Eastern Europe, such as the hora and the polka.

Not until the early 1940s did original Israeli folk dances begin to develop. The first milestone occurred at the initiative of Gurit Kadman and Ze'ev Havatzelet, two young visionaries who organized the first national folk dance convention in 1944 with 200 dancers from fourteen dance companies; 3,500 people were in the audience. The second Dalia dance convention, held in 1947, attracted 25,000 people. The convention is still held today, but now it is known as the Karmiel Dance Festival and is the largest dance festival in Israel.

Traditional dances of the different ethnic groups that make up Israeli society, from Africa, Eastern Europe—especially Russia—and India, also developed, joining dances belonging to the Arabs, Druze, and Circassian subcultures already developed in Israel.

In addition to folk dances, dance in Israel also borrowed from the classical ballet and modern dance of Western Europe. The first Israeli choreographer was Baruch Agadati. His dances melded many styles. One of his folk dances became the one most emblematic of Israel in the rest of the world; it became known as the "Hora Agadati."

Another prominent choreographer was Sara Levi-Tanai, who created within the Israeli dance form from the 1940s until the 1990s. She was considered the most original choreographer in Israel. Drawing from a wide range of sources, Levi-Tanai developed a new artistic language and added depth to Israeli folk dance by making it more artistic. Levi-Tanai established the Inbal Company in the 1940s, a group that focused on the dance of Yemenite Jews and incorporated spoken or chanted words into the performance. In 1957, the Inbal Company became the first institutionalized and subsidized dance company in Israel.

Modern dance in Israel took off toward the end of the 1950s with the contributions of three significant figures: the Baroness Batsheva de Rothschild and a young Israeli couple, Berta Yampolsky and her husband, Hillel Markman, who returned to Israel after spending several years abroad dancing with various international companies.

Batsheva de Rothschild's interest in dance came from her friendship with the American choreographer Martha Graham. She decided to settle in Israel in 1958 after accompanying the Graham Company on an international tour that included Israel. She founded the Batsheva Dance Company, initially based on Graham's methods, in 1964. By the 1990s, Batsheva, under the direction of Ohad Naharin, had turned to more contemporary styles, gaining international recognition.

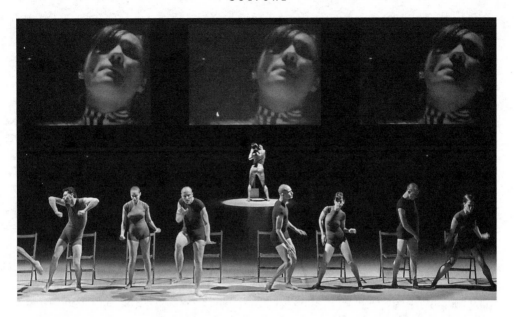

Members of the Israeli Batsheva Dance Company rehearse a scene of the play *Telophaza* on May 17, 2007, in Wolfsburg, Germany, before the Movimentos Dance Festival. (Getty Images / Image Bank.)

The Israeli Ballet was established by Berta Yampolsky and Hillel Markman in 1967 after they returned from studying abroad. They were originally appointed the lead dancers and directors of the Israeli Opera Ballet, but a disagreement between them and the company caused them to split and form an independent group—the Israeli Ballet Company. Reinforced by dancers who emigrated from the former Soviet Union, this company is composed of forty dancers and has performed all over the world. Its repertoire includes classical and neoclassical works.

The Suzanne Dalal Center for dance and theater in the Neve Tzedek neighborhood of Tel Aviv was founded in 1989 by the Dellal family in cooperation with the Tel Aviv municipality and various cultural organizations. It could be called the headquarters for Israeli dance. The Batsheva Dance Company, the Batsheva Ensemble, and the Inbal Ethnic Center for Arts all find their home there. In technical skill these companies are on a par with top dance companies around the world. The center often cooperates with the Israel Festival in Jerusalem, the Karmiel Dance Festival, and dance schools across Israel.

VISUAL ART

In 1906, the Bezalel School was founded in Jerusalem to train professional craft workers and artists. To it can be traced the beginnings of Israeli visual art. By the 1950s, the major groups in Israeli art were divided between those emphasizing the universal-aesthetics dimension of artwork (New Horizons) and those expressing the local dimensions in relation to Israel's history and society (social realism and the Group of Ten).

New Horizons (Ofakim Hadashim), established by a group of artists in 1948, dominated the art scene during Israel's first two decades. At first, it was influenced by expressionism and cubism, as well as by the Jewish Paris school—by Chaïm Soutine, Michel Kikoïne, and Marc Chagall, among others. Like many Israeli cultural movements, the group was torn between universalism and the specific reality of local society.

Eventually New Horizons moved toward abstract art, and this became the main style of artistic expression in Israel, perhaps even its canonical high art. New Horizons was perceived as a movement that emphasized universality rather than Israel's specificity. A 1958 exhibition held in honor of the state's first decade included works by New Horizons artists, among them the painting *Power* (Otzma) by the leader of the group, Joseph Zaritsky (1891–1985). When Prime Minister Ben-Gurion attended the opening, he was disturbed by the painting and asked to have it moved to a less central location since he thought it not representative enough of Israeli culture.

At the other end of the artistic spectrum were socialist realist artists, who saw their work as connected directly to society. They created representations of transit camps, demonstrations, workers, industrial developments, and life on the kibbutz and in the city. Some emphasized a link to nationalist values through symbolic images. Unlike New Horizons, these artists turned to Italian and Mexican art as well as to American painting, such as that of Ben Shahn, and Picasso's painting *Guernica*, as sources of inspiration. This heterogeneous group consisted of artists from the kibbutz, like Yohanan Simon, Shraga Weil, and Shmuel Katz; artists who had left the kibbutz, like Avraham Ofek and Ruth Schloss; and artists working in the city, like Naftali Bezem, Shimon Tzabar, Gershon Knispel, and Moshe Gat. Social realists criticized New Horizons for being egocentric and reactionary and for merely playing with form.

Another group working in opposition to New Horizons was the Group of Ten (1951–1961), which attacked abstract painting. Most of the members of the Group of Ten were former students of Yehezkel Streichman and Avigdor Stematsky, major figures in New Horizons. The Group of Ten employed figurative painting to look at local ways of living and local landscapes. Unlike the social realists, they avoided any overt social or political agenda.

The ninth exhibition by New Horizons (1959) was held at the Helena Rubinstein Pavilion at the Tel Aviv Museum of Art, and it showed not only the strength of the group but also the beginning of its demise. Others exhibited works different in spirit from the abstraction of New Horizons. These included sculpture, such as Igael Tumarkin's *Panic over Trousers:* The artist immersed his work trousers in polyester and hung them on the work's black-colored surface to look like a walking ghost. He stamped his hand on the sides, and those marks, together with the red marks on the surface, constitute a cross-composition in which the artist presents himself as a sacrifice.

An artistic organization of ten artists founded the group 10+, whose members included Raffi Lavie, Uri Lifshitz, Buky Schwartz, Ziona Shimshi, and Benny Efrat. Each retained his or her own artistic vision. Together they would set a theme for an exhibit (the color red, the figure of Venus) and invite others to participate—hence the "plus" in their name. They were influenced by the American Pop Art of Larry Rivers and Robert Rauschenberg in their use of materials and injected irony, humor, and sophistication into Israeli art. They used photographs, everyday objects, dolls, towels, and other materials innovatively to create collages and assemblages and combined different media: poetry, theater, cinema, electronic music, and fashion. Their attempts to expand the limits of art were initial steps in the anti-institutional artistic activity characteristic of the 1970s.

Postmodernism, Rebellion, and the Radical Critique

After the 1973 war, art became more political and critical in its relation to society. One event was the rebellion in the Bezalel Academy, when radical teachers abandoned painting and sculpture in favor of alternative, conceptual-material art. In the end, teachers such as Micha Ulman and Moshe Gershuni were dismissed. The institution returned to its emphasis on painting, but some students from the rebellion period—Yoram Kupermintz, David Wakstein, and Arnon Ben—retained the spirit of political art, which would become central in the future.

Artists in 1970s Israel used such industrial items as rust-proof wires in sculptures and such materials as margarine to create images with random effects. They also criticized art institutions in their work. Thus, Benny Efrat blocked the entrance to his exhibition (*Information*, 1972) in the Israel Museum in Jerusalem; Moshe Gershuni painted graffiti on the walls of the Julie M. Gallery.

The human body, suppressed by the abstract emphasis of early Israeli art, also returned to center stage in the 1970s. In 1973, Pinchas Cohen-Gan carved a male figure on the walls of the Yodfat Gallery and called it *Place as a Physical Position*. This digging into the wall in search of a nonexistent object was a testimony to the artist's process of defining and searching for his own identity as a Moroccan, a refugee, and an artist, but it also indicated the disorientation of Israel in general.

Art in this decade questioned the artist, art object, and Israel as a means of improving social, historical, and political circumstances. Most of the artists were aware of the utopianism of their performances. In 1974, Michal Na'aman reflected on the way the state dealt with its borders by placing two signs on the Tel Aviv beach bearing the words "The Eyes of the Nation." The signs were directed westward, toward the water, and were painted in the colors of the sea. The text came from a soldier's words during the last days of the Yom Kippur War and related to the capture of Mount Hermon in the Golan Heights.

A key concept of artists and cultural figures during the 1980s and 1990s, inspiring much of their radical view, was the belief that Israel could easily obtain peace if it only took the proper steps. The other side was either ignored, given sympathy, or treated as if it were not a real threat. Instead, the artists bitterly and angrily blamed conservative and religious forces for ruining Israel and extending the conflict, especially given their belief (and fear) that the conflict would bring disaster to the country.

In his 1981 painting *Sing Soldier*, Gershuni inscribes the lyrics of a 1942 song by the poet Ya'akov Orland, "Arise, Please Arise." The poet encouraged the reader to go out and fight; Gershuni erases the lyrics with layers of color that express an intense mental state and blood.

In his work *Isaac Isaac* (1982), Gershuni refers to the Biblical story of the binding of Isaac in the context of the First Lebanon War. Gershuni moves between the abject and the sublime, Christianity and Judaism, rationalism and emotionalism.

The 1982 Lebanon War and the First Intifada inspired critical political messages. David Reeb, for example, created a long series of paintings based on superimposing the violent reality in the West Bank and the Gaza Strip on the calm reality within Israel. Reeb painted cartographic images of Israel without including the territories captured since the 1967 war. In his work *Green Line with Green Eyes* (1987), he contrasted the Tel Aviv shore with a scene from the intifada. The painting is covered with images of eyes staring back at the viewer. He uses the colors of the Israeli and Palestinian flags and hints at a spreading blindness. Created by Pamela Levi in 1983, following the Lebanon War, *Dead Soldier Painting* depicts the nonheroic presence of death.

Photography

Another important development of the 1980s was the rising status of photography. Adam Baruch, Anat Saragusti, and others equated documentary photography with art and gave it an important role in describing political and social reality. Micha Kirshner shot a portrait of Aisha El-Kord from the Khan Yunis refugee camp in a series of intifada portraits that he photographed in his studio. Aisha El-Kord was a child injured in the eye by a rubber bullet. She appears in the photograph with her mother in a pose evocative of a pietà.

The contrast between calm life and violent instability is a common theme in works of this period. A good example is Gal Weinstein's installation *Slope*, which depicts small houses with red roofs buried in dark soot. The scene looks like Pompeii after the volcanic eruption, suggesting that Israel is living its last days and will soon collapse.

Similar to this is Sigalit Landau's *Swimmer and Wall* (1993), in which a tiny shiny doll swims into a wall, her head exploding in the violent encounter. The sweetness of the doll bursts when it crashes into reality. The symbol of the decade, suggested the curator of the 1990s exhibition at the Herziliya Museum of Contemporary Art, was youth aware of its own transience, of its own mortality. In a confrontation with death, there is an attempt to hold onto youth while maintaining awareness of the inferno to follow.

Khaled Zighari's *Head to Head* (1995) presents a soldier and a Palestinian civilian facing off. They are twins in a dance. A later version of this duet can be seen in Sharif Waked's *Jericho First* (2002), a series of thirty-two paintings whose point of departure was an image from the Hisham Palace in Jericho depicting a lion attacking a doe. The series develops as the violent act proceeds, and the images become denser until at the end, the lion and the doe become one body in which one can see the hanging leg of the doe. The image hovers between comic strip and abstract painting and represents a violent, mythical world filled by conflicting concepts of strong and weak, good and evil.

In 1997, Meir Gal exhibited *Nine Out of Four Hundred: The West and the Rest*. This is a color photograph that portrays the artist bursting from a dark background or perhaps immersed in darkness. The artist holds in his hand a history book from the 1970s, written by Shmuel Kirshenbaum. Of 400 pages, only nine are dedicated to the history of non-European Jews, and

Eliezer Sonnenschein (or Zonenschien), *Landscape and Jerusalem,* oil on wood, 2007. Israel Museum, Jerusalem, Israel / The Bridgeman Art Library. (Eliezer Sonnenschein / Bridgeman Art Library.)

these are the pages that he holds in his hands. The rest of the pages are hanging down. This is an effective photograph presenting a sharp message that the Mizrahim have been erased from the pages of history.

The apocalyptic mood continued into the new century. The visitor entering Sigalit Landau's October 2002 exhibition *The Country* at Tel Aviv's Alon Segev Gallery experienced a strong sense of disorientation. Descending into the basement, the visitor entered one of Tel Aviv's roofs as if excavated by archaeologists. The installation included three figures: one picking fruit, a second carrying fruit, and the third an archivist or observer who looked like an ancient Egyptian figure in the act of writing. The forbidden or poisoned fruits were fashioned from newspapers; the three figures looked like the living dead; their bodies had exposed muscles without flesh. The basement space was like a representation of hell.

Some contemporary art reveled precisely in its lack of meaning and even embraced escapism. In *Landscape and Jerusalem* (2007), for example, Eliezer Sonnenschein painted a fantastic landscape combining apocalyptic images of early European painting with the saccharine-sweet language of posters from the 1970s, together with animation effects.

Such works do not characterize all or most of Israeli art. The 1990s and the early twenty-first century also brought a new interest in beauty. The kind of magical realism that had become popular in literature also pervaded art with the use of illusion, spectacular effects, and even the use of religious ideas.

CUISINE

One of the keys to delicious cuisine is good ingredients. Israel has a wide range of quality produce available year-round, including fruits, vegetables, dairy products, fish, and other items.

Israel's small size and warm climate mean that consumers can easily find very fresh food. A distinctive Israeli cuisine—perhaps, more accurately, more than one cuisine—has emerged from a broad variety of influences.

Jewish Food

Kashrut (Jewish dietary laws) has shaped traditional Jewish food eaten by pious Jews for centuries. It continues to be a fundamental influence in Israel even for the food prepared and eaten by nonreligious people. The Guttman Report found that nearly 60 percent of all Jewish Israelis refrain from eating non-kosher meat, and 44 percent observe at least some of the dietary laws in their homes—for example, separating meat and dairy items.

Many Jewish foods are associated with Jewish holidays and become more visible in Israel during their respective seasons. On Rosh Hashana, the Jewish New Year, Jews dip apples in honey and eat honey-sweetened foods to celebrate hope for a sweet new year. Hanukkah is celebrated by consuming foods cooked in oil—including potato pancakes (also called *latkes*) and *sufganiyot* (jelly doughnuts)—to commemorate the miracle of a small quantity of oil lasting eight days after ancient Israel's independence was reestablished.

During Passover, Jews eat *matzoh*, an unleavened bread that symbolizes the food the Israelites ate on their exodus from Egypt. While religious Jews follow this practice because they believe God commanded them to do so, many less religious Jews in Israel also eat matzoh as a national and cultural custom. It becomes widely available in stores before the holiday. Many restaurants either close down during Passover—since all leavened grain must be cleaned out and kept off the menu—or feature special items. In the late spring, the Jewish harvest festival of Shavuot is celebrated. Traditionally, dairy products, including many types of cheese and yogurt, are consumed.

The importance of keeping kosher is so rooted in Jewish heritage and represents a large enough share in the market that most Israeli food manufacturers and many restaurants keep their menus kosher. Still, in today's Israel, there is a vast variety of food. One kibbutz specializes in the production of pork products; another markets a line of meat-style vegetarian foods. There is a lot of innovation and no serious coercion. Market considerations shape the opportunities and responses of businesses.

Supermarkets, hotels, and many event halls—which have a broad clientele—generally feature only kosher products. Still, upscale restaurants, especially outside Jerusalem, may be completely non-kosher, as is the Tiv-Ta'am supermarket chain created by Russian immigrants. McDonald's restaurants in the Jerusalem area are kosher, but elsewhere in the country most are not.

Muslim Food

Just as kashrut influences food options in Israel's Jewish areas, Islamic dietary law and tradition (*hallal*) influence food choices for Israel's large minority Muslim population. Religious Muslims follow dietary restrictions, such as a ban on pork products and alcohol. Food options in restaurants and supermarkets in Muslim areas reflect this.

And just as Jewish tradition influences food consumption and the atmosphere in the country during certain seasonal events, so too does Muslim tradition. For example, Muslims are obligated to fast from sunup until sundown every day during the month of Ramadan. Every night during Ramadan feasts called *iftars* are served, and the month ends with a big celebration called Eid al-Iftar. Traditional iftar foods include such Middle Eastern favorites as lamb shwarma (shredded lamb), falafel, hummus, tabbouleh, and olives.

International Influences

Since Israel has immigrants from so many countries, many cuisines and traditions are represented in its food. The distinctive traditional cuisines of greatest prominence in Israel are European Ashkenazic and Middle Eastern Mizrahi.

The strongest European influence on Israeli cuisine is the Eastern European one. Receiving supplies from the Baltic Sea fisheries and rivers, Jews in that area developed dishes like gefilte fish (minced carp fish patties) and smoked salted fish. Another popular Eastern European Jewish dish is *cholent*, a slow-cooked stew containing meat, potatoes, and beans, as well as anything else the cook wants to add. Chicken soup is another common dish, enriched with different ingredients, including matzoh balls. These types of food are still eaten in traditional homes, especially on the Jewish Sabbath. However, there are no longer very many restaurants that serve these foods, and Ashkenazic food is not generally regarded as high cuisine.

The most common elements of "Eastern European Jewish" food enjoyed in North America—delicatessen meats, lox, and bagels, for example—rarely exist in Israel, where bagels, for example, are seen as American cuisine. The Israeli *begele* is distinctly different, being drier and often saltier.

Moroccan cuisine is the most prominent Middle Eastern cuisine in Israel. It features, for example, fruity meat stews served over couscous. In addition to couscous—a grain made from semolina and usually served with vegetables, soup, and meat—other popular Mizrahi dishes include *hamin* (similar to the Ashkenazic cholent), falafel, and hummus. Falafel are deep-fried patties made of ground chickpeas and spices, originating in Egypt and popular throughout the Middle East, often eaten with pita bread. Hummus is another dish made out of chickpea paste. It is served with olive oil and different kinds of spices and is eaten with pita bread. Falafel and hummus are considered the two most popular dishes in Israel. These two dishes also find themselves on fast food menus. Another popular form of fast food is grilled meats, generally lamb or turkey, served as kabobs or shwarma (shredded).

Two main types of foreign cuisine have become especially prevalent throughout Israel: Italian, with pizza challenging the popularity of more traditional fast food items, and Asian, including Thai, Chinese, and Japanese—the restaurants often have foreign cooks. Especially in Tel Aviv, there is also the import of trendy ideas from abroad in high-end restaurants such as nouvelle cuisine, fusion, higher-quality ingredients, attractive appearance, and celebrity chefs. In short, Israel has become part of global cuisine movements. In Tel Aviv, there has also been a strong interest in Mediterranean cooking.

Mediterranean food with hummus and baba ganoush at a restaurant in Tel Aviv. (Getty Images/Image Bank.)

One popular Israeli beverage is a tangy drink called *limonana*, a refreshing combination of lemonade and mint leaves (*nana* means "mint" in Hebrew). Alcoholic beverages are also drunk. Israel is a leading producer of commercial and boutique kosher wines. Beginning in the 1990s or so, Israel's wine industry expanded dramatically, with many new boutique labels starting up in places like the Jerusalem Hills and quickly meeting high standards.

Consumption of beer and spirits—and alcohol in general—is low among Israelis in comparison with consumption in other Western countries. The average Israeli is estimated to consume about 4.5 gallons of beer per year at most, compared to 26 gallons for the average American. Israel produces two commercial beers, Goldstar and Maccabee, but many prefer foreign imports. Local microbreweries also offer other beer alternatives.

The national Israeli drink is undoubtedly coffee, drunk in regular, *hafuch* (similar to cappuccino), instant (*nes*), filtered (*natul*), and expresso (*botz*) forms. Israelis take their coffee very seriously and prefer it to be strong. Foreign café chains with their emphasis on flavored coffees have not done well in Israel.

MEDIA

The history of Israel's media predates the 1948 establishment of the state. Hebrew newspapers were an integral part of the Jewish revival in the Land of Israel, beginning in the middle of the nineteenth century. The first Hebrew newspapers were established in Jerusalem in 1863. *Ha'aretz* (The Land), was founded in 1918 and still exists. The most popular daily today, *Yediot Aharonot* (Latest News, usually referred to as *Yediot*), was established in 1939. Radio service in Hebrew started in 1936.

Today, the media world in Israel includes four major general daily newspapers in Hebrew and one in English; three daily financial newspapers; hundreds of local newspapers and magazines; three national television channels; two popular cable and satellite companies, which each make many stations available; two public radio networks; fourteen regional radio stations; four major Internet providers; four mobile phone companies; and thousands of websites and portals. This diversified media world, especially in broadcasting and new media, has emerged only since the 1990s with technological, economic, and political changes. Until the early 1990s, there was only one television channel and two public radio networks. The political establishment resisted efforts to open up the electronic media market, because it wanted to exercise some political control and influence over the institutions regulating and operating television and radio broadcasts.

Since the 1990s, Israeli media has undergone a complete transformation. Most of the political and ideological party newspapers have disappeared, and the single public television channel has lost a substantial share of its audience to commercial television channels and those—many international or foreign—available by cable or satellite. New social media have also stormed the country, and the ratio of Israeli households connected to the Internet, approximately three-quarters of the population, is one of the highest in the world.

Print Media

Major Israeli newspapers are currently published in four languages: Hebrew, English, Russian, and Arabic. Four major independent daily Hebrew newspapers appear in Israel today. Three additional dailies are financial papers. Although over the years many newspapers have closed, especially party dailies, a new daily newspaper started in 2007, and a new financial newspaper began publication in 2008. *Ha'aretz* is an elite newspaper. *Yediot*, *Ma'ariv* (Evening), and *Israel HaYom* (Israel Today) are popular tabloids, except that unlike similar papers around the world, these devote substantial space to news (including foreign news) and analysis. Traditionally, *Ha'aretz* was a morning newspaper while *Yediot* and *Ma'ariv* were evening newspapers, but today they all are published and distributed in the early morning hours.

In 1995, *Yediot* published about 350,000 copies on weekdays and about 600,000 copies on weekends. *Ma'ariv* published about 150,000 copies on weekdays and about 250,000 copies

Newspaper	Language	Owner	Year Founded
Independent Newspapers			
Ha'aretz	Hebrew	Schoken	1918
Yediot Aharonot	Hebrew	Moses, Fishman	1939
Ma'ariv	Hebrew	Nimrodi	1948
Israel Hayom	Hebrew	Adelson	2007
Israel Post	Hebrew	Nzor, Weisman	2007
Financial Newspapers			
Globes	Hebrew	Fishman	1983
*The Marker**	Hebrew	Schoken	2008
Calcalist	Hebrew	Moses	2008
Party Newspapers			
*Hatzofe***	Hebrew	National Religious Party	1938
Hamodia	Hebrew	Agudat Israel	1949
Yated Ne'eman	Hebrew	Degel Hatorah	1985
Al-Ittihad	Arabic	Hadash	1948
Selected Other Newspapers			
Jerusalem Post	English	Mirkay Tikshoret and Canwest Global Communications	1932
Ha'aretz / International Herald Tribune	English	Schoken and New York Times	1997
Vesti	Russian	Moses	1992
Al-Sinara (weekly)	Arabic	Mashur	1983

* In 2005, *The Marker* became the financial section of *Ha'aretz,* but since January 2008 it has also been sold separately.
** Merged with *Makor Rishon* on April 25, 2007, and is no longer affiliated with the National Religious Party.

on weekends. *Ha'aretz*'s circulation was about 50,000 on weekdays and 60,000 on weekends. In 2006, *Ha'aretz* said it printed an average of 70,000 copies on weekdays and an average of 94,000 copies on weekends. *Israel Hayom* publishes approximately 350,000 copies every day; they are distributed free of charge in major population centers.

As in other countries, newspaper readership is in decline, with exposure—that is, those reading part of an issue—falling 13 percent for *Yediot* and *Ma'ariv* between 2001 and 2009, according to a Tele-Gal survey. On the other hand, the newest newspaper, *Israel Hayom*, has gained about 5 percent of exposure every year.

Yediot is still the most popular paper in Israel; *Israel Hayom* occupies second place, and *Ma'ariv* is in the third place, with *Ha'aretz* lagging far behind. In 2005, exposure to *Yediot* both on weekdays and on weekends was larger than that for all the other newspapers combined. Today, this is no longer the case, but *Yediot* and *Israel Today* account for about 60 percent of exposure to daily newspapers. *Yediot* calls itself the "country's newspaper," and *Ma'ariv* calls itself "a newspaper for everybody." *Ha'aretz* has done the exact opposite by attempting to appeal mostly to elites; its slogan is "a newspaper for thinking people." Historically, *Ma'ariv* was a conservative newspaper, but *Yediot* and *Ma'ariv* are no longer partisan. *Ha'aretz* is largely on the political left. It also publishes an English-language edition.

Television

Israel began television broadcasts only in the late 1960s. The founder of the state and first prime minister, David Ben-Gurion, thought that watching television would corrupt culture and arts and reduce the reading of books and attendance at theaters, concerts, exhibitions, and other cultural events. Also, the Israeli economy was weak, and people consumed only basic commodities. The market could not sufficiently support commercial television networks, and the government did not want to spend tax money on television. This attitude changed in 1965, when for the first time the government authorized privately funded educational television broadcasts.

Another significant change occurred after the Six-Day War. During the war, Arab television networks enjoyed a monopoly over pictures from the battles. They mainly broadcast coverage that was highly distorted and misleading. Consequently, the Israeli government decided to establish a public television station, Israel Television, which began broadcasting in 1968. Israel Television and Educational Television shared the same channel, with the former broadcast in the evenings and the latter in the mornings. In 1994, Israel Television established a second public channel (Channel 33).

The first commercial channel, Channel 2, began broadcasting in November 1993. A second commercial channel, Channel 10, began broadcasting in January 2002. With the introduction of commercial television channels, Israel Television became Channel 1. Only Channels 1 and 2 are based on direct transmission; the others are available only through cable or satellite services. Multichannel cable television started in 1989, and DBS (Direct Broadcasting Satellite) began in 2000. Both services are operated by private commercial companies, HOT and Yes, respectively.

Until 1989, all the television and radio networks were public. Since then, the government has adopted a mixed model. It kept the public channels but awarded broadcasting licenses to

The Twenty-Five Top-Rated Television Shows by Genre, October 2009

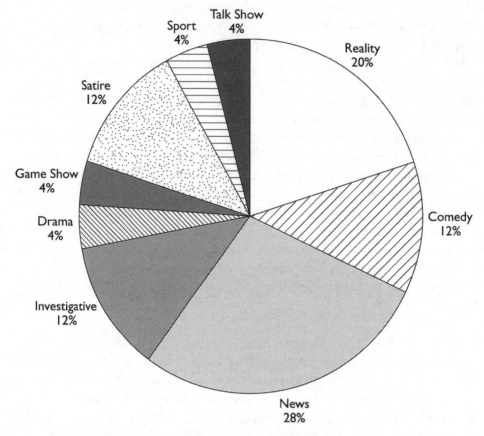

Programs aired between October 25 and 31, 2009.

The twenty-five top-rated television shows in Israel by genre among those aired in October 2009. (Data: Israel Audience Research Board, Tele-Gal, TNS. Chart: Eytan Gilboa. Drawing by Bill Nelson.)

private television and radio companies. The two commercial channels, 2 and 10, are financed via advertising revenues and regulated by the Second Authority for Television and Radio (SATR). In 2008, about 75 percent of all multichannel subscribers received digital television service; this is one of the highest ratios in the world.

In 2005, about 92 percent of Israel's 1.7 million households had televisions, those who did not consisting mostly of Haredi Jews and Bedouin. Surveys by Israel's National Statistics Bureau found that in 2008 over 50 percent of households owned a DVD player, and 40 percent owned video equipment.

The figure here shows the distribution of top-rated television programs by genre. In 2009, most viewers preferred to watch news (28 percent), reality TV (20 percent), satire (12 percent), and comedy (12 percent). This result is not surprising given the rapidly changing events in

Israeli politics, security, and economics. Israelis are addicted to news, and because of the tensions in daily reports, they frequently escape to the world of reality television and comedy. Except for news programs, the distribution of the highest-rated programs in Israel is similar to that in the United States and other developed countries.

Israeli programming is shaped by lower budgets than are available in other countries. Sometimes, however, relatively lavish productions are mounted, such as the soap opera *Ramat Aviv Gimmel*, named after an affluent Tel Aviv suburb, and multipart dramas on the Mizrahi immigration and other aspects of Israeli history. Another popular program, airing in the 2006 to 2009 seasons, was *The Champion*, about the lives of a group of soccer players, based clearly—as the audience recognized—on real people.

An interesting example of how the culture takes in and adapts Western ideas in its own image is how popular Israeli television shows develop from imported ideas. Among programs given this treatment have been *The Bachelor; Beauty and the Geek; The Biggest Loser; Dancing with the Stars; Big Brother Israel; Survivor; Master Chef (Top Chef); TLV (The Apprentice)*; and *Race for the Million (The Amazing Race)*. Perhaps most successful of all has been *A Star Is Born* (*American Idol*), which, since beginning in 2003, has produced several singing stars, including Shai Gabso, Shiri Maimon, Boaz Ma'uda, Harel Moyal, Harel Skaat, and Ninet Tayeb.

These programs generate a great deal of interest and debate over the respective merits of contestants who—Israel being a small country—are often personally known by viewers. But Israel also initiates programs keyed to its special interests, issues, and concerns. For example, one reality show was *The Ambassador*, in which a diverse group of young people competed in different trials and tests to prove they could best represent Israel abroad. During the Lebanon War of 2006, *A Star Is Born* broadcast from the missile-targeted north and has also made special provisions for religious contestants. In contrast, the local version of *Top Chef* was quite non-kosher.

In the Israeli version of *The Office*, a British situation comedy also copied in the United States, the employees of the office supply company include a mix of secular Jews, Datim, Arabs, and Russian and Ethiopian immigrants. *Srugim* (referring to the knitted kippot, or skullcaps, worn by Datim), follows the lives of several young Datim living in Jerusalem as they pursue love and career success. The show has gained a following since that group sees it as an accurate depiction.

Some Israeli programs have been bought by American networks, including *Ramzor* (Traffic Light), a hit situation comedy that started in 2008, about three male friends in their midthirties whose personal situations are said to correspond with a traffic light. Itzko (red) has problems with his wife and daughter; Amir (yellow) gets along well with his girlfriend although there are also tensions, and Hefer (green) is a playboy. Another series, *Tal and Greenbaum*, follows the adventures of two partners—a cheating husband and an aspiring cinema director—in a company that films weddings and bar mitzvahs.

One popular format for programs is the political discussion show, in which success often seems to be marked by the extent to which people raise their voices and speak at the same time. Other popular shows are pointed political and social satires featuring skits on current events, such as *Eretz Nehderet* (Wonderful Land), which started in 2003, and *Matzav HaUma* (State of the Nation), which started in 2010. Regular comedy shows include *Ktzarim* (Short Ones), which began in 2004 and features a variety of comedians doing skits.

Radio

The largest radio network in Israel is Kol Israel (Voice of Israel), which began in 1936. Today it operates several channels: A, culture and education; B, news; C, popular Israeli music; D, Arabic-language network; Kol HaMusica (The Voice of Music), classical music; and Reka, foreign languages for new immigrants. Kol Israel also supervises more than fifty local FM educational radio stations located primarily in universities, colleges, and high schools. These stations are used for teaching and training purposes.

Galei Zahal (IDF Radio, owned and operated by the Israel Defense Forces) was established in 1950 and operates two channels. The main network broadcasts primarily news, talk shows, and music, and the second (Galgalatz) focuses on music and traffic reports. The junior staff are mostly young soldiers. The station is popular among young people primarily because of the informal presentation style and modern music. For many years the station has served as the main training school for broadcast journalists, and today former professionals at the station occupy many leading positions in the Israeli media.

The communications revolution in broadcasting facilitated the establishment of commercial regional radio stations, beginning in September 2005. Today there are twelve regional stations and two national stations designated for specific audiences, one in Arabic for Israeli Arabs and the other for Orthodox Jews.

There are also about 150 pirate radio stations. Most are operated by religious, ethnic, and ideological groups—Orthodox Jews, Arabs, and Jewish settlers in the West Bank, for example. They are financed by advertisements and donations from supporters. The pirate stations claim that existing stations do not represent their groups, and they are forced to operate illegally because the government has refused to allocate them legal frequencies. The government rarely shuts down these pirate stations unless they interfere with vital communications systems, such as air traffic control.

New Media

Israel's international high-tech reputation is closely related to Israelis' fascination with the new media. Four major and about fifty smaller Internet service providers serve about four million users over the age of thirteen, including two-thirds of households and three-quarters of businesses. Mobile phone companies introduced wireless Internet in 2001. A study by Strategy Analytics found that in 2008, broadband household penetration in Israel reached 77 percent, placing Israel in seventh place in the world, ahead of the United States, the United Kingdom, France, and Canada.

Using social media and the Internet generally requires an ability to use English, a language widely understood in Israel. A number of Hebrew-language news sites, notably Ynet, run by *Yediot*, have emerged. Given the tremendous interest in Israel internationally, English-

Households' Connection to the Internet, 1997–2008

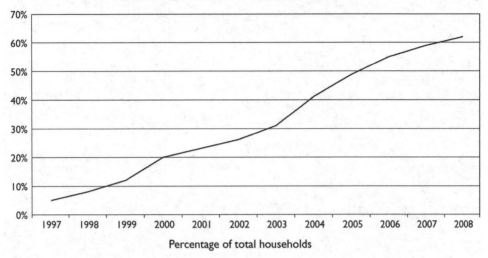

Percentage of total households

The percentage of Israeli households with connection to the Internet, 1997–2008. (Data: Israel Central Statistics Bureau. Chart: Eytan Gilboa. Drawing by Bill Nelson.)

language Israeli newspaper sites are among the most frequently visited in the world. A large number of blogs also exist in both Hebrew and English.

SPORTS

Israel's most popular sport is soccer (football), although basketball has gained a following, particularly among the higher economic strata. Israelis closely follow international competitions when their national team competes or when individual Israeli players or even coaches are involved. Games with country's leading teams—Beitar Jerusalem, Maccabi Haifa, Hapoel Tel Aviv, and others—regularly draw crowds of thousands. Top soccer stars are household names.

Yet Israel's achievements in international soccer competitions are modest. The high points in history occurred in 1970, when Israel qualified for the World Cup, and in 2003, when Maccabi Haifa beat Manchester United 3–0 in the Champions League. But a number of Israeli players have risen to top levels in Europe, notably Yossi Benayoun, Eli Ohana, and Eyal Berkovic.

Sports are not a part of Jewish tradition. It was only in the late nineteenth century that this changed, when modern-oriented European Jews, mainly university students, became interested in athletics. The roots of modern Israeli sports are in the international Maccabi movement, a coalition of sporting groups that became part of the Zionist organization during the pre-state period. The Maccabiah Games, an international Jewish sporting competition equivalent to the Olympic Games, began in 1932 and is an important event in Israel.

Given the political organization of the pre-state era and in the country's early days, many of the soccer and, later, basketball teams represented parties and political movements: Hapoel represented Labor; Beitar, what is now Likud; Maccabi, centrist parties; and Bnei Yehuda, the National Religious Party. While these names remain, they have little significance except for

Soccer fans cheer the national team at a World Cup qualifying game in Ramat Gan Stadium, March 2009. (Getty Images / Image Bank.)

joking references that sometimes carry a nasty edge in slogans shouted at games. Perhaps only Beitar Jerusalem is still seen by its supporters as having ideological significance. Otherwise, fan preferences follow geographic rather than political lines. Israeli Arabs are fully integrated into the league system. As in other countries, the televising of games draws bigger audiences but reduces the number of spectators who attend games.

Generally, the leading soccer teams over the years have been Hapoel Tel Aviv, Beitar Jerusalem, Maccabi Haifa, and Maccabi Tel Aviv, although others have done well and won league championships. The main team representing an Arab town is Bnei Sakhin—a team has both Jewish and Arab players. In 2004, it won a national championship. Each team is allowed to have up to five foreign players. Aside from the top Toto League, there are many other professional and semiprofessional leagues at lower levels.

Sometimes politics intervenes in sports, most notably the Arab-Iranian boycott that has resulted in Israel playing internationally in European rather than in Middle Eastern or Asian leagues. Israel was one of the founders of the Asian Football Confederation (AFC), but when Arab states began to join the AFC, they pressed for Israel's expulsion, which happened in 1976. Thereafter, Israel tried to join the European Football League (UEFA), but Communist bloc countries prevented this until 1991, after the disintegration of the Soviet bloc.

In international competitions, athletes and teams that refuse to recognize Israel refuse to play and at times have forfeited games as a result. Places refusing to admit Israeli players or teams may lose the opportunity to host international competitions. And at times foreign teams cancel visits to Israel because of security concerns.

Basketball is Israel's second sport, and local teams draw enthusiastic crowds. Several American-born players were especially important in the early years: Tal Brody, Be'eri Leibowitz, and Steve Kaplan. Foreign players have remained important. Israeli basketball largely developed after the fall of the Soviet Union, when European competition was completely open to Israeli teams. Maccabi Tel Aviv and Hapoel Jerusalem are the most well-known teams.

Basketball is also the arena in which Israeli teams have been most successful internationally, with the Maccabi Tel Aviv team winning the Euroleague championships in 2004 and 2005 and reaching the finals again in 2007. In 2009, an Israeli player, Omri Caspi, was drafted by the Sacramento Kings and became the first Israeli to play in an National Basketball Association game.

Tennis is popular in Israel and is one of the sports in which Israelis have been most successful in international competition. The Israel Tennis Center has fourteen branches around the country, and there are many other courts. Shahar Peer is the best-known Israeli player, ranked thirteenth worldwide in 2010. Denied a visa by the United Arab Emirates in 2009, she was unable to play at the Dubai Tennis Championship. Other players include doubles partners Andy Ram and Jonathan Erlich, who reached the semifinals at Wimbledon in 2003. In 2006, Ram, this time teaming up with a Russian, Vera Zvonareva, became the first Israeli player to win a senior Grand Slam event at Wimbledon.

A number of other sports have developed followings, including professional handball, which has been growing in popularity. There is even a small amateur ice hockey league. Israel has also done well in sailing, especially windsurfing, and the martial arts. All seven Olympic medals won by Israelis are in these sports.

Cricket and rugby are played by English-speaking immigrants, as is baseball, although attempts to start a professional league have failed. Swimming, both in the sea and at pools, is popular, as is surfing and paddle ball. And while winter sports are understandably rare in Israel's climate, downhill skiing is done at Mount Hermon.

Israelis have excelled in chess competitions, often producing world champions. Boris Gelfand, winner of the 2009 World Chess Cup, like many other leading players in Israel, immigrated from the former Soviet Union. Among Mizrahim, backgammon (*sheshbesh*) is a popular pursuit. A unique Israeli sport is the Bible quiz; competitions draw interest especially among the Datim. In 2010, the competition was won by Avner Netanyahu, Prime Minister Benjamin Netanyahu's son.

Israel has competed as a nation in the Olympics since 1952, and Israelis begin winning medals in the 1990s. They have won medals in judo, sailing, and canoeing. Yael Arad won the first medal for Israel in 1992 for judo; Gal Fridman gained the first gold medal in 2004 for sailing.

BIBLIOGRAPHY

Adelman, Tzvi Howard. "Modern Hebrew Poetry and Jewish History and Culture." Jewish Agency for Israel, Department for Jewish Zionist Education, http://www.jafi.org.il/JewishAgency/English/Jewish+Education/Compelling+Content/Jewish+History/Cultural+History/week+11.htm.

Agassi, Uzi. "'Aesthetic Distance,' in Contemporary Israeli Poetry," November 1, 2004. Israel: Poetry International Web, http://israel.poetryinternationalweb.org/piw_cms/cms/cms_module/index.php?obj_id=3149.

Aharoni, Sara, and Meir Aharoni, eds. *People and Deeds in Israel: The Jubilee Book*. Kfar Saba: Miksam, 1998. [In Hebrew.]

Anderson, Elliot, and Robert Friend, eds. *Contemporary Israeli Literature: An Anthology*. Philadelphia: Jewish Publication Society of America, 1977.

Avigal, Shosh. *Studies in Theatre*. Tel Aviv: Tel Aviv University, 2003. [In Hebrew.]

Avraham, Eli. *Behind Media Marginality: Coverage of Social Groups and Places in the Israeli Press*. Lanham, MD: Lexington Books, 2003.

Avraham, Eli, and Anat First. "I Buy American: The American Image as Reflected in Israeli Advertising." *Journal of Communication* 53, no. 2 (2003): 282–299.

Ballas, Gila. "The Artists and Their Works." In *Social Realism in the 50's*, 171–178. Haifa: Haifa Museum, 1998.

Ballas, Gila. *The Group of Ten: 1951–1960*. Ramat Gan: Museum of Israeli Art in Ramat Gan, 1992.

Ballas, Gila. *New Horizons*. Tel Aviv: Reshafim and Papyrus, Tel Aviv University, 1980. [In Hebrew.]

Ballas, Gila. "The Sixties in Israeli Art." In Zvi Zameret and Hanna Yablonka, eds., *Israel: The Second Decade*, 228. Jerusalem: Yad Ben-Zvi, 2002. [In Hebrew.]

Ballas, Gila. "Social Realism in the Test of Time." In *Social Realism in the 50's*, 155–170. Haifa: Haifa Museum, 1998.

Baruch, Miri. *Child Then, Child Now*. Bnei Brak: Sifriyat Hapoalim, 1991. [In Hebrew.]

Barzel, Hillel. *A History of Hebrew Poetry*. Vol. 5, *Avraham Shlonsky, Nathan Alterman and Lea Goldberg*. Tel Aviv: Sifriat Poalim, 2001. [In Hebrew.]

Ben Zvi, Tal. *Contemporary Palestinian Art and Biographies—Six Solo Exhibitions at the Hagar Art Gallery*. Jaffa: Hagar Association, 2006.

Bogen, Amir. "Eli Ohana: The Champion of Images." *Ynet*, May 27, 2002. [In Hebrew.]

Brinn, David. "Introducing Israeli Food to the World: One Recipe at a Time." *Israel21C*, July 22, 2007. http://www.israel21c.org/people/introducing-israeli-food-to-the-world-one-recipe-at-a-time.

Buchweitz, Nurit. *Generation Shift in Israeli Poetry: From the Modernism of Zach to the Late Modernism of Wiezeltier*. Ph.D. diss., Tel Aviv University, 2001.

Buchweitz, Nurit. "Permit to Pass." In *Generation Shifts: Meir Wiezeltier and the Poetry of the 60s*. Bnei Brak: Hakibbutz Hameuchad, 2008. [In Hebrew.]

Caspi, Dan. "Israel: From Monopoly to Open Sky." In David Ward, ed., *Television and Public Policy: Change and Continuity in an Era of Global Liberalization*, 305–320. New York: Taylor and Francis, 2008.

Caspi, Dan. "On Media and Politics: Between Enlightened Authority and Social Responsibility." *Israel Affairs* 11, no. 1 (2005): 23–38.

Caspi, Dan, Hanna Adoni, and Akiba A. Cohen. "The Red, the White and the Blue: The Russian Media in Israel." *Gazette* 64, no. 6 (2002): 537–556.

Caspi, Dan, and Yehiel Limor. *The In/Outsiders: The Media in Israel*. Cresskill, NJ: Hampton Press, 1999.

"Casspi Scores 15 in Dream NBA Debut." *Jerusalem Post*, October 29, 2009. http://www.jpost.com/Home/Article.aspx?id=158908.

Chinski, Sara. "Silence of the Fish: The Local vs. the Universal in the Israeli Discourse of Art." *Theory and Criticism* 4 (1993): 105–122. [In Hebrew.]

Cohen, Akiba A., Dafna Lamish, and Amit Schejter. *The Wonder Phone in the Land of Miracles: Mobile Telephony in Israel*. Cresskill, NJ: Hampton Press, 2008.

Cohen, Jonathan. "Global and Local Viewing Experiences in the Age of Multichannel Television: The Israeli Experience." *Communication Theory* 15, no. 4 (November 2005): 437–455.

David Reeb: Works, 1982–1994. Tel Aviv: Tel Aviv Museum of Art, 1994.

Dayan, Nissim. "From the Bourekas Back to the Ghetto Culture." *Kolnoa* 11 (1976): 54–56. [In Hebrew.]

Doron, Gideon. "The Politics of Mass Communication in Israel." *Annals of the American Academy of Political and Social Science* 555 (January 1998): 163–179.

Edelsztein, Sergio. "Israeli Art and the Media in the Last Decade." In *Blanks*. Tel Aviv: Center for Contemporary Art, 2006.

Elias, Nelly, and Leah Greenspan. "The Honey, the Bear, and the Violin: The Russian Voices of Israeli Advertising." *Journal of Advertising Research* 47, no. 1 (2007): 113–122.

Embassy of Israel, Washington, DC. "Did You Know? Israeli Cuisine." http://www.israelemb.org/education/publications/Cuisine.pdf.

Fisher, Yael, and Orit Bendas-Jacob. "Measuring Internet Usage: The Israeli Case." *International Journal of Human-Computer Studies* 64, no. 10 (2006): 984–987.

Foster, Hal. "The Return of the Real." In *The Return of the Real: Art and Theory at the End of the Century*. Cambridge, MA: MIT Press/October Books, 1996.

Furstenberg, Rochelle. "The State of the Arts: Israeli Literature." *Israel Review of Arts and Letters*, 1998. http://www.mfa.gov.il/MFA/MFAArchive/2000_2009/2000/2/Israeli%20Literature%201995–1998.

Gilbert, Andrew. "The Israeli Jazz Wave: Promised Land to Promised Land." *Jazz Times*, May 2008.

Ginton, Ellen. "'The Eyes of the Nation': Visual Art in a Country without Boundaries." In *Perspectives on Israeli Art of the Seventies: "The Eyes of the Nation."* Tel Aviv: Tel Aviv Museum of Art, 1998.

Govrin, Nurit. *Reading the Generations: Contextual Studies in Hebrew Literature*. Vol. 3. Tel Aviv: Gvanim, 2002. [In Hebrew.]

Grossberg, Daniel. "An Introduction to Modern Israeli Literature." *Midstream Journal*, May–June 2003.

Halper, Jeff, Edwin Seroussi, and Pamela Squires-Kidron. "Musica Mizrakhit: Ethnicity and Class Culture in Israel." *Popular Music* 8, no. 2 (May 1989): 131–141.

Harris, Daniel. "Idan Raichel Project Unites the Sounds of Israel." *Times Online*, August 25, 2008. http://entertainment.timesonline.co.uk/tol/arts_and_entertainment/music/article4566384.ece.

Havatzelet, Zeev. *Our Dance Together: Reflections on Israeli Dance*. Tel Aviv: Gilboa, 2003.

Holtzman, Avner. *Road-Map: Hebrew Narrative Fiction Today*. Tel Aviv: Hakibbutz Hameuchad, 2005.

Hopkins, David. "Postmodernism: Theory and Practice in the 1980s." In *After Modern Art, 1945–2000*, 197–231. Oxford: Oxford University Press, 2000.

Hunt, Peter, and Sheila G. Bannister Ray. *International Companion Encyclopedia of Children's Literature*. London: Routledge, 1996.

Institute for the Translation of Hebrew Literature. "Nathan Alterman." 2004. http://www.ithl.org.il/author_info.asp?id=13.

Institute for the Translation of Hebrew Literature. "Yehuda Amichai." October 5, 2010. http://www.ithl.org.il/authors.html.

Institute for the Translation of Hebrew Literature. "Hayyim Nachman Bialik." November 10, 2008. http://www.ithl.org.il/authors.html.

Institute for the Translation of Hebrew Literature. "Avraham Shlonsky," 2004. http://www.ithl.org.il/author_info.asp?id=250.

Institute for the Translation of Hebrew Literature. "Natan Zach." September 30, 2010. http://www.ithl.org.il/author_info.asp?id=290.

"Israel." In Don Rubin, Péter Nagy, and Philippe Rouyer, eds., *The World Encyclopedia of Contemporary Theatre*, vol. 1: *Europe*, 496–520. London: Taylor and Francis, 2001.

Israel-Travel-And–Tours.com. "Israel Food, the Unspoken Reason for Your Travel." http://www.israel-travel-and-tours.com/israel-food.html.

Katsman, Aaron. "Dining in Israel: Food That Reflects Jewish History." *Israel Newsletter.com*, April 22, 2009. http://israelnewsletter.com/2009/04/22/dining-in-israel-food-that-reflects-jewish-history/.

Katz, Elihu. "Television Comes to the People of the Book." In Irving Louis Horowitz, ed., *The Use and Abuse of Social Science*, 249–271. New Brunswick, NJ: Transaction Books, 1971.

Katz, Yaron. "The 'Other Media': Alternative Communications in Israel." *International Journal of Cultural Studies* 10, no. 3 (2007): 383–400.

Katz, Yaron. "Protecting Local Culture in a Global Environment: The Case of Israel's Broadcast Media." *International Journal of Communication* 3 (2009): 332–350.

Katz-Freiman, Tali. "Fata Morgana: The Magic Lantern of Consciousness." In *Fata Morgana: Illusion and Deception in Contemporary Art*, 166–176. Haifa: Haifa Museum of Art, 2006.

Kedem, Moshe. "The Evolution of Dance in Israel." In *People and Acts in Israel: The Anniversary Book*. Kfar Saba: Miksam, 1998. [In Hebrew.]

Korat, Yael. "Indigenization of Modernity and Inventiveness of Tradition: The Case of Israeli Hip-Hop." *Journal of Popular Music Studies* 19, no. 4 (2007): 359–385.

Koren, Haim. "The Arab Citizens of the State of Israel: The Arab Media Perspective." *Israel Affairs* 9, nos. 1–2 (Autumn–Winter 2003): 212–226.

Kristeva, Julia. *Powers of Horror*. New York: Columbia University Press, 1982.

Lachman, Dan. "The History of the Israeli Theatre." http://www.e-mago.co.il. [In Hebrew.]

Lehmann, David, and Batia Siebzehner. "Holy Pirates: Media, Ethnicity, and Religious Renewal in Israel." In Birgit Meyer and Annelies Moors, eds., *Religion, Media, and the Public Sphere*, 91–114. Bloomington: Indiana University Press, 2006.

Lehman-Wilzig, Sam, and Amit Schejter. "Israel." In Yahya R. Kamalipour and Hamid Mowlana, eds., *Mass Media in the Middle East*, 109–125. Westport, CT: Greenwood Press, 1994.

Leider, Philip. "Israel's 'Guernica.'" *Art in America* 91, no. 5 (May 2003): 60–63.

Lemish, Dafna, and Akiba A. Cohen. "On the Gendered Nature of Mobile Phone Culture in Israel." *Sex Roles* 52, nos. 7–8 (2005): 511–521.

Levi, Shimon, and Corina Shoef. *The Israeli Theatre Canon: One Hundred and One Shows*. Tel Aviv: HaKibbutz HaMeuhad, 2002. [In Hebrew.]

Levi-Faur, David. "The Dynamics of the Liberalization of the Israeli Telecommunications: Policy Emulation and Policy Innovations Outside the Joint-Decision Trap." In Eliassen Kjell and Marit Sajovaag, eds., *European Telecommunications Liberalization*, 175–192. London: Routledge, 1999.

Levitt, Avraham. "Israeli Art on Its Way to Somewhere Else." *Azure* 3 (Winter 1998). http://www.jafi .org.il/JewishAgency/English/Jewish+Education/Educational+Resources/More+Educational+ Resources/Azure/3/3-levitt.html.htm.

Lewis, Bernard. *The Jews of Islam*. Princeton, NJ: Princeton University Press, 1984.

Liebes, Tamar. "Acoustic Space: The Role of Radio in Israeli Collective History." *Jewish History* 20, no. 1 (March 2006): 69–90.

Liebes, Tamar. "Performing a Dream and Its Dissolution: A Social History of Broadcasting in Israel." In James Curran and Myung-Jin Park, eds., *De-Westernizing Media Studies*, 305–324. London: Routledge, 2000.

Limor, Yehiel. "Israel and the New Media." In Philip Seib, ed., *New Media and the New Middle East*, 157–169. New York: Palgrave, 2007.

Limor, Yehiel, and Chanan Naveh. *Pirate Radio in Israel*. Haifa: Pardes, 2008. [In Hebrew.]

Limor, Yehiel, and Hillel Nossek. "The Military and the Media in the Twenty-First Century: Towards a New Model of Relations." *Israel Affairs* 12, no. 3 (2006): 484–510.

Lubin, Orly. *Women Reading Women*. Haifa: University of Haifa Press and Zemora Bitan, 2003. [In Hebrew.]

Mann, Izi. *Voice of Israel from Jerusalem*. Jerusalem: IBA and Printive, 2008. [In Hebrew.]

Mann, Rafi, and Tzipi Gon-Gross. *Galei Zahal on the Scene*. Tel Aviv: Yediot Ahronot, 2002. [In Hebrew.]

Margolin, Yaron. "The History of Dance in Israel." Israel Dance Company, http://www.israeldance.co.il. [In Hebrew.]

Mendelsohn, Amitai. "The End of Days and New Beginnings—Reflections on Art in Israel, 1998–2007." In *Real Time, Art in Israel, 1998–2008*. Jerusalem: Israel Museum of Art, 2008.

Ministry of Foreign Affairs, State of Israel. "Culture: Dance." November 28, 2010. http://www.mfa.gov.il/ MFA/Facts+About+Israel/Culture/CULTURE-+Dance.htm.

Ministry of Foreign Affairs, State of Israel. "Culture: Literature." November 28, 2010. http://www.mfa
.gov.il/MFA/Facts+About+Israel/Culture/CULTURE-+Literature.htm.

Ministry of Foreign Affairs, State of Israel. "Culture: Music." November 28, 2010. http://www.mfa.gov.il/
MFA/Facts+About+Israel/Culture/CULTURE-+Music.htm.

Ministry of Foreign Affairs, State of Israel. "Culture: Theater and Entertainment." November 28, 2010. http://
www.mfa.gov.il/MFA/Facts+About+Israel/Culture/CULTURE-+Theater+and+Entertainment
.htm.

Moshe, Mira. "Right-Wing Pirate Radio Broadcasting in Israel: The Political Discourse about Channel 7,
1993–2003." *Journal of Radio Studies* 14, no. 1 (2007): 67–83.

Na'aman, Michal. "Artist-Society-Artist." In *Art about Society in Israel, 1948–1978*. Tel Aviv: Tel Aviv
Museum of Art, 1978.

Ne'eman, Judd. "The Empty Tomb in the Postmodern Pyramid: Israeli Cinema in the 1980s and 1990s."
In Charles Berlin, ed., *Documenting Israel*, 117–148. Cambridge, MA: Harvard College Library,
1995.

Ne'eman, Judd. "The Modernists: Genealogy of the New Sensibility." In Nurit Gertz, Orly Lubin, and
Judd Ne'eman, eds., *Fictive Looks—On Israeli Cinema*. Tel Aviv: Open University Press, 1998. [In
Hebrew.]

Ne'eman, Judd. "Zero Degree Cinema." *Kolnoa* 5 (1979): 20–23. [In Hebrew.]

Nossek, Hillel, and Hanna Adoni. "The Social Implications of Cable Television: Restructuring Connections with Self and Social Groups." *International Journal of Public Opinion Research* 8, no. 1 (1996):
51–69.

Ofek, Avraham. "Wall Painting: The Way to Folk Painting." *Massa*, August 21, 1952.

Ofrat, Gideon. "The Sixties: The Rise of External Influences: 10+." In *The Story of Art in Israel: From the
Days of Bezalel in 1906 to the Present*. Tel Aviv: Modan, 1980. [In Hebrew.]

Open Source Center. *Israel—Hebrew- and English-Language Media Guide*, September 16, 2008. Media
Aid, http://www.fas.org/irp/dni/osc/israelmedia.pdf.

Or, Amir. "Hebrew Poetry in the New Millennium." *Eurozine*, November 2, 1999. http://www.eurozine
.com/articles/1999–11–02-or-en.html.

Or, Miriam. "Landscape." In Mordechai Omer, ed., *90 Years of Israeli Art: A Selection from the Joseph
Hackmey–Israel Phoenix Collection*, 272. Tel Aviv: Tel Aviv Museum of Art, 1998.

Oryan, Dan. "Theatre and Society: The Israeli Theater." In *The Israeli Theater: Democratization Processes
in the Israeli Society*, 83–89. Tel Aviv: The Open University, 1999. [In Hebrew.]

Perri, Tal. *It Is Not the Same Valley*, 18–19. Tel Aviv: Yediot Ahronot, May 2005. [In Hebrew.]

Piterberg, Gabriel. "The Nation and Its Raconteurs: Orientalism and Nationalist Historiography." *Theory and Criticism* 6 (1995): 81–104. [In Hebrew.]

Popovsky, Michal. "The Country." *Studio* 138 (2002): 61–63. [In Hebrew.]

Rabina, Doron. "Killing Time." In *Eventually We'll Die—Young Art in Israel of the Nineties*. Herzliya:
Herzliya Museum of Contemporary Art, 2008.

Regev, Motti. "Ethno-National Pop-Rock Music: Aesthetic Cosmopolitanism Made from Within." *Cultural Sociology* 1 (2007): 317.

Regev, Motti. "Israeli Rock, or a Study in the Politics of 'Local Authenticity.'" *Popular Music* 11, no. 1
(January 1992): 1–14.

Regev, Motti. "To Have a Culture of Our Own: On Israeliness and Its Variant." *Ethnic and Racial Studies*
23, no. 2 (March 2000): 223–247.

Regev, Motti, and Edwin Seroussi. *Popular Music and National Culture in Israel*. Berkeley: University of
California Press, 2004.

Rogov, Daniel. "The International Israeli Table," February 15, 2004. Israel Ministry of Foreign Affairs,
http://www.mfa.gov.il/MFA/Facts+About+Israel/Israeli+Cuisine/The%20International%20
Israeli%20Table.

Rogov, Daniel. "Israel's Wine Industry." Jewish Virtual Library, http://www.jewishvirtuallibrary.org/jsource/Food/wine3.html.

Rovner, Michal. *Against Order? Against Disorder?* Exhibition catalogue of the Israeli Pavilion, curated by Modechai Omer, at the Venice Biennale, 2003.

Salhuv, Shva. "Deserted Still-Life, 1955." In *"Hebrew Work"—The Disregarded Gaze in the Canon of Israeli Art.* Ein Harod: Museum of Art, 1998.

Saperstein, Moshe. "The Development of Israel Rock." *Jerusalem Post*, May 21, 1990.

Saradas-Trutino, Sarit. "Israel Becomes Sushi Mecca." *Ynet*, January 28, 2008. http://www.ynetnews.com/articles/0,7340,L-3499855,00.html.

Schejter, Amit. "The Evolution of Cable Regulatory Policies and Their Impact: A Comparison of South Korea and Israel." *Journal of Media Economics* 20, no. 1 (2007): 1–28.

Schejter, Amit, and Akiva A. Cohen. "Israel: Chutzpah and Chatter in the Holy Land." In James E. Katz and Mark A. Aakhus, eds., *Perpetual Contact: Mobile Communication, Private Talk, Public Performance*, 30–41. Cambridge: Cambridge University Press, 2002.

Schorr, Renen. "Sabra Reflection in the Films of Uri Zohar." *Kolnoa*, nos. 15–16 (1978): 100–108. [In Hebrew.]

Shaked, Asaf. "Eli Ohana: 'The King.'" Beitar-Jerusalem.net, http://beitar-jerusalem.net/article_655.

Shaked, Gershon. *Hebrew Narrative Fiction: 1880–1980.* Jerusalem: Keter, 1998. [In Hebrew.]

Shaked, Gershon. *Modern Hebrew Fiction.* Bloomington: Indiana University Press, 2000.

Shechori, Ran. "Avigdor Stematsky, Gordon Gallery." *Ha'aretz*, May 15, 1970.

Sheffi, Smadar. "New-Horizons: Ten Years of Art." In Zvi Zameret and Yablonka Hanna, eds., *Israel: The First Decade*, 285–286. Jerusalem: Yad Ben-Zvi Press, 1997. [In Hebrew.]

Shohat, Ella. *Forbidden Reminiscences.* Tel Aviv: Kedem, 2001. [In Hebrew.]

Shohat, Ella. *Israeli Cinema—East/West and the Politics of Representation.* Austin: University of Texas Press, 1989.

Strategy Analytics. "US Ranks 20th in Global Broadband Household Penetration," June 18, 2009. http://www.strategyanalytics.com/default.aspx?mod=PressReleaseViewer&ao=4748.

Swoden, Dora. "The State of the Arts: Israeli Dance." *Israeli Dance, 1995–1998.* July 23, 2000. http://www.mfa.gov.il/MFA/MFAArchive/2000_2009/2000/7/Israeli%20Dance%201995–1998.

Tal, Rami. "The Israeli Press." *Ariel: The Israel Review of Arts and Letters*, nos. 99–100 (July 1995).

Tammuz, Benjamin, Dorith LeVité, and Gideon Ofrat, eds. *The Story of Art in Israel: From the Days of Bezalel in 1906 to the Present.* Ramat Gan: Modan, 1980. [In Hebrew.]

Te'eni-Harari, Tali, Shlomo Lampert, and Sam Lehman-Wilzig. "Information Processing of Advertising among Children: The Elaboration Likelihood Model as Applied to Youth." *Journal of Advertising Research* 47, no. 3 (2007): 326–340.

Teleseker/TN-TIM Survey, February 2008.

Tenenbaum, Ilana. "Eleven Notes on Political Art in the 1990's." In *Social Realism in the 50's*, 142–148. Haifa: Haifa Museum, 1998.

Tenenbaum, Ilana. "The Israeli Context: Between the Private and the National Body." In *Video Zero: Live Acts Performing the Body.* Videostoria series. Haifa: Haifa Museum, 1998.

"10+": The Ten-Plus Group, Myth and Reality. Tel Aviv: Tel Aviv Museum of Art, 2008. [In Hebrew.]

Toledano, Gila. *A Story of a Company: Sara Levi-Tanai and Inbal Dance Theatre.* Tel Aviv: Resling, 2005. [In Hebrew.]

Torstrick, Rebecca L. "Culture and Customs of Israel." In *Culture and Customs of the Middle East.* Westport, CT: Greenwood Press, 2004.

Trajtenberg, Graciela. *Between Nationalism and Art: The Establishment of the Sphere of Israeli Art during the Early Settlement Period and the Early Years of the State.* Jerusalem: Magnes Press of the Hebrew University of Jerusalem, 2005.

Vinitzky-Seroussi, Vered. "The Decade of Indifference." In *Real Time: Art in Israel, 1998–2008*. Jerusalem: Israel Museum of Art, 2008.

Weimann, Gabriel. "Cable Comes to the Holy Land: The Impact of Cable TV on Israeli Viewers." *Journal of Broadcasting and Electronic Media* 40, no. 2 (Spring 1996): 243–257.

Weimann, Gabriel. "Zapping in the Holy Land: Coping with Multi-Channel TV in Israel." *Journal of Communication* 45, no. 1 (Winter 1995): 96–102.

Weitz, Shosh. "Theatre and Society in Israel." *Skira Hodshit* 7 (1986): 1–13.

Ya'ar, Ephraim, and Ze'ev Shavit, eds. *Trends in Israeli Society*. Tel Aviv: The Open University, 2003. [In Hebrew.]

Zalmona, Yigal. "New Horizons: The Impresario Experience." *Kav 1* (June 1980): 79–82. [In Hebrew.]

Zalmona, Yigal. "To the East?" In *Kadima—The East in Israeli Art*. Jerusalem: Israel Museum, 1998.

Zimmerman, Moshe. *Hole in the Camera: Gazes of Israeli Cinema*. Tel Aviv: Resling, 2003. [In Hebrew.]

Zimmerman, Moshe. *Signs of Movies: History of Israeli Cinema in the Years 1896–1948*. Tel Aviv: Tel Aviv University Press, 2001. [In Hebrew.]

For Further Reading: Literary Works

Oz, Amos. *My Michael*. Orlando, FL: Mariner Books, 2005.

Oz, Amos. *A Tale of Love and Darkness*. Orlando, FL: Harvest Books, 2005.

Shalev, Meir. *The Blue Mountain*. Edinburgh, UK: Canongate, 2010.

Yehoshua, A. B. *Mr. Mani*. Orlando, FL: Mariner Books, 1993.

Chronology of Israel

1860	The first Jewish communities are established outside the walls of Jerusalem.
1878	The first Zionist settlement is established, at Petach Tikva.
1881–1900	First Aliya. Russian pogroms trigger the first wave of immigration to Israel: 30,000–32,000 Jews come in this *aliya*, but 15,000 of them go on to other destinations.
1897	Theodor Herzl organizes the first Zionist Congress in Basel, Switzerland. Prior to the congress, such groups as Hovevei Zion (Lovers of Zion) initiated Zionist activities, but with no central direction or political program. The Basel congress is the foundation of a mass Zionist movement.
1903–1914	Second Aliya. The Kishinev Pogrom and the Russian pogroms of 1905 trigger the Second Aliya. This immigration wave of about 40,000 Jews is organized by the Zionist movement and is characterized by the immigration of workers and by the establishment of communal settlements (*kibbutzim*). The Second Aliya lasts until World War I. This group of immigrants plays a central role in establishing the founding institutions of the State of Israel.
1909	The city of Tel Aviv is established as the first modern Jewish city in the world.
1910	The first *kibbutz*, Degania, is established near the Sea of Galilee.
1912	The Technion, Israel's institute of technology, is founded.
November 2, 1917	Britain issues the Balfour Declaration, promising a "National Home" for the Jews in Palestine.
1919–1923	Third Aliya. This ideological aliya brings about 35,000 Zionist pioneers to Israel, mainly from the area of the former Russian Empire.
1921	The first two *moshavim* are established: Nahalal and Kfar Yehezkel.
1923	The British Mandate for Palestine begins.
1924–1929	Fourth Aliya. The fourth wave of immigrants mainly consists of Jews from Poland and central Europe, motivated to leave partly by the failing European economy.
1933	The modern port of Haifa is established under British auspices. It is now the principal port and industrial center of Israel.

1939	A British White Paper severely restricts Jewish immigration to Israel.
May 9, 1942	Zionist leaders, headed by Chaim Weizmann and David Ben-Gurion, convene at the Biltmore Hotel in New York to declare their postwar program. In the so-called Biltmore Program they demand an end to the British Mandate—that is, to British rule over Palestine—and, in addition, Jewish control over immigration with the aim of founding a Jewish state.
July 22, 1946	Members of the United Resistance Movement—made up of the Jewish underground movements Haganah, Irgun, and Lehi—bomb the King David Hotel in Jerusalem, the central office of the British Mandatory government.
November 29, 1947	The United Nations General Assembly passes Resolution 181 to partition the Palestine Mandate, the region under British Mandatory government, into Jewish and Arab states, with Jerusalem to be an international city.
May 15, 1948	The British Mandate for Palestine officially ends, Israel's independence, declared the previous day, is implemented, and the British depart. Egypt, Syria, Iraq, Lebanon, Jordan, and Saudi Arabia declare war on Israel.
May 15, 1948– January 7, 1949	War of Independence.
May 1948– November 1949	More Jews arrive: 340,000, a number equaling almost half of the existing citizenry. The arrivals include about 270,000 Holocaust survivors and 50,000 Yemeni Jews.
March 11, 1949	Israel is admitted to the United Nations as a member state.
April 3, 1949	Israel and the Arab states agree to an armistice. Israel gains about 50 percent more territory than it was originally allotted in the UN Partition Plan.
Early 1950s	About 113,000 Jews arrive from Iraq, and large parts of the Jewish communities of Romania, Syria, Libya, Afghanistan, and Egypt arrive.
January 1951	The Knesset (Israel's parliament) approves negotiations with Germany for reparations for Jewish property seized, forced labor, imprisonment in concentration camps, and killings during the period of Nazi rule. The negotiations lead to a treaty, ratified in March 1953.
1952	Israel's Atomic Energy Agency is founded. In 1953 processes for extracting uranium from the Negev desert and producing heavy water are developed. In the late 1950s, Israel receives help from France in designing and building a nuclear reactor in the southern city of Dimona.
October 29, 1956	Suez War. In retaliation for Egypt-backed border raids by Palestinian gunmen and the closure of the Straits of Tiran (connecting the Gulf of Aqaba to the Red Sea) and the Suez Canal to Israeli shipping, Israel invades Egypt's Sinai Peninsula and occupies it for several months. After this Suez campaign the straits and the canal are opened again to Israeli shipping until 1967.
1958	Another wave of immigration begins from North Africa, mainly Morocco, bringing 160,000 people to Israel in a very short span of time.
May 23, 1960	The capture of the Nazi war criminal Adolf Eichmann is announced. He is convicted and hanged on May 31, 1962.

1964	Haifa University is founded in the new port city.
1964	Construction of the National Water Carrier is completed. A huge conduit, traversing two-thirds of the country, the National Water Carrier transports 845 trillion gallons (320 million cubic meters) of water per year.
May 1964	The Palestine Liberation Organization (PLO) is founded with the aim of destroying Israel. The Palestinian National Charter of 1968 officially calls for liquidation of Israel.
May 1967	President Gamal Abdel Nasser of Egypt closes the Straits of Tiran to Israeli shipping and dismisses the UN peacekeeping force. Negotiations to reopen the straits fail.
June 5–10, 1967	Six-Day War. Israel defeats Egypt, occupies the Sinai Peninsula and the Gaza Strip, and takes the West Bank and east Jerusalem from Jordan and the Golan Heights from Syria.
June 19, 1967	The Israeli cabinet votes to approve offering Syria and Egypt a trade of territories conquered in the war in return for full peace.
October 6–25, 1973	Yom Kippur War. Egypt and Syria launch a surprise attack on Israel on Yom Kippur, the Jewish Day of Atonement. After the Arabs make initial gains, Israel pushes back the Syrians and threatens Damascus. Israeli forces cross the Suez Canal, cutting off Egypt's Third Army. Israeli casualties are high. Despite the outcome, Syria and Egypt celebrate the anniversary of the war as a victory.
1975	Beta Israel aliya. Israel officially recognizes Ethiopian Jews (Beta Israel), and groups of them begin to come to Israel in the 1980s.
May 17, 1977	Election upset. The Labor Party loses power for the first time in the election of 1977, and a government led by the Likud Party takes office.
November 1977	Egyptian President Anwar al-Sadat addresses the Knesset.
September 1978	Egyptian President Sadat and Israeli Prime Minister Menahem Begin reach an agreement: Israel will return the Sinai Peninsula to Egypt in exchange for full peace.
March 26, 1979	Egypt and Israel sign a peace treaty.
June 7, 1981	Israel destroys an Iraqi nuclear reactor at Osirak to prevent Iraq from developing nuclear weapons.
October 6, 1981	Egyptian President Sadat is assassinated.
June 6, 1982	First Lebanon War. Israel invades Lebanon to expel the PLO forces there. The offensive is called Operation Peace for Galilee.
Second half of 1983	Israel has a severe monetary crisis characterized by soaring inflation.
1987–1991	First Intifada. There is a Palestinian uprising against the Israeli presence on the West Bank and in the Gaza Strip.
January 17, 1991	Iraq begins firing rockets at Israel shortly after a U.S.-led coalition attacks Iraqi forces in Kuwait.

1991	Aliya from the former Soviet Union. With the collapse of the Soviet Union, radical Arab states lose their superpower sponsor, and post-Soviet governments develop relations with Israel. Large numbers of Jews are able to leave the territory of the former Soviet Union. In the 1990s about 1.1 million people immigrate to Israel, increasing Israel's population by approximately 15 percent.
September 13, 1993	Oslo Accords. Israel and the PLO sign the Declaration of Principles (Oslo Accords): this is the beginning of a peace process that ultimately failed in 2000.
July 1, 1994	The Palestinian Authority (PA) begins to rule the Gaza Strip and Jericho.
October 26, 1994	Israel and Jordan sign a peace treaty.
September 28, 1995	Israel and the PLO sign the Interim Agreement.
November 4, 1995	Prime Minister Yitzhak Rabin is assassinated. Shimon Peres succeeds him.
September 1996	The PA initiates rioting over Israel's opening of a tunnel near the Temple Mount—the peak of violence during the peace process.
January 18, 1997	Hebron Accords. Israel and Palestinians agree that Israel will turn over 80 percent of Hebron—a part Jewish, part Palestinian village in the West Bank—to the Palestinian Authority.
October 1998	Wye River Accord. Israel agrees to turn over more West Bank territory and to release Palestinian prisoners if the Palestinian Authority stops inciting anti-Israel activities and terrorism.
March 2000	Israeli-Syrian peace negotiations falter after Syrian President Hafez al-Assad rejects the Israeli offer in Geneva.
July 2000	Camp David summit. A summit meeting at Camp David, Maryland, fails when Palestinian leader Yasir Arafat rejects all Israeli offers for a framework for further talks, including the proposal of an independent Palestinian state with its capital in east Jerusalem.
2000–2005	Second Intifada. Palestinians launch a second uprising on September 28. During the next several years there are many terrorist attacks within Israel.
March–April 2002	Operation Defensive Shield. Israel carries out Operation Defensive Shield in the West Bank to root out Palestinian terrorist infrastructures.
June 2002	Construction of a security fence to protect Israel from terrorist attacks from the West Bank begins.
March 28, 2002	Arab Peace initiative. Saudi Crown Prince Abdallah proposes a peace plan, which is watered down in an Arab summit.
December 18, 2003	Prime Minister Ariel Sharon presents the idea of unilateral Israeli withdrawal from the Gaza Strip and parts of the West Bank in a speech at the Herzliya Conference, an international conference of world leaders held annually at an Israeli institute to discuss global strategies.

October 25, 2004	Disengagement. The Knesset approves the Disengagement Plan for unilateral Israeli withdrawal from the Gaza Strip and part of the West Bank and a law to compensate displaced Jewish settlers. The withdrawal takes place in August 2005.
November 11, 2004	Yasir Arafat, leader of the Palestinian Authority, the PLO, and Fatah (a nationalist Palestinian group), dies.
January 9, 2005	Palestinians elect Mahmoud Abbas to head the Palestinian Authority.
November 20, 2005	Prime Minister Sharon announces that he is leaving the Likud Party to start his own party, Kadima.
December 18, 2005	Sharon suffers a stroke. A second stroke on January 4, 2006, leaves him in a coma. Minister of Finance Ehud Olmert takes over as acting prime minister.
January 26, 2006	Hamas (the Islamic Resistance Movement) wins the elections to the Palestinian Legislative Council. It later agrees to a coalition government with Fatah in negotiations held in Doha, Qatar.
July 12, 2006	Second Lebanon War. Hizballah terrorists cross into Israel, killing three soldiers and capturing two. Hizballah begins rocket attacks on northern Israel. Israel retaliates with bombing and, later, a ground offensive.
August 14, 2006	UN Security Council Resolution 1701 provides for a ceasefire with an enlarged UN force to keep Hizballah from resuming armed control over southern Lebanon.
June 2007	Hamas ousts Fatah from the Gaza Strip in an unprovoked attack and thereafter governs the area.
November 26–28, 2007	Annapolis summit. The United States convenes a summit meeting with Israeli and PA leaders at Annapolis, Maryland.
February 12, 2008	A leading Hizballah activist, Imad Mughniyah, is killed by car bomb in Damascus.
December 27, 2008–January 18, 2009	Operation Cast Lead. Israel undertakes Operation Cast Lead, a military operation in the Gaza Strip to stop Hamas rocket attacks.
April 2009	An election brings Benjamin Netanyahu back as prime minister.
November 2009	The Netanyahu government agrees to a ten-month moratorium on construction in Jewish settlements in the West Bank in an attempt to restart talks with the Palestinian government. The Palestinian Authority refuses to negotiate.
May 2010	A flotilla of small ships organized by Hamas supporters tries to break the Israeli trade embargo on the Gaza Strip. Nine Turkish participants are killed after they attack Israeli soldiers. Under international pressure, Israel drastically reduces the extent of the sanctions against the Hamas-governed Strip.
January 2011	The Labor Party splits. Its leader, Ehud Barak, forms a new party called Azmaut.

Glossary

Ahdut HaAvoda—Labor Zionist party formed in the pre-state years as a faction of Mapai. It ran independently in the 1955, 1969, and 1961 elections and became Mapai's favored coalition partner, running on a joint list with Mapai in 1965. It eventually joined with Mapai and Rafi to form the Labor Party in 1968.

Aliya—Literally, "ascension"; Jewish immigration to Israel. *See also* First Aliya; Second Aliya; Third Aliya.

Arab Democratic Party—The first solely Arab party to gain representation in the Knesset, which it did in 1988. It became part of the United Arab List in 1996.

Armistice agreements—Bilateral ceasefire agreements between Israel and Egypt, Syria, Lebanon, and Jordan negotiated in 1949 that ended the fighting but not the state of war between them.

Ashkenazic—Refers to Jews of European origin as well as the form of Jewish religious practice in most of Europe. The name originates from the Jewish word in the Middle Ages for areas of what later became Germany.

Balad (National Democratic Alliance)—Nationalist Arab political party established in 1996 that calls for the creation of a binational state in Israel. Attempts have twice been made and overturned by Israel's Supreme Court (2003 and 2009) to ban the party for supporting terrorist organizations.

Balfour Declaration—The 1917 declaration by Great Britain proclaiming support for the establishment of a Jewish homeland in Palestine.

Basic Laws—Laws passed by the Knesset that have superior authority, on the level of a constitution.

Bedouin—Semi-nomadic Arabs organized on a tribal basis who in Israel live primarily in the Negev and Galilee.

Beta Israel—The name by which Ethiopian Jewish immigrants to Israel refer to their community.

Bourekas films—Films popular in the 1960s and 1970s that dealt with ethnic tensions between Mizrahi and Ashkenazic Jews.

Camp David Accords—The 1978 agreement between Israel and Egypt in which Israel agreed to return the Sinai Peninsula to Egypt in exchange for full peace. This led to the 1979 Egypt-Israel peace treaty.

Camp David summit—Negotiations in July 2000 between Israel and the Palestinian Authority, with the United States hosting, during which Arafat rejected Israel's offer for opening comprehensive peace negotiations.

Clinton plan—The December 2000 proposal accepted by Israel and rejected by the Palestinians that would have established a Palestinian state in 95 percent of the West Bank, made east Jerusalem the Palestinian capital, ended the conflict between Israel and the Palestinian Authority, and resettled all Palestinian refugees in a Palestinian state.

Dati (plural: Datim)—Literally, "religious"; refers to those Jews who couple full religious observance with the integration of modern ideas; generally called Modern Orthodox in the West.

Dayan (plural: dayanim)—Religious judge who sits on a rabbinical court.

Democratic Movement for Change—Political party that called for reform and won fifteen seats in the 1977 election, costing the Labor Party the victory. It disappeared from the political scene in subsequent elections.

Diaspora—Literally, "dispersion"; refers to Jewish communities outside the Land of Israel. It is, however, a Greek word. Traditionally, Jews referred their dispersion from their historical homeland with the word *galut* (exile), signifying the centrality of the Land of Israel in their lives and religion.

Disengagement—The unilateral Israeli withdrawal from the Gaza Strip and part of the northern West Bank in August 2005.

East Jerusalem—The section of Jerusalem captured by the Jordanian army in 1948. The army expelled the Jewish residents and annexed the section. Israel captured it in 1967 and subsequently annexed it to reunify that part of the city. The Palestinian Authority seeks to make it the future capital of a Palestinian state.

Economic Stabilization Plan—A 1985 program dealing with the economic recession of the time. It led to privatization and the beginning of the end for Israel's socialist era.

Fatah—Palestinian nationalist group established in 1959 to destroy Israel and replace it with a Palestinian Arab state. Fatah took control of the PLO in 1969. It formed the government of the Palestinian Authority. Though defeated by Hamas in the 2006 elections, it continued to run the Palestinian Authority and rule the West Bank after Hamas seized power in the Gaza Strip.

First Aliya—The first wave of Jewish immigration from Eastern Europe to the Ottoman-ruled Land of Israel during the last two decades of the nineteenth century (1881–1900): 30,000–32,000 Jews immigrated.

Gaza Strip—A strip of land 25 miles (40 kilometers) long by the Mediterranean Sea bordering Egypt on the south. It is the part of the Palestine Mandate captured by Egypt in 1948, by Israel in 1956–1957, and again by Israel in 1967. Israel unilaterally withdrew from the territory in 2005, turning it over to the Palestinian Authority. Hamas seized it in 2007.

Golan Heights— Mountainous region on Israel's northeast border captured from Syria in 1967 and annexed to Israel in 1981. Israel has offered citizenship to the region's Druze residents. Syria demands its return.

Greater Israel—A nationalist concept of the State of Israel during the 1970s and 1980s that included the West Bank and the Gaza Strip in its territory, either annexed or permanently controlled.

Gush Emunim—A religious political movement whose members believed that settlement in Greater Israel would bring about religious redemption. It was officially formed in 1974, but it had largely faded away as an organized movement by the late 1980s.

Ha'aretz—Israel's left-leaning newspaper.

Hadash—An Arab Communist party founded in 1977 that replaced the Rakah Party.

Hamas—The Islamic Resistance Movement, an Islamist Palestinian group founded in 1988 that now rules the Gaza Strip. It is linked to the international Muslim Brotherhood, which rejects Israel's existence and seeks to establish an Islamist state stretching from the Jordan River (the eastern border of Israel) to the Mediterranean Sea—that is, encompassing the territory of Israel. Hamas is responsible for scores of terrorist attacks and for launching missiles into Israel from the Gaza Strip, which it seized after an election victory in 2006.

Haredi (plural: Haredim)—Literally, "somone in awe or fear of the power of the divine"; refers to Jews who adhere strictly to religious law; traditional Orthodox Jews, often translated into English with the misleading phrase "ultra-Orthodox."

Hasid (plural: Hasidim)—Jew who focuses on a charismatic, hereditary rabbi and follows a partly mystical approach to Judaism. One of the Haredim.

Herut—A conservative nationalist political party formed in 1948 that grew out of Revisionist Zionism and the Revisionist Zionist militia, the Irgun. Herut led the opposition from 1948 to 1977, when it won its first election. It merged into the Likud in 1988.

Histadrut—Israel's trade union federation, established in 1920. It owned many enterprises and institutions.

Hizballah—Iranian-financed and Syrian-backed organization based in Lebanon that is committed to a Shi'a Islamist Lebanon and Israel's destruction.

Intifada—Palestinian uprising against Israel. The first was from 1987 to 1991; the second, from 2000 to 2005.

Islamic Jihad—A Palestinian Islamist organization backed by Iran and Syria. Formed in the 1970s and committed to the destruction of Israel, it has carried out many terrorist attacks.

Israel Defense Forces (IDF)—Israel's "people's army." Conscription is mandatory with the exception of Haredim and Arabs. The IDF has defended Israel in conventional and nonconventional warfare.

Jewish Home (HaBayit HaYehudi)—A religious Zionist right-wing political party formed in 2008 from a merger of the National Religious Party and Tkuma, a right-wing party. It won three seats in the Knesset in the 2009 elections.

Judea and Samaria—The historical Jewish name for the area now known as the West Bank.

Kach—Extremist right-wing political party founded by Meir Kahane in the 1980s that advocated the deportation of Israel's Arabs. It was banned from participating in elections in 1988.

Kadima—Centrist party founded by Ariel Sharon in 2005. It became the first party other than Labor or Likud to form a government.

Kashrut—Jewish dietary laws.

Khartoum Resolution—The 1967 declaration by Arab states in which they agreed not to make peace with, recognize, or negotiate with Israel.

Kibbutz (plural: kibbutzim)—Communal farm or agricultural community.

Kibbutz galuyot—Literally, "ingathering of the exiles"; the idea that Jews can immigrate to Israel and be integrated into a nation.

Kinneret—Hebrew name for the Sea of Galilee, located in Israel's northeast.

Kippa (plural: kippot)—Also called yarmulke. Skullcap worn by religious Jewish men—the size and color are identifiers of religious orientation.

Knesset—Israel's legislative body; parliament.

Labor—Liberal-social-democratic political party with socialist roots that dominated Israeli politics from the 1930s until 1977. It has often led the government or been in government coalitions.

Labor Zionism—Ideology that espouses the creation of a Jewish state through socialist ideals; the dominant Zionist ideology from the 1930s to 1977.

Land Day—Annual commemoration by Arab Israelis of the events of March 30, 1976, when Arab Israeli protests against land expropriation turned violent, and six people were killed.

Law of return—Israeli law that is the basis for Israel's immigration policy. According to the current law, which has been changed several times, any Jewish person (later defined as someone born of a Jewish mother or someone who has converted to Judaism and who is not a member of another religion) who does not endanger the public has the right to immigrate to Israel. Article 4A of the law lists as eligible for immigration the "child and a grandchild of a Jew, the spouse of a Jew, the spouse of a child of a Jew and the spouse of a grandchild of a Jew, except for a person who has been a Jew and has voluntarily changed his religion."

Likud—Conservative political party formed from Herut and three other small groups in 1973 that first gained control of the government in 1977 and has held control sporadically since then.

Ma'abara (plural: ma'abarot)—Temporary residential camps set up for immigrants until permanent living arrangements are made. The term usually refers to those established for Jews arriving from Middle Eastern countries in the 1950s and early 1960s.

Ma'ariv—Israel's second-largest daily newspaper.

Madrid Conference—International peace conference held in 1991 including Israeli, Syrian, Lebanese, and Jordanian-Palestinian delegations.

Magav—Border Police, the military branch of the police force. The Magav deals with counterterrorism and riot control.

Mapai—The Workers' Party of the Land of Israel, the Zionist socialist political party founded in 1930. Dominant from the Yishuv period until 1977, it merged with Ahdut HaAvoda and Rafi to form the Labor Party in 1968.

Mapam—United Workers' Party, the Marxist-Zionist party of Labor Zionism formed in 1948. Initially the second-largest party in the Knesset, its popularity continually declined, and it merged with Shinui and Ratz in 1992 to form the Meretz Party.

Meimad—A liberal religious party that is close to the Labor Party on security issues.

Meretz—A left-wing Zionist political party that advocates separation of religion and state along with concessions to the Palestinians. Formed in 1992 from the Ratz, Shinui, and Mapam parties, it declined in popularity with the failure of the peace process, dropping from a high of twelve seats in the Knesset in 1992 to a low of three by 2009.

Mizrahi (plural: Mizrahim)—Literally, "Eastern"; refers to Jews and Jewish customs and culture of Middle Eastern and North African origin.

Moshav (plural: moshavim)—Cooperative agricultural community.

Mossad—The organization responsible for foreign intelligence gathering, comparable to the U.S. Central Intelligence Agency (CIA).

National Religious Party (NRP, Mafdal)—A Modern Orthodox (Dati), Zionist political party established in 1956 that served in every government coalition until 1992. Its popularity began declining in the 1980s, and it ceased to exist as an independent entity in 2008, when it joined with Tkuma to form the right-wing nationalist Jewish Home Party.

National Union—An alliance of several small religious right-wing nationalist parties opposed to territorial compromise formed in 1999 by a merger of Moledet, Herut, and Tkuma.

Negev—The desert region of southern Israel.

Operation Defensive Shield—The Israel Defense Forces offensive in March and April 2002 against the Second Intifada. *See also* Intifada.

Operation Peace for Galilee—The Israel Defense Forces offensive against the PLO in Lebanon in 1982, also called the Lebanon War and later the First Lebanon War.

Oslo Accords—The 1993 agreement, officially called the Declaration of Principles, between Israel and the Palestine Liberation Organization outlining a process intended to lead toward full peace. It culminated in failure in 2000.

Palestinian Authority (PA)—Body formed in 1994 to govern Palestinian-controlled areas of the West Bank and the Gaza Strip.

Palestine Liberation Organization (PLO)—The group formed in 1964 to lead the Palestinian national movement. After 1969 it was led by Yasir Arafat and Fatah. It signed the Oslo Accords with Israel in 1993. As a separate entity, it has declined in importance with the emergence of the Palestinian Authority and later the death of Arafat.

Palestine Mandate, British Mandate for Palestine—The era of British rule in Palestine, under a League of Nations mandate, from 1922 to 1948. The territory ruled for most of this period was that of present-day Israel, the West Bank, and the Gaza Strip. The original mandate, before 1922, also included present-day Jordan and the Golan Heights.

Partition Plan—UN proposal of 1947 to divide British-ruled Palestine into Jewish and Arab states with Jerusalem as an international city. It was accepted by the United Nations on November 29, 1947, and by the Yishuv leaders but rejected by the Arab countries and the Palestinian Arabs.

Popular Front for the Liberation of Palestine (PFLP)—Nationalist, semi-Marxist Palestinian group founded in 1967 and sponsored by Syria.

Progressive List for Peace (PLP)—The first independent Arab party, established in 1984, which promptly won two seats in the Knesset. It won only one seat in 1988, none in 1992, then dissolved.

Qadi (plural: qadis)—Muslim or Druze judge in a religious court.

Rabbinate—The official religious body that oversees Jewish religious issues in Israel, such as conversion to Judaism, marriage, and divorce.

Rafi—The more centrist faction of Mapai that broke away to form a separate party led by David Ben-Gurion in 1965. After winning ten Knesset seats, it merged with Mapai and Ahdut HaAvoda to form the Labor Party in 1968.

Ratz—Movement for Civil Rights and Peace, a political party that split from the Labor Party's left wing in 1973. It advocated separation of religion and state, eventually joining with Shinui and Mapam to form Meretz in 1992.

Religious Zionism—Ideology supporting the creation of Israel as a mandate of religious Judaism. Most Datim are religious Zionists, and the ideology is historically connected with the National Religious Party.

Resolution 242—A UN Security Council resolution of November 22, 1967, calling for full peace based on the Arab states' recognition of Israel and Israel's withdrawing from territory it captured in 1967.

Resolution 425—UN Security Council resolution of March 1978 that called for full Israeli withdrawal from Lebanon. The United Nations announced that Israel had fulfilled the terms of the resolution terms after its pullout from southern Lebanon.

Revisionist Zionism—A Jewish nationalist ideology developed by Ze'ev Jabotinsky that is the ideology of the Herut Party.

Right of return—The Palestinian demand that all Palestinian refugees who left what is now Israel in 1948 and their descendants, wherever they currently reside, be allowed to live in Israel.

Road map—The three-phase peace plan presented in 2003 by the Quartet of the United States, the European Union, the United Nations, and Russia.

Sabra—Literally, "prickly pear," the nickname for a native-born Israeli, denoting a hard exterior but a soft interior.

Second Aliya—The wave of Jewish immigration to Israel (more precisely, to the Palestine Mandate) from 1903 to 1914. About 40,000 Jews, mainly from Russia and Poland, immigrated.

Security fence—Also called the Separation Barrier. A barrier, mostly an electronic fence and in some sectors a wall, between Israel and most of the Palestinian territories in the West Bank whose construction began in 2002. Its purpose is to prevent terrorists and other anti-Israel militants from entering Israel.

Sephardic—Literally, "Spanish"; properly refers to Jews expelled from Spain in 1492. Specifically, it refers to the slight variations in religious practice by Jews from the Middle East, North Africa, and the Balkan countries compared with the religious practices of other Jews. It is sometimes used interchangeably with *Mizrahi* to indicate Jews from those places.

Shaba Farms—Area in the Golan Heights on the Lebanese border. Internationally it is considered to be part of Syria, but Hizballah claims it as part of Lebanon and uses Israel's presence there to justify its attacks on Israel.

Shabak. *See* Shin Bet.

Shabbat—The Jewish Sabbath, observed from sunset on Friday to nightfall on Saturday.

Sharav—A hot, dry wind that commonly blows in the Middle East during the summer months and during the transition from spring to summer and from summer to fall.

Shas—Sephardic religious political party founded in 1984 that has become one of the largest parties in the Knesset. It conducts social welfare activities for its supporters.

Shekel—Israel's currency, officially called the New Israeli Shekel (NIS).

Shin Bet—The Israel Security Agency, which is responsible for Israel's internal security and also for intelligence gathering and security in the West Bank and the Gaza Strip. The agency is equivalent to the American Federal Bureau of Investigation.

Shinui—A secular, centrist political party established in 1974, a faction of Meretz from 1992 to 1997 that reemerged as an independent party in 1997. Shinui was successful in the late 1990s and early years of the twenty-first century but disappeared after failing to win any seats in 2006.

Shirei Eretz Yisrael—Nationalist folk songs.

Sinai Peninsula—Desert region of Egypt captured by Israel in 1956, returned in 1957, captured again in 1967, and returned as part of a 1979 peace agreement.

Six-Day War—The 1967 war in which Israel captured the West Bank and east Jerusalem from Jordan, the Gaza Strip and the Sinai Peninsula from Egypt, and the Golan Heights from Syria.

Suez War—The attack on Egypt in 1956 by Israel, France, and Britain following Egyptian nationalization of the Suez Canal and cross-border attacks on Israel.

Tami—Small religious party that split from the National Religious Party in 1981 to represent Mizrahim. Its popularity declined in 1984 with the emergence of Shas; it won only one seat that year and merged into the Likud.

Tehiya—Small nationalist political party formed in 1979 to oppose the peace agreement with Egypt. It won two to five seats in the Knesset throughout the 1980s but failed to win any seats in 1992 and disappeared.

Third Aliya—The wave of Jewish immigration to Israel (the Palestine Mandate) after World War I (1919–1923) in which about 35,000 Jewish immigrants arrived, mostly from Eastern Europe.

Tsena—Literally, "austerity"; the period from 1949 to 1953 when rationing was required to deal with the new state's precarious economic situation.

Tzomet—Right-wing nationalist political party established in 1983 that opposed yielding territory to the Palestinians. The party won eight seats in the Knesset in 1992, its peak number, but has failed to win any since 1996 despite running in every election.

Ulpan—Intensive Hebrew language class for immigrants.

United Arab List—Israeli Arab party established in 1996 and controlled by the Islamic Movement that advocates the transformation of Israel into an Islamist state. The United Arab List sometimes runs in elections in alliances with other Arab parties.

United Nations resolutions. *See* **Resolution 242; Resolution 425.**

United Torah Judaism—The political party, made up of Agudat Israel and Degel HaTorah, that represents the Haredim. It was formed in 1992.

West Bank—Area on the west bank of the Jordan River captured by Jordan in the War of Indepence in 1948. Israel took it back in 1967 and ruled it until 1994, when much of the area was yielded bit by bit to the Palestinian Authority. Israeli settlements are also located there.

Wye River Accord—A 1998 agreement between Israel and the Palestinian Authority on Israeli departure from the West Bank in exchange for Palestinian cessation of anti-Israel actions.

Yediot Ahronot—The Israeli newspaper with the largest circulation.

Yerida—Literally, "descent"; refers to Jewish emigration from Israel.

Yeshiva (plural: yeshivot)—School or seminary for the study of Jewish texts.

Yishuv—The Jewish community in the Land of Israel, reestablished in the late nineteenth century.

Yisrael B'Aliya—A Russian immigrant political party established in 1996 and led by Natan Sharansky. It initially won seven seats in the Knesset but had just two by 2003. It joined the Likud after the 2003 elections.

Yisrael Beiteinu (Israel Our Home)—A nationalist Russian political party founded in 1999 and led by Avigdor Lieberman. It was in an alliance with the National Union from 2000 to 2006. It won fifteen seats in the Knesset in 2009.

Yom Kippur War—The 1973 war in which Egypt and Syria attacked Israel by surprise on the Yom Kippur holiday.

Zionism—Nationalist movement supporting Jewish sovereignty; a belief in the right of Jews to have a state in their historical national homeland.

Index